Wordy

Also by Simon Schama

HISTORY AND ART HISTORY

Patriots and Liberators: Revolution in the Netherlands

Two Rothschilds and the Land of Israel

The Embarrassment of Riches:
An Interpretation of Dutch Culture in the Golden Age

Citizens: A Chronicle of the French Revolution

Landscape and Memory

Rembrandt's Eyes

A History of Britain, Volume I: At the Edge of the World?

A History of Britain, Volume II: The British Wars

A History of Britain, Volume III: The Fate of Empire

Rough Crossings:
Britain, the Slaves and the American Revolution

The Power of Art

The American Future: A History

The Story of the Jews: Finding the Words

The Face of Britain

Belonging

ESSAYS

Hang-Ups: Essays on Painting (Mostly)

Scribble, Scribble, Scribble:
Writing on Politics, Ice Cream, Churchill and My Mother

FICTION

Dead Certainties: Unwarranted Speculations

Wordy

Sounding off on high art, low appetite and the power of memory

SIMON SCHAMA

**SIMON &
SCHUSTER**

London · New York · Sydney · Toronto · New Delhi

A CBS COMPANY

First published in Great Britain by Simon & Schuster UK Ltd, 2019
A CBS COMPANY

Copyright © Simon Schama, 2019

1 3 5 7 9 10 8 6 4 2

Simon & Schuster UK Ltd
1st Floor
222 Gray's Inn Road
London WC1X 8HB

www.simonandschuster.co.uk
www.simonandschuster.com.au
www.simonandschuster.co.in

Simon & Schuster Australia, Sydney
Simon & Schuster India, New Delhi

A CIP catalogue record for this book
is available from the British Library

Hardback ISBN: 978-1-4711-8009-5
Trade Paperback ISBN: 978-1-4711-8010-1
eBook ISBN: 978-1-4711-8011-8

Typeset in Stone Serif by M Rules
Printed and bound by CPI Group (UK) Ltd, Croydon, CR0 4YY

To my editors, colleagues and friends
at the *FT* who, for a decade, have indulged my
wordiness and kept me in the pink

CONTENTS

WORDY

Sometime around the age of five I stopped talking; for perhaps a month, just long enough to put the wind up my poor parents who were driven to distraction by the sudden, inexplicable muting of their hitherto garrulous little boy. That, of course, was why I did it: this wicked act of oral retention. I can't recall the exact moment of up-shutting; but I can certainly remember resenting being shown off as a freakishly precocious verbaliser. 'Take them round the garden, Simon, there's a good boy,' my dad would say, and off I'd toddle, trailing the relatives behind me, announcing not just the names of the flowers clumped in the herbaceous border but their Latin names, memorised from those little wooden sticks that stayed with them after planting. On command I could do the weather and/or shipping forecast; the opening of *The Wind in the Willows*; or, if you asked nicely, King David's grief over his dead rebel son. 'Oh, Absalom, my Absalom' I would pipe and the guests would fall about with startled hilarity, which I was unsure was a good thing, though I found myself nervously giggling along. I was such a chatterbox, my parents had no trouble, and no qualms, lying about my age to get me into school at four rather than the statutory five.

At some point I must have had enough, or sensed that withholding was power, and tied the tongue, good and proper. My sister, thirteen years older and often stuck with babysitting, glared at me over my mother's 'Taste of Eden' soup as if she was on to me. I was carted round to speech doctors, head doctors and one heavy-set lady elocutionist whose witchy, spinach-green eyes and bristling, gun-metal grey hair, a few of which had migrated to

her chin, thrust herself so close to my complacent little face that I
was nearly frightened out of my Trappism. But I shook my head at
everything sent my way, nice or nasty, sticking to the silence until
some day or other (I remember it was spring because the yellow
broom was out on the cliffs) I graciously returned to voice. Don't
even ask me why. Instead of getting a good hiding, my tormented
parents hollered with overjoyed relief, enfolded me in laughing
embraces, and walked me to the local sweetshop to buy marzipan
fruits. Relieved at having escaped the larruping I richly deserved
(in fact my father, as he often reminded me, 'never laid a hand'),
I went back to being wordy, performing for all and sundry at the
drop of a gobstopper.

My reward for never going mute again was what I now
realise was a great gift: a serial story, entirely of my father's
invention, which he would narrate every Saturday morning.
Before breakfast and synagogue, I would climb into bed with
him and get another ten-minute episode in the long-running
epic of Knockemdown Ginger. 'Knock knock Ginger' I later
discovered was the name of an unsubtle nineteenth-century
prank in which boys rapped on random doors and ran away
shouting 'GINGER'. But my dad converted whatever memories
he had of the game into a character, based somewhat on the
similarly freckle-faced, mischief-prone boy who appeared in
Richmal Crompton's 'Just William' stories. But should Ginger
ever come conker-to-conker with William in some cat-peed
alley, it would be no competition at all. Ginger, after all, had
Pieface Laroon and Godfrey McWillikins (yes, one fat, one thin)
as his two lieutenants, not to mention Molly O'Bloomer, the
wild-eyed tomboy who tagged along for the mayhem. Although
Old Poultice the warty neighbour would summon PC Shredd
to apprehend the underage criminals who'd trampled his petu-
nias, chasing after a city goat, the nice Misses Crabapple would
always get Ginger and the gang off the hook. 'They mean well,
Sergeant, they really do.' Besides, both Rabbi Farfel and the

Reverend Mincing had a soft spot for the snot-nosed rascals and could be relied on in extremis to plead mitigating circumstances when things – say a smashed shop window, or a bonfire out of control – went horribly wrong.

Anything to keep me listening and chatty. Five or so years after the speech strike my father would coax me into memorising and reciting passages from favourite books, many of them historical novels – *The White Company* or *The Master of Ballantrae*. It was as though these exercises would be vocal lubrication precluding the pipes from seizing up ever again. A few years later, we went Shakespearean, Arthur and I reciting 'All the world's a stage' or (a favourite, complete with crazed Olivieresque snarling) 'Now is the winter of our discontent' till the women of the family begged for mercy.

Then there was rhetorical self-defence. Channelling his East End Brady Boys Club Cicero, he coached me in the art of debate. ('Don't forget the peroration! The exordium? Don't worry but remember everything depends on your peroration!') All round London and sometimes beyond, our Jewish youth teen-team went, dolled up in Prince of Wales check suits and white-on-white knitted ties, mouthing off about independent nuclear deterrence or the Mau Mau.

But in English classes at school something odd was happening, or, rather, not happening. Along with Shakespeare and Balzac's *Human Comedy*, my father's cynosure was, unsurprisingly, Dickens. Sunday after tea in the childhood years was Dickens time: readings out loud, either as a family or – more usually – with Dad taking all the parts. Not just the expected items: *The Pickwick Papers*, *Oliver Twist*, *David Copperfield*, *Great Expectations*, but the tougher reads: *Our Mutual Friend*, the opening of which scared the daylights out of me even more than Magwitch; *Barnaby Rudge* and of course those *Two Cities*. (Arthur went to town as Mme Defarge executing terrible guillotine effects, involving overripe melons and a hatchet.) But at school, there was no Dickens at all. There was Shakespeare galore; there was Poe, Eliot George and Eliot T. S.; Austen, Brontës, Gerard Manley Hopkins for Christ's sake, but no Smike, no Estella, no Jellabys, no Bumbles. One day, feeling exactly like Twist asking for more, I asked why this was. 'Oh', came the raised-eyebrow reply from the English master who had handed me fourteen consecutive detentions for talking out of turn (a school record), 'he [Dickens] so overdoes it.' If we really wanted that sort of thing we could at a stretch have a shufti at *Hard Times*, the sole novel approved by the high priest of the New Criticism, F. R. Leavis, as, somehow, acceptably un-Dickensian.

Naturally, then, Dickens in all his intoxicated flamboyance became a secret pleasure. The more the critical priesthood pursed its lips at his word-gaming, the more I delighted in it. In particular I loved those cartoonish names on which were inscribed whole characters and destinies: Steerforth and Sowerberry; the Pardiggles and Tite Barnacles; Uncle Pumblechook and Herbert Pocket; Bentley Drummle and Vincent Crummle – high-coloured characters who processed before the reader like stage actors bellowing into the darkness or wringing their hands in the lime-light. I couldn't get enough of exactly the qualities the Leavisites thought most vulgar: the gravity-defying word-juggling; the somersaulting syntax; the tumbling diction; the orgies of adjectives, the manic alternations of broad comedy and dismal terror; the whole unembarrassed sense of literature as performance, written of course by an author who was so compulsively drawn to showtime that he would eventually be consumed by its brutal exertions.

Or, to put it another way, what I have always loved is literary abundance.

So did Erasmus. The year 1512 saw the publication in Paris of his *De duplici copia verborum ac rerum* (*On the Foundations of the Abundant Style*). It had been written during the early months of his stay in Cambridge where Erasmus taught Greek, worked on his purified New Testament, and complained a lot about the dreadful ale, the 'unsatisfactory wine' that did nothing to help his tormenting gallstones (he asked a friend to send the best Greek wine ASAP), the miserable biting fenland weather and the loneliness when much of the population fled the town to escape the plague. Copiousness of any sort was in scant supply. So he wrote up the manual on rhetoric, both oral and written, for students, which he had already sketched some years before. One of his great publishing successes, especially in England; revised periodically, it went through thirty-three editions in Erasmus's own lifetime. Its opening exordium was to think of words as 'surging in a golden stream, overflowing with an abundance of words and thoughts'. But this beautiful abundance was not to be confused with 'futile and amorphous verbosity', which far from embodying richness of imagination and elasticity of argument betrayed, paradoxically, the kind of vacuousness that lent itself to tiresome repetition.

The key was variety, which 'everywhere has such force that nothing is so brilliant as not to seem dim when not commended by variety'. Nature itself rejoices in variety. And the opening short chapters of the book demonstrate in the most accessible and spirited way what its author has in mind. Just as dress should be neither dirty nor badly fitting or slovenly set on the body, so abundant style ought to suit its object. Variety did not mean incongruousness of the kind that would serve garlic along with Attic sweetmeats at a feast (no danger of that at Queen's College, Cambridge). And literary furnishings need careful selection, not just as if the room was packed with branches of 'willow and fig' alongside Samian pottery ware.

What gladdened Erasmus was expansiveness; a piling-up of possibilities; the better to land on the bon mot. Chapter 33 of (what is commonly known as) *De Copia* offers the student multiple variations on *tuae litterae me magnopere delectarunt* ('your letter has so pleased me'), but also 'from your affectionate letter I received unbelievable pleasure'; 'from he who handed me your letter I received a heap of joy'; 'by your letter wrinkles were wiped clean from my brow'; 'what laughter, what joy, what exultant dancing your letter caused me'; 'your letter was pure honey to me'; 'the letter of my dear Faustus was more sumptuous to me than Sicilian feasts'; 'what clover is to bees, what willow-boughs are to goats, what honey is to bears, your letter is to me' (steady on); 'when I received your letter you would have said that Erasmus was drunk with joy' – and about 150 other versions.

In the Erasmian universe, whole worlds could burst forth from a single observation; but he also relished the multifarious. With the geographic expansion to parts hitherto unknown, to Europe, to China and Africa, with the unearthing of classical sculpture, and ancient texts preserved through Arabic editions, European singularity was left behind, at least for adventurous minds like those of Erasmus and his friends Colet and More.

Renaissance wordiness ensued, the mind going magpie. Hither and thither it flew, picking up what the wide world had to offer without troubling too much, for the time being, to arrange its trove through some sort of ordering morphology. Intake was paramount. Hence the sudden popularity of commonplace books in which anything and everything that came the writer's way could be set down – epigrams spoken and written; observations from the natural world; curiosa; an agate whose veining seemed to disclose a celestial landscape; a mandrake root resembling the likeness of the Saviour or Alexander the Great; the mystical signs of the Kabbalah; news from abroad of two-headed men.

In due course, the itch for plethora turned literary, and the long reign of Wordy was inaugurated. The original master of multiplicity was François Rabelais, who in one person had combined many kinds of vocation and thus languages: those of the Benedictine monk he briefly was; those of the lawyer he thought he might be; and especially that of the medicine he practised. It seems inconceivable that Rabelais would not have read Erasmus's *De Copia*, and although the one work is schoolmasterly while

Gargantua seems anything but, the two works share the same marriage of studious teaching with comic uproar along with an insatiable appetite for lists; that device that tries to register the infinite richness of the world and its words by accumulation. Listlessness is abhorrent to Rabelais; of its opposite there could never be excess. So when Epistemon is brought back to life from his decapitation by miracle medicine applied by Pantagruel's friend Panurge, he feels compelled to list the fate of all the famous people encountered in the underworld of the dead, and whose condition, if truth be told, while something of a comeuppance, could have been worse. Not much, though, as conveyed by a marvellously extended list of the new occupations: Alexander the Great, eking out a living by patching old breeches; Xerxes, a mustard vendor; Agamemnon, a licker-out of casseroles; Darius, a cleaner of latrines; Justinian, a seller of knick-knacks; Julius Caesar, a scullion; Arthur of Britain, a cleaner of greasy headgear; Pope Sixtus, a greaser of syphilitic sores. 'What?' says Pantagruel. 'Are there syphilitics in that other world?' 'Indeed there are,' replies Epistemon. 'I never saw so many, over 100 million. For you should believe that those who don't catch the pox in this world will get it in the next.' 'Golly,' says Panurge. 'That lets me off the hook then.'

What all the most unbuttoned wordies – from Rabelais through Leopardi, whose *Zibaldone*, or 'hodgepodge' book, ran to thousands of pages, from Herman Melville to James Joyce, Salman Rushdie and David Foster Wallace – have in common is gutsiness, in the sense of their shared instinct for carnality, meaning the connection between sensuality and meaty-eatiness. Their imaginative lair is as much the alimentary canal as the cerebellum. You won't get very far in Boccaccio, Sterne or Hazlitt before you hit the aromatic empire of chow: the hunting and devouring of it; its digestion, indigestion, coagulation, excretion; the re-fertilisation of the earth-matrix from which all this fecundity comes. When Shakespeare's Prince Hal and his epitome of Gargantuan earthiness, Falstaff, conduct one of

their insult-slams (always playful but also pointed) in *Henry IV*, Part
I, they do it as a version of Carnival versus Lent, the stuffed against
the meagre. And they go at it, needless to say, listily:

> PRINCE: This bed-presser, this horseback-breaker, this huge
> hill of flesh.
> FALSTAFF: 'Sblood you starveling, you elf-skin, you dried
> neat's tongue, you bull's pizzle, you stockfish!

It's natural, almost mandatory, then, for wordies to be foodies,
but the kind of foody who actually plunges into the cooking and
lets the roasting aroma fill the kitchen of his pages. Think of
all the edibles in Dickens: Maggy's chicking; the Pickwickian
Christmas; the Manichean alternation between starvation and
gluttony in *A Tale of Two Cities*; entire novels built around the
denial or gratification of appetite: the terrible opening of *Oliver
Twist*, or the cornucopian vision given to the miserly Scrooge of
his own lodging:

> Heaped up on the floor to form a kind of throne were turkeys,
> geese, game, poultry, brawn, great joints of meat, sucking pigs,
> long wreaths of sausages, mince pies, plum puddings, barrels
> of oysters, red-hot chestnuts, cherry-cheeked apples [two fruits
> in one]; juicy oranges, luscious pears, immense twelfth cakes,
> and seething bowls of punch that made the chamber dim with
> their delicious steam.

The words themselves chomp, chew, suck, swallow and belch.
They sound themselves into life. Doctor Rabelais has his baby
giant Gargantua enter the world through the chamber of hearing
(his mother Gargamelle having blocked most of the exit ways
through an inordinate consumption of tripe close to her time).
Add to that the intervention of a blundering midwife ('a dirty
old crone') and the infant sprang through the cotyledonary

veins of the womb, into the vena cava, 'and clambering through the midriff, took a left path and emerged through her left ear'. Instead of a newborn mewling, the baby announced his arrival with a shouted, quintessentially Rabelaisian invitation: 'Come and drink, drink, drink!'

For true wordies life is flooded with gusto. William Hazlitt — himself a virtuoso of many genres from political reporting to sports writing to art criticism and one of the wordiest of all English writers — devoted an entire essay to gusto, which he defined as 'power or passion'. Sorting through art history, Hazlitt lined up the painters he thought embodied the vital quality: unsurprisingly above all, the famous flesh-masters Titian, Rubens and of course Rembrandt, who had it 'in everything; everything in his pictures has a tangible quality . . . his furs and stuffs are proof against a Russian winter'. Besides Michelangelo, all anatomical gusto, Correggio was lovely but limp since in his figures 'we see neither bones nor muscles' — only the spiritually disembodied matter of 'soul'. In literature, Hazlitt commended Shakespeare and Milton for gusto galore. But 'gusto', of course, derives etymologically from words denoting taste, exactly at the point where 'tongue' itself doubles inseparably as both language and the organ of flavour-capture. In his toothsome *Dictionnaire de Cuisine*, Alexandre Dumas père (himself a bit of a porker) explicitly brought story and cookery together through the serendipity of the alphabet, so that calape — a turtle stew he cooked and sampled on a voyage between Africa and Sicily that involved artful removal of the gall bladder and the addition of dry Madeira, poultry quenelles, anchovies and spring onions — directly precedes a potted romantic biography of the great chef, Marie-Antoine Carême — born in a woodshed as one of fifteen children of an indigent carpenter, and left to fend for himself by his father in the middle of a street at the age of eleven.

All the virtuosi of abundance have this Rabelaisian relish for literary mouthfeel, the echoing, sometimes shouty resonance of words way beyond their mechanically assigned function as vessels of description or argument. In the nineteenth century, practitioners of the abundant style took it to operatic heights of exclamation, so that the only way to read or even to make sense of Thomas Carlyle's *French Revolution*, or the coloratura passages of John Ruskin's *Modern Painters*, is out loud. At its most extreme, the grand style of Victorian writing approaches a sonorous equivalent to Gothic Revival buildings; profusely embellished spires shooting through industrial dimness. But at its best it achieves a kind of intense poetic illumination. Ruskin ends his autobiography, *Praeterita*, in the hills near Siena with a stupendous threnody, a perfect execution of what Erasmus classified as *superlatio*, which depends for its power on a song-like cadence, the dancing motion of the words matching the bobbing fireflies that give off its supernal radiance:

> We . . . walked together that evening on the hills above where the fireflies among the scented thickets shone fitfully in the still undarkened air. How they shone! moving like fine-broken starlight through the purple leaves. How they shone! through the sunset that faded into thunderous night as I entered Siena three days before, the white edges of the mountainous clouds still lighted from the west, and the openly golden sky calm behind the Gate of Siena's heart, with its still golden words, 'Cor magis tibi Sena pandit', and the fireflies everywhere in sky and cloud rising and falling, mixed with the lightning, and more intense than the stars.

All those works and words build into epic vision. But much (not all) of what follows is journalism, and newspapers and magazines aren't in the epic business. Long form isn't a licence to be long-winded. Deadlines and page layouts are merciless disciplinarians, and we working stiffs ignore those responsibilities at our peril. But many of the pieces have appeared in the pages of the weekend *Financial Times*, where the brief is to deliver economical hits of pleasure along with argument and provocation. That, in any case, has been the vocation of all the virtuoso essayists whom I have most admired – Montaigne and Hazlitt; Orwell and E. B. White; Hunter Thompson and David Foster-Wallace – all of whom, even at their wordiest, have made every sentence count, every paragraph convey whole worlds of experience. All of them, too, were artful practitioners of the double (indeed contradictory) sense of an *essai*: on the one hand, licence to take a crack at something without quite knowing where the writing will end up; on the other, a trial proof of material, a rigorous testing of its mettle. So, while not deluding yourself that you're anything other than a journeyman shuffling along in the footsteps of giants, you get going: a thousand words, a few days, an anxious editor out there, one hand crossing its fingers, the other readying the pruning shears. You write, you file, you wait, all the time knowing that, but for the acute kindness, the generosity tipped with salutory brutality, all you would ever be is not so much dithyrambically wordy as just prolix.

Remembrance

History's relationship to Memory is supposed to be that of the sober daughter giving shape and meaning to the indiscriminate recollection of her flighty mother. Look at their portraits and you can see the difference. Dante Gabriel Rossetti's Mnemosyne (Memory) has the powerful body of the Titaness, born of Gaia and Uranus, and is in fact the artist's adulterous lost love, Jane Morris, brought to perpetual remembrance. She comes unbidden, dark brows heavy with melancholy, carrying the torch of her haunting. Images of Clio, her daughter, the fruit of a week of passion with Zeus, are sterner, for she represents history instructing posterity. Accordingly she is invariably shown with the open book that is her opportunity and her confinement: the matrix on which she must form indiscriminate recollection into a purposeful chronicle of fame. The Kings of France liked it that way. Is history, then, the severe bluestocking saddled with disciplining her mother's dishevelled garment of memory into an enduring narrative?

Not quite. In the strongest, most enduring books of the past — Herodotus, Gibbon, Michelet — the two kinds of recall flow together. Memory's stream carries the rich sediment of wordly experience — stories, documents, the physical lie of the land towards History's pool of considered reflection. Memory without history is random recall; history without memory is just interrogation.

When history is summoned for acts of public remembrance, especially if the deeds to be kept alive in the collective mind are cautionary enormities, we assume that sobriety will rule over spontaneous recall.

But that's not how it works. The indifference of future generations is only stirred to tragic empathy by imaginative re-enactment. And for that, personal narratives are necessary — a company of men fallen into the panic of war; a town of widows mourning their lost ones; a city disintegrating into anarchy as epidemic overwhelms its fragile order; a landscape scarred by natural calamity, or deformed into Otto Dov Kulka's 'metropolis of death'. History's eloquence is inseparable from witness. 'I was there', such and such witness says, 'now you must be too; let me take you into the company of the past and I will, in a while, return you to the living, more of a human than when you answered merely to the flashy beckoning of Now.'

MATZO BALL MEMORIES

It was when my friend Sid took a razor to the smoked salmon sandwich that I realised being a fourteen-year-old Jew in London was more complicated than I'd assumed. He did a good job on it, too, slashing it to greasy ribbons in an adolescent frenzy of red-faced fury, impressive when the weapon was just a pencil-sharpener blade. Once I'd got over the shock of the assault on Cohen's finest Scottish hand-sliced, I tried to grab it back. The blade skidded across the palm of my right hand, opening a 3-inch wound below the fingers. I howled while dripping blood onto the rye with caraway but, many stitches later, I swaggered back, cocky with cred, to bestow magnanimous forgiveness on the glumly penitent Sid.

Frankly, I blamed my mum. Smoked salmon sandwiches for lunch every day: how was that going to square me with the Gentiles? There were days when I envied the *goyim* their mince and their frogspawn tapioca; and hungered for the dark and dirty freedom from *kosher*. But the awful truth is that until the sandwich pogrom, it had never occurred to me that a daily smoked-salmon lunch – worse, complaining about having to eat it all the time – might get up the nose of boys doomed to Shippam's shrimp paste, or the steak'n'gristle glop served by Doris in the hairnet, and that they might think, as Sid did, just for that one moment, and never again so far as I knew, *Christ, bloody Jews*.

It wasn't that we were the kind to throw around our money or our weight, because we didn't have much of either. We were in Golders Green in the early 1950s because my father, Arthur, had come down in the world a bit; taken one of his periodic falls from grace in the schmatte trade, steep enough for us to have to sell off, in a hurry, the Tudor-ish villa by the sea.

So we said so long to the half-timbered Jews of the Essex littoral in their gold-buttoned blazers and weekend convertibles; to the cliff walk with the gorse bushes where cheeky Jewish dachshunds sniffed Gentile retrievers; to the sunken rusticated garden with its winsome stone Cupid and heavily composted gardener Bill, who, pipe clenched between his shag-stained teeth, gruntingly tended the antirrhinums; farewell to the matronly house help to whose apron clung a faint but unmistakeable whiff of transgressive bacon; toodle-oo to the walnut-fascia Rover; to the loud parties where, in front of innumerable uncles and aunts who'd come down from London, Dad would shamelessly do his Jack Buchanan soft-shoe shuffle and tell the odd off-colour Max Miller joke; *shalom* to all that and hello to a hill of pebble-dash semis in NW11.

My mother Trudie, in shock, railed at my pa for his commercial failings, invoking Wilkins Micawber a good deal. When he couldn't take any more, Arthur would march off down the hill, coming home slightly tiddly, playing worryingly with the soup noodles at supper.

But Golders Green was just fine with me. Sixty years ago it was an island of cosmopolitanism between high-minded Hampstead and gritty Cricklewood. In Golders Hill Park and on the Heath you could catch the cultured end of the Jewish immigration of the 1930s – from Berlin and Vienna – reading poetry on the benches. The Jewish flavour of the place was no more than just that: the bakeries where you could get gleaming challah bread and poppy-seed-filled *hamantaschen* at Purim; killer strudel; and properly boiled, chewy flat bagels, not the bloated, puffy monsters that have taken over the world; kosher butchers where the customers haggled about the brisket; and Cohen's, that temple of smoked salmon and pickled cucumbers. Golders Green Road also had survivors from the traditional, bosky suburban village it had long been: flower shops; tailors; the kind of groceries where the assistants stuck money into whizzing overhead pneumatic tubes. Other tweed-free communities, Asian and Italian, had settled in. I saw my first urban turban and inhaled my first hit of roasting coffee beans on the Road. This was where I wanted to be.

So when a bus conductor shouted, 'Gol-ders Green: get yer passports out!' I chuckled along with everyone else. I loved being one of Them: the loudmouths, the violinists, the wide boys with the sharp suits, the showmen. I didn't want to blend in with the tea-cosy people of Macmillan's Britain, shuffling patiently forward in the bus queue, muttering about the weather. I was happy to be a Brylcreem boy, a jiving Jew from the Green, from my gleaming winklepickers to the white knitted ties and the snap-brim trilby worn with an attitude on the way to *shul*. Mind you, I didn't want to be in the company of the *frum*, either, the ultra-orthodox with their deep swaying and knee-bobbing, the corkscrew sidelocks and fringed *tzitzit* worn on the outside; the pallor peeping from beneath the homburgs.

But, in the 1950s, they weren't often to be seen in Golders Green. On the Monopoly board urban geography of Jewish London, the frum were mostly still stuck in the purple squares of Stamford Hill. Brown was Whitechapel and Stepney, where both my father and mother had started life; their parents coming from the Turkish Balkans, Romania and Lithuania. The oldest of my father's twelve siblings were still stuck in the East End, and when we went to see them it was like a trip to some sort of mournful immigrant antiquity: their dreaded sponge cake, and the tall glasses of lemon tea, sipped with spoonfuls of plum jam.

At the other end of the Jewish Monopoly board was Park Lane, where, miraculously, one of my mother's cousins, the ones who had gone from running Soho pubs to importing pink champagne, had settled in unimaginably high bourgeois splendour. The sofas alone would swallow one's small behind in their downy cushions. Somewhere in between, on the red and yellow Monopoly squares, were 'comfortable' Hendon and Finchley, where yet more uncles and aunts shovelled the strudel in living rooms still misty with last night's Partagás cigar fumes.

The home I always made a beeline towards belonged to the handsome tie manufacturer with a Chekhovian line-up of daughters: the chatty oldest one, the creamily beautiful but scornful youngest, and, in the middle, the merry, tan-skinned teaser with just enough of a hint of wicked glinting from the golden chain about her neck to put a boy right off his bar mitzvah rehearsals.

So there we all were in various degrees of comfort or modesty but, at least, unlike some of my mother's mother's Vienna family, we were alive. By the time we moved back to London, the war had been over barely ten years. The 'Holocaust' wasn't even a word used about the slaughter. We seldom talked about it, except for fleeting analogies on Passover and Purim, both commemorating the destruction of early editions of Hitler: Pharaoh, Haman, the perennial *mamzers*, the bastards. There wasn't even much to read until Lord Russell of Liverpool, a lawyer at the Nuremberg trials, published his *Scourge of the Swastika* (1954), which we devoured in the upstairs synagogue library, aghast and fascinated by the hecatombs of bones; the naked women running before the grinning guards. My mother spat ripe and terrifying Yiddish curses at the whole idea of Germany (exempting only a small town on the Austrian border, where, in 1921, aged nine, she had been taken in by a kindly Burgomeister when she missed her train connection en route to her uncle in Vienna).

My father took the high road and concentrated on the good fortune of having been born British, especially gifted with the priceless, indestructible power of the English language. It was as though Shakespeare, not Monty and the troops, had beaten the Nazis. 'A Jew's best weapon is his mouth,' he would say to me, though his own had been on the receiving end of many a knuckle sandwich courtesy of the Blackshirts. But out of devotion to the biggest mouth-makher of all – Winston Spencer Churchill – he made sure I was schooled in oratory before I was even in my teens. To Arthur's energetic, hand-wagging stage direction, I did Crispin Crispian from *Henry V*, or 'All the world's a stage' in the living room while my mother fried the gefilte fish.

So the fit between being British and being Jewish seemed to my parents, and to their two children – to whom they had given the very British names of Simon and Tessa – utterly natural, *beshert* even – historically fated. As well as Dickens and Shakespeare on the bookshelf at home, there was Fielding, George Eliot, Austen, the Brontës, Hardy, Wells and (a special passion of Arthur's, who spoke as if he had known him personally) anything written by G. B. Shaw.

Parliament was still something to revere; an indomitable institution that, for all the appeasers, had stood fast when European democracies across the Channel had crumpled into murderous fascism. They took delight in the number of Jewish MPs (most of them Labour): Barnett Janner, Manny Shinwell, even the alte-Bolshevik Sydney Silverman, and, as far as my dad was concerned, Benny D'Israeli, too. Even some of the notoriously nose-holding British peerage who thought Jews frightfully entertaining but preferably not in their clubs were co-opted as sympathisers.

During the war, Arthur and Trudie had decamped to Knebworth in Hertfordshire, partly to get out of the way of the bombs and partly so my mother could be closer to her job at De Havilland aircraft, where she was secretary to racy test pilots who flirted with her over a whisky and splash in the local pubs. In the village, Trudie, a storyteller who could charm the birds off the trees, was on tea-shop and shopping-basket terms with Lady Lytton of Knebworth House, whose name she would ever after intone with glowing admiration, in the plummy accent she would switch on when chatting with the upper crust. Every so often this included the Queen Mother, who would visit the Stepney Jewish Day Centre where my mother made a second career, and, less probably, her pal John Profumo in his long atonement phase volunteering at Toynbee Hall in the East End.

Vocalised English in all its various glory was music (literally) to their ears. My mother's idea of a lullaby reflected exactly her twin passions for the cockney and the kosher: Marie Lloyd music hall one night, Sophie Tucker ('The Last of the Red Hot Mamas') belters the next. The result was that I was the only six-year-old in Essex who could give you a powerful rendering of 'My Old Man' and 'Some of These Days' in kindergarten, whether you wanted me to or not.

On sunny Sundays my dad would don his raffishly striped blazer and go into Jerome K. Jerome mode on the Thames, somewhere between Old Windsor and Datchet. Sitting me at the tiller of a small craft, he would tilt his boater at a jaunty angle and tune up his Noël Coward medley.

In Golders Green, our oak-panelled and stained-glassed syna-gogue had an air of late Victorian ecclesiastical grandeur about it: 'wardens' in ceremonious top hats, installed in a special boxed-in pew at the front of the congregation. The reading desk, instead of being in the middle of the synagogue, was removed to the far end in front of the ark, more like an altar table at the end of a church nave. High up above the ark behind a metal screen, a massed choir, featuring my cousin Brian as the star tenor, poured the operatic melodies out on to the congregation below, a flock that, on Yom Kippur, would include singer Frankie Vaughan, who we kids secretly willed to burst into a chorus of 'Green Door' right in the middle of the service.

And yet there were moments when the force of ancestral memory cut right through the solemnities. I'd learned to read Hebrew when I was quite small, had even gone on to teach it at the local synagogue Sunday school. So when, on the Sabbath, I grasped the silver *yad* – the pointer made in the form of a finger to remind us that the only aspect of the disembodied God revealed was the finger that, according to Leviticus, had written directly onto the stone tablets at Sinai – I became, through the mere act of chanted reading from the Torah, connected to the great chain of endurance embodied in Hebrew writing.

I would stray, far and wide. Bar mitzvah done with, I'd spend more time hanging round the Golders Green telephone booths (remember them?) angling for long-lashed girls than in pondering the Talmud. For much of my teen years, being Jewish meant Zionist socialism on the Finchley Road – where the girls wore no make-up and danced with abandon – while being expert in dialectical materialism, the polemics of nuclear disarmament, the halutz pioneers' songbook, avant-garde films and prolonged making out. Both that impassioned secular Zionism and the easygoing Judaism of the oak-panelled synagogue, unconflicted about its co-existence with the Gentile world around it, now seem relics of the lost innocence of half a century ago. Both now are fighting rearguard actions against more adamantly separatist constructions of Them and Us.

I am not especially happy about this. But there are moments when, sometimes, abandoning a film crew or a conference, I find myself wandering towards a synagogue wherever I happen to be: to the grand doors beyond the tough Israeli security detail in Rome; to the shuttered slats of Cochin; the wrought-iron balconies in Shanghai; the bulbously beautiful brass candelabra in Amsterdam; the pale tiles of Marrakech. If there is a congregation, I will find a seat, open a prayer book, and know my place right away. If it is empty, as is so often the case, I will fill it with remembered melodies, first learned in Southend and London, summoned as easily and instinctively as breathing. '*Etz chayim hee la'machazikim ba*', my remembrance sings, 'A tree of life for those who hold onto it . . .' Somehow I still do.

OTTO DOV KULKA IN AUSCHWITZ

It is commonplace that in the matter of the Holocaust, words fail us. Language, especially the wrought language of literature, struggles to register atrocities unrecognisable as the acts of sentient humans. Yet however unequal to the task, writers persist in their efforts to give form to smoke; to match words to madness. Sometimes, pardonably, fiction writers fall into the error of encompassing enormity by acts of literary violence. Monsters of prosody result, which, with every shriek amid the bloody mire, only draw attention to how far they miss the mark.

But, silence being the handmaid of oblivion, nothing is not enough. The memory-vacuum will quickly be filled by the lies of deniers, whose numbers are increasing not diminishing. So chroniclers of what Otto Dov Kulka calls the 'Great Death' continue to be torn between redundancy and futility. The dilemma is particularly acute among the dwindling band of survivors whose personal testimony is unreproducible by second-hand accounts, yet who are traumatically burdened with the indecency of adjectives; the sense that writing may never be more than an artificial simulacrum of what remains buried in their nightmares like deep-lodged shrapnel.

Kulka, professor emeritus of Jewish history at the Hebrew University of Jerusalem, is one such survivor. In *Landscapes of the Metropolis of Death* he recalls reading, after considerable reluctance, a much-praised account of the extermination, which nevertheless provokes in him only a total failure to recognise anything remotely close to his own experience of Auschwitz-Birkenau.

Was that book, one wonders, the work of Primo Levi, who may himself have been a fatal casualty of the struggle between word and memory? Like Levi and H. G. Adler, Kulka has long wrestled with what he should do with his burden of recall, some of it, like the sense of being perpetually returned to the gates of Auschwitz, mercilessly involuntary. Like Adler (in his sober non-fiction), Kulka has elected to steer clear of anything resembling autobiography and to address the horror instead with the analytical tools of the historian. But that turns out not to have given him peace. So over the years he confided to a tape recorder his dreams, nightmares and memories, which so far from being shrouded in the wraithlike indeterminacy of phantoms, have, for better or worse, remained visions of unsparing precision and concreteness.

Fortunately for us all, he has been persuaded by friends and the promptings of his own formidable decency to turn those spoken recollections and meditations into the astonishing book that is *Landscapes of the Metropolis of Death*. In its essence this is not so much a book about Auschwitz as one about coming to terms with the shock of survival. Like the eleven-year-old Kulka, who came within a few hundred metres of the crematoria, assuming that he would perish there, the writing hovers around the incineration, as he puts it, 'like a moth circles a flame'.

The origins of the book in Kulka's patient but exacting self-interrogations; his post-war circumlocutions and confrontations; the visit to the camp, once with his father who also survived; the attempts to liberate himself from the nightmare of obligatory return by doing just that – all mean that Kulka's style is bony and austere, with scarcely a note of literary striving in the hundred-odd pages. His prose is halting and broken as befits its subject; interspersed with black-and-white photographs, which in their amateurishness make no attempt to frame the magnitude of what they ostensibly record: the stoved-in remains of the crematoria; the 'forest of concrete pillars' once supporting the barbed-wire electrified fences that held the population captive.

W. G. Sebald, acknowledged as one of those encouraging
Kulka to write and publish, is an obvious and appropriate
model for wrestling quietly with the infernal. Kafka, too, supplies sympathetic correlates for Kulka's perplexities. Yet amid
the fragmentary, digressive impressions are images of terrible
poetic concreteness: the black stains of the Death March that
resolve into corpses shot by the Germans and dumped at inter-
vals by the snowy roadside; the 'speck' of his mother in 'a thin
skirt that rippled in the breeze' as she walked off to a labour
camp without ever turning her head to look back one last time
at her son; a prisoner attempting to dodge the rain of blows
beating down on him from the SS through a kind of 'grotesque,
bizarre dance'.

What, ultimately, makes Kulka's book unlike any other first-
hand account written about the camps is the authenticity of its
vision of an eleven-year-old boy. By some freak of fate (the logic of
which is explained at the end of the book), Otto and his mother,
who had volunteered to go from the notoriously fake 'resettlement' village of Theresienstadt to Auschwitz, were exempt from
the usual merciless division between those swiftly destined for
the crematoria, where 'the living, who enter in their masses in
long columns and are . . . transformed into flames, into light and
smoke, then disappear and fade into those darkening skies', and
those fit enough to slave until they too, after six months, shrink
into the skeletons covered by yellow skin he sees carted away each
day from the barracks dump. Instead, Kulka and his mother are
mysteriously lodged, with thousands of others, in a *familienlager*, a
family barracks where they are spared the shaven heads and camp
uniform; where the boy even gets to sleep beside his mother.
The barracks turns into a true school, where the future historian
learns for the first time of Thermopylae and Salamis; where the
children perform an opera and, in an act of stupendous defiance
of their fate, sing Schiller's words and Beethoven's melody of
'Ode to Joy'.

But this miraculous capsule of cultural survival within Auschwitz is, of course, a calculated contrivance of Nazi propaganda, designed to persuade Theresienstadt prisoners that these were the conditions that awaited them upon resettlement to the east, and to convince inspectors from the International Red Cross that reports of torture and immolation were baseless slanders. Once the IRC had fallen for the propaganda stunt at Theresienstadt, there was no further need for its Auschwitz counterpart. Five thousand mothers and children sharing Kulka's barracks were taken at one fell swoop to the gas chambers, leaving room for another group who in six months would be similarly disposed of. By one of the strokes of luck that Kulka recognises as determining the fate of the doomed, he and his mother were in the camp hospital with diphtheria when the rest of the *familienlager* were murdered.

There are other moments of fortune that left Kulka possessed by a sense of reckoning suspended rather than obviated. Handing his father a bowl of soup through the electrified fence, his hands (curious to see if the touch was fatal) stick to the wire. The boy assumes he is already dead and is amazed to discover that the landscape of Birkenau remains in his sight in the afterlife. Then he has to ensure that the burns, which turn lacerating and pus-swollen, are not discovered, since his unfitness for labour would send him summarily to the crematoria.

All this is unimaginably horrifying, yet through the eyes of little Otto we can, again, apprehend it. In a particularly moving passage, he considers himself spared the 'acute, murderous, destructive discord and torment felt by every adult inmate who was uprooted and wrenched from his cultural world . . . and which was almost always one of the elements of the shock that often felled them within a short time'. For him, he writes, that shock 'did not exist because this was the first world and the first order I had ever known: the order of the selections, death as the sole certain perspective ruling the world.'

Whether or not setting all this down has done anything to relieve the unrelenting grip the 'metropolis of death' holds on his mind, or whether it has tightened that hold, Kulka does not say. But since he has done the rest of us – and the world – so great a kindness by writing his book, one hopes for his sake the former. Ending in Jerusalem with his going 'to usher in Shabbat with the children of the sons and daughters of Job the Just', he offers the barest glint of sunlight amid a thunderous darkness.

THE EMPEROR OF LIES

I suppose it's too much to ask for a moratorium on the publication of Holocaust novels, but perhaps we might take a breather from having to read them, and especially those that parade their literary pretensions. As if 2009's prime offering in the genre, Jonathan Littell's radically over-hyped *The Kindly Ones*, was not enough, along comes another, the Swedish writer Steve Sem-Sandberg's *The Emperor of Lies*, all puffed up with the kind of 'fine writing' that succeeds only in drawing attention to the emotional and moral void at its centre.

The emperor in question is Chaim Mordechaj Rumkowski, the 'Eldest of the Jews' who held dictatorial sway over the Łódź ghetto in Poland after it had been sealed by the Germans in May 1940. By practising a policy of slavish co-operation, and by turning the ghetto – in which 200,000 souls were packed – into a complex of small factories and workshops, making goods in return for food supplies, Rumkowski claimed to have saved Łódź from earlier extermination. It was indeed the last of the ghettos to be liquidated in the summer of 1944; but it was also the place in which nearly 50,000 died from disease and malnutrition and from which tens of thousands were sent to the first mass-murder camp of Chelmno, 60 kilometres away. Rumkowski was deported to Auschwitz on one of the last transports out of Łódź.

Rumkowski has remained a subject of agonising and bitter contention ever since, not least because we know so much about him and the utter wretchedness of the Łódź ghetto (in effect an urban labour camp) over its four years of existence. Apart from the sometimes formulaic *Ghetto Chronicle*, a daily record of doings official and unofficial, there are the photographs by Mendel Grossman, the personal diaries of Josef Zelkowicz and Dawid Sierakowiak. Sem-Sandberg knows, and has used much of, this material and wears his research with an air of almost pedantic studiousness. But the mercilessness of the truth is impossible to reinforce with the novelist's hand. When Rumkowski is faced in September 1942 with an ultimatum to surrender the elderly (the over 65s that is) and small children, to save the 'healthy' occupants of the ghetto fit for work, he spoke with terrible candour. 'A broken Jew stands before you,' he said. 'I must cut off limbs to save the body . . . I come to you like a bandit to take from you what you most treasure in your hearts.'

The fact that Sem-Sandberg quotes verbatim from some of these documents in no way mitigates the question: what is the point of fictionalising any of this? Or of adding to Rumkowski's already appalling resumé – rumoured to include the molestation of girls – the graphically described paedophiliac abuse of an adopted son? Is there not enough cruelty, desperation and terror in the truth to forbear from the luxury of fiction? The only justification would be if the novel yielded some sort of understanding that the archive resists. But no such augmentation of empathy occurs at any point in the course of this relentless, and ultimately tedious, book.

Worse than the defensively carried historical baggage is the matter of the writing itself. There is no doubt that Sem-Sandberg is a technically gifted writer. Passages in the book that sketch in a landscape of the ghetto – streets and buildings, the children's home where much of the action unfolds – are done with a kind of ashy poetry. But this is scant relief in a book that turns on the style when Sem-Sandberg wants to shove our faces in the unsparing detail of the horror. People are tormented, mutilated and done to death in every imaginable fashion – as indeed they were – but in case that's not enough, Sem-Sandberg makes sure to add elaborately stylised massacres of cagebirds and rats.

When a grotesque figure called 'The Belly' has his eyes torn out with an iron hook by a Jewish policeman, Sem-Sandberg has a high old time with the imagery: 'As the blood flowed, the gouged-out eye dangled on its string like an egg coated in an oily brownish membrane.' You want to ask the writer: did writing that particular sentence, that particular simile, give you special satisfaction?

There is much in this vein running through *The Emperor of Lies*, although the German perpetrators of the atrocity remain for the most part a distant presence. What there isn't is any memorable characterisation (least of all of Rumkowski himself), any gathering tension of plot, or any grain of redemption amid the wall-to-wall cruelty, suffering, treachery and malice, much of it inflicted by Jews on fellow Jews. The fact that so much of the book turns on the fate of children only makes its failure of tenderness the more distressing.

It makes you wonder what Sem-Sandberg thought he was doing when he perpetrated this lumbering monster of a novel. Also it makes one meditate on the relationship between personal experience and moral power needed to take on this kind of subject. I am not of the school that believes a writer must have survived the camps in order to have written decent fiction about them. But one can't help reflecting that when works such as Alexander Solzhenitsyn's *One Day in the Life of Ivan Denisovich*, Primo Levi's *If This Is a Man* and H. G. Adler's astonishing *Panorama* draw the strength of their narrative from direct memory, and their own non-fiction accounts, there may be something to the connection. Beside their raw witness to an evil so unspeakable as to be all but unwriteable, Sem-Sandberg's misbegotten effort is just a 672-page cautionary footnote.

THE REMAINS OF THAT DAY

What are public memorials for? Are they meant to perpetuate the sorrow of loss, pay a debt of respect, or set a boundary about grief by turning it to public reverence? Must their primary obligation always be to the immediately bereaved? Should such places be no more than a site where those victimised by slaughter can find consolation in a community of mourning? Or is a public memorial, by definition, created to make something more universally redeeming from atrocious ruin? Does remembrance invite instruction or forbid it? Should it make mourners of us all, bow the heads and stop the mouths of all who stand before it? Is it greatly to their credit that Presidents George W. Bush and Barack Obama will stand at that haunted site on the tenth anniversary and not utter a word? Or is that silence a missed opportunity for reflection?

For some of us these will never be purely academic questions. I was in New York on 9/11 and in London on 7/7. I am a citizen of both of these unapologetically secular, mostly tolerant, rowdily cosmopolitan cities that the exterminating apostles of destruction chose as their target. I am at home in both places: I think of them as 'the mansion house of liberty' – in John Milton's fine phrase from *Areopagitica*, the poet's passionate 1644 defence of freedom of publication – and the temerity of that liberty was, in the mind of the murderers, cause enough for immolation.

Like so many others, I knew someone who was the victim of the massacre. She was not a close friend but the sister of one of my closest; a woman our family knew well from firelit evenings in a Massachusetts suburb, someone who had taken my children in her arms, had shoved cupcakes into their crumby mouths, who was the epitome of humane affection. Ten years on, without any effort whatsoever, I can close my eyes and see her face, hear her soft voice, and register the warmth of her distinctive presence. My 9/11 will always be more than a news event; it will always bear the imprinted portrait of the wide and gentle face of the murdered Laura attached to it. But Laura's own family, especially her distraught sister Terry, a good strong intelligence, has from the start been determined to make something more from her tragedy than agonised remembrance. Journeying to Iraq, talking to people who have undergone their own forms of undeserved assault, Terry has wrestled with understanding.

At the World Trade Center site this week, I search for Laura's name, cut into the blackened bronze lip that overlooks the cascades of the 9/11 memorial, pouring into the two immense basins of grief that outline the phantom towers. The names file endlessly along the perimeter, gathered, by wish of their families, in what the memorial's designers call 'meaningful adjacencies', which, in English, means in groups of passengers, firefighters, office colleagues – the working cells of the human beehive. It is those waves of names that drift through the place like spirits. The memorial's architect originally wanted them to be inscribed on the granite walls of the cascades, washed by the fall of his tear-drop waters. But that would have been a victory for classical aesthetics over simple emotion; it would have made them remote from their nearest and dearest who, rightly, insisted they be lifted to the living space of the memorial plaza, accessible to touch, to the fingertip trigger of love's memory.

Does that suffice, for decency's sake? Or do we owe it to their sacrifice and to our own future to make a translation from yesterday's torment to tomorrow's resolution, and bend ourselves to something more thoughtful than the periodic brandishing of the military fist? At the risk of vulgar presumption, ought we to meditate on what, exactly, it is about the free life of a democracy that we would defend it to the death in the face of theocratically sanctified mass murder?

The competing claims of lamentation and instruction were embodied in the guidelines provided for the memorial by the Lower Manhattan Development Corporation. Every victim of the attacks – in New York, Washington and aboard flights 11, 77, 93 and 175, as well as the six casualties of the abortive bombing in 1993 – was to be given recognition. Provision was to be made for visitation and contemplation, and the footprint of the towers was to be left forever exposed. More sententiously, the document also called for a work that evoked 'the historical significance' of 9/11 and would create 'an original and powerful statement'. It was this last invitation that unloosed gushing fountains of quasi-spiritual vapour, even among the finalists chosen – from more than 5,000 submissions – by a panel that included Maya Lin, designer of the Vietnam Veterans Memorial, and the great African-American sculptor Martin Puryear.

Gisela Baurmann proposed a Memorial Cloud; its 'top surface . . . a translucent bandage healing a wound . . . during the day the cloud like an undulating veil, a sinuous surface forming cathedral-like vaults'. Pierre David prefaced his plan for 'A Garden of Lights' by declaring, in the breathless manner usually reserved for the trailers of disaster movies, 'There was a last hour, a last minute, a last second, that 2,982 stars went dark.'

But even these overwrought exclamations pale in comparison with some of the more egregious submissions (which can be read in their entirety on the WTC website); including an 'enormous white marble Carrrara rock' suspended 30ft above the ground on a titanium chain; a colossal question mark entitled 'Who Did That? What Did That?', and, most appalling of all, a proposal featuring 25ft-long sculptures of silhouetted bodies 'punched out of stone . . . hurtled as if in a trajectory or force field . . . These silhouettes,' explained Eric Staller, who came up with this ghastly notion, 'will be perceived as floating or flying forms in space at peace.' Well, no, Eric, they won't.

By comparison, 'Reflecting Absence', the project of architect Michael Arad and landscape designer Peter Walker, is a model of moral tact and poetic indirection. A play of dialogues lies at the heart of their design: between the deep granite well of sorrow and the animated plaza filled with the living, between the fugitive quality of the waters and the regenerative growth of the hundreds of swamp oaks planted about the upper level. Arboreal resurrection is a commonplace of memorials – though no bad thing for that – and very often, as here (and at the deeply moving Oklahoma City National Memorial to the victims of the 1995 bombing), features a single 'survivor' tree (in this case a Callery pear) that acts as a living, vegetable hero of the blast. But the trees are planted in relentless military rows, which, together with the tomb-like granite slabs dotted around the plaza, make that space more dutifully mournful than you would wish, especially since the deciduous oaks will be little more than bare branches during the long months of New York's merciless winter.

It's hard, amid the welter of construction noise and the relentless testing of the emergency public address system, to conjure up the tonal character that will compose the memorial's tragic euphony: the soughing of Hudson valley winds through the foliage, the muffled downrush of the waters. The falling that is inescapably at the heart of the remembrance is echoed poetically in the 30ft drop of the cascades. Bravely, instead of allowing those waters to collect and recycle from a limpid pool, Arad has them drain away into abysmal sinks, a darker stain of granite than the basins, akin to the unfathomability of the desolation. Notwithstanding their name for the memorial, perhaps Arad and Walker understand that, by definition, absences can never be mirrored except as phantom visions, so that the reflection triggered by their work, however unforced, will be more philosophical rather than optical.

But what form will that reflection take? Arad and Walker understand, I think, that multitudes will come to the memorial, unphilosophically, first and foremost as an act of empathy; to suffer vicariously terror and pity; and then to share in common elegy. But, inevitably, people, especially from beyond New York, will be drawn to experience the history-shudder that comes from walking on a site where an act of unconscionable horror took place. The shock will be sustained in the on-site museum housing explanatory materials and a collection of remains: scorched phones, ragged fragments of clothing and personal testimony. The museum will not open until 2012, but its graceful armature, at once luminous and hard-ribbed, is already apparent and something of a reproach to the nondescript towers rising around it. And it has at its core something of a transformational marvel: twin surviving steel columns about 70ft tall, coloured a burnt coppery hue and surmounted with a distinctive webbed 'trident' that forms a kind of heroic capital. The first thing any visitor to the museum will see, the columns will, like the pear tree, be taken to heart as emblems of unbowed endurance.

But how eloquent can dumb steel be? Is there something else to be said? For, truly, there are no value-neutral memorials. One of the most grandiloquent, the Lincoln Memorial – designed by Henry Bacon and dedicated in 1922 – in Washington DC, is dominated by the martyred president, literally colossal in stature but also in the ideals he articulated. He is seated as if in profound thought; and the most solemn of those thoughts are duly inscribed on the walls of his enshrining temple. Not far away is the most recent addition to Washington's monumental statuary, in the form of a 30ft-high statue of Martin Luther King – inaugurated, appropriately, by the first African-American president.

Memorialised heroes could be wordy or mute. But how to remember Joe and Jane? It was only when the twentieth century ratcheted up the scale of atrocity that high and mighty minds gave systematic thought to what forms the remembrance of ordinary mortals might most decently take. After the First World War, there was already some sense of the incommensurability trap, that traditional figurative monuments with their dauntless bayonets were somehow feebly inadequate to the scale of the tragedy. How could the dead, whether of an annihilated city or a slaughtered army, be represented as unbowed in bronze when they had been bloodily exploded in the Flanders mud or entombed in the burning wreckage of Coventry or Dresden?

The aptest responses were those that either abandoned figuration for a kind of elemental simplicity – like the grave of the Unknown Warrior buried in Westminster Abbey in 1920 – or else aggressively distorted it in keeping with the wounds inflicted on the classical ideal of the human body by modern savagery. Pablo Picasso's *Guernica* – created for the pavilion of the beleaguered Spanish Republic at the Paris Exposition of 1937 – continues to be harrowing because its Cubist language for once stopped being a medium for formal ingenuity and instead carried the sense of art, as well as humanity, helplessly imploding. Ossip Zadkine, a Jewish survivor of both world wars, was commissioned by another Jewish survivor, Dr Gerrit de Wal, owner of the Bijenkorf department store, to make a memorial to the incineration of Rotterdam by the Luftwaffe and in *The Destroyed City* produced an unsparingly confrontational sculpture, a limb outstretched to the merciless sky, both defiant and vainly protective.

But there have been annihilations so total, such as the Nazi genocide of European Jews, that any sort of figuration has invited bathos. The most successful memorials have instead been emblematic inversions of what was destroyed – such as Rachel Whiteread's monumental, millennial Vienna library of negative-cast books – or summarising analogies – such as the Berlin Holocaust Memorial's ramped field of 2,711 stelae erected in 2004, beckoning the visitor into a descending, darkening universe of interminable tombs. The thoughtfulness with which Peter Eisenman and Buro Happold rose to a daunting commission did not preclude one of its organisers from describing it as a 'tourist magnet', nor does it stop children from using it as a hide-and-seek playground. Whoops come from the world of the dead.

In the hands of the uninspired, of course, poetic abstraction can be as inadequate as cartoonish figuration to the work of giving shape to emptiness. For the vocabulary of abstraction – hollowed spheres and discs, the brutally soldered girder, the lacy spray of spokes – has been so depleted by overuse as to risk innocuousness. For the London 9/11 Educational Project, Miya Ando has fashioned a sculpture, also from ruined columns, that no one, I think, could accuse of being an abstraction of convenience.

The urge to say something moves restlessly amid the ruins. But in the case of 9/11 some of the proclamations have been numbingly banal. Daniel Libeskind, whose original design for a 'freedom tower' complete with a 'wedge of light' to be illuminated every 9/11 has been disastrously compromised by the requirements of commercial space and defensive security, claimed that retaining the slurry wall that prevented flooding from the Hudson River would reveal 'the heroic foundations of democracy for all to see'. More fatuous still is the obsession with the tower's toothpick mast reaching 1,776ft, as if one measures the genuine grandeur of the Declaration of Independence by the altitude of a skyscraper.

If we must speak as well as weep, then let us speak thoughtfully as befits the magnitude of the onslaught on the 'mansion house of liberty' and the enduring nobility of the ideals that the 9/11 terrorists were so avid to demolish. Of those ideals none, wrote Milton, were dearer than freedom of conscience. His vision of a 'vast city, a city of refuge' where 'there be pens and heads . . . sitting by their studious lamps, musing, searching, revolving new notions and ideas' utterly unchained by guardians of conformity, *is* New York, *is*, at its best, the American Republic. And Milton's passion to dissociate sin from crime, to deny the state any authority in matters of belief – 'The State shall be my governors, but not my critics,' he wrote in *Aeropagitica* – had an American heir, albeit in the anti-urban person of Thomas Jefferson. So if we wish – and perhaps we should – to make a 9/11 memorial not merely out of concrete and cascades but from the living body of the idea that most clearly separates us from the death-drive of the intolerant, let it be Jefferson's, written for an Act for Establishing Religious Freedom in Virginia, drafted in 1777, that 'truth is great and will prevail if left to herself [for] she is the proper and sufficient antagonist to error and has nothing to fear from the conflict unless by human interposition disarmed of her natural weapons, free argument and debate, errors ceasing to be dangerous when it is permitted freely to contradict them'.

And there is another high principle, dear to New Yorkers, abhorrent to the armed evangels of purity, be they fanatical jihadists or racist Nordics – one on which the immigrant Republic of the United States was founded: pluralism. The survival of that ideal lives on at the memorial, and not in any tablet of text but in the names inscribed on its rim, the neighbourliness of the beautiful impurity of cosmopolitanism: Shakhar Kumar; Whitfield West Jr, Marianne Liquori Simone, Helen Crossin Kittle and Her Unborn Child. The world music of those names is perhaps all the eloquence we need.

NEIL MACGREGOR:
GERMAN MEMORIES

'Suppose', I say to the director of the British Museum, as we sit in his office, 'I want to write the history of Neil MacGregor in three objects. What would they be?'

'Golly!' he says. 'One never thinks of oneself in those terms.' The animated voice, at once posh and populist, tails off in amused reflection, but only for a moment. Then, like the sport he is, he plays the game. 'Yoghurt,' he says, decisively, 'a pot of Danone yoghurt.'

And then the story of Neil MacGregor – where he came from, what he became, the marvels he makes for British culture – begins.

'My parents' – both Glasgow doctors – 'were of that generation completely marked by the war.' For many Britons, that meant a recoil from Europe – but not for MacGregor's father and mother: 'They were absolutely determined I should be brought up as a European.' And thus, at ten years old, began the Glasgow boy's *wanderjahre* – the making of the roving, endlessly curious, marvellously cosmopolitan mind Britain is lucky enough to have had presiding, successively, over two of its greatest cultural institutions: the National Gallery and the British Museum.

'I was sent to France, on my own', to a family in Paris and Arcachon, that lovely Atlantic seaside town south of Bordeaux. There, young Neil had his epiphany with Danone yoghurt and life was never the same. 'There was no such thing as yoghurt in Glasgow in the 1950s . . . salt in the porridge, yes, but not yoghurt, much less "*yow-uhrt*" as I learned to pronounce it.' A dreamy, happy look comes into his eyes as he intones, as if about to burst into song, '*Yaourt, dessert agréable et sain.*' 'That was the first French phrase I learned! I wandered happily around Paris by myself, then, back in Glasgow in 1957, I said – hopelessly pretentious as I was and wanting to be somebody else – "I just can't go on without yoghurt." My parents took a dim view of this but realised it was their fault for having introduced me to sophistication. There was only one place I could get yoghurt and that was the Jewish delicatessen, so off I went, armed with my pocket money, and that was my first encounter with European Jews.'

There in the Glasgow deli, buying yoghurt from the white-aproned Jewish refugee, inhaling the aroma of sausage entirely unrelated to bangers, the boy MacGregor became, heart and soul, a cosmopolitan. That the shopkeepers spoke German was itself unexpectedly thrilling. 'In general, in the social hierarchy of Scotland, you didn't expect shopkeepers to be polyglot.'

The Glasgow deli – simultaneously Jewish and German, and this just twelve years after the great extermination – was the threshold of a life that would be devoted to the exploration of cultural paradox; to what MacGregor calls 'the complication of history'. His own history has not been uncomplicated.

After reading French and German at Oxford, he was set to write a thesis at the École Normale Supérieure in Paris. The subject was Denis Diderot, the sceptical philosopher and playwright whose omnivorous, encyclopaedic intellect and droll temper would have been a perfect match for MacGregor. Instead, he was summoned back by his father to solid professionalism in Scotland: a law degree and then, for some years, practice. It was while he was a lowly apprentice in one of the grandest Glasgow law firms that he remembers one of his young colleagues being told, as a Catholic, that while he was welcomed as an apprentice, he must never dream of making it to a partnership. (He did.)

Perhaps it was this sudden revelation of stifling narrowness that sent MacGregor, at the comparatively late age of twenty-seven, back to his true calling. While a student of art history at The Courtauld, he received the benediction of Anthony Blunt. From editing *The Burlington Magazine* he became, at forty-one, the director of the National Gallery. Over fifteen years he wrought a mighty transformation, turning a slightly forbidding cathedral of art into the people's treasure house without the slightest compromise of aesthetic or scholarly standards. He could work this wonder, as he did again at the British Museum, because in a markedly unBritish way, Neil MacGregor is unafraid to care, and care intensely. And what he cares about most is the museum as more than a lodging house of masterpieces. For MacGregor, the purpose has always been historical and anthropological, to make a place where people rethink their place in the world and rediscover, richly, just what it means to be a human.

MacGregor is about to embark on what may be his most challenging exercise yet in cultural education: a thirty-part series of weekday programmes for BBC Radio 4, coupled with an exhibition at the British Museum, modelled on the phenomenally successful 'History of the World in 100 Objects'. But instead of a Minoan bull-leaper or a Hawaiian feather helmet, this show will feature an Iron Cross, a Gutenberg Bible, the great Tischbein portrait of Goethe, the inscription from the gates of Buchenwald concentration camp, and a wetsuit in which fugitives from the Stasi hoped to make it to freedom across the Baltic in a dinghy. For MacGregor's subject is Germany – from nebulous, scattered, medieval beginnings, via passages of cultural glory and unparalleled brutality, all the way to the twenty-fifth anniversary of the demolition of the Berlin Wall and the latest iteration of the protean, endlessly mutating thing that is Germany arriving at the status of the senior power in Europe.

MacGregor senses the project may be a hard sell. He says, a mite defensively – as if anticipating the tabloid headlines

'Germans Occupy Bloomsbury, Don't Mention the War' — 'I've really no idea whether people are going to be interested. The British, on the whole, don't travel to Germany and don't read German literature.' But then he says he also wondered, at the time it was being planned, whether the great Shah 'Abbas Iranian exhibition of 2009 would appeal to the public. 'The culture was unfamiliar and there was such a legacy of hostility.' Come, they did, however.

It is just because the public's general knowledge of German history, such as it is, is so dominated by one immense and hideous narrative — that of the Third Reich and the Holocaust — that MacGregor wants to open minds to something broader and more complex. Those horrors he calls — provocatively — 'extraordinary historical anomalies'. What he wants to present to the listener and the visitor to the exhibition is, rather, a strikingly under-determined national identity — one not, from the beginning, driving inexorably on the Autobahn to annihilation. This Germany was more often than not uncertain about what it was, where its borders, especially east and west, lay; a Germany hostile rather than hospitable to centralising power. MacGregor believes this characteristic serves Germany well in its understanding of what a federal Europe needs; when to step in and when to step back. The first section of the exhibition will, he hopes, undermine the stereotypes right away by presenting objects that speak to what he calls 'the floating frontier'. The series begins in Königsberg where, right now, 'there is not a single ethnic German', and the show will include a handcart of the kind pushed by millions of women (for the men were gone) expelled from the eastern lands in 1945 and 1946. Nearly 14 million had to be somehow housed: 'It was as though the entire population of Canada or Australia arrived all at once in Britain.'

His own journey to this particular cultural destination also began in the yoghurt-and-sausage years. Hamburg in the early 1960s was the next place in the making of the historically engaged mind-expander. MacGregor was sixteen, on a school exchange and, like all of us in that generation, most of the Germans he had encountered were the caricatures of war movies, kitted out in SS caps, screaming '*Halt!*' from watchtowers. In Scotland, his parents had friends who had been prisoners of war who felt that their incarceration was, on the whole, 'an honourable recollection'. But it was otherwise in France, where the bitterness and fury were implacable and intense. 'There were people one met whose whole family had been deported; there I learned what it meant to be occupied.'

Given those preoccupations, the depth of the unhealed wounds, Hamburg was astounding in its silence. 'I expected them to talk about their Blitz. The city was almost completely rebuilt – there were still people living in the big old house where I stayed, who had been there since the years when people had to take in the emigrants, but they lived a separate existence on the top floor . . . But at school no one spoke about the war; *nicht sprechen*. It's not as if I expected the children to ask, "And what did you do in the war, Papa?"' – he laughs one of his endearingly self-mocking chuckles – but, 'on the borderline between cowardice and courtesy', he stayed silent for a while too.

Then one day he realised that the German boys of his own age had no idea that the war had begun when the Reich invaded Poland. 'When I did talk to them, they said it had been because Poland attacked Germany!' (More laughter.) No modern history was taught in the German schools. 'This didn't surprise me, because we didn't do the twentieth century in our schools either, so I mentioned it to the teacher and we had a remedial class on it.' MacGregor is at pains to say that this was not a one-boy educational reform project (though the rest of us might say it presaged it): 'I was just puzzled.'

The puzzlement deepened in 1969 when, with Rudi Dutschke and the student revolts turning the world upside down, MacGregor understood that this was a generation that had had virtually no access to the history of its calamity and the atrocities it had inflicted on others. And he speaks of their struggles to remake their own history, grounded in truth, as an extraordinary exercise in engagement. I, too, remember Berlin in 1965, when the choices were, on one side of the wall, the oblivion of shopping on the Ku'damm thanks to Chancellor Erhard's *Wirtschaftswunder* and, on the other, the fairy tales told about valiant communist resistance to the Third Reich and the canonisation of its pre-war leader Ernst Thälmann. But among the young, something hungry for truth was seditiously stirring. In Vienna, on the other hand, denial danced in three-four time to a Lehár waltz.

Not so in beleaguered Berlin. There, history, torn from the bed of forgetfulness, was made to be painful, conflicted and guilt-ridden, yet critically important for the possibility of a future life. 'There could be no redemption,' MacGregor says. 'How could there be?'

But in Germany, history determined how you lived. Arguably it still does. This, he believes, is sharply different from the way in which history is routinely consumed in Britain. This may be about to change as our own country goes through its own painful shape-shift but, mostly, he says, it's about 'good things done in the past'. 'It's in our architecture, our churches, a kind of solace', sometimes on the verge of sentimental self-celebration. German memory, on the other hand, is dangerously, inescapably explosive. From one side of the Siegestor in Munich, the victory arch built in the 1820s, 'it looks exactly like Hyde Park Corner, but on the other side it's completely blown away'. In the very centre of Berlin, in the heart of the capital, is 'a monument to ineradicable shame, the Holocaust memorial. I can't think of any other monument like it in history, a monument to their own shame. Where in Paris is a monument to French imperialism; where in Britain a monument to our own wrongdoings?' There are, I remind him, museums of slavery and empire. 'Yes, but not in *Whitehall*,' he says.

Is he worried that his enthusiasm might tip over into vulgar boosterism for the latest edition of democratic Germany; that it will be all Goethe and no Goebbels? 'Yes, I was – and am.' But it would be hard to accuse MacGregor of running away from the pain and horror, any more than he feels modern Germany itself has done.

There is a huge, hideous anti-Semitic poster advertising '*Der Ewige Jude*' (The Eternal Jew) exhibition of 1937; and that gate inscription from Buchenwald, '*Jedem das Seine*' (To Each his Own). MacGregor's subtle unpacking of the multiple, hideous ironies of that display is itself worth the price of admission and characteristic of his method. First, an evocation of its setting – the camp just outside Weimar, home both to Goethe and the great burgeoning of free modernism in the 1920s. Then, the physical thing itself, letters of iron assiduously repainted every year by the Nazi regime, so that inmates would have to read it every day from inside the camp parade ground. Then the swerve into unintended resistance: the lettering made in a Bauhaus font by one of its designers, implying the torturers, too, would get their just deserts. And then a succession of twists: the author of that little act of subversion, Franz Ehrlich, released in 1939, goes on to have a flourishing career under the Nazis, and in 1948 Buchenwald is recycled as a communist gulag, where a quarter of the inmates perish.

There is a point in the exhibition, he says, from which, in one direction, the visitor will be looking at the beautiful portrait of Goethe by Tischbein – with the great man, a slouch hat on his head, recumbent in the warm light of an Italian landscape, the epitome of humanely learned Germany – while the other direction takes the eye to that Buchenwald inscription. In the Buchenwald essay MacGregor himself raises the awful, essential question of how one kind of Germany turned into the other. But he doesn't offer an answer: 'I don't understand it myself,' is all he says.

His humility is moving but, all the same, there are ways to try. The Holocaust was made possible precisely because earlier figures who had shaped German culture had dehumanised the Jews and made them objects of murderous hatred. MacGregor wants to present Martin Luther as the father of the German language, and so he was. But what he also fathered, all the more potently for that status, was an obsessive anti-Semitism that described the Jews as 'full of devil's feces which they wallow in like swine'. 'If they could they would kill us all,' he raved, proposing in *On the Jews and their Lies* a programme to burn their synagogues and raze their houses, so as to dispose of the 'poisonous envenomed worms' that they were.

Luther's anti-Semitism is not in this show. But its illuminations are no less deep for being less relentlessly grim. The Iron Cross, often taken to be the emblem of Prussian militarism, was, MacGregor reminds us, invented in a moment of reformist egalitarianism, following the traumatic defeat and humiliation by Napoleon in 1806. Its consequence was to trigger a period of reform. The Cross was iron, not of a precious metal, because it was the first decoration that could be awarded to all ranks. Sanctioned by King Friedrich Wilhelm III, it became the symbol of a new, comradely patriotism.

The Imperial Crown featured in the exhibition is not the original medieval crown, said to have been worn by the Holy Roman Emperor Otto I at his coronation in Rome in 962 and then reused by successive HREs all the way to the liquidation of the empire in that fateful year of 1806. That was the object MacGregor wanted for the show, but he was 'politely' turned down by the Vienna Museum on the understandable grounds that it 'doesn't travel any more'. In an inspired move, MacGregor remembered that Kaiser Wilhelm II's request had also been declined around 1906, causing the Hohenzollern emperor to make his own version. Showing the replica allows MacGregor to turn the story into a tale of competition for the legacy and memory of Charlemagne, not just between

Austrian Habsburgs and Prussian Hohenzollerns but between the Germans and the French.

These are the sort of memory riffs, back and forth across time, that MacGregor loves and at which he is the peerless virtuoso. His eyes shine with a boyish glee when he brings off one of those complications that makes us rethink stereotypes. The damage done by mutual tribalism is very much on my mind as I talk, referendum looming, to the Glaswegian who might one day soon become a foreigner to his own country. I ask him whether Germany is a prism through which we can all think harder about what it means to give our allegiance to a national community. He does not take the bait: 'I think it's very sui generis to Germany.'

All the same, there is no doubt that he does think of the British Museum as a place with a vocation inherited from its founders like Sir Hans Sloane all the way back in the mid-eighteenth century. Even then that mission was comparative anthropology; the liberating notion that by looking at objects from a range of cultures, separated by geography and history, one would come to understand more about the single object at hand. Sloane collected shoes, all of which had in common the universal need to protect feet but were radically different in every other respect. 'One pair of shoes is not interesting; a huge collection of them an illumination.'

The insatiable curiosity to collect and inquire into other cultures, to learn their languages and understand their traditions in their own terms, was largely pre-imperial, which, MacGregor says, makes the museum descended from Sloane 'perfectly suited to a postcolonial world'. It was and is the museum that resisted the ignorant assumptions of cultural and racial superiority displayed by the proconsuls and generals of the Victorian empire. MacGregor's dauntless belief in the humanising effect of looking at the work of others, rather than endlessly at our own reflection caught in the mirror of time, could not be more timely as the fires of wounded nationalisms burn down the house of common culture.

I ask him the question on many people's minds: it is widely rumoured among the chattering classes that he will not stay much longer in this job. He gives no indication of departure any time soon but smiles and says, 'I've been here a long time – twelve years.' But then we talk a bit about what kind of exhibition within our own history might have the same salutary effect of raising questions, facing hard truths through the eloquence of objects, and he says right away, 'Ireland.'

I can't quite tell whether he has just thought of this or whether he has the next great project already under way. All I know, as I step out into Great Russell Street under a kindly drizzle, forgetting that, in the brightness of our voluble conversation, we only got to one of the three objects in the history of MacGregor, is that times being what they are, neither the British Museum, nor whatever is left of the house of Britain itself, can afford to do without Neil MacGregor.

ORHAN PAMUK:
THE MUSEUM OF INNOCENCE

I am hunting *huzun*, the state of collective melancholy that, in his lovely memoir, *Istanbul*, Orhan Pamuk says is the soul of his city. *Huzun* was 'covered women who stand at remote bus stops clutching plastic shopping bags and speak to no one as they wait for the bus that never arrives . . . the patient pimps striding up and down the city's greatest square on summer evenings in search of one last drunken tourist . . . the little children in the streets who try to sell the same packet of tissues to every passer-by'.

But from where I'm sitting, in a Tesvikiye tea house, a stone's throw from the Pamuk Apartments where the writer lived as a child, huzun is in scant supply. Perhaps it's the season, the time of day, the moment in history. It's Ramadan; the July heat has abated into nothing more than a late afternoon cheek-warmer. The Bosphorus, which Pamuk often describes as turbid and dangerous, the graveyard of cars and burnt-out shoreside houses, glimmers blue and gold. Sidewalk cafés are packed with animated Istanbullus, sipping honey-coloured tea from tulip-shaped glasses. Istanbul's famous packs of urban feral dogs are nowhere to be seen. Only the canine senior citizens, long since retired from snarling at taxi cabs, lie fat and floppy, snoozing beneath the café tables, a puff of contentment periodically escaping their slack upper lips as if exhausted by the work of doing absolutely nothing.

Evening draws on. The muezzin calls and a thin line of the

faithful responds, walking unhurriedly through the doors of the Tesvikiye mosque. This was the first mosque to which Pamuk was taken by his nanny, comforted by the rugs that seemed to him just another kind of domestic furnishing. Though he never became the poet he aspired to be, his father's gods were Sartre and de Beauvoir. 'He used to go to small Left Bank hotels and write existentialist diaries, which he gave me before he died,' Pamuk recalls. In his Nobel Prize lecture in 2006, Pamuk paid lyrical tribute to that suitcase of writings.

Piety still has an uphill battle in fashionable Nisantasi. Not long after the mosque opens, a lone fiddler establishes himself a few hundred feet away. After one number he is loudly upbraided by an indignant street cleaner, but whether for impiety or impeding the passage of his truck, it is impossible to say. This is about as raw as the battle of faith gets on this side of the city. Even politics conspires to relax the agitated. In the end, Taksim, the square that for many years was the hub of Pamuk's own life, avoided the rolling disasters of Tahrir. After the tear gas and the outrage that brought more multitudes into the square in June, Prime Minister Recep Tayyip Erdoğan, whom Pamuk compares to a vainglorious sultan in his twilight years, has since beaten a tactical retreat. 'He was politically and economically successful, old, perhaps sick, so now like an Ottoman ruler he decided he'll do monuments, and he'll do it inside [Gezi] park, recreating the barracks – which was nothing, ugly – then some architects and Greens began to resist. Erdoğan thought "nothing will come of it" – he mismanaged the whole thing, attacked them with tear gas, burnt their hands, and the "Tahrir" effect took over; people tweeted to defend themselves against the disproportionate attacks.'

Erdoğan's plans to rebuild the former barracks and open a mall are on hold. So for now, Islamists and café people are content to avoid lethal collision, tacitly agreeing to live in separate worlds, rubbing shoulders rather than throwing stones. An occasional headscarf goes by but the Nisantasi women make their own statement by wearing their hair shoulder- or even waist-length. Wherever they are, they fondle it, threading the tresses through manicured fingers as they chat on their mobile phones. Their hair is black, blonde and every so often blazing red, exactly the hue of pul biber, the Aleppo pepper, which, like much else here, is less hot than it looks.

Orhan Pamuk himself is a virtuoso of delight: good-looking in his early sixties; voluble, intellectually as well as personally hospitable. The assignment is to talk to him about Turkey after Taksim, caught between the pulls of tradition and modernity, nationalism and liberalism. Who better to do this than the Nobel Prize winner, sometimes in trouble with self-appointed guardians of National Honour, but also the writer who has featured these conflicts in a number of his books. When I try to get him to talk about his positions on such matters, he agrees that 'Turkey's record on free speech is not good and still is not good', but insists that it's in his fiction that the most radical statements are to be found. 'I don't like to make strong statements. I want to write strong novels . . . I keep my deep radical things for my novels.'

It is in them that, in obedience to the good writer's rule that 'you identify with people not like you', he makes the utterances and actions of all his characters equally credible. 'I write a world where everyone is partly right', even 'the Islamist who shoots people. He's not crazy, he has a point of view . . . the novel is a place where you make such people understandable.' In two of his novels, it is the conflict between past faith and new fashions on which the drama turns. In *My Name is Red*, set in the late sixteenth century, miniaturist painters are required to produce work in the new perspective-framed 'Frankish' manner that would be likely to impress the Venetians. In *Snow*, a westernised poet encounters impassioned Islamists in a remote provincial town. In both stories the question of the true Turkish way becomes a matter of life and death.

So I have my agenda for discussion. But then, on a side street in

Çukurcuma, once a run-down district of hilly alleyways, houses left behind by Greeks, victims of riots in the 1950s and expulsions in the '60s, changed now by the arrival of boho buyers, I step into the house that Pamuk has turned into his Museum of Innocence and right away I forget all about Erdoğan, Taksim, Gezi Park and Islamism. I am, instead, knocked over by something that seems altogether more important: the capture of love's time.

A grandfather pendulum clock, uncased, hangs between two of the three storeys. The Pamuk Apartments had one but the grandparents did not 'like so much the dong dong ding' violating the quiet of the night and fastened its pendulum, making it keep company with the other moribund objects: the piano that was never played; the glasses too crystalline to drink from. The museum's walls are lined with sixty-odd display cabinets, each designed by Pamuk, containing the objects and emblems that are the memory traces of each significant moment of the love affair that is the tragicomic heart of his novel, *The Museum of Innocence*. The progression begins with the love-object Fuzun's shoes and a handbag from the shop where the narrator, Kemal, a rich relation, discovers her. On the ground floor is the *pièce de résistance*: some 4,000-odd cigarette ends smoked by Fuzun, most bearing her lipstick smudge, each inscribed below with the exact day, time and circumstance of their smoking. Smoke of course is one of the oldest emblems of the fugitive nature of worldly experience. But in *The Museum of Innocence*, Fuzun's fag-ends live on, anything but spent, each one a little burst of recollection. 'So who wrote all these inscriptions?' I ask Pamuk, who is showing me round. He looks incredulous. 'Me!' 'All of them?' I reply, astounded. 'All of them!' He beams, proudly, boy-scoutishly. 'How . . . long?' I say. 'Oh, just the summer of 2011.'

It seems crazy and would be, had not Pamuk created in this old house what may be the single most powerfully beautiful, humane and affecting work of contemporary art anywhere in the world, at once poetic and darkly comical; tender and, case by case, space by space, aesthetically ravishing. You can spend the rest of your life going round contemporary art fairs and never experience anything remotely like this: connecting chambers of memories and dreams, objects embalmed in loss, suspended in a medium of agonised longing, brought into mysterious, telling juxtapositions – an abandoned glass of tea immensely out of scale with the harbour scene into which it leans. On such visions, waking and dreaming, by night and by day, passion feeds. The whole place is inhabited by the recognition that the most intense moments of love are marked by the desperate craving to halt time.

From childhood until the age of twenty-two, Pamuk was a painter, making streetscapes of the city, especially tumbledown half-ruined buildings, districts or glimpses of the Golden Horn seen from gaps between the houses of Cihangir, where the family retreated after their fortunes faded. 'The second child is always the bad, imaginative boy and I was that,' he recalls. Amused by his son's sketchings, his grandly feckless father praised him and there was no stopping Orhan. But in the '60s there was no Istanbul art culture to speak of to nourish the gift except in the derivative ways Pamuk came to despise. 'I realised if I wanted to be a painter I would have to leave Istanbul as the [art] culture there was very weak and the galleries very limited.' Hating the trap by which he seemed condemned to be 'someone else' in order to be his own artist, and while studying architecture at university, it came to him that he should be a writer. 'I told myself I had a screw loose and I stopped painting and switched to novels.'

The museum, however, proves that the two vocations were not, after all, mutually exclusive, and perhaps that was the whole point of it for this most painterly writer. Within the displays the production of words is inseparable from the gathering of images. There are genuinely old newspapers and then some faked by Pamuk to be exactly as they were in the late '50s and '60s; real movie posters and imposters, advertisements, street signs; even a mock anatomical chart of the physiology of love-pain. Art stalks

almost all his writing. *My Name is Red* had its genesis in his urge
to write about the paintings of the sixteenth-century miniaturists
in compelling, concrete detail. 'Most of the book is ekphrasis,' he
says – the thick description of the works. At some point Pamuk
decided that this might not be enough to hold the reader, and a
murder story (about which he feels wistful) was introduced.

I am about to talk about this to him when, as if by some act
of Pamukian magic, we glance through a window and there,
standing before an easel, is a young woman, her hand and arm
extended, swooping decisively down over the surface, in the
unmistakeable action of someone blocking out the early stages of
a composition. It is too good to be true, echoing as it does photographs of the young Orhan seated at his easel doing much the
same thing. Painting he loves, still, as the dominion of instinct;
a release from the cerebral calculation of writing. 'I wrote *My
Name is Red* just to remember painting, where the hand does it
before the intellect. When I'm captive to it I'm a happier person.
Kierkegaard tells us that a happy person is someone who lives in
the present; the unhappy person someone who lives either in the
past or the future. When I paint I definitely live in the present,
like someone in a shower whistling or singing.'

Pamuk doesn't whistle but he laughs at the serendipity of the
artist at the window. Laughter comes easily, punctuating the flow
of his eloquent English. If the shadows of huzun sometimes lie
long and dark over his fiction, they coexist with artfully wrought
black merriment. The run of his impassioned sentences darting
back and forth between the highest of high culture – Nabokov,
Tolstoy, the Russian formalist Viktor Shklovsky – and boyish glee
in the trivia of daily life. A whole chapter in Istanbul is devoted
to the inadvertent comedy of street signs and homespun oracular
declarations in the press. 'It has been suggested that, to beautify
the city, all horse-drawn carriage drivers should wear the same
outfit; how chic it would be if this idea were to become a reality.'
But he loves to sweat the small stuff, to get it exactly right. To

enshrine the soda pop, Meltem, favoured by Fuzun and Kemal, he went to the length of making a fake black-and-white television commercial, complete with a blonde emerging from a convertible happily grasping her bottle of the gazoz. I notice that not only her hair-do but her mascara is perfect '60s. 'Of course!' he exclaims.

It was Shklovsky, he tells me, who declared that 'a plot is something connecting things one happened to like'. And contrary to my naive assumption that it occurred to Pamuk to create the actual museum after he had written the fictional one, as a kind of literary vanity project, the process happened the other way about. The outlines of the inconvenient passion, kindled in Kemal just as he was getting engaged to someone else, had laid themselves out in Pamuk's imagination, but that was about it. It was enough, though, for Pamuk to go looking for a house in which the objects of the obsession would be preserved before there had been much work on the novel. His original idea was to write a catalogue of the objects with entries so long and digressive as to form the novel itself. While getting on with other work – *Snow*, *Istanbul* – he haunted local flea markets for clothes (Fuzun seems bodily present in a bright-red printed rayon dress in the centre of one of the cabinet-shrines); for old maps, postcards; a bust he turned into his image of Kemal's father; anything that would construct the wraparound world of Kemal's passion, even toothbrushes, which for Pamuk had to be of just the right period. 'What kind of collectible-vendor (or junk shop) stocks very old toothbrushes?' I wonder out loud. 'I know, I know,' he agrees, chuckling, but someone did. Another vitrine was born. Out of all these objects came characters. The rat-packing hoard became so overwhelming that a warehouse was needed to cope with the overflow.

In his 'office' – a stunning, book-lined space on the summit of a Cihangir street, where the curtain window reveals an impossi-bly spectacular panorama over the Golden Horn, I ask him if he's addicted to lists (as am I). 'Oh,' he says, 'that's what novels are, drama plus a list . . . now we're approaching the list part so you have to make the list dramatic, then you have to stuff the drama with another list.' It's what children do, he says, faced with 'so much complexity, so many black parts you can't understand, but you can name them and once you name them it's the first attempt to exhaust them. I like the epic artist, who has taken a brush, who wants to take the whole world and set it in an encyclopaedic book.'

The sheer baggy plenitude of life still entrances him and makes him sympathetic to the great list-makers of literature: Rabelais, Sterne, Melville, Eco. Minimalist he is not; *de trop* is never enough. Does that come from a kind of benign greed, I ask? He admits to this, in a *Museum of Innocence* kind of way: the possibility of somehow absorbing and embodying the whole abundance of the world through the singularity of its sensuous detail. 'It's a greed for power; once you have a list you have power. As Foucault said, you categorise it, it's in your world, you own it like a collector. Kemal wants to be powerful and collect . . . a novel is a story that collects everything in the list.' But lists can weigh heavily too. One of the saddest cabinets of the museum is covered with photographs of all the places around Istanbul where Kemal imagines he's glimpsed his missing Fuzun but had been mistaken: a map of proliferating illusions.

We've done the tour of the museum; now we take in the *tour d'horizon* of the Istanbul that lies before us. Pamuk points to the graceful little pavilion at the water's edge beneath the greenery of the park surrounding Topkapi. 'See that? That's where the sultan would go and bid farewell to the fleet off to some battle or God knows what. Bye-bye fleet,' and the turbans and kaftans suddenly seem to materialise – in miniature naturally – down below. I am happily adrift in a Turkish memory mist, feeling oddly at home. A fish supper with Pamuk's girlfriend Asli and his daughter Ruya impends. He offers me a glass of wine. And then he doesn't.

'You know, Simon, we haven't really talked of Taksim, have we? Wouldn't your editor think this a bit odd?' Gloomily I acknowledge she probably would. 'Right then.' The bottle is recorked, I snap to attention as best I can, but Pamuk really saves me the bother by proceeding to interview himself on Subjects of Contemporary Importance. He was, in fact, away when the great demonstrations in the square took place but because so much of his life, child and adult, has revolved around Taksim Square – 'half Times Square, half Hyde Park Corner' – he feels the drama keenly and personally. 'Gezi Park, it's not much but it belongs to everyone who's been there; a neighbourhood place so they would resist with everything they could just cutting one tree down, never mind the whole place, and for what? A mall, a barracks, which everyone knows was nothing, nothing.' What then unfolded was for Pamuk something poetic, a spontaneous outpouring of feeling, shared by many who shared not much else. 'There was no idea of overthrowing the government, it [Taksim] was just anti-authoritarian, it was amazing, great, wonderful,' he says. 'I respect and like the poetry of that moment.'

There have been other ways in which Erdoğan has been testing his power to impose norms on Turkey: not just the restriction on alcohol sales, but the banning of abortion and, most ominously for Pamuk, the application of a discreet kind of censorship in which writers who give offence are not, as was the case for him, put on trial but summarily fired by newspaper editors. 'Arms are twisted to fire and fire and fire anyone critical,' he says.

To ask which side might ultimately prevail in Turkey is, he thinks, beside the point, not least because allegiances are so complicated. There are nationalist conservatives who are secular in the Atatürk mould and then there are those who are not. All of his instincts hanker after a Turkey that was not monocultural or monolingual, rather an imperial polyglot Istanbul of Greeks, Armenians and Jews. But whatever happens in formal politics or even in Taksim Square, the deeper conundrum remains and, as he says, is by no means unique to Turkey. 'There's always a clash, always the modern betrays history and culture, and always tradition betrays modernity. There's no solution.' If you lean forward into modernity you betray the authenticity of your past; if you lean backward into tradition you betray the principles and philosophy of, say, freedom of speech and pluralism, to which any writer has to be committed.

The question hangs in the air, unanswerable for the moment. Asli and Ruya arrive and the sardines and anchovies await my greedy attention. At this minute it is hard to remember that across one border, in Syria, tens of thousands have been slaughtered in a relentless civil war; across another, in Iran, theocracy still reigns with unelected Guardians vetting political candidates for their moral orthodoxy. Suddenly, Turkey's problems seem manageable, even enviable. But it's not this placebo philosophy that stays with me that night and on the flight back to London; it's the ultimately bigger thing, the tenderly human thing: a lipstick trace on a cork-filter cigarette; a glass of undrunk tea; a girl standing beside a lamppost who may or may not be there except in the haunt of memory where she will always lodge.

ART, ARTISTS AND CRITICS

It was Camille Corot's landscapes that drew from Paul Valéry the con-
fession that 'we should apologise for daring to speak about art'. Perhaps
it was the incomparable purity of Corot's light, captured by painting
outdoors in the Forest of Fontainebleau, which made a poet feel inad-
equate about rendering it in prose. But any honest writer about any
kind of fine art will share Valéry's sense of clumsiness at the futility of
translating vision into text.

Nevertheless, we try. Why? Partly, I suspect, from enthusiasm's
overspill: the urge, not necessarily egotistical, to share insight born of
accumulated knowledge, but also released by what Duchamp (mean-
ing it unflatteringly) described as the 'retinal shudder': the visceral
response that takes place in the material presence of the work itself.
Walter Benjamin was wrong. The aura of a work of art 'in the age of
mechanical reproduction' has only become more unreproducible with
digital ubiquitousness. So even with the ancient task of ekphrasis —
thick description — as its calling, non-academic art writing still has
useful work to do.

It positions itself somewhere between the monstrous heaviness of
catalogue essays, their ball and chain of theoretical solemnity clanking
along behind the work itself, and the necessarily summary captions on
the wall. The most memorable art writing is often the most personal;
a transmission from the moment of fresh encounter. My late lamented
friend Robert Hughes was incomparably brilliant at delivering those
quick, rich exclamations, and was (as were we all) horrified and

depressed when Time magazine decided it could do without art criticism altogether.

I began writing art criticism for the TLS (a new editorial departure launched by its then editor John Gross) in the 1970s; principally but not always about Dutch painting. The challenge then, as it has remained – through the years of writing reviews for the New Yorker – was how to be invitational and instructional at the same time; to deliver an impression of what awaited the beholder but also to supply the modicum of knowledge and questioning that would make for a richer gallery experience. Some of the pieces here add to that mix, visits with contemporary artists themselves. Artists can be notoriously laconic about their work, as they have every right to be. I spent one of the most tortuous hours of my life trying, at the Hay Festival, to extract from Howard Hodgkin (whom I had known for years) any kind of insight about his painting, an excruciating ordeal some of the audience enjoyed as a priceless moment in the theatre of cruelty, the verbose critic undone by the obdurate silence of the master. But just as many – especially the women artists featured in the pieces that follow, who gave me the time of day – can be thrillingly eloquent about their art and how they came to conceive and execute it. It's their creative hospitality that gets critics, especially this one, off the hook of Valéry's embarrassment.

THE PALACE OF COLOUR

How blue can it get? How deep can it be? Some years ago I thought I'd hit ultimate blue at the Guggenheim Bilbao where a sheet of Yves Klein's blue was displayed on the gallery floor. Klein had a short career (dying at thirty-two), much of it obsessed with purging colour of any associations external to itself. Gestural abstraction, he thought, clotted with sentimental extraneousness. But in this search for chromatic purity Klein realised that however ostensibly pure a pigment was, its intensity dulled when mixed with a binder such as oil, egg or acrylic to make useable paint. So he commissioned a synthetic binder intended to resist light-wave absorption and to deliver instead maximum reflectiveness. Until that day in Bilbao I'd thought him a bit of a monomaniacal bore, but Klein International Blue (as he patented it), rolled out flat and elsewhere pimpled with saturated sponges embedded in the paint surface, turned my eyeballs inside out, rods and cones jiving with joy. This is it, I thought. It can't get any bluer, ever.

Until, that is, YInMn came along; the fortuitous product of an experiment in Mas Subramian's materials science lab at Oregon State University. Oxides of magnesium, yttrium and indium were heated together at 2,000°C with the idea of making something useful for the electronics industry. Instead what emerged was a brand-new inorganic pigment, one that absorbed wave lengths of red and green, leaving as reflected light the bluest mid-blue ever. Subramian made sure to send a sample to the Valhalla of pigments, the Forbes Collection at Harvard University, where it sits with 2,500 other specimens of pigment documenting, visually and materially, the whole millennia-long history of our craving for colour. Among the blues on its shelves are 'Egyptian Blue', a modern approximation of the very first synthetic pigment engineered five millennia ago, probably from the rare mineral cuprorivaite, heated with calcium and copper compounds, silica and potash, to around 850–950°C, and used for faience, the decoration of royal tomb sculpture, and the wall paintings of temples. After that ancient technique was lost, blues strong enough to render sea and sky were made from weathered copper carbonate: azurite (from Persian izahward), known to the Greeks as *kuaonos*, in Latin *caeruleum*, our vision of cerulean. Azurite was crystalline bright but liable to fade in binder and when exposed to light and air. But in 1271, Marco Polo saw lapis lazuli quarried from a mountain at Badakshan in what is now Afghanistan, which, elaborately and laboriously prepared to remove impure specks of glinting iron pyrite, became ultra-marine, the blue from 'over the seas', as expensive, ounce for ounce, as gold and so precious that it was initially reserved for the costume of the Virgin. In addition to all these, the Forbes Collection also has poor man's blue for the jobbing painter – smalt made from crushed cobalt, brilliant when first laid down but notoriously fugitive, fading over the centuries to a thin green.

The Forbes Collection owes its existence to the belief in the interdependence of art and science, but it is also an exhaustive archive of cultural passion. For as much as high-minded theorists over the centuries have condescended to colour as retinal entertainment rather than high concept, painters themselves have often had a different view. In a modernist rehearsal of the ancient quarrel between *disegno* (drawing) and *colore*, Wassily Kandinsky, no conceptual lightweight, characterised colour as fully occupying painted space, in contrast to line, which he argued merely travelled through it. At any rate there is no doubt that colour wars can get serious. The Forbes Collection, which acquires newly minted pigments along with its trove of historical specimens, has a display of Vantablack, which absorbs so much – 99.6 per cent – of light waves that it has to be grown on surfaces as a crop of microscopic nano-rods. Originally invented for military use (those disappearing aircraft flying through Donald Trump's starwars dreams), the sculptor Anish Kapoor saw that it might produce spectacular vacuums for his own work; a collapse of light that would work as a designed black hole. But working with Vantablack's producer he reserved the pigment for his own use. An outcry spurred the invention of a competing 'Singularity Black', marginally less absorptive but also translatable into paint. More dramatically, the artist Stuart Semple was driven to create a 'Pinkest Pink', making it freely available to the art world with the express exception of Kapoor. Undaunted, Kapoor found a way to obtain a sample: coat, not his pinky, but a middle digit and flip the pigment bird online to Semple and his critics.

While enjoying these pigment brushfires – and displaying them in a vitrine for the public – Narayan Khandekar, the head of the Straus Center for Conservation and Technical Studies at the Harvard Art Museums, knows he presides over something immeasurably more serious: a priceless resource for understanding the construction and preservation of works of art. The vast library of colour is housed along with technical laboratories in the airy, steel and filtered-glass addition the architect Renzo Piano designed for the Fogg Museum. Rows of them stand and sit in tubes, jars and bowls, visible through floor-to-ceiling glass-fronted cabinet doors. Khandekar, learned and expansively eloquent, had the winning idea of displaying them as a line unspooled from the classical colour wheel, reds at one end, greens at the other. There are the showy products of nineteenth-century chemical innovation: viridian green, cadmium orange, and the chrome yellow with which van Gogh was infatuated but, over time, has begun to fatally darken his sunflowers. But the unique heart of the Forbes Collection are the natural and historical pigments that were the staples of a painter's inventory before chemically synthesised paints replaced the impossibly esoteric, the dangerously toxic, the prohibitively expensive and the unreliably fugitive.

Among those relics is Dragon's Blood, reputed in antiquity and the Middle Ages to have got its vividness from the deep wounds of dragons and elephants locked in mortal combat. The pigment actually owed its intense redness to resin secreted from trees growing on the islands of Socotra (in the Arabian Sea) and Sumatra, especially the rattan palm and the draecena draco. But the Forbes sample of Dragon's Blood has faded, most likely from exposure to ultraviolet light, to a dusty rose, not much different from the blushing nineteenth-century pigment named '*cuisse de nymphe émue*' – thigh of an excited nymph. But the light fastness of Dragon's Blood has always been as unreliable as its mythology. Even in the early fifteenth century, Cennino Cennini's practical manual *Il Libro dell Arte* had warned artists, beguiled by its reputation, that its 'constitution will not do you much credit', meaning it was likely to prove fugitive in light and air. Better to stick to madder root, red ochre or red lead minium, in use since classical antiquity.

But many of the Forbes specimens preserve the poetic mystique of their origins. There is a murex shell from the eastern Mediterranean, a quarter of million of which were needed to make a single ounce of 'Tyrian purple', the colour edging the togas of magistrates, senators and generals in the Roman Republic, and a whole lot more toga in the case of the emperors. There too is a loaf of toxic tawny-red cinnabar, for centuries the indispensable ingredient of vermilion. Buy it in solid cakes and give the top of it a little tap, Cennini advises, lest some scoundrel pass off stuff adulterated with brick dust. Here too is the copper-arsenite Scheele's Green, synthesised at the beginning of the nineteenth century and more dazzlingly vivid than traditional verdigris, the latter laboriously made from the particles given off by copper when eaten by vinegar or strong red wine. A variant, manufactured a little later, Emerald or Paris Green was so cheap to manufacture and so dazzling to behold that it coated Victorian wallpapers, children's toys and, according to the colourman (a preparer and vendor of artist's materials) George Field, who was horrified at it getting into the hands of the young, even confectionery. Bonapartists mourning the death of their hero believed the British had poisoned Napoleon passively but deliberately by having him sleep in a room papered with the deadly green, the damp of oceanic St Helena conspiring to produce the arsenic exhalations that did for the captive Emperor.

Here too are two tubes of Mummy Brown, made from the rendered gunk of the Egyptian dead, thought to be rich in bituminous asphalt used in embalming and as a shield against insects and fungal decay. Pounded and mashed Mummy had been in continuous demand in Europe for medicinal purposes at least since the sixteenth century, as it was thought to cure pretty much anything, from gastric pain and menstrual obstruction to epileptic fits. An early Mummy trader, Sir John Sanderson, shipped 600lbs of assorted bits and pieces in 1586 to satisfy an eager market. Colourmen and druggists often shared the same inventory and the same slightly occult alchemical reputation for possessing exotic secrets unavailable to the common run of men. 'Bitumen' – a cover-all term for the asphaltic muck – was prized for its tawny glow, but the romantic taste for the oriental macabre in the nineteenth century had a lot to do with its reputation as a unique pigment. Costume paintings of the kind fashionable in the 1830s and 1840s were gravy-brown (and heavily varnished), as if patina conferred historical authenticity. You could reach for the cuttlefish sepia or burnt umber, but if Turner needed loamy richness, he reached for Mummy. Eugène Delacroix, an arch-orientalist, is said to have used Mummy in his ceiling painting for the Salon de la Paix in Paris's Town Hall in the 1850s, though since the chamber was destroyed in the Paris Commune of 1871 we will never really know. Its vogue was short-lived. By the middle of the nineteenth century, Laughton Osborn's *Handbook for Young Artists and Amateurs in Oil Painting* advised 'there is nothing to be gained by smearing our canvas with part of the wife of Potiphar'. Specialists in history pictures like Alma-Tadema loved it, but according to Edward Burne-Jones's wife, Georgina, when he told the pre-Raphaelite that he was about to go see pieces of Mummy before they were turned into pigment, Burne-Jones snorted that the name was just a childish fancy. On being assured the Mummy was real enough, Burne-Jones insisted on giving his own tubes of the paint a burial in the garden, planting daisy roots to keep the Mummy company, rather in the spirit of Egyptian resurrections. Alison Cariens, the learned Harvard Museums' conservation coordinator, who showed me withered chunks of desiccated Mummy in the collection, explained that while no DNA had been found in samples to suggest ground-up human bones, the millennia may well have degraded biological material beyond reliable analysis. And in any case, she added, humans were often accompanied by mummified animals for their journey to the afterlife, so that a tube of Mummy Brown might well be constituted from the remains of long-gone crocodiles or cats.

The Harvard Collection is not confined to jars or the collapsible tin tubes invented by an American artist in London, John Goffe Rand, in 1841, superseding pigs' bladders, which had for centuries been paint containers but, when pierced to squeeze the paint, had a tendency to dry out notwithstanding their stoppers. The Forbes shelves contain a whole universe of paint sources: cuttings of red madder root, the most common source of red dyestuff, convertible into pigment when cloth clippings were dissolved in alkali, then combined with alum to make insoluble red lake. The minute silvery bugs heaped in a glass bowl like a crunchy bar snack are the Mexican *Dactylopius coccus* – scale insects that swarmed on prickly pear cacti and whose crushed bodies produced the lustrous carmine-crimson that so excited Caravaggio and Rubens. After the Spanish conquest of Mexico and the discovery of the brilliant colour in native painting and textile dyes, buggy cochineal almost immediately supplanted traditional red from the *Kermes vermilio* scale louse found on evergreen oaks in eastern Europe, but they were expensive and laborious to harvest, a two-week window after the feast of John's Day at the end of June being the only time the kermes would swarm in multitudes enough for commercial production in Poland and Armenia.

Seductively beautiful pigment sources abound on the Forbes shelves: rocks of arsenic-sulfide realgar and orpiment, blazes of flame-orange locked within the crystals. Cennini attached a health warning to his advice about the twin perils, though mysteriously he also claimed orpiment to be just the thing to cure a sick sparrowhawk. Too spellbinding not to get a closer look, I stuck my head in the cabinet. 'Don't breathe, dont touch,' warned the kindly, vigilant, Alison.

Further along the row is a greyish-greenish wrinkled ball, about the size of a baseball, a section sliced open to reveal yolk-bright Indian Yellow. Yellow of any kind never had much traditional purchase in Christian iconography, where gold signified the aura of sanctity. But when Baroque masters experimented with extreme effects of light and dark, the hunt for a light-fast deep yellow became urgent. Rough, intense yellow was the colour of choice for Caravaggio's plebeian coarsely clad rumps, thrust through the picture plane at the beholder in the *Crucifixion of St Peter* or kneeling at the feet of the *Madonna of Loreto*. The cheapest, most widely available traditional yellow was made from unripe buckthorn berries but was too fugitive for the likes of Rembrandt. Instead, the pigment supplying the bloom of yellow on the luxurious costume of Lieutenant van Ruytenburgh in Rembrandt's *Night Watch* and the scrim of primrose light hanging over Vermeer's *Woman with a Pearl Necklace* in Berlin is the gracefully pale lead-tin yellow, which, despite being in common use in the Netherlands as 'massicot' in the seventeenth century, went into oblivion until being recognised once more as a distinctive pigment in the 1930s. In the early eighteenth century antimony combined with lead became the base for one of the first synthetic pigments – known in England as 'Naples Yellow'. But when the European powers made invasive inroads into India in the eighteenth century they would have seen the deep, rich, glowing yellow used to paint walls and images on them, as well as Mughal book illustrations. Botanical pigments like saffron and turmeric had been used in Persian and Turkish art for centuries, but this was something altogether more chromatically vibrant. The first samples of the pigment available in Bengal, Bihar and in some centres of Rajput painting, like Jaipur, were known by many Indian names – *piuri*, *puri*, or *gowgli*, a corruption of Persian *gangil*, meaning, significantly as it would turn out, 'cow-earth'. The amateur artist Roger Dewhurst recorded buying and using it in 1786. But it was in the early nineteenth century that Indian Yellow established itself as something special in the Romantic palette. Especially beautiful in watercolours, Turner used it for the washes describing the limpid radiance of Venetian dawns and sunsets. The infatuation could lead him astray. His romantically imagined Jessica, Shylock's daughter, painted for the Earl of Egremont, stands in front of a wall so screamingly yellow that facetious critics called it 'woman standing in a mustard pot'.

And then there was the smell. Depending on the sensitivity of your nostrils, the aroma of unrefined Indian Yellow was either interestingly pungent or rank and disagreeable. To a number of those getting a nostril-load of it, the pigment had a distinct whiff of castoreum, the aroma, prized by some, of a secretion from a gland close to the anus of beavers – which can't be that bad since it's still used in commercial ice cream as a substitute for vanilla. But for those who didn't care for it, the odour proclaimed the origin of Indian Yellow in animal urine. George Field and many others thought the animal in question was the camel; others speculated about elephants, water buffalo and cattle. During the nineteenth century, this whole matter became an ongoing controversy. Failing to discover nitrous traces, a chemical analysis in the 1840s argued that Indian Yellow was much more likely to originate in a plant, possibly the *Mycelium tinctorium*, as its name suggests in common use as a dye, and notorious for its pissy odour.

In 1883, however, in response to a query from a German chemist, the director of the Royal Botanical Gardens, Sir Joseph Hooker, was able to shed light. An expert on the materials of Indian arts and crafts, T. N. Mukharji was sent to the village of Mirzapur in the Monghyr district of Bihar where he had met gwala workers who produced the Indian Yellow sold in Calcutta. He had also seen with his own eyes, he reported, cattle being fed on decaying mango leaves (and water); this yielded the strong urine that, evaporated in earthenware pots set over a fire and after further baking in the sun, produced the precious yellow powder. The gwala trained these cows to urinate four times daily by stroking them where it counted, but understandably the cattle didn't look too healthy on this regime. Periodically, 'to keep up their strength', Mukharji wrote, they would get a diet supplement, but the pigment would lose something of its startling, fiery intensity. By the turn of the century the suffering of the animals led the British-Indian government to ban production, and certainly by the 1920s Indian Yellow had pretty much vanished from colour-men inventory. But was any of this true? When Victoria Finlay, the author of *Colour: A Natural History of the Palette*, travelled to Monghyr around 2002, she failed to find any local memory of cows fed on mango leaves for the brightness of Indian Yellow and decided that the whole thing must have been yet another fable in the great treasury of colour lore. But that story hasn't ended.

In any event, the great collection on the fourth floor of the Harvard Museum is more than a treasury of colours and stories. For Edward Waldo Forbes, director of the Fogg from 1909 to 1944, pigment hunting and gathering was not just a matter of encyclopaedic entertainment: the creation of an archive of lost or languishing colour; it was all about the union, urgently needed, as he believed, of art and science. His own pedigree spoke to the paradox: Boston Brahmin but with one grandfather a railway magnate, the other the metaphysical philosopher-poet, Ralph Waldo Emerson. With a Massachusetts schooling, culminating, inevitably, at Harvard, Forbes was a typical product of the generation that believed that gilded age materialism could be redeemed by the 'western civilisation' eulogised by Professor Charles Eliot Norton, himself a friend of John Ruskin. The moral purpose of that civilisation, they assumed, was the conversion of raw wealth into beauty and humanism, and the place to understand how that miracle came about was of course Italy. But while this made Ruskin's Oxford (two years) and the Renaissance tour mandatory, Forbes also shared the fin-de-siècle American resentment at condescending European assumptions that the New World would never really rise above breathless cultural tourism. Serious art history was supposed to change that, and in 1900 Wellesley College was the first in America to offer a degree in the subject. But teaching at Wellesley and Harvard had to make do for the most part with lantern slides and plaster casts.

In Rome, the 26-year-old Forbes bought his first Italian painting, a half-ruined flaking altarpiece attributed to Giròlamo di Benvenuto. Many other paintings followed, all intended by the altruistic young collector for museum loans, above all to his alma mater. Well aware that Yankee buyers were being treated as easy marks, Forbes realised he needed to educate himself in the material construction of Old Master paintings if he was to avoid being swindled. It was at this point that the claims of art and science converged. The romance of originality, the inimitable hand of the master, passionately upheld by Ruskin, presupposed that to feel the transcendent force of great painting, it was necessary to recover (or even imaginatively re-enact) the artist's magic moment of creation. Strip away the varnish, then, both physical and cultural, for what had been intended to seal in the freshness of the completed painting had in fact trapped it beneath a yellowing skin. But what lay beneath? And how to recover its purity without inflicting yet more damage? Modern archaeology with its patient, fastidious excavations seemed to offer a promising model. There were also Victorian manuals on the material structure of pigments, one on *The Chemistry of Paints and Painting* by Arthur Herbert Church, the first true scientist to hold a position at the Royal Academy in London. In 1928, Forbes invited a Harvard chemistry professor, Rutherford John Gettens, to create and run a lab in the newly rebuilt Fogg Museum. Close by the pigment collection is a monumental legacy left by Gettens, a cabinet of thousands of cards: colour samples of paint, showing how each would be altered in shade, depending on binding medium – egg yolk, egg white, the whole egg, or oils – the kind of optically concrete visual information that loses its subtlety of differentiation when digitised.

For Forbes, painterly re-enactment, using materials as close to the originals as could be found, was the precondition of true understanding. Pigment-hunting commenced. But he also planted madder in his private garden at Gerry's Landing on the Charles River, and taught the lab section of his courses at home where students could brush gesso and lime onto an assigned patch of wall and, using pigments ground at MIT, have a stab at Boston fresco. His passion for authenticity encompassed the globe. Resins came from Singapore and Indonesia; Japanese woodblock colours from his diplomat brother William, stationed in Tokyo in the early 1930s. The pigment collection grew and grew, and Forbes set a small selection in a cabinet display for students to inspect.

I knew about this modest exhibit when I was teaching art history at Harvard in the 1980s, but never thought to seek it out, much less bring students to it. All art historians respect conservation, but its working practices, other than the X-radiography and spectroscopy used to reveal under-drawing and painted designs invisible to the naked eye, were pretty much a closed book. But Narayan Khandekar is all for accessibility. Up to a point. A small free-standing vitrine is available to the public. But the long parade of pigments marshalled visible through the glass cabinet doors can only be glimpsed tantalisingly from the opposite side of the fourth floor across the open space of the atrium courtyard. This is partly because they are not just there for show but are actively used during conservation. A life-size portrait of King Philip III of Spain from the workshop of the court painter Juan Pantoja de la Cruz from around 1605, acquired by the Fogg a century ago, is a perfect example of an official image multiply copied to promote royal authority throughout the Spanish realms. Visible, though much darkened and deteriorated, are passages of cochineal carmine and quite possibly Mummy Brown, the palette thus encompassing a whole empire of pigment from Egypt to Oaxaca.

More notoriously, the large Rothko murals given by the artist to Harvard in 1962 were installed in a modernist office tower where they were subjected to an unfiltered flow of light and the kind of casual abuse likely to be inflicted by chairbacks and college catering. Recognising the extent of the damage, the murals were taken down in 1979, but on their public outing in 1988, Harvard found itself on the receiving end of brutal criticism for the neglect. Rothko's use of rabbit skin glue as the binder for his colours has been mentioned as a culprit, but even with that paint laid onto raw unprimed canvas, Khandekar says that wasn't the problem at all. Nor was Rothko's choice of Lithol Red for his monumental portal-like forms, since the synthetic pigment is famed for its light fastness. Further research (along with work on the Seagram murals at the Tate in London) leads Khandekar to believe that the trouble was Rothko's mixing a calcium salt red with mineral ultramarine – to make the purplish indigo the artist loved so much in these saturnine years of his temper. Unpredictably, the synthetic and the natural pigment reacted badly to each other. Physical restoration using those colours would have made matters worse, not least because they would have bled directly into the raw canvas. But using one of the surplus-to-requirement paintings Rothko added to his commissions as template, the conservation scientist Jens Stenger was able to design a digital 'colour map' of both the original appearance and its faded-out damage. Since passages of the murals, depending on how exposed they had been to window light, had degraded differentially, Stenger's reparatory light projections had to be absolutely precise, but the result, shown with the murals in 2014, was a revelation.

This is just the kind of complex, painstaking project that gives Khandekar and his colleagues at the Straus Center most satisfaction; science summoned to do what Ruskin and Forbes wanted: bring the work back as close to its inception as possible. He is himself a modern personification of the Forbesian mission: a hardcore scientist converted almost mystically to the imperatives of art. 'Art didn't play much of a role in my upbringing,' he says, somewhat wistfully, and his first degree from Melbourne University was in marine chemistry. 'But I realised there had to be something important about art in Australia with all those enormous government buildings devoted to it.' His curiosity triggered, he went to the National Gallery of Victoria (where he could have seen one of the greatest early Rembrandts – a disputation between Peter and Paul, the former silhouetted in a red ochre cape, Paul illuminated in a blinding flash of lead white with perhaps a touch of lead-tin yellow). Enchantment built to the point where Khandekar asked himself, 'How can a scientist spend his life with art?' The conservation course at the Courtauld answered the question, followed by practice at the Hamilton Kerr Institute at the Fitzwilliam Museum in Cambridge; then a spell at the Getty Museum before landing in the techno-paradise of the Straus Center.

To listen to Khandekar and his colleagues in the labs talk about pigments (as well as the other physical matters that, far more than is usually supposed, determine the way we experience paintings) is to share a response that is at once technically sophisticated and disarmingly naive. Like Ruskin, they too are devotees of the innocent romance of creation: when all went according to the artist's plan; the colours were fresh; everything dried as it was

supposed to; and there was no thought of the hostile work of
time. (Interestingly, the one artist who mournfully did anticipate
the fade of time was Vincent van Gogh, who argued that that
was all the more reason to trowel on the colours in resistance.)
Khandekar winningly – and rightly – says that while many artists
fight shy of entering the interpretative fray, all of them will be
eager to discuss materials; the physical exercise of executing their
designing idea. From personal experience I know this to be true,
and there are contemporary artists like Michael Craig-Martin,
once a specialist in delivering drolly indirect meditations on the
distance between expectation and representation, who have now
turned a corner into radical, almost violent chromophilia. Cy
Twombly went from automatic writing on the blackboard to oil-
stick Dionysian exuberance. The concept is the colour.

In fact, this has long been true. On the ground floor of the Fogg
are two large works, one by the Colour Field painter Morris Louis
from the 1960s, a vertical pour down unprimed canvas; the other
thick free-standing dabs of paint by Joan Snyder from 1970 called
Summer. They are the kind of statements about the irreducibility
of colour: its enthronement as the most painterly of painting
instruments, devoid of any kind of representation, which don't
wear well. But, perhaps under the influence of the treasures of
the Fourth Floor, they seemed to me unexpectedly alive. Louis's
Blue Veil – in surprisingly mint condition – lives up to its lyric title:
a cascade of sensation; Snyder's colour patches, ostensibly trial
strokes, the palette translated to canvas, are shrewdly calculated
for complements, contrasts and conflicts a one-piece sampling of
colour theory from Newton and Goethe to Albers, yet winningly
set down with impulsive nonchalance.

Given the roll call of artists for whom colour was sovereign,
from Giovanni Bellini and Titian to Vermeer and Tiepolo, Monet
and Matisse, to say nothing of the almost lurid polychrome of classical statuary, the sculpture fronting some Gothic cathedrals and
the spiritual gem-like burn of stained glass, the glories of Rajput

painting and Japanese woodblock prints, the defensiveness of colourists and their champions seems gratuitous. But the history – or
at least the mythology of condescension – is real. Recalling the
visit he made with Michelangelo to Titian's studio in the winter
of 1546–7, when both masters were working in Rome, the artist
and biographer Giorgio Vasari had Michelangelo say what a pity
it was they didn't teach proper drawing in Venice. (Titian's most
militant defender, Lodovico Dolce, would return the favour by
complaining how regrettable it was that Michelangelo couldn't
really paint.) For the Florentine theorists like Leon Battista
Alberti (though not as fanatically as is sometimes assumed),
disegno, drawing – especially from classical exempla – was the
vehicle of the noble idea; the philosophical concepts transform-
ing art from artisanal craftsmanship to the noble visualisation
of humanist ideals. In his breakthrough years before the First
World War, producing works like the *Red Studio*, which dissolved
plane and line completely in a bath of flat colour, Henri Matisse
was patronised by the Cubists as lightweight. Later his cut-outs,
which he called sculpting directly in colour, were treated as a
sure sign that the old boy had entered second childhood. Over the
centuries it is precisely the instinctive demotic appeal of colour
as the driver and modeller of visual experience that has led to its
being discounted as so much retinal entertainment: the painter
as showman. Cennini, after all, gave advice in his book on gild-
ing and heraldry, making no distinction between any sort of low
and high art.

Embedded in the criticism was an implied attack on naturalism
as a lower order of artistic thinking. When the Venetian champions of *colore* praised Titian and Giorgione for their unsurpassed
representation, especially in oils, of nature – landscape and
human flesh – the compliment was made to seem backhanded
by the champions of the drawn Idea. The implication was, that
whether it was Leonardo's *Treatise on Colour* advising artists working in the open air to try to match samples of their paint with

what their eyes beheld (a principle he hardly followed himself) or, according to Joachim von Sandrart, Claude Lorrain's habit of getting up before dawn to experience the sunrise, staying through changes in light and then racing back to the studio to match it in paint, the strenuous attempt to replicate optical vision with painterly practice was a fool's errand. All those books of which there were plenty in the seventeenth and eighteenth centuries giving detailed (and actually fascinating) advice about which pigments to use for grassy fields, flowing water or a fall of hair, were treated as manuals for journeymen.

But throughout the history of art – and most evident outside the west – colour has always carried with it a heavy freight of non-naturalistic value. The power of Byzantine mosaics was self-evidently iconic; Gothic stained glass and polychrome statuary was offered a vision of the Heavenly Jerusalem. Colour effects of Baroque painting, which to the casual eye might seem straightforwardly naturalistic, were often the result of calculated jarring contrasts or interlocking harmonies as sophisticated as anything that would be dreamed up by Monet or Matisse. The brilliant force of red ochre, made more intense with a red lake glaze that describes the sash of Captain Banning Cocq in *The Night Watch*, was used conceptually by Rembrandt because contemporary theory believed red projected sharply forwards, so that the axial dynamic of that astounding painting, from back to front, in keeping with its 'march out', would feel, as it does, unstoppably propulsive.

Colour can be social and moral, too. To read the writings of colourmen like George Field is to be made aware that he thought his vocation a redemption of sight from the murk of industrial obscurity; what Field called 'foul air'. He thought of himself as a colour reformer, manufacturing reds, greens and yellows free of the toxins of cinnabar and orpiment. When he inveighed, with Dickensian wrathfulness, against the poisonous, child-killing horrors of Scheele, Paris and emerald green, and championed viridian as a replacement, the ethical integrity of his contemporary society seemed to be at stake. Conversely, when science and industry supplied a new and safe colour, Field, who had his own factory of artist's materials near Bristol, took it as providential vindication. Mauveine, discovered by William Perkins in 1856 as a residue of coal tar, drew from him an outpouring of Ruskin-strength joy:

> After its long winter of neglect there sprung from coal tar the most vivid and varied hues like flowers in the earth at spring ... at a touch of the fairy wand of science the waste land becomes a garden of tropic tints ... the world rubbed its eyes with astonishment and truly it seemed as wonderful to produce the colour of rainbows from a lump of coal tar as sunshine from a cucumber.

The redemptive force of colour-driven painting was taken to a revolutionary extreme by the failed lay preacher Vincent van Gogh, whose idols were those ancestral colourists, Rembrandt and Delacroix. The halting tongue that had betrayed him in the Belgian mines turned, with the help of the revelations of Japanese prints, into ecstatic illumination. More than any artist since Delacroix his letters are famously full of chromatic calculations and inspirations (even when, as in *The Night Café*, he used jarring clashes of red and green to signify the depths of drunken despair); almost as if van Gogh were reinventing church glass for the modern age. All the sadder then that some of those calculations served him poorly. The Fogg self-portrait poses him against a turquoise-celadon green background, which van Gogh (as well as unscrupulous re-branders) described as 'Veronese', but was in fact lethally toxic emerald mixed with white.

Instinctively, van Gogh belonged in the company of those – like William Morris, and, more improbably, Kandinsky – who thought colour acted directly on the soul. Van Gogh's Bible paintings like *The Good Samaritan*, a variant on Delacroix's composition, are usually sidelined as sentimental embarrassments. But arguably they lie at the heart of his late work, when the cypresses shake from some primordial upheaval and the firmament boils in the night skies of Provence. Van Gogh set down bristling muscular stabs and dense ponds of paint as the antidote to any kind of academic art, or even the optically mixed snowfall of pointilliste dots. Instead he would offer something for which there would be no need of visual tutorials, a kind of chromatic democracy, a rush of radiance for the masses toiling in their umbrous slog.

Staring at Vincent's jacket, edged with the bright blue trim of his imagination, posed against his poisoned teal, made me think of the sheer labour that had made all those Forbes pigments possible: the women (as Cennini recommended) endlessly rinsing, knead-ing ('day in and out' he says), sieving and drying the pulverised lapis lazuli so that Giovanni Bellini or Titian could clad the Virgin in ultramarine; Amsterdam labourers shut into airless sheds, waist deep in horse manure, the vapours of which hastened the flaking of lead buckles, thus producing the white that allowed Hals and Rembrandt to make visual symphonies of linen and lace. I thought of van Gogh claiming to recognise more than twenty blacks in the portraits of Hals, the best of them created from charred bones. Cennini, needless to say, thought nothing would do except the thigh bone of gelded lambs. And then bright pigments made in grim captivity: the forzado convicts, augmented by north African slaves, condemned to lung-hacking labour in the mercury mines of Almadén so that the Spanish Crown could market its cinnabar; inmates of the Amsterdam House of Correction, rasping away at unyielding brazilwood to produce a red dye that would in any case become notoriously unstable; and the deep blue indigo trans-planted from its native subcontinent to the Caribbean, where its culture and harvest was the product of mercilessly worked slaves.

And, of course, those gwala 'milkmen' (as they were known) in Bihar, whose livelihood, it turns out, came to an end not because of some sudden welling of official compassion for the mango-leaf fed cattle, but because of the rise of Hindu cow-protection politics in late nineteenth-and early twentieth-century India. As for the rest of the story, it turns out, after all, that T. N. Mukharji was a reliable reporter. In addition to his publication he had sent samples of both purified and unrefined Indian Yellow to the Kew Botanical Garden along with one of the earthenware collecting pots and a specimen of the cloths used to strain the urine before evaporation. Some of those samples, in addition to the Forbes balls of Indian Yellow, have recently been subjected to rigorous analysis by scientists at the Conservation Department at SUNY Buffalo State and the Conservation Department of the Indianopolis Museum of Art, using a whole array of investigative techniques from ultraviolet fluorescence and Raman spectroscopy to pyrolosis and a whole host of analytical tools I won't pretend to describe. The results will be published – where else? – in *Dyes and Pigments*. Ruefully conceding that not that many people are likely to read it, the conclusions nonetheless excited Narayan Khandekar. 'Guess what?' he exclaimed happily, waving the paper reporting that the tested samples of Indian Yellow have been found to contain traces of the hippuric acid associated with animal, especially ungulate, urine; as well as the euxanthic acid that could have resulted from the metabolic processing of mango leaves.

I have no idea why, on leaving Harvard's palace of colour, this little vindication should have made me so cheerful. But I do know that if you're so minded you can order a synthesised version of Indian Yellow from Bob Ross, the friendly TV painting tutor, for a mere $7.29 a tube. He uses it, he says, to 'paint the sun in the sky'. Which, as Turner, who did the same, would say, is only as it should be.

GOLD

A mask of hammered gold from Chichén Itzá in Yucatán has its toothy mouth open but its eyes shut. The closed lids are engraved with stubby crosses: the glyph in the native tongue of Nahuatl for teocuilatl or 'excrement of the gods', which is what the Mixtecs and later the Aztecs called their gold. That says it all, really. Dug from the bowels of the earth (often by miners believing that the first humans emerged from caves), the intensity of its light-absorbing radiance transmutes an earthy ore into the emanation of the sun. Early South American goldsmithing, four millennia ago, reinforced this elemental transformation since it was mostly achieved by hammering raw nuggets into fine sheets, at once softly beatable yet still a sunray made metallic.

An unparalleled wonder, in fact, so that, from one end of the world to the other, gold has been associated with immortality since, unlike silver (associated with the moon), it never tarnishes or corrodes. It's this resistance to corruption that has allowed gold treasure to survive from remote antiquity, and, when cleaned, to shine out with blinding lustre. So we have astonishing beaten crowns, ear flares and nose ornaments from the cultures flourishing in coastal Peru 4,000 years ago; the gold that covered the mysterious bronze masks of Sanxingdui in western Sichuan (in, but not of, ancient China, which seems to have been relatively indifferent to gold); and the British Museum's goat standing on its hind legs nibbling its favourite shrub.

Something about the dazzle lures archaeologists into swoons of wishful thinking. Leonard Woolley, who excavated the sites of Ur and Uruk in the 1920s, called the goat 'ram in the thicket' as if it could be associated with the biblical sacrifice of Isaac even though that scripture was written at least a millennium later. When Heinrich Schliemann found a mask of finely beaten gold in the midst of the staggering trove he uncovered at Mycenae, he convinced himself that he was looking at the death mask of Agamemnon.

Gold can be not only a deceiver but a fatal lure. When the Spanish conquistador Hernán Cortés and his men were lodged by the Aztec king Moctezuma in the quarters of his predecessor, they broke through what appeared to have been a recently sealed door-way and found themselves in a storeroom piled high with golden jewels, sculptures and sacred objects. Needless to say, they made short work of the treasure, ripping the layers of gold from objects that had become worthless to them, and melting the metal into portable bars. But when, at the end of June 1520, the Spanish and their Tlaxcalan allies decided to make a night exit from captivity in Moctezuma's palace, their departure was weighed down by the swag. Ordinary soldiers for whom the gold would be the medium of elevation from peasant to grandee were described by Bernal Díaz (who was there) desperately tying the bars to their bodies with strips of cloth. Attempting a retreat along causeways, and fiercely attacked by the Aztecs, many of the gold-luggers drowned in the canals, gold still attached to their bodies.

But gold has also been represented as weightless, a misty, glowing medium in which sacred forms float as they take on physical presence. The first panel of a Marwar school triptych, painted in the early nineteenth century when the Raja was under the influence of the hatha yoga-practising Nath sect, is nothing but a ravishingly brushed patina of golden paint; a universal void out of which forms – human and natural – gradually resolve themselves as the rippling sea of gold washes about them. Centuries earlier, a Byzantine mosaicist working for the Basilica of the Assumption on the island of Torcello in the lagoon in which Venice would arise, produced an immense bowl of gold in which the Virgin and Child are suspended, upright, as if perfectly balanced on a sacred surfboard.

Christian iconography used precious gold for the halos of male and female saints alike, but in pagan mythology and its endlessly recycled imagery, golden effusions were the projections of male self-glorification, especially when directed at female objects of desire. Ovid tells the story of King Acrisius of Argos, who when told by the oracle he would be killed by his grandson, locked up his daughter, Danaë. As usual this was no barrier to Zeus, who entered Danaë's cell and the maiden herself in the form of a shower of gold. In response to the more elaborate version of the story written by Boccaccio, the image of the virginal captive receiving the auric insemination that would produce the hero Perseus, inspired some of Europe's most voluptuous paintings.

Titian painted a Danaë at least six times; the most sensual (at the Capodimonte Museum in Naples) has the velvety nude reclining as the golden cloud bursts above her like the jackpot from some divine fruit machine.

Rembrandt, who was besotted with the Venetian master, made his own gorgeous variation, which did away with cash flow, instead euphemising the gold as a flood of hot light pouring through a parted curtain and washing Danaë's naked belly and face as she stretches out an arm of welcome to the penetration. The great masterpiece, in the Hermitage Museum in St Petersburg, is, however, now a glorious ruin since in 1985 its erotic urgency pushed a crazed Lithuanian to attack it with both acid and knife.

Could these two golden atmospherics – the sacred and the sexual – ever be brought together? Gustav Klimt certainly thought so. In 1903, he beheld the Byzantine mosaics in Ravenna and the epiphany is usually invoked as firing his 'golden' work, climaxing with *The Kiss*, exhibited in Vienna five years later. But, like so many of his contemporaries, Klimt had already been pulled into the golden stare by the championship of oriental ornament in the work of the art historian, curator and authority on carpets and textiles, Alois Riegl. Decoration, for Riegl, was in no way a lesser form of art. It could concentrate within it complex drama. So Klimt's 'Judith', her mouth parted in post-decapitation excitement, registers the force of her sadomasochistic coupling of death and sex by being mantled in an armour of gold tiles, hard metal laid over her voluptuously aroused body, the tight curls of her victim's head brushing against her blushing breast.

Klimt's women are no longer Danaës, their bodies opened in gratitude for divine impregnation. They have themselves becomes the sovereigns of realms of gold enfolding, embracing and engulfing both lover and beholder. The tiles and whorls of gold sheathing Adele Bloch-Bauer turn her costume into a throne from which all-seeing eyes look out with an authority more imperial than anything coming from the court of the Habsburgs.

And though in that kiss, the hunky male mantled in a tiled costume pulls his floral lover to him, it is her face (and her feet clenched in rapture) that are revealed to us while the picture translates the magnetism of their union into churning pulses of golden sensation. The couple dissolves into the kiss on the verge of a formless oceanic mist of gold that the Byzantine mosaicist and the Rajput painter alike would, I think, have recognised as the swimming radiance within which light generates the germ of life.

BLUE

Except for the perverse poet Mallarmé, who called on ashy fog to obscure the aggravatingly impassive azure, we all like a little cerulean in our lives: the sky above, the gentler kind of ocean below, limpid and warm. But do we want to wear it? I have a pair of sky-blue brogues, three words that don't really belong in the same sentence, but they make walking like treading on air. I also have an Alexander McQueen boxy sky-blue jacket, which may have been a mistake, and a whole suit in the same colour from the crazy-great Boston store Alan Bilzerian. But if you want heavenly blue (which is what cerulean means, more or less), you'll need to go to Amsterdam, to the Rijksmuseum, to the *beddejak* bed-jacket worn by the girl in Vermeer's *Woman Reading a Letter*.

One of the most sublime things the hand of man has made, Vermeer's painting is bathed in a crystalline serenity that even screeds of literal-minded articles pondering whether the profile curve is a pregnancy or not can't spoil, not so long as you gaze at the radiant blue at the centre of the picture. Vermeer was prodigal with his ultramarine, the most expensive of all pigments. Most Dutch painters resorted to the much cheaper smalt, made from cobalt oxide. Over time smalt blue goes fugitive, fading to green, but it was all that artists like Jan van Goyen, dependent on high volume for his livelihood, could afford. But Vermeer was the opposite of a production line, painstakingly producing just thirty-six paintings over his career. The best of them concentrated maximum intensity of light and colour, and nothing delivered saturated radiance like ultramarine.

The pigment was costly because the lapis lazuli that was its base was originally obtainable only from Badakshan in what is now Afghanistan. In 1271, Marco Polo saw the mountain from which lapis was mined and marvelled at its beauty. The very term coined for the colour, 'ultramarine' – beyond the seas, carried with it a charge of the magical-mythical so precious that it could only be used sparingly for sacred painting, in particular for the dress of the Virgin. The central panel of Duccio's c. 1315 trip-tych in the National Gallery in London is a communion of the two sacred colours: ultramarine and gold. Fra Angelico applied it in economic patches. An apocryphal story had Michelangelo leaving his *The Entombment* unfinished for want of the expensive pigment. Conversely, slathering on the ultramarine was a coded boast: done exuberantly by Titian in the drapery of the wine god in *Bacchus and Ariadne*; excessively by the prolific seventeenth-century Roman painter Sassoferrato in *Virgin after Virgin*. It was a sign of Sassoferrato's confidence that a self-portrait sets off his ostensibly modest black and white attire against a ground of spec-tacular cerulean.

The genius of Vermeer, in a culture that had removed religious images from its Protestant churches, was to transfer sacred lumi-nosity to what were ostensibly domestic scenes – the pouring of milk, the reading of a letter – so that they became an intimate epiphany. Given the piety of Vermeer's faith, it's hard not to see the Dutch letter-reader as a disguised Annunciation with the Immaculate Conception euphemised into the reception of the letter. Looking into the heart of the blue we are dwelling simul-taneously in an earthly and a heavenly world.

This optical transport was scientifically planned. During a recent restoration, the Rijksmuseum conservators discovered an undercoat of copper green above the primer and beneath the ultramarine, and it may be that extra layer that accounts for the sustained intensity of the colour. But the whole picture is a diffused rhapsody in blue: the leather backs of the chairs are blue (in all probability they would have been green); the rods holding the map of Holland and West Friesland (those parchment and flesh tones work optically with the blue as foil, much like Duccio's gold) are, in another departure from realism, a dark glowing blue. More important than any of these details is the filtered light itself, which Vermeer has made into an ethereal veil of the utmost, pearly delicacy, so that the shadows of the chair backs and the ball-ends of the map rods fall in dark blue hues against the blonde wall.

There's only one other being that manages the same degree of celestial-blue radiance, and that's the Morpho butterfly. It has the same colour contrast of pale brown and brilliant cerulean as the Vermeer but deployed more functionally. The creamy-brown underside of the Morpho's wings work as protective camouflage as it flits through the South American rainforest, feeding and mating. It has just 115 days to get this done but the odds of success-ful reproduction may actually be enhanced by the startling fact, discovered by Nipam Patel at UC Berkeley, that many Morphos are gynandromorphs, with both male and female cell tissue pres-ent in their wings. But those wings are, by butterfly standards, enormous – 12 centimetres wide – and when fully displayed by the male, are the flashiest bolt of colour in the forest.

After the invention of synthetic chemical pigments, starting in 1826 for ultramarine, but industrially produced later in the nine-teenth century, blue-struck artists – Cézanne, Renoir, Picasso and, especially, Matisse – could use variations of ultra and aqua-marine lavishly. Cézanne could chill his blues, almost cruelly where, as costume or background, they make the portraits of his wife inanimate. (It was not a happy marriage.) Or as in the Provençal skies over Mont Sainte-Victoire he could make them tumid with heat.

But the Morpho of modernism was Yves Klein, for whom the perfect ultramarine came to serve as the be all and end all of his work. For Klein (much taken with Zen) that peerlessly rich blue was the visualisation of impassive infinity, the colour that liquidated line, edge, space. In quantities that would have made Duccio and Vermeer faint, Klein produced works that were nothing but blocks of blue. There was a totalising madness about his quest for a hue that would exclude the slightest trace of the mineral impurities found in lapis lazuli. Klein bound the pigment in a synthetic resin he had specially commissioned, which he believed would retain the saturation of the colour in purer concentration than if it were suspended in any oil emulsion. When he had nailed it he patented the colour as International Klein Blue (IKB). In 1958, his fetishism extended to a controversial attempt to drown the obelisk on the Place de la Concorde in blue light; to creating IKB versions of Louvre icons like *The Winged Victory of Samothrace*; and to exhibiting the saturated (he liked to say impregnated) sponges as sculptures in their own right. The obsession made him a poster-boy for minimalist contempt for any kind of gestural art as well as figuration, the liberator of colour free from the presumptuous intervention of an artist's hand.

However tediously compulsive the serial Blues seem on the pages of catalogues and monographs, when you are in the actual presence of the work Klein made in the last few years before his fatal heart attack at the age of thirty-four in 1962, the intensity of the paintings does deliver the retinal punch of its sensory force-field. Few of the paintings are, in fact, perfectly flat. Many of them are textured, pitted, studded and in some cases incorporate those sponges. The paintings that raised most eyebrows were done with what Klein called the 'living paintbrushes' of naked female bodies, daubed in that same blue and then rolled over sheets of white paper. The best of them are actually very beautiful, flowing with a kind of balletic, exuberant vitality.

Blue can calm but, turning cold, blue can also kill. The calming hue can turn into the herald of mortality as blue stains appear on rosy flesh. It's a bad sign when your lips go blue. And the

colour is of course dense with sadness; the spectrum's equivalent of the long sigh. As an expression of melancholy, 'the blues'
apparently came from the 'blue devils', which, in seventeenth-
century English, were said to possess those suffering from alcohol
withdrawal.

But when the Blues are sung with that paradoxical union of
joyful mournfulness – by Bessie Smith or Muddy Waters – they
somehow make us happy. Yet if you want the all-time moody
howl, there's only one performance to have in your head while
you're hunting for blue suede shoes. That would be 'Blue Moon',
sung, to the soft clip-clop of a cowboy's horse, by Elvis: the
only version of the song that drops Lorenz Hart's unpersuasively
golden ending.

HERCULES SEGERS

Among the shattered slabs of landscape etchings that dominate the spectacular show at the Metropolitan Museum of Art, lost amid the erupted geology, it's easy enough to miss the one ostensibly unassuming image that tips you off that something startlingly peculiar is going on with Hercules Segers. It's a heap of books, four of them, page ends towards the viewer; one a sheaf of unbound pages, sinuously bent atop the pile. This etching is the very first graphic still life in all of western art and one of the most startling ever made. The books lie in darkness, printed either in yellow or pink, crowding the picture space so massively that we have a bookworm's eye view, wriggling up the cliff face of their pages for a nibble.

Rembrandt, who owned eight paintings by Segers and who obviously admired his waywardness, liked to paint heavy volumes as well, notably in his portrait of the Mennonite preacher Cornelis Anslo and his wife. But, as befitted that subject, Rembrandt was interested in the living breath of words, so that the pages of Anslo's Bible rise and flutter as if self-speaking.

Segers, whose family were close to Mennonite circles (if not actual Mennonites themselves), is also a visual rhetorician but in a very different tone. He is consumed by the sculptural materiality of things, broken surfaces especially, so his books subordinate any sort of external meaning to the impression of their physical substance: the soft frill of the page-ends; the heft of the bindings, the metal drop of their fasteners. And he will push the comparatively

young art of etching further than anyone before or after, to make
the work itself, complete with stains and foul bites, additions and
subtractions, part of the image. He is the virtuoso of the mystery
of making.

Does this make Segers sound modern? Be careful not to say
so or the anachronism cops will be on your case. He was, they
will say, entirely a man of his time and place, namely the early
seventeenth-century Netherlands. Art history abhors a vacuum
and it gets hot and bothered by any suggestion that sometimes
there are rogue players whose idiosyncrasies are completely unex-
plained by historical context.

Segers's first, anecdotal biographer was Rembrandt's pupil
Samuel van Hoogstraten, who must have seen paintings and probably prints in his master's studio. But Hoogstraten was barely a
teenager when Segers died, some time between 1633 and 1640, so
that his portrait of a genius so unappreciated in his lifetime that his
prints on cotton and linen were used to wrap soap and butter and
who died from a drunken fall down a staircase, must have been
based on anecdotal hearsay. Which, however, doesn't necessarily
mean they were wholly untrue. Segers, who had married well and
bought a house on the Lindengracht, did fall into poverty extreme
enough to force a foreclosure.

But it is a myth that Segers, like Vermeer, fell into centuries of
neglect. He was barely cold in his grave when his 'painted prints',
as Hoogstraten accurately calls them, were eagerly sought after.
One buyer in particular, Michiel van Hinloopen, was enthusiastic
enough to own forty of Segers's works.

And Segers had a relatively well-to-do if uprooted background.
His father was a merchant and buyer and seller of pictures, one of
the thousands of Flemish refugees who fled north after the Spanish
conquest of Antwerp. Hercules grew up in Amsterdam and was
apprenticed by his father to the painter Gillis van Coninxloo,
known for darkly mysterious woodland interiors. But the Flemish
immigrants brought with them a taste for spectacular bird's-eye

view landscapes in which broad, rugged valleys were enclosed by jagged Alpine peaks. Pieter Bruegel the Elder popularised those landscapes, half real, half imaginary, in large-format prints.

Some of Segers's early work follows the Bruegel format, but before long he transformed conventional subjects – ruined castles and abbeys that had become excursion sites – into heady visual experiments. A view through a colossal entrance gate of one of those sites, Brederode Castle, looks onto broken archways and walls that make little or no spatial sense except as a trance of brickwork. Whether or not Segers is using direct visual description, back in his studio he is already working primarily from his supercharged imagination as if transcribing from dreams.

At some point Segers pulls away entirely from the norms of his day, dissolving the distinction between paintings and prints, not least by adding brushed-on details to the impressions. Instead of multiple impressions from a single plate he makes every print an individual work of art. He goes colour-crazy, printing the same image in different coloured inks and differently tinted grounds; some of them so dark – grey and blue – that rocks, themselves made granular and crumbly, or clotted vegetation resemble the phantom impressions of a photographic negative.

The colour effects were just the beginning of the experiments. Segers kept trials that other more fastidious artists would have thrown away, which are some of the most dramatic things here: 'maculatures' (impressions made just to blot excess ink from the plate) and 'counter-proofs' (made not directly from plates but from wet impressions printed again on cloth or paper so that the image would face the same way as the original plate). To deliver a loose and velvety line he would use 'lift' solutions of ink and sugar that would blister open the ground on the plate.

This must have baffled even broad-minded buyers. Segers may have kept the wolf from the door with more conventional topographical prints and paintings of towns in the Netherlands. But he was in the grip of a gambler's instinct that flouted all the norms of finish: making differently coloured versions of the same image, each of which consciously displayed its own imperfections, additions, even trial scratch marks of his instruments.

Every so often he finds equipoise amid the whirlwind of experiment. His most famous image is a mossy tree in delicate tones of pink, green and blue. Such trees had appeared before in the prints of Albrecht Altdorfer, but not like this. Although the tree rises from beneath the brow of a grassy hill, we see neither its base nor its top. On closer inspection the thing is entirely trunkless, just an ascending construction of dripped threads floating in misty space.

Nothing like it had ever been imagined, much less executed, before, and it would be centuries before such visions would make their way into art's vision. Sometimes, a Segers comes along and all the footnotes disappear.

HOKUSAI

For those of us in the springtime of our dotage there is heartening news (as well as numberless pleasures) to be had from the British Museum's radiant, entirely octopus-free, Hokusai show. The supreme master of multiple artistic personalities (thirty changes of name; at least ninety-three changes of address) didn't, so he tells us, hit his stride until late. On the colophon page of *A Hundred Views of Mount Fuji*, at the age of seventy-five, he confessed that until seventy his drawings were beneath notice. 'When I reach eighty I hope to make increasing progress; at ninety I will see the underlying principle of things . . . at 100 I will have achieved divine status as an artist and at 110, every dot and stroke will be alive.'

He only made it to eighty-nine but that bounding animal vitality and leaping line never left him. Perennially hard-up, housed in rough lodgings, 'old man crazy to paint' as he signed himself, crouched over the *tatami*, dressed in a ratty lice-run quilt, helped by his gifted pipe-smoking daughter Eijo, he worked ever harder, faster, deeper.

Hokusai, who died in 1849, is often thought of as the last genius of the woodblock colour print revolution, a people's art if ever there was one, which had begun over a century earlier. But his long life stretched all the way back to the middle of the eighteenth century when the supply of woodblock prints – costing about the price of a double helping of noodles – transformed how art was consumed. It was a genre invented to satisfy the cultural appetite of the biggest city in the world, the million-plus population of Edo (now Tokyo).

Ostensibly the power and the authority of government belonged to the Tokugawa shogun immured in his urban castle. But to keep the nobility out of mischief they were required to stay in Edo, along with their retinues and families. Inevitably, as at Versailles, an emasculated, over-dressed, politically pointless class compensated for its impotence with stupendous conspicuous consumption. That led to the rise of a merchant class to service their ever more extravagant needs. Although the chonin were officially at the bottom of the social hierarchy (in moral status, beneath peasants and artisans), they were the ones who held the moneybags and called the cultural shots, and what they wanted above all was entertainment: the courtesans of the Yoshiwara pleasure quarter; the star actors of the kabuki; copiously illustrated ripping yarns and epics. Prints from cherrywood blocks with their runs of hundreds and then of thousands – many in eye-popping colour – catered to this visual greed. Like all brilliant entertainment cultures drenched in feel-good fantasy, it gorged on sex and celebrity, sentimental romance and over-the-top dramatics.

Hokusai played his part in this. For all his exalted sense of vocation and Buddhist devotion, he was, in his own way, an outrageous showman with art as his magic. Summoned to perform before the shogun he laid down a thick band of blue, then pulled a live chicken from a basket which hopped around in the paint. Hokusai declared the result 'Autumn leaves at Tatsuta river'. In 1804, before an audience come to see a temple sculpture, Hokusai used a hemp broom and 54 litres of ink to make a colossal, 20-metre-long portrait of the founder of Zen Buddhism.

It is hard to think of any artist more indifferent to some notional line (alien, in any case, to Japan) between high art and pop culture. There was nothing he couldn't or didn't do: comic book illustration, travel guides, haikus, paintings of sparrows on grains of rice, designs for netsuke, epic battle scenes and military lives, devotional images of holy men, spooks and tigers, raccoon-dog priests and giant flowers.

His adoptive father was a high-end mirror maker to the sho-gun's court and Hokusai began fairly quietly, mastering the traditional arts. Like all conscientiously exhaustive shows this one wants us to look again at the screens and scrolls. But Hokusai's own judgement was right. An elegant hand is evident but nothing compared with the dynamite to come.

In the 1820s he began experimenting with liberated surges of waves and whirlpools, some of them decorative designs for combs and pipes. The great themes make an early appearance: a spectac-ular woodblock stained with the Prussian Blue that would become a tonal obsession, fishing skiffs racing down heaving waves, the churning water flooding the whole field of vision. He surfed between fine calculation and free impulse. An enigmatic still life features a halved watermelon, set on no visible means of support, the nakiri knife that cut it resting on a finely translucent piece of paper veiling its surface. Above the fruit, lengths of rind like curtain cords hang from a rope. The whole thing is delicate and somehow violent at the same time, appetising and inaccessible, the visual conceit as tantalising as a Donne sonnet.

The accessibility of the woodblock masters, and their instant appeal to western artists and connoisseurs when they arrived in Europe, is sometimes assumed to be connected with their apparent worldliness: the brilliant patterning, the dancing line, the elaborately posed, gorgeously costumed seductiveness of the working girls. When needs must, Hokusai could be as skilled a fluffer as the rest. But the great constant of his life and career was at the opposite pole of sensibility: a deep devotion to Nichiren Buddhism, the cult of the North Star, which brought together the daily doings of the mortal world with intimations of the infinite.

That yoking together of the physical with the metaphysical, the bounding sea and the arcing heavens, is all there in *Thirty-Six*

Views of Mount Fuji. As the seat of immortality, the site was a place of pilgrimage for every sort of Japanese and one of the prints on show has a group of them, some in the ragged clothes of the humble, seen from the rear, standing on the viewing platform of a temple. The mountain is framed in their enthralled beholding like the frame of the picture we have before us, and the composition is designed along orthogonals implied by the gesturing figures so as to converge at the distant conical peak. It is both beautiful and exceptionally clever, as much a meditation on the machinery of sight as on the pull of reverence.

And, this being Hokusai, it comes with a human touch, a boy too small to enjoy the view tugging on the hand of his mother. Like the very greatest masters (Rembrandt comes to mind over and over again in this show), an observant fondness for the human comedy – including his own part in it – somehow deepens the spirituality of the work.

The Mount Fuji prints are deservedly famous for their dramatic manipulation of space and form: the thrilling collision of colossal nature with toiling humanity; those crab claws of the titanic wave frozen at the moment before the crashing break. But Hokusai's most radical experiments in the compression of depth – something the flat bias of woodcuts was made for – are eight startlingly stylised woodblocks of waterfalls.

Hokusai could do guidebook scenery but these are no postcards from the cascade; rather they are little art revolutions, not so much representations as translations of nature into quasi-abstract inventions. The subtle gradations of light and shade that mantle the Mount Fuji paintings, especially those in which the peak stands alone in rosy or reddened sunsets, disappear. So does modelling. The flowing pool at the grassy summit from which the water drops is rendered as a perfectly flat, dazzlingly marbled disc. The downpour is sometimes rendered like the pulsing veins of a body, sometimes as tightly folded drapery. Either way Hokusai has landed us a wholly new universe of representation.

In his eighties, Hokusai portrayed himself not as some patriarch, heroically wasted by his exertions, but rather as an inexhaustibly animated imp, his baggy eyes still bulgingly bright and eager. Reciting sutras on daily walks, he took to painting the engulfing forms of the Buddhist cosmos. A stunning pair of painted panels made for a festival cart heaves with giant waves, between which a spray of spattered paint forms a dance of stars. In what might be his last work, he found the strength to sign off with a dragon soaring into the sky above Mount Fuji, the snaking form rhymed in a dark wraith of smokey storm-cloud. The valediction pierces to the quick. To the very end of his days Hokusai never ran short of sublimity, just of time.

MONDRIAN AND DE STIJL

One of the photos of Piet Mondrian in this life-changing Pompidou show is packed with emblematic cunning. Shot by André Kertész in Mondrian's Paris studio in 1926, it shows him as both the creator and the personification of his art – austere, sharply angular, pressed into the tight containment of his three-piece suit. The coal-dark eyes burn confrontationally from behind rimless spectacles. Behind him, all is uncompromisingly rectilinear. It is a study in the Deadly Earnest.

So why would anyone want to surrender a Paris afternoon to the contemplation of Mondrian's philosophical severities, much less be locked up with the hard-edge utopianism of De Stijl, the Dutch group of artists, architects and designers devoted to fashioning a modern urban aesthetic that criminalised the curve? It might seem about as welcoming as Gerrit Rietveld's notorious chair, bright to behold but brutal on brain and bum.

But the stereotype of Dr Grid isn't the whole story. The exhibition throbs with vibrant colour, beyond the holy trinity of the primaries. Not even Matisse could produce so many delicately modulated greys; nor the panes of etheral, washed-out robin's egg blues; the dusty rose pinks; the toasty burnt orange; and the greens, yes greens, from sour acid lime to deeply bottled, that were the staple of his abstraction before the trinity took over.

Even in the classic period, from the early 1920s to the mid-1930s, when Mondrian was intent on fastening his geometric minimalism to utter flatness, there is more action going on than you might suppose. The black lines of the armature swell or contract; sometimes they falter and halt short of the edge; the edges themselves are rubbed away so that they dissolve seamlessly into the painted sides of the physical frame. The scarlets, cobalts and chrome yellows are intense in some passages, depleted in others. The craquelure that laughs at illusions of timelessness webs the surface of everything, a conservator's nightmare.

The only awkwardness in this spectacular show is an installation that tries, with occasionally claustrophobic results, to accommodate both the masters of De Stijl – van Doesburg, Bart van der Leck, Vilmos Huszár, all of whom were revolutionary geniuses in their own right – and Mondrian in the same space.

At the outset this makes sense because in the first decade of the twentieth century they all shared an enthusiasm for theosophy, the modernist metaphysics that proposed a return to the elemental mathematics that revealed the essential mysteries of the universe. Photographs of the bearded young Mondrian looking half-Rasputin, half-yogi, along with Dutch translations of the lucubrations of Madame Blavatsky and Annie Besant, may make the Dutch theosophists seem crankier than they were. For what was theosophy other than a modernist edition of neo-Platonism, which, since the Greek philosopher's own musings in the Timaeus, had always been at the root of classical aesthetics?

Stylistically, the group thrashed around for a visual idiom that would express their odyssey from base matter to celestial illumination. Mondrian tried the wilder shores of fauvism – literally – converting the wind-scoured Dutch littoral into expressionist mindscapes, the dunes painted in heaving lavender rising into a turquoise sky, church towers drenched in gorblimey pink. The footprints of the dead god of Dutch pantheism, Vincent, are everywhere, in the skeletal trees at Oele, whose spike-branches puncture the face of a full-fat-dairy Dutch moon, the expressionist urge to scream in pigment both liberation and burden as they were for van Gogh himself.

Drawn to Paris, both conceptually and residentially, the group then discarded fauvism for cubism, the disintegrated facets of figuration offering a bolder escape from surface form towards inner structure. But it was never really more than the warmed-over remains of Braque and Picasso, if given a flintier northern aspect with forms smashed into shivers and shards.

Something then happened, and that something was the First World War. The Netherlands stayed neutral, but Doesburg and Mondrian in their different ways responded with therapeutic meditations on the sublime. An entire room in the show is given over to stained-glass murals that Doesburg made for Dutch clients, each built from bricks of coloured light: it is a hypnotically numinous space.

Although Mondrian produced the odd canvas of mosaic-like checkerboard colours, pinks, greens and oranges, his most profound impulse led him in an entirely different direction, one that was drastically to alter the course of modern painting with the generation of true abstraction. Mondrian had come back home from Paris; the old Dutch instinct for seeing celestial patterning in nature may not have been consciously on his mind when he stared out at the North Sea in 1914–15, and translated waves into a rippling field of horizontal hatch-marks. But the translation of natural form into purely abstract language, the flicker of sunlight denoted with dilute chalky accents on the horizontal stab-strokes, went well beyond anything in the vocabulary of Paris cubism. The 'Pier and Ocean' series was an epic inauguration of an entirely new art: contrapuntal, rhythmic, cumulatively spellbinding, something that preserved a relation with natural origin without describing it.

Manifestos followed, always a bad sign. In 1920, Doesburg, van der Leck and Mondrian all issued statements proclaiming the new aesthetic of 'Neo-Plasticism', a label of such empty grandeur that it was guaranteed to undermine its own cause. In the same year Mondrian began to assemble his flat panels depthlessly nailed to the picture plane. The early examples, exceptionally beautiful with their delicate and complicated pavements of greys, slate blues and yellows, are short-changed if seen as just a prelude to primary colour purism, for they are exceptionally beautiful. But as early as 1921 he was purging the compositions of anything but elemental blocks, thickening the black grid so that it became not just a containing membrane but an organic agent of the construction; by the end of the year, the grids resolve themselves into works of adamantine power and simplicity. Just when you think, 'Oh, who needs the modernist moment?', you discover, with giddy exhilaration, that we do.

That's because of the endless variousness of the compositions. While Mondrian's working brief was formulaic, the paintings never are. In *Composition* (1922) a white panel dominates the entire field intruded on by a yellow vertical, a timidly trespassing stripe of scarlet in one corner and a presumptuous edge of blue. Ten years later, in *Yellow-Blue*, the colour blocks press hard against their confinement, generating exactly the tension without which Mondrian's pursuit of equilibrium would have been frictionless. They are, in their way, all perfect.

Mondrian's obsession with purity of form verged on the comical when, in 1925, outraged by De Stijl's flirtation with – no! – the diagonal, he broke with them for good. The De Stijl masters went on to preoccupy themselves principally with architecture and visionary urban design, based on what they insisted were 'elemental forms'. The galleries at the end of the double-exhibition do justice to the utopian sweep of their shared imagination, with a brilliant computer animation of an interior house constructed with great panels of primary colour; blueprints of cafés and city streets, a wonderful display of De Stijl furniture including a Rietvelt sideboard of dark wood and steel pulls that must be one of the most elegant pieces of furniture ever made by modernism, giving some inkling of the dream they had of sleek, functional, machine-age form.

But De Stijl's design has held up less well than Mondrian's paintings. And as they were becoming more rigid, Mondrian was loosening his grid. From 1935 the itch to complicate and syncopate gets to him. He doubles and triples the armatures to make fretworks on which the colours hang, no longer motionless but with a faint thrum and tremor as though beginning the tune-up for full Boogie-Woogie. He loses purity but gains animation. The Mondrian section of the show ends with Pompidou's own *New York* painting of 1962, where, discovering the ultimate grid-city, Mondrian happily surrendered to its jive. (He was himself a dandy ballroom dancer.) The late *Manhattan* paintings replace the black scaffolding with brilliant ribbons along which chatter an electric buzz of colour, making Mondrian, as much as Jackson Pollock, a patriarch of action painting.

They were in fact anticipated by compositions Mondrian made before taking ship for New York in London. One of the jazziest is called *Trafalgar Square* and it makes abstract music out of urban commotion. But don't go looking for it in this otherwise exhaustive and glorious show, which is, after all, a heartfelt celebration of the modernist furnace that once was Paris — even if it took someone as resolutely Dutch as Piet Mondrian to distil abstraction from its fizzing alembic.

ROBERT HUGHES

Robert Hughes's thrilling book on the British painter Frank Auerbach, written at the peak of the author's powers in 1989, begins thus: 'Frank Auerbach's career says little about the "art world", except that it may not matter much to a real artist's growth.' The single sentence, set off as a paragraph, announced that this was not so much an opening as a manifesto. Hughes's prodigious gifts – his lynx-like perception; the sharpness of his analytical acumen; his raw, Promethean literary power – were devoted to saving art from the art world: that fawning, narcissistic, vampirical, trivially fashionable, commodity-obsessed universe he believed was sucking the life out of the thing itself, cheapening the challenge of making great work, and flattening the distinction between novelty and originality. He wrote the Auerbach book at the close of the '80s, which he thought the most despicably meretricious of decades for art: the time of 'supply-side aesthetics', in a typically Hughesian coinage. Ronald Reagan and Andy Warhol he often announced were meant for each other: the twin, winsomely coiffed sovereigns of the realm of the deeply shallow.

Darkly pessimistic towards the end, he despaired of ever liberating art from the art world. The '90s turned out, in his view, to be still worse, though he hailed the giants – Kiefer, Richter, Freud – who towered above the pigmies. He was, like the Victorians he admired – Hazlitt, Ruskin – a fighter-writer. While he was acutely aware of the social matrix from which art arose and to which it would be directed, he was the adversary of all reductionism. Those who thought art the mere extrusion of a set of theories, positions and class concerns, he pitied as intellectually obtuse, compensating for their inadequacy at registering the ultimately irreducible force of art itself, by shackling it to social theory and wishing away (how he chortled at this) the notion of authorship, genius, beauty, those ancient qualities modern muttering had decreed were fictions. Had they never actually opened their eyes in front of, say, Cézanne's *Mont Sainte-Victoire* or Rembrandt's *Bathsheba*, he once growled to me? Or were their eyes somehow locked into an inward glance, lost in the empty spaces of vain self-regard and third-rate speculation?

The Victorian patriarch of the family was Thomas Hughes of County Roscommon, no convict but an emigrant to Australia in search of better things. From running a grocery store he became The Mustard King of Sydney, and it's tempting to think the hot tang and keen snap of English mustard passed down the line to Bob and lodged in his intellectual temper. To be sure, he was no cultural condiment but the meat of the matter itself. But the Irish-Australian stayed in him wherever he went – Italy, England and New York – as a deeply democratic, populist instinct. Detesting insider-dom, academic or art-worldly, and despising the language, at once obscurantist and vacuous, by which those insiders sustained the exclusiveness of their priesthood, Hughes gloried in the trenchant plainness insisted on by his cynosure, George Orwell. 'To see Chardin's work en masse in the midst of a period stuffed with every kind of jerky innovation, narcissistic blurting, and trashy "relevance"', he wrote, in full Orwellian mode, in a *Time* magazine review from 1979, 'is to be reminded that lucidity, deliberation, probity, and calm are still the virtues of the art of painting.'

The same resolute belief that accessibility was not to be confused with triviality, and that hard, complex ideas could be delivered in language that was not ashamed to trigger delight at the same time that it yielded illumination, informed his television masterpieces *The Shock of the New* and *American Visions*. In *Shock*, time and again Hughes gave huge audiences moments of startlingly fresh insight into the ancient warhorses of modernism that he somehow made seem self-evident. The sequence on Seurat, for instance, reflected not just on Those Dots, but on the overall composition as the ambition of a modern painter, obsessed with the frieze and a kind of monumental gravity. And suddenly the compositional weight of the work made perfect sense. It was not the flicker and mottle, the instantaneity of Seurat that ultimately mattered, but the massive statuesque immobility of those figures. Modernism may have been a heady project, but it could never escape the paradoxical longing to become museum classics.

To work this magic – to bolt together keenness of perception and eloquence of reading – you need to be an exceptional writer, a quality not invariably on display in the work of art criticism. More's the pity, he thought, for the challenge of writing about art – as of writing about music – is peculiarly daunting. It is above all an act of translation: the conversion of image into prose with an inevitable loss of substance as one kind of expression is turned into the other. Given this inescapable flaw, the justification for doing art criticism is the opportunity to bring before readers enough of the essence of the work to encourage them to go see for themselves, as well as provoking them to think anew about the implications of that encounter. That provocation inevitably involves an element of performance. Even when the Abstract Expressionist paladins of 1940s and '50s New York (the Bergs, Green- and Rosen) affected ascetic remoteness, they were in fact performing.

Bob Hughes not only made no bones about his own prose performance – despite his commitment to Orwellian simplicity, he revelled in his muscular, swashbuckling sentence-fashioning: shamelessly exhilarated by its energy surge, high on its wit.

Open almost any page of the anthology *Nothing If Not Critical*, or *The Shock of the New*, or *American Visions*, and you will be lit up by the dazzle. But the light is always put at the service of exactness. Illumination for Bob was pleasure. On Picasso's erotically loaded paintings of Marie-Thérèse Walter: 'In the paintings her body is re-formed, not so much as a structure of flesh and bone but as a series of orifices looped together by that sinuous line: tender, composed, swollen, moist, and abandoned. The point is not that Picasso managed to will himself into the thoughts of this woman. He was interested in no such thing. Instead he depicted his own state of arousal, projecting it on to his lover's body like an image on a screen. Her body is re-composed in the shape of his desire and the paintings that result describe a state of oceanic pleasure.'

Stirred to eloquent fury by what he thought was contemporary art's entrapment by the public-relations industry, Hughes was happiest when away from its garish posings and off by himself considering the incommensurable power of a particular master. 'Never go to openings,' he counselled me when I became the *New Yorker*'s art critic in the 1990s. 'It's just white whining. Go when a show is being installed or with the public.' This aversion to the glitz was not his only sin against form. Hughes delighted in an unrepentant, deeply unfashionable allegiance to ancient notions of genius – not in the simple-minded sense of a pantheon of supermen, but in the assumption that there was indeed something unmistakeably heroic about the needful sweat involved in creating art. He was one of the last romantics of tough toil, both its celebrant and its exemplar, and he despised cheap facility and outsourced execution as a betrayal of the principles of the craft.

A gifted carpenter himself, he was happy to confess his admiration of manual skill – and to insist on the sheer labour needed to achieve true artistic power. That inexplicable miracle of a work's force field, instantly registered as a tremor on our senses, he thought not a pathetic fantasy but the perceptual truth. And it could not be achieved with anyone else's sweat. Strenuousness, what Renaissance theorists understood as *difficoltà* – both conceptual and technical – would never of itself guarantee great achievement, but without it, without respect paid to the rugged work needed to extract from the recalcitrant raw material the shape and substance of a particular vision, the result was likely to be facile, and its imprint trivial and fleeting.

Hughes's sticky-fingered relish for the material texture of life, for its savours and flavours, its warp and woof, always immersed in the thick of being, and the skilled gusto with which he set it all down, ought never to be mistaken for indifference to complex ideas and deep analysis. Bob's beef with much (though not all) of conceptual art was the vacant banality of the concepts. Jenny Holzer's visual utterances he memorably compared, and not to her advantage, with the homilies embroidered on an embroidery sampler. He could, if he chose, do duelling discourse at dawn with the best of them, but he preferred instead to invite the regular Janes and Joes who thronged the Met or MoMA into the subtle web of his thought, and let them emerge more thoughtful, more attentive, before the work itself. He was the benevolent enabler of Everyman's epiphany.

Bob could be a good hater, but mostly he was fierce in his loving. The object of that loving was *Homo sapiens*, even when he gagged incredulously on the cruelties of which it was capable. That deep compassion for the rest of us, living and dead, glowed through the pages of his imperishable masterpiece *The Fatal Shore*, the history of the convict settlement in Australia, in which both the victims and the martinets are sketched in all their massively tragic indomitability. But some of the most beautiful passages of that book fix on the landscape itself, where the terrible theatre of atrocity and endurance was played out. 'On top of the cliff, the soil is thin and the scrub sparse. There are banksia bushes with their sawtooth-edge leaves and dried seed cones like multiple jabbering mouths. Against this austere gray-green the occasional red or blue scribble of a flower looks startling.' And Hughes of course knew his koalas:

'Not the winsome cuddly teddy bears of the Qantas commercial but slow, irritable aldermanic creatures with furry ears and a boot-heel nose which ate 2lb of fresh gum leaves a day, and when captured, scratched furiously and drenched the offending hand with eucalyptus-scented piss.'

It took a force of nature to understand how geography and power broke against each other in the Australian epic. And Hughes met his own appalling calamity in 1999 – described in terrible detail in his memoir *Things I Didn't Know* – a head-on collision that he was lucky to escape alive, but from which he never quite repaired his broken body. The nightmare alienated him from Australia – especially after he was put on trial for responsibility for the accident – an estrangement not helped by his intemperate but loudly broadcast view of the proceedings. The shadow was long and lasting, though in the pain of Goya, he found an affinity that let him write a magisterial book and make a haunting, spellbinding television film. Ten years earlier, reviewing a well-meaning Goya show in Boston that attempted to turn the master into an exemplary liberal, Hughes gently demurred, arguing correctly that the painter was as much pulled by the demons of the *pueblo* as committed to exorcising them in the name of a Spanish Enlightenment.

He ended the piece with a statement of the kind of bleak truth he always refused to duck. 'The liberal message was that . . . Man is born free but is everywhere in chains. Goya's message late in life is different. The chains are attached to something deep inside human nature: they are forged from the substance of what, since Freud, we have called the id. They are not the "mind-forged manacles" of which William Blake wrote: they are not a social artifact that can be legislated away or struck off by the liberating intellect, they are what we are. In the end there is only the violated emptiness of acceptance of our fallen nature; the pining of the philosophical dog whose master is as absent from him as God is from Goya.'

Those of us who bitterly mourn him not only as an irreparable loss to art writing and history but also as a friend and inspiration – our old high-voltage mate who turned the intellectual temperature up in any room he entered, and whose lovely, rich Aussie voice sounded from that barrel of a chest made us merrier, wittier, cleverer, better natured than we actually are – want him to have ended with something other than Goya's awful Nada, the world turned to slurry. We hope that he knew how he'd changed the game, opened eyes, sharpened perceptions – how he ensured we never confuse value with auction price, how he'd shared the eureka with us who would never have got it by ourselves, how this most gloriously profane adventurer in the life of the mind and art was an incomparable blessing for us all.

SALLY MANN:
PHOTO TRACES OF CY TWOMBLY

'What will survive of us is love,' declares Philip Larkin in the last line of 'An Arundel Tomb'. The medieval recumbents seemed to him stony until he noticed a gauntlet, faithfully sculpted, removed so that the knight could, in death, take his wife's hand in his. Stony is the last word you would ever use in connection with Sally Mann, that most poetically passionate of photographers, and, as readers of her wild and careening memoir *Hold Still* know, she also comes equipped with a brilliantly exuberant writing style to match. Her title is torn from a beautiful but mercilessly dry-eyed time's-up-fellas poem called 'The End' by Mark Strand. 'When the weight of the past leans against nothing, and the sky/Is no more than remembered light . . .'

But the 'no more' quietus is not Sally Mann's style, especially not when big Cy Twombly was so close to her for so many years: neighbour, pal, fellow crew member on all those ships sailing into classical memory. Her photos make the most of that toasty Virginia light; admitted through the slats of Venetian blinds; a peachy penumbra sliced every so often by a sharp blade of radiance. From what she does with that light – whether it shines on a plaster flamingo or on the crowded tabletop necropolis of sculptures, whether it's a scrim or a shaft – we do somehow infer the mighty force of Twombly's creativity from all the leftovers, smears and stains, and an absence turns into a presence.

Do artists imprint themselves on remains left behind after they have gone? Or do we project our own version of their presence into those empty rooms? Either way, it's a communion. Dante Gabriel Rossetti's paintbox, pre-Raphaelite clottings of emerald, gold and umber, preserved in coagulate thickness, still lie on the table of his studio bedroom at Kelmscott Manor, where he spent one summer in the embrace of his passion for Jane Morris, if not actually in her arms: a crusty mausoleum of desire. The Australian artist Arthur Boyd's studio is crowded with an astonishing number of brushes and palettes, hog bristle to squirrel, as if he restlessly changed his materials every week. The box of colours Turner took with him on the Thames in 1805 when he daubed on little panels, as well as in his sketchbook, is a little pack of painterly brightness, almost two centuries on.

Then there are the stains and splatters that were a conscious extension of the artist's modus operandi: the whiplash drips of Pollock's allover floor; the brush- and knife-wipes covering yards of Lucian Freud's studio wall, a storm of marks he incorporated into some of the late pictures. All this incontinent spillage extends the force of the work way beyond any ostensible framing.

So it was with Twombly. His manner, as Sally Mann fondly recalls in her memoir, was that of a Virginia gent, grandly courteous and wry even when the powerful engines of the demiurge were tuning up and getting ready to play. He never lost the elemental force; the oil sticks stabbed and punched; the paint for the Lepanto series was flung and splashed like sea spray on the canvas sails; in his hands, the smear and the scribble turned lyric. Some of the loveliest of Mann's photographs have that dribble and bleed, so much part of his picturing, running on down beyond the work surfaces, down the skirting boards almost as if the thin, bright flow had never been stanched.

Remembered Light is as much an artist's exploration as it is the house wandering of a bosom pal and creative co-conspirator, barefoot on the floor, pushing open the door of affectionate memory.

'I miss him now each spring and fall, the seasons when he would alight in our valley . . . I miss our afternoons at the kitchen table over his favorite meal, tart apples fried on the woodstove in a cast-iron skillet with bacon fat, cinnamon, salt, and brown sugar.' He is present here through inanimate alter-egos: one of those green pottery frogs, hands clasped about the belly, which is somehow uncannily him, studious and mischievous at the same time; and a pair of Moroccan slippers, the heels squashed in.

Twombly spent half the year in Gaeta, Italy, but knew that he always had to come back to Lexington. The voyages of his work set off from Gaeta, but very often the grandest of them needed to be finished in a big storefront working space in his Virginia home town. If he was among the most poetically charged artists of our time, he was also the least precious. And Mann's pictures fit that temper, being so luminously oblique. In 'Hold Still' she tells the story of Brancusi's exasperation with Stieglitz's relentless photographic artification of his work, to the point where he, Brancusi, turned instead to a cheap camera to catch the makeshift moment of creativity.

Mann captures that same quality here. There are a few documents of improbable discipline: tubes of paint laid out in rows; cleaned brushes reporting for duty in their pots. But these give way to the explosion of fecund mess. There are the marks of Twombly's Rabelaisian appetite for raw colour; but also the lightning strike of the loopily musical blackboard cursives; and the epic one-room panorama of sculptures in both Twombly's priapic-stalagmitic and nubbly-knobbly modes. Like Rauschenberg and Johns ('the dickheads from Dixie', as he called them, and among whom he included himself), Twombly had a dumpster-diver's appetite for junk; for the teeming abundance of life, without which art was just so much modernist asperity. Even more than the other dickheads, he was all about the layering of memories: instinctual, learned, classical and historical; sensual; a feeling that we are what we stain. But many of the photographs here go beyond poetic remembrance of a dear pal, evenings spent on the wisteria-draped deck, and deliver a kind of independent grace. The picture facing Strand's lines, which insist cheerlessly that 'Not every man knows what is waiting for him, or what he shall sing/When the ship he is on slips into darkness, there at the end', is an act of resistance to engulfing obscurity. Instead, the empty room is bathed in a velvety radiance; hot light coming through the window, a gentler gleam on the floor; an open door; and, somehow, full of the man who is gone.

THE NEW WHITNEY

There's art, and then there's Artworld. Artworld is buzz, style, money, blockbuster openings, gallerista-fashionistas eyeing each other; theory-clotted higher drivel struggling to attach critical ballast to the lightweight and the forgettable, auction porn, vanity architecture, the carnival of the meretricious; the twinned inflation of hokey-jokey ephemeral sculpture and prices; art appreciation as a term of investment rather than understanding, anxiously acquisitive billionaires from the Far East, Near East and Slavic East all trying to outscore their rivals, padding around galleries as the fancy eyeware ushers them to the Next Sure Thing. The Meatpacking District of New York is the epicentre of Artworld Manhattan. When the new Whitney Museum opened its doors in the neighbourhood on 1 May, the question was always whether it would be sucked into its black hole of glamour.

The old Whitney was the puritan on Madison Avenue. Penetrating the gloom of Marcel Breuer's stacked concrete boxes was generally an act of faith. Even the basement café tried its best to block out the fun along with the light. Come the biennial, the puritan would put on a fancy frock, adopt a whoop of a meaning-lessly provoking title, and hoochy-coochy around a bit. The old Whitney's farewell show, as if to demonstrate it had had enough of modernist gravitas, was the falsetto giggle of a Jeff Koons retrospective. But there was something about the fight that the art had to put up against the enveloping murk of the building, which sorted out the weak from the strong and commanded the respect that comes from prolonged concentration. Would Renzo Piano's new Whitney, with its airy openings to the river and to the thrum and thrust of the city, make it too easy; turning high-minded machines of abstract expressionism into metrosexual playground ornaments?

A number of critics have complained that this is exactly what has happened. Those outdoor terraces are just a mini-High Line; the plump couches hotel-lobby fodder; the glittering bars an invitation to a hookup. Just wait, they warn, for the Twomblytinis and the Rothkoritas. So why was I, who can curmudgeon with the best, wandering around it with an expression of stupid bliss on my face, not quite able to believe how hospitable to the art, not the Artworld, the new Whitney actually is? An opening show of 600 of the museum's holding of 22,000 works gets its title from a Robert Frost poem of uncharacteristically whimsical couplets about Columbus's predicament: 'America is Hard to See'. That itself speaks of a gutsy confidence on the part of Donna De Salvo, the chief curator, that with new room and new thought, this might no longer be the case. I did see, literally in a new light, work I've never much rated before: a Georgia O'Keeffe abstraction; a captionless Lichtenstein; and – ye gods – an Eva Hesse dangler of resinated cords that positively dances its broody sorrows. There are knockout masterpieces that somehow have eluded me; above all, a moving Jacob Lawrence series of small war paintings, made when he came back from the battle in 1946. There are more familiar numbers that expand before your eyes: Hopper's *Early Sunday Morning*, storefront parallel to the picture plane, caught in its bell jar of frozen time.

The exhilaration is in part due to the light, which, on the fifth floor, pours down from filtered skylights; and with the tripling of space. But, on reflection, the very features lamented by the party-poopers as low diversions – those openings to the city – turn out to be the secret of its newfound élan. They set up a dialogue between the world and the art, so much of which, even when it is abstract, feeds off the impatient percussion of American life: the roaring start of Whitman's 'Song of Myself' or the opening sentence of Saul Bellow's *The Adventures of Augie March*. If we were looking at, say, Fra Angelico, this would be all wrong. But we are not. We are looking at a 'Jack the Dripper' Pollock; at Alex Katz's blaze of *The Red Smile*; at George Bellows's merciless punching.

The most magical museums all have this same unforced affinity between urban place and art space. In the Rockox House in Antwerp, you see van Dyck and Rubens as its owner did; in the mottled-mirror bling of the Doria-Pamphilj gallery in Rome, you sample the baroque confectionery of Correggio and Carracci. Amid the jet-fuelled Artworld, the shopping mall of the mega-rich – here a Warhol, there a Warhol, everywhere a Warhol – perhaps it is not so very bad to have a place in Manhattan where the art can jump for joy because it finds itself at home.

PRINTS USA

American nightmares are never very far away from the American dream. One image in the British Museum's compendious and absorbing new show of prints from the 1960s to now embodies the perpetual national passion play of light and darkness with startling vividness. Ed Ruscha's take on the Hollywood sign, pictured not from below but along the brow of its hill, makes it subside into the slope, shrouded in ambient twilight of a smoggy, sulphurous orange. Other images lurk devilishly on the dark side: Andy Warhol's screenprints of an electric chair repeated in ten shades like an interior decorator's sample book – peach and azure, rose and slate – the artist claiming with his usual sly disingenuousness that multiplication dilutes the charge, when the opposite is true. Prettiness kills.

Like the place and time it documents, the British Museum show is not wholly given over to broken dreams. Brightness abounds in the abstractions of Richard Diebenkorn with their patches of California sky blue, and in the swimming pool splashiness of the adopted Angeleno David Hockney. But it's another work of Ruscha, the swooping and scarlet lines of a gas stop in *Standard Station*, that brought back to me the exhilaration of my first encounter with America more than half a century ago.

A 140ft-high steel globe encircled by ninety-six fountains, the 'Unisphere' was the focal point of the World's Fair held in New York in 1964. Along with saucer-shaped observatories perched on tall stalks, the globe beckoned Americans into a technologically streamlined, harmoniously connected future, an emblem of the country's long-lived truism that its destiny lay with the rest of the world: when I first saw the 'Unisphere' that summer, mists from the fountains obscured its base so it looked as though it was floating freely in space.

That calculated spirit of levitation was everywhere in the sprawling complex of the Fair, the pet project of the omnipotent parks commissioner Robert Moses, whose earlier attempt in 1939 had been inconvenienced by the war in Europe. A quarter of a century later, the gates of America's domesticated utopia opened wide again. Satellite national pavilions (scrubbed pine for the Scandinavian countries, for instance) dotted the fairgrounds in anodyne modernist constructions like courtiers around the true sovereign: America's mighty automobile industry. I rode Ford's travelling pavement, the last word in people-moving, undulating above the steel and glass structures together with well-upholstered families burying their faces in multi-decker sandwiches. In the General Motors pavilion students stood proudly beside the Studebakers, wearing blazers and broad smiles – themselves dazzling exhibitions of world-beating American dentistry. US tech-nology, engineered for the suburban home, was at hand: a jumbo freezer for every kitchen, in a choice of wheat or avocado. The future was middle class: soda-fizzing, popcorn-buttered, eternally and stupendously American.

But then history pooped the party. Not long after I disembarked onto Manhattan pier, on a steamy stretch of Ninth Avenue slick with the grease of hot dog drippings, I saw a newsboard bearing the mysterious legend: BAY OF TONKIN! This turned out to be the provocation of convenience that allowed Lyndon Johnson to push through congressional authorisation to prosecute an undeclared war in Vietnam. On a bus in Virginia, where my travelling pal and I had mistakenly seated ourselves in the back, the enraged driver ordered us to sit up front where we belonged.

But even as the first shots were fired (both metaphorically and literally) in what would be America's decades-long cultural and political civil war, it was impossible not to respond to the raw, exclamatory exuberance of the country. Everything howled and kept on wailing: Allen Ginsberg's chanted epic of impassioned profanity; Jimi Hendrix's guitar torturing 'The Star-Spangled Banner' in the stoned-out dawn of muddy Woodstock; Lenny Bruce's satirical outrages on decorum; Coltrane's sax on 'A Love Supreme'; Janis Joplin's bourbon-sluiced tonsils screaming through 'Cry Baby'.

Independently, but not coincidentally, this was the time, too, when something big happened to American art, the moment when, in the critic Leo Steinberg's perfect phrase, painters such as Jasper Johns and Robert Rauschenberg 'let the world back in'. For a decade or more, American art had been dominated by vast heroic abstractions on which artists inscribed their impulses in intuitive, gestural marks. The aim was to take the beholder as far away as possible from the raucous din of American street life into some metaphysical space occupied only by the sublime intersections of line and colour. The heresy of Pop artists such as James Rosenquist, Roy Lichtenstein and Andy Warhol was to adopt the disregarded objects of everyday life, the more garish the better, and present them as independent constructions of shape, colour and chirpy text. They were visual wisecracks, but the cracks cut deep. Instead of turning its back on the urban charivari, art kissed up to it and from the sexy union was born a new kind of visual drama.

Not that this meant abandoning the ancient techniques of art-making. On the contrary, the brassier the images, the more painstaking the process of composition. Lichtenstein compulsively painted every Ben-Day dot of his mega-cartoons; James Rosenquist made huge elongated murals as grandiose as the friezes commissioned for government institutions in the late nineteenth century. But, instead of poses recycled from classical antiquity, Rosenquist scrambled together F-111 bombers, exploding munitions and a small girl grinning under a helmet hairdryer resembling the nose cone of a rocket.

The appropriation of the messaging icons of American life – the flag, the map of the US, commercial advertising and supermarket packaging (Rosenquist had been a painter of billboards for Times Square) – is often taken to be ironic. But the irony was directed more at the priestly pretensions of traditional and abstract art than at the soup can and the gumball machine. There was – and is – a good deal of celebration about the fierce dynamism of American life in these elaborate capers. In 1969, Rauschenberg was invited by NASA to go to Cape Canaveral to witness the launch of the Apollo 11 moon mission and the result was two-way rapture. His riotously erupting series *Stoned Moon*, with its mash-up of launchpad burns and bouncing astronauts, is itself a kind of disorderly lift-off into gravity-free visual space.

American dreaming: the green-light promise of better tomorrows, upward social mobility, a democracy of opportunity, is so ingrained in the national psyche that, until very recently, it has been able to survive the bitterest disenchantments. As American expansiveness retreated into a defensive crouch after Vietnam and Watergate, the hollow hulk of the 'Unisphere' was left to decay like a leftover set from *Blade Runner*, gently rusting on the edge of a Queens cemetery. Somehow, it escaped the wrecking crew, money was found for its lengthy renovation, and in 2010 the restored fountains played once more at its base. Downtown New York arose from the toxic ashes of 9/11; the economy, even the automobile industry, with an infusion of Obama-supplied capital, came roaring back after the crash of 2008.

The inspirational high of the Obama presidency has been succeeded by an administration bent on obliterating all its accomplishments, but it too has presented its politics as a return to an ur-America. The thrusts and counter-thrusts of the culture wars may not have been good for the disunited states of America, but they released phenomenal forces of creative energy in image-making. That imaginative rush has not been all nonstop polemics. Between Philip Guston's scabrous post-Watergate caricatures and Jenny Holzer's exposure of egregious censorship, making pictures of blacked-out paragraphs, some of the most inventive artists turned out studied exercises in photorealist cool: Chuck Close's monumental heads, Richard Estes's storefront reflections, organised with the formal compositional geometry of a latter-day Poussin.

But American art, for all its flirtation with minimalism, is no more capable than its writing or politics of simmering down into resignation. Every crisis in the world of power has triggered another round of fighting images, sometimes wry, sometimes as fulminating as an evangelical sermon. Amid all the kitschified Marilyns and Maos manufactured by Warhol's prolific assembly line, it's easy to forget how razor-sharp his most acute takes on the meretricious vanities of the powerful could be. The most luridly gripping of his images of Richard Nixon borrowed the leering face from a *Newsweek* magazine cover but then printed his skin in the colour of his wife's dress taken from the same photograph: a curdled, luminous teal.

In contemporary America, activist art is alive and kicking. But many of its most powerful images draw on older traditions of visual preaching and teaching. The psychiatrist-artist Eric Avery, who treated patients broken down by the onslaught of Aids, went back to expressionist woodcuts for *Blood Test*, a devastating print of a raised arm and fist clenched for the needle, revealing through deeply incised lines all the veins and arteries. Kara Walker turns the genteel form of the nineteenth-century silhouette inside out for her images of sexually brutalising mischief inflicted on slaves by their masters. Her *No World* takes a sailing vessel, not unlike the one featured in Turner's *Slave Ship*, and retains as well the image of a drowned body lost in the waves, but has a pair of black hands rise from the waters to raise the ship high above the swelling sea. Other pictures reprise themselves and the inaugurating years of

post-abstract art, but now in a wistful strain, none more affecting than Ruscha's ghostly 'DEAD END' signs, coloured with the
decrepitude Donald Trump could have used as an emblem for his
visions of industrial desolation.

But we're not in Kansas any more, Toto. The hard-right
Republican majority in congress has long assumed that the 'liberal' in 'liberal arts' tells them all they need to know about the
irreligiosity – and thus the un-Americanism – of the humanities.
Notorious examples of offences against piety and decorum in the
arts, such as Andres Serrano's *Piss Christ*, are routinely trotted out
to justify the elimination of public support for the arts. Universities
other than those instituted around a religious ethos are suspected
as citadels of subversion where lefty academics hound patriotic
young conservatives into silence. So the National Endowment for
the Arts, along with the National Endowment for the Humanities
and the Corporation for Public Broadcasting – stigmatised as 'elite'
institutions, notwithstanding that millions flock through the museums and galleries and watch in numbers only dreamt of by the likes
of Fox – are targeted for total defunding. Before his resignation as
director of the Metropolitan Museum of Art, Thomas Campbell
pointed out in the *New York Times* that the defunding of the NEA
will make it impossible for provincial museums to come up with
the insurance needed for loans to prospective exhibitions. The
result will be the stunting of national culture, the closure of public
broadcasting stations, the withering away of arts and humanities
in exactly those parts of the country the Trump administration
purports to champion.

How will American art respond to the assault? Doubtless there
will be many among the galeristas who will greet fat tax reduc-
tions for the rich and the gross inflation of prices in contemporary
art with rejoicing. There will be others who may retreat once
more into an airy world of pure aesthetics.

My hunch (or hope) is that the march of the philistines will
be catnip for creativity in the arts and that a new era of public

engagement is upon us. One thing American art does brilliantly is inventive disrespect, and the relentlessly self-congratulatory vanity of Donald Trump presents the fattest target imaginable for its satirical artillery. The challenge, as with all such imaginative counter-attacks, is the capacity to project the message beyond the halls of college and museum and into the street where it counts. Prints lend themselves perfectly to poster polemics but the most effective challenge may yet come from creative adventures in the digital media, where inspired derision coupled with the defence of truth can go viral. Should that happen, the complacent dismissal of resistance art as the self-indulgent playtime of a defeated 'elite' will die on the faces of the powerful. *Aux armes, les artistes!*

CINDY SHERMAN

Sometimes you can overdo the prep. I realise this when Republican wives, mobilised to do their duty for the cameras in the primaries circus, all begin to look like Cindy Sherman in light disguise. The doll-like gestures; the inhumanly exquisite coiffure; the lip-glossed smiling; the desperation behind the adoration; all seem to leap shrieking from a Sherman show yet to be posed, shot and exhibited. No living artist I can think of has more exactly nailed the masquerade we perform when we go about our business, public and private, social and erotic. No one has caught the futile compulsion to self-brand, to lock down an identity, with quite Sherman's psychological acuteness. As an anatomist of self-consciousness, a collector of living masks, she has no peer. No one else catches those moments of sudden disarray, when the identity-performance begins to fall apart and delusions of grandeur tip into comedy.

This is why the retrospective at New York's Museum of Modern Art was a sure-fire smash. For although Cindy Sherman's work, over four decades, has been catnip for heavy-duty poststructuralist theorists who sometimes embalm her antic mischief in solemn lucubrations about the Lacanian 'gaze' and the commodification of the body, her popular appeal is much simpler. In a culture drunk on the vanity of images, Sherman's universe of characters appear with the skin of their appearance deeply and multiply punctured, so that all kinds of repressed humanity leak out: apprehension, fearfulness, garish over-confidence;

lust, disgust and furtive terror. No one makes such brilliant art by pulling our insides out. Though not a portraitist, much less a self-portraitist, her subject is something that has always exercised the most perceptive of those picturers: the artifice of self-presentation. In the age of YouTube and Instagram, the call to perform has gone epidemic. But she's no enemy of the image industry; just its clever jester. Her take on the unceasing caval-cade of personae works so well because she is unapologetically of the pop culture she ironises and occasionally torments. She manages, sometimes within the same image, total immersion and cool distance; the frontal challenge and the sidelong glance; the gasp and the giggle.

She does all this, by and with, herself. Not only has she been, over many decades, her own model, but she works without pla-toons of assistants. She takes justifiable pride in having no one but herself executing the work. Sherman is an old-fashioned art maker. There are no lens-shleppers, no lighting people; no dressers or make-up artists; there is just Cindy. The perennial tease of her shape-shifting is that she is everywhere and nowhere; peekaboo-recognisable and as often totally unrecognisable; her performances thematise the hunt for identity without herself having one. She simply disappears into the murderous ogress; the centrefold model done in by visual abrasion, the foundation-pancaked tennis queen of the Hamptons. Look for True Cindy and you will never find her.

So naturally I wonder, as I ride the elevator to her studio, which Sherman of the countless variations will be doing the interview? I half-imagine one of her personae – edgy, mournful, fierce, reticent, wearing a ghastly grin or a sociopathic scowl, heavily wigged, exotically made-up – to be lying in wait behind the door at the end of the concrete Chelsea corridor. But, surprise, the person who greets me is none of the above. Instead, a woman slighter than I had imagined; no make-up, softly attractive, wearing the kind of smile that kicks the Manhattan winter into the Hudson, shows me in. She talks a lot; she laughs a lot; she is generous with time, tea and funny, voluble conversation. There is not a trace of defensive taciturnity or jokey condescension. Good grief, can she actually be a contemporary artist? But then there's something invitational about much of Cindy Sherman's work, even when the party gets wickedly out of control and you're confronted with stuff designed to prod the gag reflex. Her pictures beckon the imagination into mysteries, horrors, suggested conversations, vaguely intimated consummations. They will not leave you alone.

Her studio, as you'd expect, is as much a theatrical dressing room as art workspace – awash with costumes hanging from garment rails, sequins and satins, masks and hats, feathers and wool, props and wigs, bits of mannequin. The drapery of drama; everything she might need for a new character. It is her playground of personality and she has, she says, always been one for dressing up. 'At school the teacher always seemed to wear a different outfit every day and I was so impressed. I had this little pegboard and I'd figure out my outfit for the whole week! I was so neurotic.' Her art began with making drawings of her own clothes; the beginnings of something that, as an art student at Buffalo State College, would become a booklet of Cindy-doll.

If in some of her early photographs characters look lost, or anxiously alert in the big city, it may be because she was kept from it by her parents, even though they were living close by in suburban Huntington, Long Island. 'There was this family fear of Manhattan . . . monsters in the manholes. We never came in, not to museums, not to the theatre. The only time I remember was at Christmas, to see the Rockettes.' I suggest that the fishnet-stockinged, high-kicking chorus line may have left its own imprint and she laughingly agrees that in retrospect it is a distinct possibility. Perhaps it was also telling that her first dabbling in art was to make copies: of news pictures, any images that took her fancy. Her enduringly haunting masterpiece album of black and white *Untitled*

Film Stills has been described by Rosalind Krauss as 'copies without originals'.

Parental Manhattanophobia dictated where she would go to study art: upstate at State College, Buffalo. The city was a gritty place in the 1970s, though with handsome Victorian buildings and, more important, the Albright-Knox Gallery, one of America's great modernist and contemporary collections. The college itself was a let-down: 'no contemporary art and no interest in it'. But in Hallwalls, an artists' space co-founded by Sherman in an old ice-packing warehouse across town, she found sympathetic comrades who opened her up to the reinventions of the 1970s: conceptual art, minimalism, body art, earth art; Vito Acconci and Robert Smithson. The college art department hated the upstart. 'They felt threatened. My photography teacher gave us an assignment to go to Hallwalls, pick out something we were drawn to and copy it . . . because [he said] that's what they do, they just steal other people's ideas. Wow, what a nasty man.' With hindsight that condemnation of the playful copy only made Sherman more excited about experimental work that engaged with the immense carnival of American images. Something could be cut from this matrix, and made over into a fresh take: askance and off-kilter.

The first partly made object she worked on was herself. *A Play of Selves* (1975) was at once a mini-theatrical performance of a murder mystery and a game about multiple identities and disguises. She dressed herself up as all the members of the cast; the preppy, the ingénue, and so on, photographed the characters, cut each one out and reassembled them in a single composition, and then, as if making a film strip, did it all over again. The results are wittily playful but the laborious process of making them took the zing out of the invention.

When Sherman got to New York in the mid-1970s, 'I wanted to work alone,' she says, partly because she was the only model she could afford but also to please her solitary streak. At Hallwalls she liked the creative companionship – up to a point. Now she wanted to do a solo act with the rest of the world just out of frame. 'I wanted to tell a story that implied I'm not alone.' From that bud of an idea blossomed the seventy *Untitled Film Stills* that remain some of the most stunning work done over the past thirty years, not least because so many of them are formally very beautiful while being noirishly atmospheric. Sherman claims to be 'a little sick of them', which is too bad because no one else is. The earliest pictures, which originally were meant to follow the career of a single blonde actress, were made romantically grainy by 'being developed in hotter chemicals than you're supposed to use. The film cracks so it looks like the crappy B movies I had in mind.' It's called 'reticulation', a term so grand it draws another chuckle from her. In a justly famous image, from 1977, the blonde stands in a barren corridor against a shut door, face turned in profile, eyes closed, a late-1950s short coat slung over her shoulders, her right hand clenched in a fist, raised against the door, her weight on the back foot. Is she knocking? Is she just stopped in the moment of anticipation? We will never know but we sway with her on the tightrope of possibility.

All that happens is a slight tremble on the power lines of our imagination. Sometimes it's done with gesture. A swimsuited woman sitting on a folding beach chair turns her head – we are made to think, suddenly – to check out something we can't see. A big-eyed brunette (a favourite of mine) looks up from the kitchen floor, where her grocery bag has spilled its eggs and cans, to challenge anyone who's going to make something out of it. The Hitchcock and Antonioni inspirations are obvious. Real albums of stills, many of them from European cinema, triggered her inventions. You can have innocent fun spotting a Jeanne Moreau set of the lips, an Anna Magnani jut of the hip. But while most of the stills featured turning points in the plot – a scream, a fit of weeping – Sherman was hunting for the moments before, after and especially in between the turns of event. She wanted the blanks on which we can write the action. It's these freeze-frame actions that spill from the cinema screen into the inner projection of the little dramas we play in our own heads. The effect is as unsettling as a dream, and as enigmatically stirring.

The series was all the more remarkable for being so simply done, especially the lighting. 'For interiors I'd just use a lamp or a screw-in bulb, just cheap aluminium parts.' Exteriors, if anything, were even simpler, relying on serendipity. The famous 'hitchhiker' (*Untitled*, 1979) with its Tippi Hedren ash blonde in gingham check skirt, standing on a road under a low western sky, a dauntless little suitcase by her side, was taken by Sherman's father on a family road trip through Arizona. She packed her costumes, many of them scooped from discount vintage clothing stores in New York, and equipped herself with a new telephoto lens. When she spotted a suggestive location, she would stop the car, get kitted out, pose, wave at Dad and shout, 'Okay, now!' The party line on these one-shot dramas is that they are not 'photographs' in the sense of the fixing of an arbitrarily happened-upon event or place. But of course the entire history of the medium has been one in which happenstance yields to the framed, staged design, and there was a lot going on in New York art of the late 1970s – Warhol, above all – that was shamelessly stagey. *Untitled Film Stills* were shown first at the downtown Artists Space where Sherman was working as a receptionist. She got a nice review in *ARTnews* by a name she can never forget – (who would?) – Valentin Tatransky – and then the work came to her.

Even then, in her mid-twenties, Sherman was wary of losing her edge to fashion. One of her strongest instincts has always been to bite against the glamour. When *Artforum* approached her in the early 1980s to do one of their 'centrefolds' playing with the girlie mag format, they were probably anticipating a feminist commentary on the female body as a grazing field for the voracious male eye. But what the magazine got when Sherman adopted the big horizontal format in colour was less a polemic than a baroque drama of fear, exhaustion, vulnerability and damaged reflection and, just occasionally, cool defiance.

The centrefolds are, in their way, a strike against the captivity of the ogled; but their poignant intensity comes from substituting for erotic intimacy an altogether different kind of proximity; the body in distress. What she was after, Sherman says, was 'someone expecting to open a centrefold and then "oops, sorry, didn't mean to disturb you"'. The Cindies, some blonde, some not, are post-posed, hair matted, beads of sweat hanging on their face and body, psychologically stripped bare, even when clothed, emotionally disarrayed. Laid out on off-pastel towels and cheap blankets, the women register a palpable sense of suffering from some sort of violation, or dispossession. They are utterly still yet caught in a psychological shiver and the expressions are among Sherman's most astonishing pieces of acting. 'They make me want to . . . cook them soup,' I say. She laughs again.

Sherman followed her woman's version of grandes horizontales with a visual coda; a small series of the same persona this time in upright format, an unmade-up Cindy clad in a red terry-towel robe, as though 'beaten up by the photographer', that are among the most affecting pictures she has ever made. Alert to becoming flavour of the month, Sherman turned more confrontational. She began to experiment with uglification. This was the moment when the fashion house Comme des Garçons flew her to Paris to pick out outfits for the shoot. But instead of sending back the numbers she chose, 'they picked really boring wool stuff'. Off she went to the Halloween fright shops to stock up on scar tissue, raw-meat lips and cups of blood, and then posed in the wool jobs with a calculated vengeance. A black suit-dress is modelled with an unkempt peroxide wig covering all but one angry eye and clenched fists; a crimson wool number has her with greasy psychopath hairdo and bloody fingernails, and the most fabulously demented of all has her sitting in zebra stripes and floppy tie with an expression of deranged glee on her androgynous mug. 'I dare you to print this in French *Vogue*,' she thought. 'And of course they didn't; they wound up hating everything. To get them off my back I did a few I knew they would like.'

As she became a Name in the late 1980s, Sherman tripped deeper into realms of horror and disgust, two of her favourite resorts. Her *Fairy Tales* series, not the kind you want your seven-year-old to see, are elaborately staged phantasmagoria, shot on beddings of gravel, dirt, moss and sand that she brought into the studio. A bloody-toothed hag in Norman Bates granny-wig, ancient fishnets half-rolled down, scrabbles obscenely in the pebbles. A naked giant ogress fingers her blood-soaked tongue against a background of tiny figures: her lunch. 'Oh, they were the little people model railway buffs buy for their sets,' Cindy says cheerily. But all this was Bambi compared with what followed: still lifes of a tidal wash of puke and cupcakes; bluebottles crawling around in their favourite kind of yummy habitat.

'It was my little rebellion,' she says with a cherubically art-less smile. But it doesn't do to tangle with Cindy. Provoked by sanctimonious congressional condemnation of Andres Serrano's *Piss Christ* and Mapplethorpe's homoerotic photography, as well as the way Jeff Koons modelled his porn-star wife – 'so lame' – Sherman responded with a *Sex Pictures* series (1992) that is definitely not lame but ferociously combative. For once she removed herself from the shots, but used anatomically correct medical mannequins to make poses of savage absurdity: it was all ingeniously economical. By unplugging certain parts from their allotted position she could suggest massively gaping orifices; switching others around made a composition of separated heads, one male and one female lying on satin sheets beside a trunk equipped at one end with a penis and at the other a densely bushy vagina complete with tampon string; the whole thing circled by a silky bow tied around the midriff. When some unhinged minds actually found this a turn-on, their creator was horrified: not what she had in mind at all, she says.

There would be other passages of mayhem: action figure toys melted, burned and mutilated. 'There was an anatomically correct model of a gay man with a giant penis so I had to have that – think he was called Gay Bob. A year later they brought out his friend who naturally had to be Latino.' Cindy did terrible things to Bob and his friend, but 'I was going through a divorce. It wasn't like "I hate you"; it was kinda fun, like a science project.' But there would also be more meditative engagements: with the old masters in her *History Portraits* (1988–90) – witty impersonations in which the canon gets stripped of its pretensions and pushed towards the circus. The exposed breast of a Fouquet Madonna; the emblem of intercession of sin, is straight out of the novelty shop; the head of Botticelli's Holofernes is a Halloween decapitee.

Sherman is often mistakenly thought of as a one-note impresario of the grotesque, working in a range from neurosis to horror. For sure, the eloquent, impish person I've been talking to has always had a yen for the weird and the wondrous, but I tell her how struck I am by the sheer range of human types she manages to print on her face. Hers is the real Facebook (the one we all mistake for human connection, she avoids like the plague). The writing about her work, preoccupied as it is by the post-modernist mantras of quotation, allusion and ironic instability, seldom pays much attention to the astonishing versatility of her performance, the protean elasticity of face and body. Occasionally, with the mirror set beside the camera, this gift unsettles her. 'Sometimes I'm awestruck by how little I look like myself and say, "Wow, that is so not me." But I do feel empowered by the spooky thing that is happening.' She's right, but the capacity to take on the entire cast of the human comedy is actually not a symptom of post-modern distance from its cavortings, but its opposite: sympathetic total immersion.

The first thing visitors to the MoMA saw was an enormous mural in which five monumental Cindies pose in the horticultural neo-classical style against the background of a park and pond. But instead of Demeter and Diana, she gave us a gently wry procession through the aeons: from nude body-suit Cindy through faux-medieval to Big-Bra-Jane-Russell Cindy of the 1950s. Has heroic megalomania struck? Quite the contrary. The statues are all nebbishy nobodies wearing expressions that range from prune to pudding and their costumes are, as ever, discount-shop tat. The sweetly mocking parade is, like a lot of her work, a sly reproach to the besetting sin of contemporary art: its callow, orgiastic narcissism. Cindy Sherman looks at herself and sees everyone else. No other living artist manages so generously to exemplify the Roman playwright Terence's dictum: 'I consider nothing human as alien to me.' Well, okay, maybe the ogress.

TACITA DEAN

Immerse yourself in the films of Tacita Dean and your sense of the world shifts. As in all exceptional art, vision remakes itself. In Dean's work, the play of sound is intrinsic to that remaking. A hum of unseen traffic drones while magpies flit in a web of trees; an orthopaedic boot attached to an elegant oldster clumps percussively over polished parquet in a deserted art deco villa. Often, the commonplace is suddenly revealed as miraculous. The plod of brindle Friesians into a Cornish pasture turns into a ceaselessly flowing rump river; a branch weighted with rosy apples caught by the breeze bobs and curtsies in the autumn light; a backlit fringe of white hair on an old artist's mottled crown becomes his halo. Everything is heightened, quickened, poetically illuminated in more than the purely kinetic sense, and charged with the intense beauty that is conditional on the presentiment of loss.

'The old men I film', Dean says, with witchily dark merriment, as we sit on the terrace of her Berlin studio, 'seem to die just afterwards.' And indeed they do depart: the poet Michael Hamburger; the artists Mario Merz and Cy Twombly; the choreographer Merce Cunningham. But they will never be granted more subtly revelatory obituaries.

Now Dean is facing an extinction against which she is fighting with everything she has: the death of film – real film, that is; 16-milimetre celluloid, the indispensable medium of her work, the material that gives her art its uncanny presence. The laws of the marketplace have decreed that digital rules supreme; that film is no more than a quaint relic, and the champions of its immeasurable distinctiveness are deluded romantics. Dean grieves and rages against this smug indifference. Although (exasperatingly, for both of us) Tate Modern has forbidden us to discuss her imminent installation in its Turbine Hall in any detail, she lets on that it will be a vehicle for her impassioned last stand on behalf of the survival of film: 'Otherwise, we won't see a projected film again, except in archives and museums.' It strikes her as an appalling irony that *Edwin Parker*, her lovely film about Cy Twombly, just made it under the wire for processing before Deluxe – owned by the Twombly collector Ronald O. Perelman – stopped printing 16-milimetre negatives at its Soho Film Lab in London last February.

Dean speaks about the end of film as a 'heartbreaking bereavement. Very soon, maybe, I won't be able to make my work if they have their way.' It's as if Rembrandt received a letter informing him that, as of next week, oils would no longer be available . . . but not to worry, since acrylic would do the job just as well. Digital is 'not the same!' she storms, as the Berlin sky above us dramatically darkens, as if to her prompting. 'You watch it differently, you handle it differently, you experience it differently.'

Dean is no Luddite though. She has used digital from time to time, but only film – 'made with chemistry, alchemy, light' – has drawn great work from her. Her vision, she says, is inseparable from the physical character of the medium, but also from the discipline it imposes on the filmmaker. With one roll of stock lasting three minutes, 'you have to make decisions. I like the flaws in it that trip you up; the lack of ability to lie.' She regards digital filmmaking, on the other hand, as sloppily forgiving, indulgent. Sound – so vital to Dean – comes willy-nilly with the digital camera. Film, though, is silent and sound has to be superimposed, fashioned, given its particular timbre and resonance. She thinks the lazy user-friendliness of digital must have something to do with why movies these days 'bore the pants off me'. And don't get her started on 3D!

The digital supremacists had better watch out, for Tacita Dean is not only one of the greatest living British artists but also one of the most eloquently headstrong and volubly articulate. She claims to be 'voiceless', but if anyone can rescue her beloved medium in much the way that vinyl sound recordings were brought back from the tomb, she can, and perhaps her Turbine Hall installation will turn the tide of doom. 'It's not what people are expecting,' she warns. 'Am I going to like it?' I ask, suddenly nervous that the force of her polemic might blunt the poetic subtlety of her images. 'I dunno,' she says, giving me one of her mischievous cat-lady grins. 'Maybe not.'

If that's the way it turns out it will be a first, although, inevitably, there are some of her films I love more than others, especially those made in an astonishing burst of creativity between 1999 and 2007 – among them *Bubble House*, a long, steady vision of the modernist shell of an abandoned house on Cayman Brac, in the Cayman Islands. I remember seeing it at the Tate in 1999, in a darkened space, the purr of the projector an intrinsic musical undertone, as rain crashed down on the desolate modernist vanity, an emptied egg of a structure, and the tropical tide washed in, leaving mirroring puddles on the floor. I realised then that her film had none of the slick virtuality of video art; that an element of Dean's genius lay in allowing what unfolded before her to exert its own unbidden drama on the senses. Shots are held for minutes at a time to savour the subtlety of changes of light and the motion of the waters; the camera takes up a fixed viewpoint, allowing whatever passes to come into frame.

Offer a precis of these films and you might conclude that nothing very much happens. You would be entirely mistaken. In the stunning *Banewl*, those lowing Friesians are led through a gate into a meadow overlooking the sea. They chomp to their own luxurious measure. Above them, excited swallows soar and swoop. The light fades – and little by little the animal world registers the optical tremor of the oncoming solar eclipse well before Dean and her cameraman. The cows stare fixedly at the camera as if attempting to tip off the oblivious filmmakers of the imminence of darkness. 'We sat there thinking it was about to rain,' recalls Dean. The swallows go frantic. 'Everything went to roost. It was so atavistic.' As the cows lower themselves heavily, the light turns mother-of-pearl, then pale copper, before leaching away altogether. In the gloaming, a lighthouse Dean hadn't known was there reveals itself. The scene is simply cows, birds, grass, lighthouse, sea and, as light breaks afresh, a cocky rooster straight out of La Fontaine . . . yet you'll seldom see a more cosmically loaded drama.

The effect of Tacita Dean's patient gaze, and of her exquisite talent for composition (each and every frame of hers is a living painting, a Cuyp or a Vermeer), is hypnotic, though she claims to have no feel for single images. However, it is a hypnosis not of other-worldly drowsiness but something like the opposite: an acute sharpening of perception. All the standard fetishes of modern filmmaking – hyper-ventilated hand-held cameras, antsy cutting, bloated mood music, pedestrian commentary – are stripped away, leaving exposed the tangible reality of lived experience. Her work is a palate-cleanser for our jaded sensibilities; an invitation to apprehend the fine thread of life before it slips away through our fingers. The exhilarating result could not be further away from the splashy artifice of much contemporary art, with its strenuous itch to startle or joke.

Perhaps it's no surprise that Dean's work glides above the circus of trends, for her obsessional subject is the corrosion of time. She has always been a cat who walks by herself, or, as she likes to say, 'really weird'. She is certainly that unfashionable thing – a connoisseur of anomaly, a visual archaeologist of modern relics. *Sound Mirrors* takes its name from the tracking devices planted in the Kent countryside to detect incoming German aircraft, but in Dean's imaging they seem to turn into dolmens of a more ancient world. *Gellért* features hefty Hungarian women gossiping in the steamy dimness of marble-walled therapeutic baths. Neutral-coloured shifts cling to them like second skins, casings for their sausagey bulk; Chaucer or Bruegel brought to Budapest. Dean is not above doing what's necessary to get the picture right. Knowing they were going to be filmed, the staff of the baths turned up in 'appalling swimwear'. Instead, Dean encouraged them to dress in those peculiar garments they oblige everyone else to wear.

Dean's brother, Ptolemy, is an authority on architectural restoration, and, wanting to know something about the parents who laid those classical monikers on their children, I wonder out loud about the siblings' interest in ruin. 'Maybe because my father was one,' she observes with a rueful laugh. The damage was done by her grandfather, Basil Dean, one of the founding fathers of British talking movies in the 1930s, much married, notoriously womanising, who let his son know that he had never really been wanted.

So even if the legacy had its dark side, film is in Tacita Dean's blood. Mostly, though, Tacita wanted out of the enfolding cosiness of Kent. After a foundation year in Canterbury she ended up – despite stiff parental disapproval – as a student at Falmouth School of Art: 'I chose it because it was so far away.' She arrived to find the place shrouded in deep Cornish fog, with foghorns sounding from the harbour. Dean fell for the Romantic atmospherics.

There were all of forty students in each of the three years, and the doughty Dean rowed in the 'pilot gig' races, ploughing through the waves in howling gales and heavy seas: 'wooden seats, none of this moving seat pansy stuff'. Her first circuit was round St Michael's Mount. 'What with a serious dope smoker in the bow, we were so last that they started the other race before we got back.' She laughs about it all, but that exposure to the consuming force of the sea – its power to scramble the charts, and play fast and loose with location – would become a powerful motif in her early films. Lighthouses and wrecks, abandoned boats and trembling marine horizons would shimmer through her work like Melvillean phantoms.

The sirens called to Dean from other seas, too – the Aegean, the next in her odyssey. In Athens, trying to get her artistic bearings, she endured 'a depressive Greek painter who didn't leave his room and his mad actress girlfriend . . . really crazy'. She then applied for a Greek scholarship in animation, 'which I didn't get, thank God; that would have been a false move'. Instead, Dean spent a winter on the island of Aegina, commuting by ferry to Athens.

Back in London, more applications ensued, but she was 'always falling between painting and film'. In 1990, the baronies of the art colleges (painting and media studies especially) wanted nothing to do with each other. Dean was admitted to the painting department of the Slade School of Fine Art on condition she promised never to make films. 'You lied,' I say. 'I lied,' she concedes, with an unrepentant smile. Billed by the faculty as The Troublemaker, at least one now famous woman painter, then her junior at the Slade, remembers her as a fiery role model of creative independence and the soul of friendliness.

Dean describes her career as moved along by a chain of 'miracles' and spooky epiphanies, discovering, for instance, the factory at Chalon-sur-Saône that had just stopped making film, which gave her the perfect location for its elegy, *Kodak*, one of the most visually compelling of her works. 'You're too late,' they told her when she asked to film. 'I like too late,' she replied.

It was another such time-bending coincidence that drove her to the experiments in fact and fiction that are at the heart of much of her strongest work. On discovering a photograph from 1928 of an Australian girl stowaway, bound for Falmouth, Dean began to spin the story in her imagination: first, the photo disappeared along with her bag from a Heathrow X-ray machine when she was about to board a flight to Glasgow. The picture and bag turned up mysteriously on a carousel at Dublin airport, at which point Dean decided to fabricate a newspaper story in the style of the 1920s, imagining the girl and the ship both bound for Ireland. Digging a little deeper, she discovered that a ship called the *Herzogin Cecilie* had in fact run aground in 1936 off the Devon coast. Fearing that the reek of salt-rotted grain cargo would get up the noses of holidaymakers, the local authorities had it towed to a less conspicuous mooring in Starehole Bay, where it was promptly wrecked.

Pursuing the story, Dean went to film the ruin, completed her shots on a July morning, departed, and then learned that perhaps a few hours later a woman had been raped and murdered exactly where she had been shooting. Two wrecks, maritime and human; two kinds of reports; fact and fiction suddenly swam together in her imagination.

Girl Stowaway (1994) became her first experiment in this kind of broken story, with the narrative splintered like drift-wood on the rocks. Later, her extraordinary *Teignmouth Electron* explored the story of the eponymous trimaran entered in a round-the-world yacht race in 1968 by the delusional Donald Crowhurst, who faked his coordinates during the race before plunging into the sea. The boat beaching on Cayman Brac followed, and in turn led to Dean's discovery of the *Bubble House*.

It was a tremendous breakthrough, but its timing didn't fit the 'So what's next?' finger-tapping urgencies of the art world. In 1998, when she was nominated for the Turner Prize, all Dean had to show was the Budapest bath-house piece *Gellért*. And there was the matter of the peculiarity of her commin-gling of the modern and the archaic. YBA (Young British Artists) was quick-hit buzz; Tacita Dean has always been about the harvest of concentration. Even now she is amazed that she was approached about the Turbine Hall installation. 'I never thought they would turn to an artist like me . . . my attraction to the quiet.' At the time of the Turner, 'I was a nobody. I just wasn't part of the whole social thing.' She shrugs, amused at the memory.

She knows it was just as well. Being un-Turnered made her detachment from the YBA scene that much easier. A fellowship took her instead to Berlin, from where she produced a steady succession of masterpieces. But even in a city where she became gently embedded, if not rooted, it was the instability of location and memory that caught her muse. In *Fernsehturm* (2001), her version of the German revolution revolves in a moving restaurant at the top of the city's television tower. In this favoured watering hole of the former East German elite, overlooking the Alexanderplatz, her camera is still; but the place turns, ever so slowly, a relic of a world somehow preserved in historical aspic. As the light beyond the windows changes from day to night an antique organist strikes up 'The Girl from Ipanema'. Even here, Dean had a little 'miracle'. A group of tables remained empty while its occupants were delayed playing the casino tables (as customers always did in the Old Days), so there is room for her camera to do its gentle surveying. It is the most tender take one could imagine on history as human comedy, even in the lingering shadows of Stasiland.

There are so many beauties for anyone unfamiliar with Dean's work to dive into as an introduction that to choose one seems invidious. However, *Boots* has the Dean alchemy working to perfection. Boots was Tacita's sister's handsome godfather, nicknamed for his clumping orthopaedic shoe. His history was raffish enough for Dean to bring Boots – sticks, pacemaker and all – into a deserted Portuguese art deco villa, where she imagined him playing its architect. As strong-minded as his goddaughter, Boots thought he would do better as the lover of Blanche, the model for whom the villa had been built. Up its steps he stumps, through its elegant columns; the sweet music of erotic memory coming to him. 'She was quite a good lover,' he says by her marbled bathroom. 'We did interesting things together. Simple sex doesn't amuse me. [Pause.] It didn't amuse her either.' Outside, birds warble; a golden light washes through the blonde rooms and Dean's humanely expansive lens allows this little flood of make-believe to seem utterly true.

That's why Tacita Dean is so passionate on the subject of film. For, in our digitally meretricious age, film retains – though only perhaps in the hands of her particular genius – the priceless gift of poetic truth.

RACHEL WHITEREAD

All it takes is a couple of dollars and a five-minute ferry ride to sail from the southern tip of Manhattan to a dramatically different world: leafy Governors Island, right in the middle of New York harbour. Once an army base and a military prison, the island fell into weedy neglect after the Coast Guard left in 1996. But following its transfer to New York State, a firm of Dutch landscape architects has made it into a park for day-trip recreation, complete with stunning wrap-around views of the southern tip of Manhattan, Brooklyn and New Jersey.

A toasty August morning found hundreds of schoolchildren on the island rambling, bike-riding, shooting down a giant slide, slurping soda pop. None of them was paying much heed to a pale grey hut standing on the slope of one of the island's new hills, raised from the demolition debris of pulled-down buildings. On a site full of abandoned structures: two churches, a theatre, long lines of brick-faced barracks, the pitch-roofed hut on the hill must seem like just another left-behind ruin. A moment's sustained look, however, reveals something odd: blank windows that project from the exterior rather than being set into it. The phantom shack is Rachel Whiteread's *Cabin*: the latest of her negative casts of interior space and one of the most spellbinding things to be seen anywhere in New York.

It's easy enough to misread Whiteread, especially if all you've seen are photographs of her monumental inside-out rooms, stairwells and, in one stupendous case, an entire house. Blind, filled

windows (only Michelangelo did those on the staircase of the
Laurentian Library in Florence), interior air and space translated
into a solid mass, can give the impression of forbidding impenetra-
bility, a tomb-like hermetic sealing. And, indeed, intimations of
mortality are never far from Whiteread's instincts and thoughts.
Embankment, her colossal 2005–06 installation in Tate Modern's
Turbine Hall, was prompted by her artist mother's death. She and
her twin sisters were 'so devastated we couldn't pack her house
up. It took us about a year to get around to it and when we did
I found an old Sellotape box, used for decorations. I pressed it
flat and brought it back to the studio and so it [*Embankment*] came
from that.' A box of grief, then, mountainously multiplied. 'There
should have been more,' she tells me in her Camden Town studio,
a big light-drenched space filled with pieces from every stage of
her career, including the hypnotic drawings that are her elegant
forethoughts. 'But, Rachel, there were hundreds,' I say. 'Well,
thousands actually,' she says in reply (14,000). 'Still, there should
have been more.'

Even so, and despite her volunteering as a teenager for a job at
Highgate Cemetery, I think of her work as dominated by memory
rather than memorial, and marked by traces of warm life as much
as chill death. On Governors Island you make your way through
a jungly mass of rambling roses, flocks of tortoiseshell butterflies
flitting through them, and the immediate impression is not of
abandoned dereliction but human occupancy, as if someone has
only just departed. Everything on and around the cabin is marked
by domestic use: the grain on the wooden shingles; the gaps
between them now extruded like blisters appearing on weathered
timber, the bricks on the hearth climbing the chimney wall; a
perfectly rendered bolt-slide on the door; window curtains that
in reverse have become corrugated but still give the illusion of
shifting softly in the breeze. Scattered around the building, half-
hidden in the scrub, are Whiteread's bronze casts of the casual
detritus of shack life: a spoon, beer cans, indeterminate bits of

machines; the casual rubbish of the homesteader-squatter as if turned into throwaways by a modern Bernini.

Cabin is not some sort of hermit's retreat (any more than Thoreau's Walden home in the woods – the prompt for her work – was a flight from society). Standing on its hill directly facing the Statue of Liberty, the little smoke-grey dwelling seems in active dialogue with the forest of commercial towers looming over the water, since 9/11 inescapably imprinted with memories of destruction and disappearance. Nothing could be more eloquent about two radically opposed ways of living, the imagined freedom of the homestead and the pullulating empire of capitalist hustle.

What *Cabin* is not is minimalist, in the sense that bone-dry exercises in sculptural austerity – Donald Judd's cubes or Carl Andre's bricks – have made a fetish of planing away all signs of the artist's mark. Critics and art historians reluctant to abandon the tag have pigeonholed Whiteread as 'post-minimalist' or a 'minimalist with heart' – a coinage she quite likes but one that doesn't do the difference adequate justice. Whiteread's surfaces are all facture: heavily imprinted with life-traces (even her mattresses cast in resin or rubber are often coloured with simulacra of human staining). Her sculptures are never self-contained. They are saturated with memory, and overflow with social comment and personal narrative. Many of them, such as *Cabin*, look solitary but, in fact, never are; they always imply habitat, always infer something bigger in space and time, namely the ramshackle lives of all of us. That is why they are so easy to connect with and why they pack such intense emotional power. Whiteread's great pieces are sighs made tangible.

So only if you were expecting a tight-lipped guardian of emptiness made solid form would it come as a surprise to discover that, in person, Rachel Whiteread is warmly voluble, the stories of her life and work told in the north London-speak of my own childhood and punctuated with bursts of merry laughter. But then her work is the opposite of disembodied.

'When I was a student at the Slade [School of Fine Art], I used my body quite a lot; I cast bits of me – a few friends have got them – bits of leg and back and arm. There were caretakers that had my breasts on the wall of their hut.' She laughs one of those big rosy-faced laughs. One of the attractions of the Slade was the accessibility of the anatomy school. 'I remember drawing a brain and holding it afterwards. What a weird feeling that was.'

Lately her body has been through it a bit. Last year in Greece, an erupting gall bladder came close to doing her in altogether. She is fully recovered but has to abide by a recuperative diet. 'No alcohol, then?' I sympathise. 'Oh, no, alcohol's fine.' 'No coffee or tea?' 'No, they're okay; just no milk . . . well, I suppose sheep's or goat's milk would be alright.' This sounds like the kind of regimen unlikely to interfere with her easy-going humour and compulsive work habits. The prospect of her big retrospective, opening in mid-September, is the best kind of tonic. But even the generous exhibition spaces of Tate Britain can only accommodate one of her monumental casts, *Room 101* – the negative of an entire room. It will, though, have a rich collection of smaller objects, many from her own personal collection and at least as dear to her: the curiosity cabinet of her own memories – the cavity of a spoon cast in bronze, for example.

For a long time now Whiteread has been the visual poet of urban flotsam. Heaps of belongings discarded on the street, grungy mattresses and upended tables always made her curious about the lives of which the used-up objects were the visible residue. Leaning against a wall of her studio is her *Rosebud*: a talismanic object found on the beach when, before the Slade, she was a student at Brighton College of Art; a petrol can flattened by a heavy vehicle and tossed away for the sharp-eyed artist to nab and that she has used as a plate to make a print. She freely acknowledges the part her father and mother played in these archaeological wanderings. Her father Thomas was a geography teacher at school and then polytechnics, fine-tuned to the eloquence of space. 'At the bottom of our garden' in Ilford 'was a field, and beyond that a Roman road. We would walk on the Roman road and my dad would talk about it.' Then, with gangs of friends from school, she explored scattered treasure: post-Second World War Portakabins, rusting farm machinery. Both her parents were drawn to the verges where town life overflowed into the country. Her mother Pat collaged diapositives of 'crap people had deposited – petrol pumps that no longer worked, oil spills' onto her landscape paintings.

The Whitereads were north London boho Labour Party campaigners so, inevitably, she and her sisters were sent to the pioneering Creighton comprehensive in Muswell Hill, where they'd moved from Ilford. 'That must have been exciting,' I offer. 'It was awful,' she shouts, and then sighs, 'truly awful, shoved together', albeit with good intentions, from secondary modern and grammar school halves that never properly fitted. 'But I kind of loved it; it was a big world soup, fights all the time, influxes of Bangladeshis, Greeks, Turks, Romanians, a really interesting bunch of people all thrown together. I wasn't good at school. I didn't behave or sit down, I mucked about, doing what I could do to get by.' And precisely because her mother was a painter, she wanted nothing to do with art. Until, in the sixth form, she discovered the art room. 'I discovered what I wanted to do and was addicted to it.'

After school she went to Brighton College of Art, an inspired choice since, although she entered as a painting student, some of Britain's most original sculptors were teaching there, among them Phyllida Barlow, Antony Gormley and Alison Wilding. Something had happened to the work of British women sculptors since the abstract refinements of Barbara Hepworth, and that something was a kind of dramatically expressive untidiness; a massing up of uncontainable forms; strong visual rhetoric often made from modest materials. Pretty soon Whiteread was embarking on her own experiments, borrowing an empty room at the top of the college – 'a window, a door, an alcove' – and papering the white walls black, hanging rolls of masking tape ('like bats, organic') from the ceiling. She tells me she didn't really know what she was doing. 'I wasn't trying to make sculpture; I was trying to make a collage in space, freeing things up in my mind.' Barlow and Wilding were sufficiently struck by its off-kilter drama to bring students working in more conventional forms to come and be provoked. She took to walking the South Downs and the beach ('I have always liked weather') struck by the 'lines' made by washed-up scrap metal and torn-apart tyres. 'That's when I realised I wasn't interested in just making something that goes on a wall.'

At the Slade, Whiteread began to raid the bank of childhood memory; some of it repressed, of how our bodies first experience the space around them: what we grow into, and what we shrink from. Whether or not the attraction of secret enclosures, at once sheltering and dangerous, are responses to expulsion from our first in utero berthing, there's no doubt that children like to hang out in hidden spaces – underneath tables or desks or inside the kind of wardrobe where the child Rachel spent a lot of time. But reconstructing furniture as lodging would have been banal doubling. Instead, Whiteread hit on the possibility of making the interior of the space visible and solid by filling it with plaster. What she calls her 'Eureka moment' took the form of a cast of the interior of a wardrobe that she then mantled in a covering of light-sucking black felt. The effect of *Closet*, as everyone who has ever written about her work has noticed, was what Freud called *unheimlich* – the uncanny sensation of being simultaneously homely and unhomely, invitational and locked-off. Though Bruce Nauman, whose work she had seen at a show at the Whitechapel Art Gallery, had cast *The Space Under My Chair* in 1965, nothing like the sustained series of such creations that followed had ever been attempted.

The spell cast by these works – the revelation of a parallel universe of domestic life, its daily respirations made solid – got

Whiteread her first solo show just eighteen months after grad-
uating from the Slade, precisely because she refused to fit the
categories designated by contemporary art criticism. 'There was a
guy, a really nasty guy, who wanted to buy the whole show, £200
each. I kept it all,' she says, smiling at the memory. She wasn't
interested in pure form, but impure associations. The cluttering
of memory had its consummation when she cast an entire room
of a house in the Archway Road, every detail – electrical out-
lets; soot clinging to the fireplace – preserved. *Ghost* was like
a reverse *studiolo*, fastidious intaglio replaced by equally scrupu-
lous reverse imprinting, and worked with the same exhaustive
handcraft, lugging all that plaster up the steep hill. But 'I knew
exactly what I'd done; it was quite other-worldly; I knew it was
special; that it was the germ of something.'

Ghost landed in a Thatcherite Britain in which demolitions
as well as constructions were just the latest chapter in a long
history of woundings and scarrings on the body of cities. In
the raw spaces opened by bombing or areas where docks and
factories were going out of use, commercial towers and luxury
apartment blocks were rising. An earlier generation of tower
blocks built in the 1960s was showing its age. Beneath them,
whole terraces were being levelled. The social geographer in
Whiteread now connected with the poet of abandonment to
tackle the ultimate challenge in urban memento mori. 'James
Lingwood [of Artangel, which specialises in art in unexpected
places] came to me and said, "Is there anything you want to do?"
To someone still in their twenties, this was amazing. "Yeah, I
want to make a house," I said.' Since it wouldn't survive the casting, it had to be uninhabitable and she found what she needed
on a street in Bow, east London, where the house of a retired
dockworker, scheduled for demolition, stood with just two half
houses on each side.

It seemed perfect. The former occupant, Sidney Gale, who'd
built DIY cocktail bars in his shed in the 1970s, warmed to the

unexpected attention. But soon enough the Promethean project began to attract a glare of publicity, not much of it sympathetic. The Young British Artists, of which Whiteread is generationally a member, had not yet emerged as the sensational *enfants terribles* of the art world. For most people contemporary art was incomprehensible, or possibly a great con, and an easy mark for the tabloids. Ten years before, Tate's purchase of Carl Andre's floor-array of ultra-minimalist bricks had drawn a tidal wave of angry derision. When they got wind of *House*, the tribunes turned the same sort of enraged sneering on Whiteread. Art? My arse! Local politicians in Tower Hamlets went along for the ride. Woundingly, and although Whiteread made sure to return personal objects, medals and the like, that she had found while working on the cast, Gale joined the chorus of chortling hatred. Et tu, Sidney? *House* emerged from its cast like a disinterred body, eerily beautiful, a perfectly formed spectral twin but also a poignant emblem of a vanishing world of terrace life.

It stood for just eighty days but Whiteread says, although 'I sealed the building off myself and loved every inch of it', she was 'sick to death of it' well before its end; the hostile publicity making it 'virtually impossible to go have a quiet moment with it'. All the dusty, toxic labour of making it against the storm of hostility made her physically ill. 'Did Artangel look after you?' I ask. 'They tried to but it made them ill too.' On the day of the demolition, she just 'toughed it out; wore a hat and scarf and just stood there' at the centre of all the nightmare circus.

Almost all art aims to nail the fugitive passing of time. But in Britain, mulling over what-has-been is the national psyche. This instinctive fit with a culture of disappearances and recollections made *House* one of the great works of British self-recognition. Despite the publicity ordeal, 'I was extremely proud of it and I still am.' Would she have liked it if it had been permanently spared the wrecking ball? 'Oh, I think it would have been a very sorry thing.' How about making something like it? 'Sometimes I think

I could make something which could live on in this country,' she says reflectively.

But the next big challenge came from elsewhere. The tabloids' target was catnip to the art world, and the afterburn of *House* inevitably produced other commissions involved with collective memory, none more challenging than an invitation from the city of Vienna to enter a design competition for a memorial to the 65,000 Viennese Jews murdered by the Nazis. Whiteread had lived in Berlin for a year and a half and become deeply interested in the memory traces of the Holocaust (or their absence). 'I went to a number of camps for my own personal research, so I was very clear about what I could touch and what I knew about. If I hadn't had that experience, I would never have tried to make a Holocaust memorial.' Above all, she knew that enormity on that scale defies any kind of figurative representation adequate to its horror. Whiteread had admired Maya Lin's abstract response to memorialising the fallen of the Vietnam War and came up with a design generated naturally from her work with negatives: a concrete library of vanished books, their spines towards the hidden wall, deckled page-ends projecting towards the viewer. When, to her genuine astonishment, she was actually awarded the commission, she plunged into it with tragically informed energy. The result is absorbingly elegiac, an evocation, not so much of a multitude of books as of their readers and everything they had brought to European civilisation.

But though Whiteread's strongest works play for high stakes, moral as well as aesthetic, she couldn't have anticipated the intensity of local resistance. Much of Vienna preferred to forget. And there were misgivings on the part of figures prominent in the commission, especially the Nazi hunter Simon Wiesenthal, to the emblematic, rather than figurative, character of the design. At the unveiling ceremony, Whiteread was asked if she herself was Jewish. Virtually simultaneously, Wiesenthal, who had an arm round her shoulder, said 'yes' while she said 'no'. Abruptly his avuncular arm dropped from her shoulder. 'I don't blame him. He was on a mission and he was duped.' But he never spoke to her again and she has never returned to Vienna.

After that experience, 'I had to be dragged kicking and screaming' into another Holocaust commemoration: the project, launched last year, for a memorial and learning centre in Victoria Tower Gardens overlooked by the Palace of Westminster. Whiteread's design is an ingenious doubling of an already standing monument to the slavery abolitionist Thomas Fowell Buxton, but with lantern lights illuminating the learning space below, though it's up against stiff competition including (full disclosure) one with which I'm associated.

Inevitably, before we part, we try to speak about the horror of Grenfell Tower, its charred architectural inside-out still standing, a colossal black tomb, above west London. Snagged in her memory is the series of prints she made in the 1990s called *Demolished* of the organised destruction of Hackney tower blocks. Before they were demolished, Whiteread asked to tour the doomed blocks, climbed twenty-eight storeys to the top floor, then descended to inspect on the ground floor the tied bundles of dynamite laid so the buildings would crumple in on themselves. The recollection trips painfully over itself. For once, with Grenfell on our minds, words fail us both.

But for all her reflectiveness on the play between vitality and mortality, her studio is packed with beautiful things, large and small, delicate and powerful, some of them in the bright colours she has recently worked with and many of them going to the Tate Britain show. As if to correct clichés about her having one string to her bow (however beautifully played), she contrasts herself with artists such as Robert Ryman and Agnes Martin (both admired), who really did do only one thing. 'Look around,' she says, 'and you'll see silver, bronze, wax, resin, paper. I've made this language and now I can play around with all the elements.'

She does indeed engage in her own way with almost all the

materials fashioning the lived spaces of the world. But in a contemporary art culture where forgettable whimsies jostle for their tinny fifteen minutes, she is always going to go for subjects, big or small, that cut to the quick of human existence: time, memory, the space we inhabit, and what remains when it's our turn to head for the exit. 'I always wanted to confer immortality on the quotidian,' she says. And after all, making the ordinary extraordinary is itself the true work of art.

BEASTS

Call me a Yahoo but if you prick up your ears you might just catch the sound of mass whinnying; the pawing of hoofs and the odd titanic neigh coming from somewhere in north Kent where Mark Wallinger wants to install a colossal gee-gee by the Ebbsfleet railway station in time for the Olympic influx in 2012. Fifty metres high, that's a hell of a fetlock. But then contemporary art seems so stampeded with equimania that an extra-terrestrial visiting Frieze (and they probably are) could be forgiven for assuming that, from queen to commoners, Britain is in the grip of an esoteric cult of the filly and the stallion.

Petrified horses are closing in on the West End of London where *War Horse* commands the stage. On Park Lane, David Backhouse's *Animals in War* memorial features a noble patriotic dobbin and, only a few months back, minding my own business at night, I caught sight of something colossal mounted on high where the Lane meets Bayswater Road. By daylight, the object turned out to be one of Nic Fiddian-Green's decapitated and slightly shattered outsize horse-heads.

But then the animal fetish to which much contemporary art is surprisingly devoted carries with it a heavy pack of associations. Wallinger's 'Angel of the South' may be an augmented version of a miniature toy horse, but let's hope Eurostar passengers aren't deep in their Homer or they may find the colossus a bit too Trojan for comfort.

While the bestiary has long been close to the heart of British modernism, its obsessions have generally been not horsey but sheepish and cow-eyed, with an ironic yen for exploring the weird connection between butchery, sacrifice and salvation enshrined in Christian iconography. Damien Hirst's *Saint Sebastian, Exquisite Pain* (2007), for example, with its bovine, arrow-pierced martyrdom, has all kinds of precedents, not just in the multiple piercings of Piero del Pollaiuolo's fifteenth-century *Sebastian* but also in Rembrandt's *Flayed Ox* of the 1650s, the latter a meaty martyrdom for the Calvinists, the carcass strung out on its wooden cross like an even more animal version of the younger Rembrandt's Passion paintings with their tragically beastly torment and howling. 'There is a kind of tragedy about all those pieces,' Hirst has said of his bisected and formaldehyded animals, and, however laconic, almost all of his strongest work taps into that most forgotten but deepest strain in British culture – its ancient perfervid religiosity.

Hirst's most famous sheep piece, *Away from the Flock* (1994), strands a little woolly jumper, pathetically and permanently separated from ewe and flock. But it means much less without summoning the ghosts of lambs past: the van Eyck brothers' 1432 triptych – the first great altar masterpiece in oils – of the sacred lamb in Ghent, for example, or Piero della Francesca's triumphant lamb of the Resurrection. Hirst might have strayed across the livestock lines by drawing on William Holman Hunt's *Scapegoat* (1854–56) but he certainly knows the whole host of strayed lamb parable paintings – whether Hunt's *The Hireling Shepherd* (1851) bringing the flock into danger by flirting with the shepherdess while his sheep wander to the alien corn, or Ford Madox Brown's lavishly lurid *Pretty Baa-Lambs* (1851–59).

Hirst's contemporary bestiary, whether fixed or butchered, pays backhand homage to the equation in Christian tradition between sacrifice and salvation; makes a meal out of it, perhaps, but also exposes what we take for granted as something infinitely strange and tragic. Today's horse-mania, however, is different, disconcertingly upbeat and heroic, even when, as in Backhouse's

Animals in War monument (2004), it is striving to be tragic. The
sculptor had the odd instinct to represent his subjects not torn
and mangled as they have been on the field of battle but as intact
ghosts, so that they seem, peculiarly, to be inspecting themselves
at the wall of their memorialisation rather like the bereaved
families hunting for names of the lost on Maya Lin's Vietnam
Veterans Memorial.

But then horse imagery goes in precisely the opposite direction
from that of the slaughtered meat-animals. Cattle and sheep graze
unknowing that they are destined for the butcher's whetted knife,
and their transcendence as symbols of our own collective sin is
in some deep sense wired to our faint but lingering awkwardness
about making meat of their innocence. Horse and rider, on the
other hand, move almost as equals, each ennobling the other. So
while sheep and cattle recur as images of Christian sin and atonement, man and horse fused together canter through history as the
unapologetic symbol of classical power.

Far better than Backhouse's confused literalism is *The Black
Horse* (2003) by the young Belgian artist Berlinde de Bruyckere, a
wry but strangely poignant take on equine pedigree and the cultish
obsession with bloodlines and breeding. Instead of a specimen
perfected by so many calculations of sire and dam, De Bruyckere
stitches together, literally, a horse of many parts that undergoes
vertebral collapse from the disaster of its misconstruction.

De Bruyckere's mischief works to disfigure the tradition,
stretching back to antiquity – Perseus and Pegasus, Bucephalus
painted by Alexander's pet artist Apelles – of the complementary
fit between horse and rider. Courtier painters such as Titian, van
Dyck, Rubens and Velázquez all followed in delivering images
of fantastic sovereignty, the prince's hand nonchalantly reining
his great horse even or especially in the perilous stance of the
levade, front feet raised off the ground. When aristocratic political cultures such as Hanoverian England dispersed that power,
the warhorse gave way to the racehorse; the courtier artist to the

sporting painter. Only George Stubbs, however, transcended the genre by delivering pictures in which horses and men were virtual peers. Stubbs changed the nature of the genre from equestrian portraits to horse portraiture. The secret of his success lay in his unparalleled mastery of equine body language: the flare of a nostril, the widening of an eye, the accurate fixing of gait and stance. Stubbs was the first to realise that, hitherto, equine representation had been conforming to templates supplied largely by the Renaissance; and that freshly exacting anatomical study, a scientific accumulation of empirical information, was the condition of individualising his subjects; of making not just horse portraits but equine genre paintings.

It was only by being a true anatomist, which is to say, using death to inform the trick of life, that Stubbs could produce *The Anatomy of the Horse* (1766), the masterpiece that made his name and fortune. Subjects would be brought to his attic studio where he would hang them in a complicated harness-contraption from the ceiling and then methodically and slowly bleed them to death, injecting the veins and arteries with tallow to painstakingly preserve their external appearance through the skin. Eventually he would proceed to a flaying and thence to a careful, systematic dissection. What a Gothic romance! It was only from this shocking, protracted intimacy in which love and death were bloodily commingled that Stubbs was able to liberate the horse from its confinement in the conventions of equestrian studies and reconstruct the pure animal as though never saddled: creating what were, in effect, equestrian nudes like *Whistlejacket* (1762) or fantasies of entire families of mares and foals gathered together in some imaginary glade like a school of Houyhnhyms (Stubbs could hardly have avoided *Gulliver's Travels*, which was published in 1726 and revised in 1735).

That moment caught on the cusp between anatomical science and romance became trapped in the next generation of saddle-sore melodramas, from Théodore Géricault's doomed *chasseurs* to Frederic Remington's cult of the cowboy. We're not far from Marlboro country now and the holy relic of Roy Rogers' stuffed Trigger. The nail in the coffin of equestrian kitsch was supplied, finally, by Maurizio Cattelan. It seems improbable that Cattelan could have been unaware of the famous story of Stubbs's contraption when he designed his own. With *Novecento* (1997), Cattelan converts a harness designed expressly to transport racehorses safely from stall to stable, to precisely the opposite: an exhibit of their lifelessness. As an end run round the long equestrian tradition, it is, I guess, a mildly amusing, ultimately banal deconstruction. But it does, at the very least, make an economical obituary.

Taxidermy (and the chemistry of the morgue) has been something close to a cult obsession for contemporary artists. We get it, we get it, you often want to howl in the presence of some of the postmodern confections, now show me something you've really pondered, not just a high-school truism about the world drowning in the bloody slops of the abattoir. And back they come as if to say, 'No, that's not it at all, actually; the reason we dip carcasses into formaldehyde, why we (or our hirelings) are so busy stuffin' 'n' stitchin', is because we're really making a point about art itself; the unselfconsciousness with which all representation is a form of gussied-up taxidermy; the fixing of fugitive moments. Art may be the victory over decay but, guess what,' the contemporary artist protests, 'it can't be done.' The end result of all that effort is merely a sub-species of deadness. So the contrary gesture is to foreground precisely the repugnant processes that the fake aesthetic of the perfect death, the immaculate mortality, belies. Instead, Damien Hirst's *Thousand Years* (1990) made decay or rather the relentless cycle of death and regeneration, the maggot and the blowfly born from the rotting head, the point of it all.

But re-creation is all it sometimes is, and you sigh and shrug and hope for something with more artful staying power. Above all, I think my occasional wistfulness about the gap between the conceptual high-mindedness of the grand titles — *A Thousand Years, The Physical Impossibility of Death in the Mind of Someone Living* — and the yield of true illumination comes from a sense of redundancy; all this feverish labouring to see off the traditional death aesthetic by substituting what in the end is an equally artificial new death aesthetic; the varnish of the Passion piece replaced by the vat of stinky chemicals.

Anyone who really knows the much-despised art historical canon will also know that, far from artists such as Goya having been unaware of the relationship between sculpture and slaughter, many went out of their way to put it down on paper and canvas. What, asks Goya over and again, are we? We are the butchers — and the chopped meat. It's also a feature of the most thoughtful artists — Rembrandt certainly — and the greatest practitioners of *nature morte* to indicate their awareness of the self-defeating quality of painterly immortality. Hence, all those butterflies: ephemera, creatures who live for the day, just one day. Which is why I'm happy to find Hirst turning lepidopterist, and to call one of the sweetest such confections — yes, I suppose with an ironic grin — *Rapture* (2003). But if his mordantly sobering take on bliss is that it always presupposes its own swift disappearance, there have been moments lately when the self-cancelling nature of art's beauty is offset by a surprising gesture of faith in its power of resurrection.

QUENTIN BLAKE

The Big Friendly Giant he is not: more like the Small Friendly Elf, tufty-haired, white-shod and beaming. But Quentin Blake, now an inexhaustible eighty-one, has been the deliverer of sweet exuberance for so long that it may come as a shock to those visiting the show of his work opening at the new House of Illustration in King's Cross, London, next month, to discover that he can also do dark, deep and brutal.

Many of the illustrations he has drawn for Voltaire's *Candide* fully match the philosopher's determination to turn hearty chuckle into mirthless cackle. Dr Pangloss, Candide's tutor, who despite a procession of slaughters and rapes will not be shaken from his optimistic dogma that this is 'the best of all possible worlds', gesticulates inanely in Blake's drawing over the mangled bodies and debris of the Lisbon earthquake, while ignoring his protégé pinned beneath the masonry. A stain of bloody light blooms on the horizon. Another image, a little masterpiece of contemporary art, equally faithful to Voltaire's mordant verdict on the human comedy, summons Blake's inner Goya, depicting a victim of the Inquisition's auto-da-fé swinging from a rope while a trio of canting friars roll their eyes to heaven. Blake's animals are not invariably Giraffe, Pelly and Cuddly. A recent lithograph series, *Girls and Dogs*, features enormous ravening hounds, heaps of carnivorous mange, squatting by the frail bodies of adolescents.

This is not to say that the octogenarian Blake has withdrawn into a cave of morbid gloom. His show, 'Inside Stories', will not be short on joy. Among the nine sets of illustrations are the *Dancing Frog*, hoofing (or webbing) with Astaire and Rogers; the wordless, funny-sad *Clown*, inspired by Jean-Louis Barrault's mime in *Les Enfants du Paradis*; *How Tom Beat Captain Najork and His Hired Sportsmen* ('a parable about education, really'); and two of the collaborations with Roald Dahl: *The Twits*, drawn with a grubby-stubby, bristly-gristly manner befitting its stinky subjects, and *Danny the Champion of the World*, which by comparison is delicately documentary.

When he shows me round the House of Illustration on a wet morning, Blake is the picture of cheerful energy. Initially, he explains, it was intended to be somewhere to show the originals of his illustrations, a place 'as it were with my name on it . . . I'm not frightened by the word museum, though some people are'. Someone then pointed out that, given the way the world is, the institution was more likely to be funded if it didn't have just one person attached to it. And, despite its name giving off a faint whiff of Petrograd collectivism, the House of Illustration conveys its multi-purpose character: as exhibition space in three generous galleries washed by the milky light of north London; rooms for lectures and seminars and workshops; a place shared by working artists and a public avid for the magic of the illustrator's mind and hand. Walking around the empty, handsome house, as students slope to their benches at the adjoining Central Saint Martins school of art and the cooks start frittering their chickpeas in the neighbouring restaurants, it already feels like a sure hit, another gem to add to London's bottomless jewel box of art.

Yet somehow 'illustration' seems too weak a term to apply to paintings and drawings that, at their strongest, are not just auxiliaries of a text, but integral to it, a full partner in the creative play between word and image. So many of those pictures have made not just the British literary imagination, but the sense of what our shared country looks, sounds and feels like. It is impossible to imagine *Alice's Adventures in Wonderland* without John Tenniel's monster loony Queen of Hearts or the towering titfer on the Mad Hatter. Pickwick and Micawber belong to Phiz (Hablot Knight Browne) almost as much as to Dickens, just as Toad and Pooh bluster and mutter according to the drawn lines of E. H. Shepard. But when I ask Blake whether those books and their illustrations were part of his own childhood, he tells me that he only got to see them when he was a teenager: 'I thought now this is a good time to read them.' Maybe he was right.

He himself has never married; never wanted children. And he bridles a little at the sentimental assumption that because his books are full of the snot-nosed happy mayhem of kids he must somehow identify with them. 'Everyone asks me that. Look, I like children. And I like telling stories. But I really like drawing.'

We sit in the temple of inspired clutter that is Blake's studio – an eruption of paints, inks, brushes, paper, books. He tells me about discovering at Chislehurst and Sidcup Grammar School how much he loved drawing, though when an art teacher ordered the boys to make 'rhythmic marks', he says, 'You were supposed to get something out of it; all I could get was octo-puses.' The first thing he saw, walking into his still-life exam, were 'little ziggurats of green apples', a dispiriting prospect until he noticed an alternative, much more to his taste. 'Thank God for that lobster.'

Recognising a precocious talent, Alfred Jackson, the husband of his Latin teacher and himself a cartoonist, asked the fourteen-year-old Quentin if he had any ideas. 'He meant jokes but I didn't know what an idea was.' Jackson encouraged Blake to send in drawings to the humour magazine *Punch*, from whom he received the laconic response: 'Not quite.' Jackson's kindly verdict was: 'That means send some more.' And eventually, at the age of six-teen, Quentin Blake's cartoons appeared in a national magazine. He brushes them off these days as awkwardly stilted, and those that survive are guffaw-challenged even by the genteel standards of *Punch*. 'As soon as I knew something was meant for print, I tightened up. First they were published. I only learned to draw afterwards!' Blake laughs at the memory, adding, 'Even then I knew the roughs were better than the finished drawing' – an early intimation that his strength would lie in a scribbly line that preserved the loose energy of the uncalculated hand, as free 'as handwriting'.

After Cambridge University he went to study with Brian Robb at the Chelsea School of Art, who drew densely hatched, strangely affecting pictures for Sterne's *Tristram Shandy*. 'He was like [Edward] Ardizzone, only more eccentric, the ideal person to do *Tristram Shandy* since he was, in fact, just like that himself.' There was, Blake says, dropping one of his many poetically focused insights, 'an element of dusk in them'. Not surprisingly, Thomas Rowlandson, the Regency caricaturist who specialised in tumbling pratfalls and amorous romps, registered with a bolting hand, is a favourite. And he loves the backhand affability of Hogarth in works such as *Strolling Actresses Dressing in a Barn*. 'It's supposed to be making fun of them. They're degraded in their awful hut but they are discreetly transformed, taking on the parts they act, becoming wonderful.'

Blake comes straight out of this eighteenth-century tradition of rococo mischief, the arabesque ride through the storyline. I ask him if he ever thought of painting full-time? He tells me that he didn't think he could make a living as a painter and then, more importantly, that his instinct was always for the marriage of words and image, the connections that propel a tale forwards. Though everyone who loves his work will have their own laugh-out-loud moments – I can't decide between the outstretched limbs and elated eyes of the frog soaring above the *corps de ballet* or the upturned snout of the cheese-dwelling rat (from his illustrations for La Fontaine's *Fables*), hypocritically deploring his inability, alas, to spare a morsel for his beleaguered fellow rodents – Blake doesn't think of himself as a humorist.

'The humour is a by-product [of the story]. You draw the scene, what people are doing, their reaction to it, and if it's funny, it comes out. There are certain books where you play it for laughs but it's always more interesting in a dramatic situation.' And there is a touch of the playful ghoul in some of his best work. Another of the La Fontaine drawings, of the man who loved his cat so much he married her – which is fine until one night a mouse gets into the bedroom – has her leaping naked and pointy-toothed from the bed to squash her prey in her fist so hard that blood spurts from its body.

Though Blakeans may think of their hero in his rumbustiously adorable mode – Aunt Fidget Wonkham-Strong, or the kids running for cover in his alphabet book where N for (Cyrano/Pinocchio strength) Nose is about to let fly with a nuclear sneeze – he resists fiercely the possibility of type-casting and embraces every chance he gets to change the mood music. Michael Rosen's *Sad Book* was one of the most dramatic of those challenges. Rosen had gone through the worst misery known to humans, losing his eighteen-year-old son to meningococcal septicaemia. The book was his attempt to cope.

'It's extraordinary he could write it. He sent it to Walker Books. They didn't know if it was a book but they sent it along to me ... You respond to something like that differently, on two levels, emotionally one way and professionally another. The problem is so interesting. How do you do it without it being completely gloomy? But he [Rosen] gives you the words – "This is a picture of me trying to look cheerful, actually I'm very sad but people don't like that."' And somehow, by a miracle of empathy, Blake makes the thin mask of cheerfulness reveal the depths of suffering behind it.

Blake had worked with Rosen before, on books of his poems, and had actually drawn pictures of his son. 'Eddie, his name was. I'd never met him but I'd drawn him from imagination. In a way I was glad I hadn't met him as it would have been too much.' He managed 'an element of humour' even in the misery, as Rosen wanted – a sense of the steady beat of indifferent routine, 'trains going past, other people getting on with their lives', the struggle to be part of all that ever again.

But it was the long tall streak of demonic genius, Roald Dahl, with whom, despite also working happily with Russell Hoban (*Najork*) and John Yeoman (*The Wild Washerwomen*), Blake will always be most closely associated. They were the ultimate odd couple, the writer fiendish to the edge of sinister, notoriously cantankerous, the illustrator a power-pack of benign creativity, the virtuoso of the human comedy: Doctor Dark and Professor Bright. 'We weren't the same kind of person,' Blake says in a massive understatement, 'but that was good' – which, since the outcome of the volatile mix was literary and pictorial gold, is indisputably true.

In 1975, when they began to work together, Dahl had not written illustrated books but his new publisher Tom Maschler suggested he try a picture book and sent Blake *The Enormous Crocodile*. 'It was still a very long text,' Blake says, summoning the patient smile he evidently needed for those years. 'We got along okay,' he says. 'But when we did meet it was always at the publisher's.'

Then came *The BFG*. Maschler thought the book would need at best a dozen or so pictures. Blake duly sent them off, to get the response: 'He's not happy.' The reason was that Dahl, unlike Maschler, was expecting many more images and 'thought I wasn't pulling my weight'. Over three days, Blake drew vignettes for each of the twenty-four chapters. 'He's still not happy,' Maschler said. Dahl wanted even more. 'So we went back and started all over again. I have a whole set of drawings [for *The BFG*] that were never printed. Then he listed the scenes he decided he wanted illustrated; I went down to Great Missenden [Dahl's home] and we talked it over.' Without being planned, everything improved. The face of the BFG, originally 'more clown-like', became almost graceful, notwithstanding the elephant ears. 'It all came out in the cooking.' I press Blake a little on the uglier side of Dahl's prejudices. 'I don't think he liked introspection. He wanted things to be practical.' There were surprises in the books, he reminds me, above all at the end of *The Witches*, when the child changed permanently into a mouse declares to his grandma that this is alright since he doesn't want to live longer than her – a moment full of tenderness.

You have the feeling that kindness comes as naturally to Blake as breathing, and that much of his work is borne along by a belief that delight is the best therapy for whatever ails us. Recent work – 'some of the most satisfying I have ever done' – has been for hospitals. Pictures for the public spaces and bedrooms of a geriatric hospital feature young and old together, an elderly dancer with one hand in the air, the other on her walking stick. Other paintings have been made for a hospital for eating disorders, one featuring a girl at the open window of her room, feeding crumbs to the birds on the sill: 'Lots of those patients are known to be very good at helping others to eat.' If a maternity hospital in Angers despairs of the 'sad corridor' taking newborns from delivery room to intensive care – call for M. Blake, who will supply *tristesse*-banishing murals of naked mothers and babies frolicking underwater amid the fishes.

No saint could produce the universe of visual mischief that is Blake's repertoire. But he doesn't have it in him to deliver the sting of cruelty. When, at the end of *Candide*, Pangloss, looking like a decrepit snail, is still droning on about the best of all possible worlds and Candide responds, 'That may very well be but it is time to cultivate our garden,' the artist has the younger man looking down at the seedling cradled in his hands, while forbearance is traced on his sweet face with a single, perfectly economical stroke of Quentin Blake's enchanted pen.

WHITNEY McVEIGH

It's a crude generalisation but, by and large, since images first appeared on the walls of prehistoric caves, the swell and hollows of the rock surface, used to model animal forms, there have been two types of artists. Many have been heroic intervention-ists (Michelangelo, say) self-consciously embattled with their material, and bent on liberating the forms embedded in the inert stone as if freeing something sublime from captivity. But then there have also been the studious, restless, wonder-struck observer-explorers (Leonardo, say), for whom natural form is not the obdurately resisting adversary but rather the settling place of creation's pulsing motions. As a result their modus operandi is less combative than collaborative. Drama is already within the natural forms waiting to be shaped and framed. When he saw, drew, or painted a glacial erratic, Ruskin thought the rock's undulations were the frozen record of their original primordial upheaval.

Whitney McVeigh's exceptionally beautiful, allusive and pro-found work evidently belongs in the Leonardo camp: not just in its fathomless wonder at the uncontainable shape-shifting of nature, but also in the way she has human habit and its semi-fossilised memories (writing, rusting, staining, foxing) lie down with those natural forms to create a marriage between the organic and the manufactured. She is much interested in refreshed vision as a kind of repair or healing and much of her loveliest work is meant to move beyond the assumption that the made and the unmade are forever in mutually depleting opposition. Again like

Leonardo she perceives the mechanical, the geological and the vegetal elements of the world as continuous and their separation into boxed-in universes of knowledge as arbitrary. For years she has been collecting manuals of technology and engineering, on which she superimposes biomorphic blots and images, making the differentiation between organic and inorganic forms moot.

Reticence can be eloquent. It's possible to mistake the poetic delicacy of McVeigh's marks, her willingness to allow ink washes to bleed and run, leach, clot and mottle, for visual modesty, a kind of self-effacing sonata form, given a hearing amid the tinny pumped-up clangour of so much contemporary art. But this is altogether wrong. While deeply respectful of what the world has to offer to the eye – and the rest of the senses – her work is in fact ambitiously visionary: grand macro-micro metaphysical specula-tions about the inconstant universe, and for that matter, our own faces and bodies that inhabit it, and the glimpses that art can give us of all those unstable mutations and metamorphoses. Nothing in her imagery is truly stony. Faces and bodies that are marked with the creases and crumpling of ancient landscapes establish a sympathetic rhyme between the geological and the biological.

There is, of course, something paradoxical about fixing, however momentarily, visions meant to suggest the provisional, contingent, quality of forms – a ship, a face, a body, a landscape. But all the meltings and re-emergences are meant, I think, to resist the temptation to equate an arbitrarily observed single appearance of an object or a human with any sort of descriptive definition. McVeigh's sensibility is creatively unsettled and, ever the itinerant pilgrim, she believes in going forth to meet blessed apparitions. Her art is an act of faith in the happenstance of illumination, but it is never random. To have a chance of encountering such happen-stance, she thinks, means finding somewhere free from the drone of life, a place where intense absorption can yield poetic truth.

Consciously or not, McVeigh's art is in the tradition of all those ambitious artists whose work has sought to reconcile our two cultural halves, Platonic and Aristotelian. Last spring she exhibited at the Getty villa along with Paul McCarthy, Mike Kelley and others devoted to the Platonic echo in contemporary art. On the one hand, with Plato the metaphysician, McVeigh sees ostensible appearance as a veil or scrim, beneath which lies deeper, immaterial truth. So the ragged, melted and motile forms she draws presuppose the rending of that veil so that the true substance of life, dwelling beneath the integument of the world, a miracle of intricate design, can become visible. Unlike Plato, though (and less explicitly recognised), her omnivorous sensibility is also Aristotelian, rooted in the physical texture of the earth; the abundance and infinite variety of its progeny. Her instincts are those of an inexhaustible, urban and rural hunter-gatherer of seemingly unrelated phenomena, from which she establishes meaningful relationships. And her field of play is the exhilarating heterogeneity of creation. Rembrandt, who was likewise addicted to multifarious collecting – bones, instruments, costumes, weapons – would have immediately appreciated McVeigh's studio, crammed as it is with the marks of every kind of human activity along with the piled-up books of memory. Her whole life, like her art, is an ongoing *wunderkammer*, prodigiously expansive: a willed overdose of epiphanies, local and remote. But the ecstatically hungry nature of her harvesting, her openness to the world's everything, is not some sort of feverish rat-pack accumulation. Rather, it is driven, as it was for Dürer or Rembrandt, by the conviction that somehow amid the array of matter there will be a moment of unanticipated fit between the countless parts, and from that fit will arise some sort of deep revelation. Put that way, her art sounds more grandiosely prophetic than she might wish. The ink washes, the lovely palimpsests and superimpositions of memories, she intends as invitational clues, a series of intimate directional nudges, like trail marks in a forest that lead to something majestically serious: a sudden numinously lit clearing in the mind.

None of this means that Whitney McVeigh is a particularly cerebral artist. The category of 'conceptual' art in its more eurekish mannerisms doesn't fit her at all. In the end, the human predicament, embedded in our mortal nature and the burden of that knowledge, is what drives her and much of her work touches, with great poignancy and compassion, on how heavily or lightly we tread the earth, the manner of our arrivals and departures. Her beautiful and moving film *Birth: Origins at the End of Life* has women, facing their death in a hospice, recalling memories of how it was to give birth. In any other hands such a scenario might have seemed instrumental. But McVeigh makes of those voices, faces and bodies something incomparably tender and compassionate. That's how her work is and how she is, and it's not idly sentimental to realise that without this obstinate belief in the ultimate grace of the world she would not have been able to produce her revelatory art.

CAI GUO-QIANG

My very first memory was pyrotechnic. I can date it exactly: 5 November 1949, 'bonfire night', in which the Catholic Guy Fawkes, who failed in an attempt to blow up the British parliament along with King James I, is commemorated with a stuffed dummy incinerated on a backyard pyre: a patriotic auto-da-fé. The gunpowder the plotters failed to ignite is transformed, every Guy Fawkes Night, into a firework display of neighbourhood merriment.

But the 1949 fire-party was, literally, beyond the four-year-old Simon. Instead of being immersed in exploding light, my anxious mother kept me indoors, restricted to a sparkler gripped in my pudgy little hand while I stood, nose pressed against French windows, to see, beyond the glass, majestic fireworks arc and burst over the back garden. So the first drama of my life was well-meant protection from the full force of creative fire. Can small children resent such barriers? You bet your life they can. I already knew that whatever and wherever the oncoming surge of life was to be found, it had to deliver something more than a two-minute sparkle.

So I understand Cai Guo-Qiang's instinct that freedom is explosive. He often speaks of the oppressive weight of confinement in his Chinese childhood. The repression was both domestic and political; during the Cultural Revolution his father regularly burned books lest the traditional culture bring down the wrath of the punishing state on his head. From his home in Quanzhou he remembers hearing the sound of continuous cannon firing on the two sides of the strait, with Kinmen Islands (governed by Taiwan) in their sights just a few miles away. His adoption of gunpowder as a medium and explosion as an artistic practice has been a way of turning confinement into liberation; robbing the state of its monopoly of fire. Composition through disintegration has a long art history, pre-dating Picasso's famous provocation (with its backhand compliment to Dada) that all his work was the sum of many destructions. The traditional process of etching invited many such erasures and amendments, gouged into the plate and bitten into constantly amended lines and shadings. The drama of Rembrandt's most compelling etchings is often to be found not in their ostensible subject matter so much as his working process, a drama of repeated reinvention preserved on the surface of his plates. Those creative onslaughts are relentless, for example, in the different states of *The Three Crosses*, the last of which mantles the Passion in a storm of drenching blackness, as Golgotha heaves with the unearthly force of sacred transfiguration. Rembrandt's fuliginous epiphany is surely an ancestor of Cai's cosmic detonations.

Contemporary art, unable to avert its gaze from global calamities, yet struggling to translate the pain of looking into something that can be decently hung on a wall or installed in a gallery, offers many such refusals of conclusive *finito*. On 9/11, Gerhard Richter was flying into New York from Cologne for a show at the Marion Goodman Gallery when the attacks precluded his landing. As Robert Storr describes it in his fine study, *September*, Richter's painting, the result of much formal struggle, was meant less as a representation of the event than the experience of witness, in this case, received by millions via digital display. Richter's monitor-sized image necessarily embodies this glossy coolness – in keeping with much of his painterly practice. But in this particular case, the licked finish seemed a prohibitively compromised aesthetic. It was only when he returned to his work, abrading and scarifying its surface, that atrocity ignited into visual life: plumes of smoke, sulphurous blooms of fire scarring any art-effect. More recently, the Colombian artist Doris Salcedo, whose work has found poetic analogies by which to represent torture and incarceration, exploded a group of kitchen and work tables, reassembling them on legs mutilated by the shock of that fire, their top surfaces broken into a filigree of scales and flakes as if shredded by flying shrapnel.

Some of these conflicting urges – a fascination with the elemental effects of explosives, above all by forces escaping the designing hand of the artist, while still anxious about the prettification of destruction – must have imprinted themselves on Cai Guo-Qiang. Working in Japan was bound to bring memories of nuclear apocalypse to mind and indeed one of his early experiments with explosions – *The Century with Mushroom Clouds: Project for the 20th Century*, executed in 1996 at Michael Heizer's earthwork *Double Negative* – abysmal crevasses cut into the desert surface – turned on exactly that tension between spectacle and apocalypse. Perhaps because of his own inescapable history (and with Chinese traditions becoming ever more central to the fate of the world), Cai is not one to shrink from history, or rather as in the extraordinary work installed in the Pushkin Museum in Moscow last year, representations of the emotive markers of official memory. That work featured one of the emblematic clichés of Soviet self-congratulation (but also of Russian literary and figurative tradition), a rolling field laid out on the gallery floor, the horizontal field of vision flanked by roomlength murals in which mashed up images and photographs of the Russian Revolution processed along the wall as if unfurling through a Chinese handscroll. Everything is reflected in reverse through the mirrored ceiling, most notably the carved emblems of hammer and sickle in the centre of the wheat field.

On discovering contemporary art in the 1980s, Cai recalls being elated by the Duchampian realisation that it could be anything and everything. Yet he has never sought to disentangle himself from cultural memory and the golden chain of transmitted practice. Gunpowder of course was brought into the world by China, but in one respect Cai's hospitable practice of creating gunpowder works in the presence of viewers and volunteers is in marked contrast to the display of hanging and handscrolls in classical China, where viewing was offered only to privileged guests of the noble or mandarin patron-owner before being secreted away again within cylindrical containers.

Cai's collaborative and immersive habits were most generously offered to our film crew for the final episode of the BBC's nine-part *Civilisations* series. One of the objectives of the series (in contrast to the great 1969 programmes authored by Kenneth Clark) was to extend the range of art beyond the western tradition and in particular to make connections, where they were valid, between different cultural traditions. *Heaven Complex* was created in the summer of 2017 in a fireworks factory on Long Island, the owners of whom descended from a long tradition of Italian pyrotechnics. But the structural base of the work was a visionary idyll common to both western and Asian traditions: the paradise garden. Its characteristic features: a woodland glade; a graceful doe and fawn; a hovering dove, wings extended above monstrously gigantic floral blooms – carnations, peonies and über-pansies – (magnified from nursery catalogues), as if seen by some over-awed caterpillar, or one of Runge's nature-children, were all set down in stencils over stretched canvas. 'I want to create a utopia,' Cai said, his face a mask of sweetness, 'and then destroy it.' The medium of that destruction sat in bowls on a trestle table, so brilliant in colour that I mistook them for pure pigments rather than the gunpowder, which I'd assumed would be, if not black or charcoal grey, then at least darkened, as if locking in their cargo of smoke. Cai loaded smaller containers with the colours he needed and freely scattered the powders along the stencil lines of the drawing, not unlike a sower strewing seed on a furrowed field. Then, finally, as if in some sort of benison to ensure all this would transpire, came the magus move. Roadside plants – the stalks and leaves of overgrown weeds for the most part, pulled and gathered from roadside sites around the Long Island suburban town – were laid on top of the powdered stencil. None of this was done in sovereign solitude. The action was collaborative, the site alive with a small army of assistants and volunteers, running back and forth carrying out the art-general's instructions, given with fiercely decisive quietness. Cardboard sheets were laid over the composition to control the explosion. 'First there is the hiss,' said Cai, softly imitating it tongue against teeth, 'then the pause.'

So indeed there was one when the fuse was lit. And then the shake (rather than a bang or a clap) of sound, and escaping white snakes of smoke and fire rushing from beneath the blanketing boards. Edges were cautiously lifted revealing that some trails of powder had not quite scorched through their intended path. More powder was applied; a secondary ignition lit. When the boards were fully removed the vision of the burned glade was so breathtaking that everyone on the site broke into applause. Cai had spoken of destruction but what had happened was a kind of hothouse blooming, the edges of petals crisped by the shock. But fire, after all, is the necessary condition of renewal, the cracking of seeds, the gestation of botanical rebirth. So when the canvases were laid against the walls, the immense blooms, crimson, gold and blue, seemed to have swollen and were radiantly backlit as if by sunlight streaming through stained glass, the note of sacred illumination, enhanced by the white dove, outstretched wings spotted with soot, but still fluttering over the inferno.

'In the explosion,' Cai had said, 'you can sense eternity.'

'So who gets the beautiful pictures?' one of the fireworks people asked me over a perfectly improvised Chinese lunch. When I told her what was in store for them in the afternoon she let out a 'NO!' of incredulous horror. For Cai now proposed to do something altogether new, full of startling potential but also great risk: he would deliver what was already a richly expressive, sublimely coloured work to a second detonation and see what might arise out of the smoke. It could be something unexpectedly thrilling or it might be too scorched. Whatever the result he wanted a mirror image of it. So in place of the cardboard panels, naked white canvases were set closely over the re-powdered composition to catch an imprint of the explosion. It seemed more powerful than the first. Clouds of acrid, choking smoke filled the space so fully that most of us, masked as we were, needed to rush for the doors to get a pull of Long Island oxygen. What we witnessed as the smoke cleared was a cosmic alteration. The radiance of the first firing had now been charred through, and sprayed with a bituminous mist, as in the aftermath of a profound firestorm or geologic upheaval; some terrible elemental combustion – volcanic or military. Beneath the flying dirt storm there were still petals and feathers, but the wings of the dove were now ragged and torn back as if riddled with shot, almost to the bare contours of avian bone. Paradise had not been regained; just blown apart, fragments of it suspended in some intermediate zone between heaven and black infinity. No merely painted vision of cosmic force could come close to this.

'Gunpowder has such a magical feeling,' Cai said. 'It brings a deeper understanding to changes in space and time . . . it is [on the one hand] an instant in time but somehow also connected to eternity.' And this second burning did in fact have a feeling of Olympian planetary space. The flowers were still glowing through the enveloping darkness, but seen as if from satellite distance; or with the flaring nubs of lit energy you see when you fly over a great city at night.

The naked canvases bearing the ghost-print of the explosion drew from us the deepest response. 'This is God's work,' Cai said, unselfconsciously as he wandered between the canvases, 'his space and his dimension for creation.' This new zone did indeed seem primordially formless, its atmospherics reduced to spectral off-white and grey, but stained with small flares of livid red, flying through the ether, together with feathery smudges of sooty black pellets whose minuteness suggested motion amid the vastness of indeterminate space. Many of those black micro-forms trailed streaking tails, jet comets in the macro world, swimming sperm in the micro: rudimentary organisms shooting towards some consummating destination. Yes, sure, a Big Bang, but also, I was bound to think, the cabbalistic moment of primordial creation when celestial vessels are shattered; falling from ethereal radiance into concrete matter as they descend, but retaining within them the lit seeds of future living energy. To stare at all this was to be launched, pod-like, into infinity. But it was also to experience a release of mystical beauty.

Cai Guo-Qiang inspected all this in a state of happy exhilaration but also with an expression of wonder, as if he had not been the maker of this stunning work at all but just the enabler of some immanent vision powered by the flowing *qi* of the universe.

But then again, that's pretty much what Michelangelo felt about marble when he sought to free forms trapped within the carapace of stone. For that matter, all great art is the result of a hard negotiation between the conceiving artist and the resistance of materials. Though Cai in his modest fashion likes to stress the ways in which powder, smoke, fire and light can and should get away from his designing hand, the fact remains that, as with every bona fide genius, his mind is the only source of the kindling spark.

RIJKSMUSEUM REBORN

At last. There they were, all my old friends, missed these past ten years, propped up against the wall, waiting their turn to be back where they belonged: on the walls of the Rijksmuseum in Amsterdam. There were the dangling legs of Gabriël Metsu's hollow-eyed sick child cradled in the arms of his mother; there was Adriaen Coorte's bunch of white asparagus, ghostly against the blackness, filaments of its bundling twine pressing against the papery skin. There was another pair of legs, belonging to Jan Steen's pretty slattern, curls escaping her soft cap, perched on the edge of a bed, garter-marked right leg slung over the left, the underside of her thigh scandalously visible, rolling her scarlet stockings. 'What do you think?' asked Taco Dibbits, then the Rijksmuseum's director of collections and the hero, along with the museum's general-director Wim Pijbes, of its exhilaratingly brilliant makeover, 'Up or down?' 'Down,' I said. 'Oh, that's settled then,' he said, wearing his knowledgeable smile.

The reunion was well under way. Earlier we'd watched as chubby-chinned Saskia, cow-eyes glittering, was hoisted back onto the wall of a room full of early Rembrandts. Already on station was the grieving Jeremiah in his dove-grey velvet coat, head slumped as the temple burns behind him; the young boho Rembrandt mugging with his unruly hair and knobbly nose half-masked by shadows to project depths of poetic melancholy.

Dibbits and Pijbes were thinking of borrowing the slogan *'weer-zien met de meesters'* ('meeting up again with the masters') from the reopening of the Rijksmuseum at the end of the Second World War. The present moment can't have quite that sense of national resurrection but it is still an emotively charged reunion of the public with works that are inseparable from the sense of who, collectively, the Dutch are. What has been done with the museum is less a restoration with some fancy contemporary design than the inauguration of a curatorial revolution. When you see those early Rembrandts or the great mannerist *Massacre of the Innocents* of Cornelis van Haarlem with its ballet of twisting rumps, you will also encounter, as would those who would first have seen them, the silver, weapons and cabinets that were the furniture of the culture that made those pictures possible. You will enter the historical world of the Netherlands at a particular moment. And, because the objects are housed in frameless, edgeless displays in which the glass is of a stunning invisibility, nothing in one's field of vision separates images from artefacts.

The objects are not there amid the paintings in the service of ornamental atmospherics. They were chosen by Dibbits and his colleagues from the vast Rijksmuseum holdings to create an active dialogue between pictures and artefacts, the material world and the cultural imagination. The idea is gently rather than dogmatically social, and it owes something to a scholarly tradition, best embodied in the work of the great Dutch cultural historian Johan Huizinga (1872–1945), who believed that images, objects and texts were indivisibly related in the creation of a common culture. In keeping with recent art history's emphasis on the creative force of a milieu in the making of a master (rather than the musings of solitary genius), the young(ish) Rembrandt is installed in the company of friends and patrons. One of those friends, the framemaker Herman Doomer, is represented by a spectacular ebony and mother-of-pearl cabinet. Another friend, the goldsmith Jan Lutma, is present in a stunning drinking bowl in the form of a slickly glistening opened oyster. Collaborations and relationships bounce from wall to wall. Rembrandt's early self-portrait is complemented by the in-your-face self-image painted by his Leiden doppelgänger and rival Jan Lievens, who also supplies a head of their shared patron Constantijn Huygens, learned secretary of Stadtholder Frederik Hendrik.

If this all sounds daunting and distracting, it really isn't. History and art have their natural companionship restored, for – although historians condescendingly suppose images to be 'soft' evidence of the past, and art historians suspect historians of obtuse philistinism – the truth is, as Huizinga knew, they need each other to reconstruct the reality of lost worlds. History without the eloquence of images is blind; art without the testimony of texts is deaf.

The Rijksmuseum isn't the first institution to bring together what should have never been separated into 'fine' and 'decorative' (by implication not-so-fine) art. But it has been museums rich in objects rather than paintings that have made a systematic effort at presenting cultures in the round. Thus in 2001, London's Victoria and Albert Museum, reflecting the conviction of such nineteenth-century writers as John Ruskin and William Morris that textiles, ceramics and so on could have an aesthetic charge every bit as potent as paintings, brought together those arts in a chronological sequence of rooms from Tudors to Victorians.

But it is another thing entirely for a place associated in the public's mind with a great procession of masterpieces and artists – Rembrandt, Ruisdael, Vermeer – to remake their house as the 'Museum of the Netherlands' as the Rijksmuseum now calls itself. Nor is it accidental that this exhilarating breakthrough has happened here: it was in the Netherlands that resistance was strongest to making the invidious distinctions between 'high' and 'low' adopted in Renaissance Italy. According to the Portuguese humanist Francisco de Holanda, Michelangelo condescended to praise the ability of the artists of the Low Countries as they specialised in such low matters as landscape. But this was exactly why, whereas art in Italy became, primarily, the possession of the church and the aristocracy, in the Netherlands it became the possession of the people. It was here that an art arose that was unembarrassed to take as its subjects not just devotional and historical matter but the earthy entirety of human existence, from the most vulgar to the most exquisite.

When we look at Vermeer's servant girl pouring a jug of milk, or a goblet of wine and a herring by Pieter Claesz, we now take for granted that ordinary acts and objects may be intensely charged with sublimity. But it was in the Netherlands that this translation of the sacred from the religious to the worldly realm was most dramatically realised.

The Calvinism that frowned on images in churches as a species of idolatry was, however, content for the picturing impulse to transfer itself onto every other conceivable subject. The Rijksmuseum is full of images that retain a charge of spiritual self-interrogation even as they seem to be full of worldly relish. A Pieter Claesz still-life gathers emblems of all the arts that are supposed to deliver worldly pleasure – among them painting itself – at the same time as it displays transcendent artistic skill. A heroic Jacob van Ruisdael windmill prompting meditations on the Cross can be deadeningly beside the point. Such visual finger-wagging may have had little more effect on the original viewers than it does on us. They may well have nodded, sighed and got on with enjoying the shimmer on the satin of a Gerard ter Borch gown or the perfectly rendered creamy surface of a Floris van Dijck cheese.

There is another reason why the popular appeal of the Rijksmuseum is rooted in national memory. For this was not just an art that mirrored the life of the ordinary people of the Netherlands; it was, to an astonishing degree, owned by them too. Valuations of household goods made for purposes of taxation and bequests tell us that whereas grandiose portraits and history paintings may have been beyond the reach of the average miller or merchant, a huge range of modest paintings that flooded the market – low-life scenes, little landscapes, still-lifes, 'merry companies' of boozers, flirters and the like – were not. Many of them could be bought for not much more than the weekly wage of a skilled artisan. There was an additional sense, too, in which painting was a civic patrimony. In Italy portrait groups were dynastic; in the Netherlands they were civic and thus part of a popular patrimony, at least among the middle classes. Every town in the country had its publicly displayed groups of militiamen, wardens of orphanages and old people's homes, syndics of the men of the clothiers guild. *The Night Watch* might be seen now as a 'masterpiece', but of what? The answer is of an idea or, rather, a civic myth: that of the undying vitality of the citizen in arms. Its form – the propulsive dynamism that throws Banninck Cocq's company forward through the picture frame and into the space of the goggling beholders, the unsettling sense of commotion of noise and chaos barely contained by the orders of officers – is perfectly fitted to its ideology. That ideology was the polar opposite of aristocratic and church paintings, which are, above all, ordered through hierarchy and authority. So while Rembrandt's picture may exist in some rarefied realm of the canon as one of the world's masterpieces, the point and, therefore, the enjoyment of it is incomprehensible without its specific, Amsterdam history.

In the spirit of giving back their history to the Dutch, a history inseparable from its art, Dibbits and Pijbes and Ronald de Leeuw, the original visionary of a historical narrative and the Rijksmuseum's previous director, have been unapologetic about this 'Museum of the Netherlands'. In an age of interchangeable international art fairs, all flogging indistinguishable contemporary art, there is something deeply stirring about a great art institution being unafraid to reassert the distinctiveness of its national culture and history, and to make it a cause for popular rejoicing rather than uncool embarrassment.

None of this has been done in any spirit of narrow chauvinism. Honouring the vision of the Rijksmuseum's original architect,

Pierre Cuypers (1827–1921), meant taking an expansive view of the Netherlands past and present. Cuypers was a Catholic from the south and he chose a vernacular that was meant, in its brick gable-towers, to echo the late medieval and Renaissance Netherlands as yet undivided between a Catholic south and a Calvinist north. Cuypers' liberal historicism, enshrined in history paintings by George Sturm and stained glass from formative episodes in Netherlandish history that decorate the museum's interiors, was thought absurd if not abhorrently parochial by subsequent generations of modernist-minded directors of the museum, who ripped up the terrazzo floor, rolled up the canvases and whitewashed the walls. But the museum was never meant to be some sort of white cube, and now it has been fully restored to Cuypers' beautiful vision. That this should have been accomplished by Spanish architects, Cruz y Ortiz, coming from the kingdom against which the Dutch fought a bloody eighty-years-long war for their freedom, is an irony not lost on anyone. For this reconstitution of a nation's history has been achieved as a pan-European collaboration, in keeping with the internationalist humanism of Erasmus and the philosopher-statesman Hugo Grotius, whose portrait, by Jan van Ravesteyn, at the age of sixteen, face lit by mercurial intellectual mischief, is one of the most winning rediscoveries of the new installation. The brilliant interior design including those dazzlingly formless display cabinets is the work of the Frenchman Jean-Michel Wilmotte; the glass and metalwork were made in Brescia, Italy; and the optically undulating star-spangled decoration of ceilings above two staircase wells has been painted by the British Turner Prize-winner Richard Wright.

Not all Dutch artists were stay-at-homes like Vermeer or Rembrandt. Painters such as the phenomenal Hendrick ter Brugghen, who went to Italy and then returned to Dutchify Caravaggio's drama of light and darkness with meaty bodies bulking up against the picture frame like Dutch football fans: going abroad for the action but always bringing the energy back home.

In the medieval and Renaissance galleries, it's possible to see a truly Netherlandish style – raw and naturalistically expressive – emerging from the matrix of international Christian sculpture.

Perhaps even more wonderfully, although the Rijksmuseum is about to be the greatest history-teaching institution anywhere in the world, it's not all homework. Around every corner is eye-popping merriment and pleasure. The 'special collections' galleries are a stupendous open treasury, a gorgeously lit Dutch Aladdin's cave in which kids of all ages can boggle at the geegaws: jewels, muskets, pikes, miniature tea services in silver; a whole fleet of model ships going back to the seventeenth and eighteenth centuries, magic lanterns, costumes, glasses, those tiles, marvel piled on marvel; wonder on wonder, a fabulous, unending inebriation of stuff.

The people who wore, used and possessed all this stuff also haunt the place, often turning up in the simplest guises. One case houses a small collection of woolly hats, many striped in vivid colours. The only other place I know where you can see anything like them is in paintings of fishermen and, perhaps, Dutch boers. But these are the hats worn by whaling crews in Spitsbergen in the seventeenth century, preserved beneath the ice, in such perfect condition that you'd expect to see them in a tray of beanies at your outerware shop of choice. So you look at the hats, you hear the sailors' shouts, the creak of ice-trapped timber, you smell the blubber vats and you commune with your ancestry. Which may not be Fine Art, but is all the more enthrallingly potent for it.

The Remains of That Day: 9/11 memorial, New York

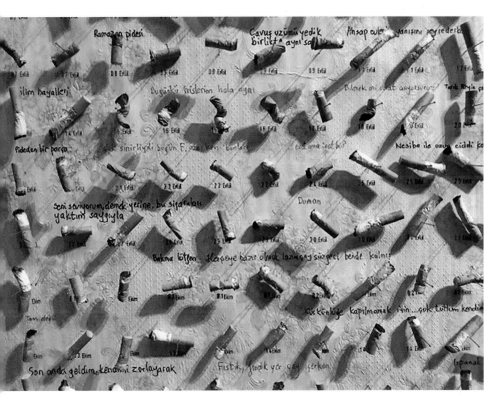

Orhan Pamuk: The Museum of Innocence: 4,213 cigarette butts

The Palace of Colour: Forbes Collection,
Harvard University

Gold: funerary mask in Mycenean gold

Blue: *Woman Reading a Letter*, Johannes Vermeer

Hercules Segers: *Still Life with Books*

Hokusai: *Kajikazawa in Kai Province*

Sally Mann: Photo Traces of Cy Twombly: *Remembered Light, Untitled (Drips and Newspaper)*

Cindy Sherman: *Untitled #86*

Tacita Dean: *Bubble House*

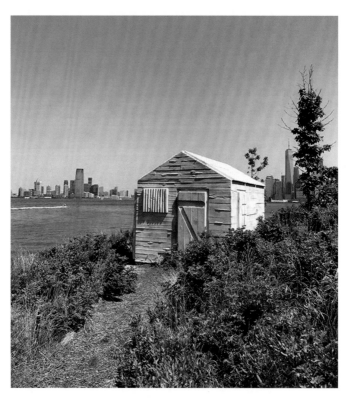

Rachel Whiteread: *Cabin*, Governors Island

Beasts: *Whistlejacket*, George Stubbs

Quentin Blake: illustration from the Folio Society
edition of *Candide* by Voltaire

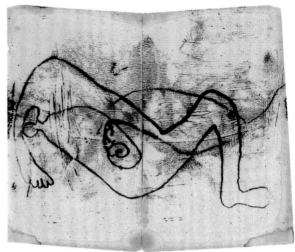

Whitney McVeigh: *You are a child (The Conference of the Birds)* and *Untitled (book page) IV*

Cai Guo-Qiang: *Heaven Complex No.1 and No.2*

Civilisations: What Were We Thinking?: collage created by Helena Mandlová, aged twelve, in the Theresienstadt concentration camp

Patti Smith

Tom Waits

Helen Mirren: *The Tempest*

Bill Clinton

Two Big Eaters

CIVILISATIONS:
WHAT WERE WE THINKING?

Half a century ago, in 1968, Kenneth Clark was in Paris, standing in front of the BBC cameras, asking, 'What is civilisation? I don't know, but I think I know it when I see it'; then, turning to Notre Dame behind him, he added, 'And, as a matter of fact, I'm looking at it now.' Then off he sailed into the majestic television series that brought millions, previously daunted by museum grandeur, to the mighty illuminations of European art. The scene that day was sunny, the temper serene. But somewhere off camera the Fifth Republic was falling apart; students were roaring protests and when not buried in the Archives nationales or dodging a light mist of tear gas in Montparnasse, I was among them. I was, in fact, part of the problem: by Clark's lights, barbarically feckless youth, stoned on self-righteousness, threatening to storm the doors of 'bourgeois' enlightenment.

So it's with a sense of irony that Clark would doubtless have relished, not to mention a cartload of hubris, that at many points along the way I too found myself asking the same question or wondering whether it was even worth being put? But towards the end of filming one particular work of art gave me the answer. It was by an artist Clark would not have heard of, though I like to think he would have felt the same way about her. She was twelve years old when she made her picture, living in Building L410, in the concentration camp of Theresienstadt, about an hour's drive north of Prague. Like the other 15,000 children Helena Mandlová had been taken from her family on arrival and put into horrifyingly overcrowded, disease-riddled barracks. But during the hours she spent as a pupil of her art teacher Friedl Dicker-Brandeis, one of the great unsung heroes of the history of art, Helena was free. Her collage, which you can see in the Jewish Museum at the Pinkas Synagogue in Prague, is a night landscape, as if seen in a dream. Mountains rinsed in moonlight look down on a huddle of houses; stars burst in a deep red sky. The white paper used for stars and mountains is office stationery, its heading, inverted by Helena so that it lies at the foot of her composition, German. The sheet is not some enumeration of transports east, one of which would carry Helena (like 90 per cent of the Theresienstadt children) to her death in Auschwitz, but simply some piece of dull bureaucratic supply of the kind needed by those who managed the efficient business of mass extermination. But for a moment, Helena had cleansed the sheet of its moral dirt. She had made art.

And this was important because Theresienstadt (Terezin in Czech) was a travesty culture. When the International Red Cross visited it in 1944 they were shown concerts, football, a children's opera. The eighteenth-century garrison town was spruced up, the grim 'lower fortress' of torture and execution hidden away. Along with the film made by the SS this was meant to show the world that Jews were being treated humanely in their resettlement. It was all a lie. The camp was just a way station to the crematoria.

Friedl Dicker-Brandeis would also be among the murdered millions, and it is unlikely she was deluded. But she had been taught at the Bauhaus by Paul Klee, Johannes Itten and Lyonel Feininger and had become herself an impassioned teacher. When she was deported to Theresienstadt at the end of 1942 she used her meagre luggage allowance to bring art materials to the camp and after her death, some 4,500 drawings, paintings, collages and sculptures were found in two surviving, hidden suitcases. She told her pupils – all between the ages of nine and thirteen – to sign their work so posterity would know them. Some of the pictures are what you would expect from children of that age; others are strikingly beautiful: an underwater scene made at the same time Matisse was cutting his own oceanic reveries; flowers painted gigantically as if from a caterpillar's point of view; a hasidic Jew flying over a bed; and many landscapes seen through opened shutters. Also, trains and, in one case, a public hanging. Some, too, are imaginative variations on paintings by Vermeer and Raphael shown to the children in photographs brought by Friedl. Thus civilisation came to the inferno, fighting back hard for humanity.

I am not someone who subscribes to the Romantic theory that torment and sorrow, whether of the artist or the world, are the necessary conditions of great art. Yet, without leaning on the scales of history, it has been striking how often a period of great creative energy either followed a period of calamity or was produced as a response to it. The first truly sophisticated landscape paintings in the history of art were made in tenth- and eleventh-century China under the northern Song dynasty following a period of catastrophic civil wars. Imperial patronage encouraged the production of scenes of mountainously imposing authority beneath which the proper order of society could proceed untroubled. But that process could be dramatically reversed. One of the most unforgettable moments of filming was in the Shanghai Museum where *Dwelling in the Qingbian Mountains* by the fourteenth-century painter Wang-meng was freed from its cylindrical storage container to cascade down the wall. Proud of his descent from the Song dynasty, Wang-Meng was one of four masters who famously refused to serve the Mongol Yuan dynasty, but who could never completely escape the pressure of politics. At the centre of the scroll is a pavilion built for spiritual retreat belonging to his own family with a single solitary figure seated there. But his place is precarious. For all around him, the great mountain writhes in tumult, as if a dragon aroused, its slabs of rocks heaving in some sort of rehearsal of its primordial creation. And all this geological and botanical havoc is registered in astonishingly expressive stabs of the brush. There was reason for Wang-Meng to paint in this disturbed mode. Wrongly accused of plotting against the new Ming emperor, he would die in prison.

Art as redeemer from calamity was of course the leitmotif of Clark's heroic narrative of European genius. Rescued from the darkness closing in on the ruins of antiquity (Clark made that age rather darker than it actually was), by the likes of the monks of Iona, the 'precious' hit its stride in the 'warming' of the twelfth century bursting into full glorious flower in the Italian Renaissance, onward and upward to the sunlit plateau of Enlightenment cheerfulness and reason. Cue Mozart. But then came the siren song of Romantic revolution and the twin exterminating angels of war and industrialisation. It is a coherent, seductive story told with eloquent persuasiveness and in many respects not at all wrong.

So what could possibly be added by a new series? And of course the answer is the rest of the world. It won't have escaped your attention that these days those who shout most loudly about the sovereign virtues of 'Judeo-Christian civilisation' (an oxymoron by the way) are generally those who are most clueless about its actual content. They are often even less aware of the countless moments when contact between the European and the non-European world seeded a blossoming of cultural creativity. The most abrasive issue of our own time, worldwide, is precisely this relationship between connection and separation, and the history of art has not been unaffected by it. Academic departments are often ghettoised into western or Asian or African or pre-Columbian specialists who seldom teach together, though the phenomena they deal with often unfolded at the same time.

At which point alarm bells will ring. But our series is not some sort of television manifesto by the Citizens of Nowhere; much less knee-jerk deference to non-western cultural constituencies.

Mary Beard, David Olusoga and I ('Hey,' Mary joked at a meeting, 'the woman, the black and the Jew, what could possibly go wrong?') instead try to give the wider truth an airing without, we hope, spoiling the view. Quite often, that truth can be one of fruitful connections. In one programme David Olusoga reveals the effect that the import of Dutch optical instruments had on the art of Tokugawa Japan; in another I look at the opposite flow: the dramatic impact that the availability of woodblock prints by Hokusai, Hiroshige and the rest had on painters like Monet, who collected more than 200 of them, and van Gogh, who borrowed them from the dealer Siegfried Bing, and his brother Theo, who sold them. Van Gogh portrayed his art materials supplier 'Père Tanguy' three times, always surrounded by those prints, and when he went south to Provence he described his migration as a quest for 'Japanese light'.

Sometimes, to be sure, the spur is competitive envy, born of mutual, wary, observation. In the middle of the sixteenth century, Mimar Sinan, the Ottoman sultan Suleyman's master builder, and Michelangelo (both of them old) were each trying to outdo the Hagia Sophia by building massive, domed houses of worship that would proclaim the invincibility of their respective faiths. Turks visited the site of the partially rebuilt St Peter's and there was an entire colony of Italians in Istanbul, so it seems unlikely that either of them would have been unaware of the other's progress. And in some respects, their designs, a vast cupola, pierced with light, resting on four colossal piers, were strikingly similar, though while Sinan got to realise his vision, Michelangelo's Greek Cross, inherited from Bramante, would be partially thwarted by his successors.

These encounters are not necessarily the rule. There are plenty of instances where cultures take root and evolve in complete isolation from the rest of the world: the glories of the Maya being a spectacular case in point. In 1986, a sacrificial grave was discovered at Sanxingdui near Chengdu in Sichuan; along with a mass of

elephant tusks, a trove of bronze masks were found, some colossal, some gilt, which bore absolutely no relationship (except in the
technology of their casting) to anything else seen in Bronze Age
China. There was a struggle to integrate the astonishing objects
within the continuity of ancient Chinese art, but one look at those
masks tells you it's in vain. Sometimes cultures just happen in
their own idiosyncratic style.

None of this is to say that we short-changed the glories of the
west. You'll find Greek sculpture, medieval stained glass, Titian
and El Greco as well as Olmec heads, Mughal miniatures and Paul
Gauguin in the programmes. But *Civilisations* makes no pretence
to being a comprehensive survey of world art. Clark had thirteen
episodes for Europe between the early Middle Ages and the early
twentieth century. We had a paltry nine to get us from the Ice
Age to last week. Inevitably, then, each of the programmes, while
delivering a feast for the eye, is driven as much by themes as well
as stories; and the questions that looking at masterpieces provoke.

But you can't always get what you want. Filming the exquisite
Iranian mosques of Isfahan was frustrated by discovering that our
American co-producer, PBS, would have been charged with violating sanctions. Many of the caves holding the most spectacular
displays of Paleolithic art are now off limits due to the damage that
human presence, especially our breath, has done to their fragile
condition, although at Tito Bustillo in Asturias we were able to
film astonishingly beautiful images of horses from 25,000 years
ago. After a day deep inside those caves I was so weirdly smitten
with a sense of their hospitable cosinesss (the temperature is a
mild 12 degrees all year round) that I had to be dragged out in
grumbling protest. On the Japanese 'Art Island' of Naoshima, the
custodians maintain such reverence before Monet's water-lilies
that no speaking is countenanced and requests to film a fine James
Turrell installation were greeted with shocked disbelief. On the
roof of St Peter's our clerical handler wasn't thrilled with my
impression of Gene Kelly's 'Singing in the Rain' between takes.

I can't imagine why not. And along the way there were the usual hazards: a car crash on the Delhi–Agra road at 4 a.m., with the colliding party evidently the worse for wear with booze. At Petra, a bolting horse thundered towards us in a narrow gorge, turning itself and its buggy over just feet away.

But there were also epiphanies: rounding the corner of a Paleolithic cave and seeing the stencilled hand of a fellow human from 40,000 years ago; sitting halfway up one of the great pyramids of Calakmul, populating the Maya plaza below in my imagination; being allowed by the owner of a print shop that has been in business in Tokyo since the late nineteenth century, to hold in my hand one of the greatest Hokusai masterpieces. And there were also powerful revelations from works I mistakenly thought I knew inside out: the poignant figure of a woman of uncertain age, trudging across a bridge, stooped under an immense pile of twigs and branches (for thatching or fuel) in Pieter Bruegel's *Hunters in the Snow*, a tiny detail that suddenly seemed an emblem of the human condition; the androgynous interchangeability that the bisexual Benvenuto Cellini contrived in the beautiful heads of both Perseus and the decapitated Medusa.

In the end we have tried to fail better, as Beckett's famous injunction has it. But I have no qualms at all about being grateful for the opportunity to bring a dazzlingly photographed art series, made on a scale only the BBC could contemplate, to realisation. Clark's original series, conceived by the then controller of BBC Two, David Attenborough, as a vehicle for the new medium of colour television, unapologetically celebrated the enduring at a time of Vietnam miseries, and political and social upheaval. Art should never be a bromide for discontent, but it can deliver things in short supply in our own universe of short attention span: attentiveness, thoughtfulness, contemplation; depth; illuminations that persist when the screen goes dark. As close as we could get to the works of art, though, I am under no illusion that what we offer is any sort of substitution for being in their material presence. So the offering is by the way of an invitation: go, see, think. Let the exhilaration, the disturbance, the power and the beauty sink in. And if in the weltering storm of the trivial we can interpose some sense of what really matters in the array of things that humans – the art animals – have fashioned, then perhaps we will be judged to have done our job.

MUSIC, THEATRE, FILM AND BOOKS

My career as a music critic began at the tender age of fifteen and ended at the still-tender age of sixteen, when the editor's daughter and I called it quits. 'Might I ask a favour?' the dad ventured when I first showed up at the flat to take the daughter to a movie. Might I help out with the odd mini-column (300 words, it doesn't get minier than that) to supplement the real concert reviews? Just the occasional trip to the Festival Hall, Wigmore Hall, all the halls, for the odd recital or chamber music concert? A treat, I imagined, furtive hand holding, Apassionata! The only snag was I knew absolutely nothing (critical that is) about Beethoven, Mozart, Bach, all the likely assignments. Buddy Holly yes, Schubert no. It wasn't that Mum and Dad weren't musical; they were in fact almost histrionically melodic, but as in musical shows rather than the stuff of Proms. In fact music resounded through the Golders Green semi at invasively inappropriate moments: renditions of 'There's No Business like Show Business' (a duet) ringing over the breakfast table while I paddled my spoon in the raspberry yoghurt and inwardly moaned.

This was different. I needed guidance. The girlfriend, who certainly did know her Brahms from her Dvořák, set past columns in front of me and together we perused useful adjectives: 'lyrical'; 'animated'; 'lively'; 'serene'; 'sprightly' and so on, inscribed a bunch of them on Scrabble tiles, shook them up in the bag, pulled a few out and there we went: 300 words on Annie Fischer's rendition of the Moonlight Sonata; another

300 for Rubinstein and the Chopin Mazurkas; Archie Camden's Big Bassoon? Lyrical, masterly and (naturally) 'deep'.

Theatre was a different story. It was where my father had wanted to spend his professional life rather than in the textiles that became a kind of prison for his irrepressible theatricality. Now I come to think of it the brilliantly coloured silks he specialised in were as theatrical as he could get in that line of business. He over-compensated by bursting into Shakespeare at the drop of a hat: between courses at dinner when he would rise to deliver Falstaff's 'sherris sack' complete with tottering booziness; or when reproved by my mother for my sub-par school report, would intercede with 'the quality of mercy is not strained'. Before I was out of short trousers he had me memorising whole speeches. So one of the most thrilling TV assignments I've ever had was, along with Sam West and Amanda Stubbs, judging the 'Off by Heart Shakespeare' competition for schoolkids (for Daisy Goodwin's Silver River Company and the BBC). To see twelve-year-old Jack throw himself literally across the stage at Stratford with 'O for a muse of fire' was to believe all over again in the inextinguishability of Shakespeare in the age of tweetomania. The winner was a fourteen-year-old girl in a hijab who nailed the hardest speech of all, 'To be or not to be', which, startlingly, she treated as self-mocking black comedy — 'that is the question?' — before becoming quietly terrified of the 'unknown country'? Sam said, 'My god, I'd hire her now for the company.' We went over to say the same to her proud parents. 'She must become an actress,' said Sam. 'Oh, no,' said her smiling dad, 'she's going to be an international financial consultant.' Hey, all the world's a stage.

PATTI SMITH

It is safe to say that Patti Smith was the only person in Greenwich Village who knew that the date of our interview, 6 January, was also the birthday of Joan of Arc. An image of Frémiet's gilded statue in the Place des Pyramides, the armoured heroine holding the fleur-de-lys aloft, appears in her volume of black-and-white photographs. There is plenty in Patti Smith's poetry and music to suggest an affinity with the Maid of Orléans: fellow warrior, possessed by visions, and tuned to the music of the angels. But in the 12 Chairs café she was wielding the pen rather than the sword. When I arrived, she had her back to the door, bent over the loose pages of a manuscript ('my café ruminations'), her hand swooping across the scattered paper. Much energetic underlining was under way, so much in fact that it seemed impolite to interrupt the studious figure in her glasses and flannel shirt, long hair streaked with grey, more the literary professor than the hellcat howler of *Horses*.

I had met her once before, in England, in another bookish setting: the Charleston literary festival, which takes place in the Sussex remove of the Bloomsburys. Something about those Bells and Woolfs, perhaps their criss-crossing between prose, painting and partners, spoke to Patti Smith – as if Charleston was the Chelsea Hotel in wellies. Patti the still-life artist took lovely photos of Duncan Grant's brushes standing in their battered paint pot. One evening, after a kitchen supper, she appeared like a phantom troubadour, hair swinging over her shoulders, and generously sang

for the tipsy chatterers: a lullaby composed for her children. The
grown-up kids, including me, melted with happiness. I remembered her as the wake-up witch; the queen of the frontal shout.
But this Patti, soft and deep, was just as real. 'It was always there,'
she reminds me now. '"Elegie" in *Horses* was a pretty tune.' So it
was, but it was also a keening lament for all those who had gone
too soon: Morrison, Hendrix and Joplin, the self-dosing ninepins
of the '70s.

She apologises for being dressed down but this hardly seems
necessary. This is MacDougal Street; it's Monday; I am not exactly
a fashion plate myself. Besides, she is under the weather, stricken
by the nasty bug that has colonised New York. I sympathise but
she adds that she's done four performances nonetheless. 'It didn't
affect my voice,' she says. 'It's funny, you can be ill but on stage
it's the adrenaline and sometimes you can just tell the people;
they'll give you what you need and you crash later.' On 5 February,
London will hear that unmistakeable voice – to judge by her latest
album, *Banga*, more beautiful than ever, by turns raw and tender.
She will perform with a small group including her guitarist son,
Jackson. He lives in Detroit, once her own home but these days a
tough place to make a living. So the European tour is pay cheque
and family. Patti the mother (and now grandmother), liberated
from the pressure of a full-on big-band screamer, gets to hang
with her boy.

These chamber concerts are called 'An Evening of Words and
Music' and feature poetry as well as song. But right from the
moment when the nasally shouted chant of 'Piss Factory' came
before the world in 1974, the two genres have been inseparable
in her work. It was through the compelling need to voice poetry
rather than just have it sit primly on the page that Patti came to
be a singer. Either way the words matter most. Anyone doubting
that Patti Smith is in her own right a fine, strong, writer should
open *Just Kids*, the memoir of her loving friendship with the artist
Robert Mapplethorpe in the late 1960s and early '70s, before

either of them was famous. Any paragraph will tell sceptics that the National Book Award jury wasn't just giving her the prize out of astonishment that a rock 'n' roller could string the odd sentence together.

When the award was announced, her publisher's publicist told me, Patti cried for a solid hour. There was no self-congratulation in the tears; rather the deep satisfaction of a promise fulfilled. A day before his death, Mapplethorpe asked her to write their story and she had said yes. How could she refuse him? But without any experience of book-length writing, it took twenty years of struggle in and out of her own ordeals and tragedies to get it done. It was hard, she says, 'because I wanted to write a book that would have real substance for the habitual reader but one which would also welcome the non-reader', not least because Mapplethorpe never read much at all. To bring those non-readers into the story she tried to make the book 'as cinematic as possible, like a little movie unfolding'.

It was worth the long gestation. The result isn't just a coming-of-age in Bohemia but a deeply affecting account marked by wry self-knowledge; clear-eyed, unsentimental, yet loving. 'We used to laugh at our small selves, saying that I was a bad girl trying to be good and that he was a good boy trying to be bad. Through the years these roles would reverse, then reverse again until we came to accept our dual natures. We contained opposing principles, light and dark.'

Passage after passage gleams with sharply nailed images: the 'slivers of ice wrapped in brown paper' given to Patti as a child by the horse-drawn iceman; the gothic 'oven crammed with discarded syringes, and the refrigerator over-run with mold' greeting her and Mapplethorpe in their first Brooklyn digs; the 'hair jigs, feathered lures and tiny lead weights' bought from a fishing tackle store and, along with lobster shells, used to make punk necklaces, since even without a dime to rub between them, they both knew how to fashion a striking look.

Patti Smith's memory bank is a cabinet of keepsakes, each object trapping a moment or a place. 'Some serve you, some are magical,' she says. A number appear in her photographs and in *Dream of Life*, the documentary made by Steven Sebring: a favourite childhood dress; the goatskin tambourine Mapplethorpe made for her twenty-first birthday. For Patti, no object is ever completely inanimate. When it was time for her mother to buy her a new toothbrush, little Patti, 'heartbroken', asked, 'But what do I do with the old one?' 'Throw it away,' came the reply. 'But I can't,' she said. 'It took such good care of my teeth.' 'You thought its feelings would be hurt?' I ask. 'Yes, exactly,' she laughs.

But she also remembers with uncanny exactness the words that passed between her and her soulmate. She tells me that this is because Mapplethorpe not only didn't read much, he didn't say much either. 'He was a listener, so when he did speak it seemed like a whole world of something . . . When he finished a piece of art he wasn't interested in any sort of spatial analysis or anything like that. It was just, "Is it good or is it not?" It seems simplistic but that's what it comes down to after all.' When he was drawing and it was going well, he would tell Patti he was 'holding hands with God'.

If Mapplethorpe's comment sounds a bit William Blake, it's no accident. These days Patti Smith is full of literature. Even the jaunty foot-tapper 'April Fool' on the new album is a nod to Gogol, whose comic genius arrived in the world on that day. Our talk does the rounds of her mentors and champions: William Burroughs, Allen Ginsberg (who gently hit on her until he discovered she was a girl), Bob Dylan as well as her long-time paragon, Arthur Rimbaud. But no one in the pantheon matters more to her than Blake. She has photographed his death mask and visited his grave.

The devotion to Blake began early when her mother gave the eight-year-old Patti a copy of *Songs of Innocence*. This was in rural south New Jersey, in a landscape of swamps and pig farms. Two generations back her paternal grandfather – 'small, bullish, Irish' – had run a steel mill in Pennsylvania while her mother's father played honky tonk piano. A year before his daughter was born in 1946, Patti's father had come back 'broken' from a brutal war in New Guinea, where he had contracted malaria. To put food on the table for their three children, he went on the production line at Honeywell while her mother worked as a hatcheck girl and waitress.

But like so many American families who had come down in the world, the Smiths made sure their children got the treasure of words along with what in *Just Kids* she calls 'the radiance of imagination'. *Silver Pennies*, an anthology of poems, became a precious possession. Its pages included poems by Yeats and his correspondent Vachel Lindsay, 'the Prairie Troubador', for whom poetry was nothing unless it could be sung. In her turn, Patti performed for her brother and sister, embroidering on stories she had read, for 'I was the little ghost haunting the library . . . I was the shepherd of my siblings,' she says, smiling her big-sister smile, 'taller, better read, their guardian . . . My mother and father were away working so I tended to my little sheep.'

Already she was won by the 'rough simplicity' of Lindsay and Blake, their amplification of the common voice. And there was something else about Blake she admired: the painting and drawing in which the words were set, the homespun determination to do everything from setting pen to paper to printing the result. 'I had a penchant myself for doing several things at once. I wanted to draw, write, speak.'

The sentinels of The Watchtower, the Jehovah's Witness teachers of her Bible school, did their best to knock the dreams out of her. Predictably, their austerity had the opposite effect. At 'twelve or thirteen . . . I fell in love with art as a calling' and made a 'conscious choice' to reject organised religion. Already she was possessed by the need to write 'not egotistically but as a kind of thank you . . . to put one more spine on the library shelf'. (No surprise, then, to learn she is not a Kindle reader.) In New York, making do on the pittance from a job in a bookstore – 'I was very resourceful; Robert was always worried about money' – she had moments of doubt about making it as a poet. Mapplethorpe, on the other hand, was certain of his artistic destiny; what he was uncertain about was his sexuality. The two parted. Patti went to Paris stalking the ghost of Rimbaud. When she saw Mapplethorpe again in New York, he was a walking ruin. They reunited after a fashion and moved into the Chelsea Hotel, which became for them, as it did for so many others, the seminary of possibilities. She kept running into people who believed and who helped: the actor-playwright Sam Shepard, Burroughs and Ginsberg, who embodied for her the poetry of direct address; verses from the gut. While she began her own reading in hospitable grunge-holes now canonised as the nurseries of punk – Max's Kansas City and CBGB's – she noticed audiences getting restless as the poets droned on. 'It was kind of boring.' She would not be boring.

She speaks of that moment in the mid-'70s as a vocational awakening. 'There was a movement, a direct line through rock 'n' roll in the '60s and '70s drawn by people who wanted to raise its level – Jim Morrison, Neil Young, Hendrix, Lennon, Grace Slick. They all had so much intelligence and they took what Bo Diddley had started and lifted it and lifted it . . . When I started singing I didn't do it to be a rock star but to keep that thread going. Hendrix and Morrison had died. Things were changing and shifting; I was worried the torch wouldn't pass, the light would dissipate. I know this sounds conceited, a bit lofty for a girl from south Jersey, but those people, what they did, was so important, it was the great American contribution. I wanted to be the kid with the finger in the dike holding things together until someone came along.'

'That someone was you,' I say, 'you and Springsteen.' 'Oh,' she says, 'Bruce was off doing his own thing. Look, we come from different parts of Jersey; he's from mid or north of the state, I'm from south rural Jersey – the starter homes and the pig farms.' When I ask her if she'd consciously fashioned the voice of *Horses* and *Easter* – the hooting and drawling and in-your-ear wailing – she laughs again and says, no, she didn't know any better. She sang nasally because 'I was a shallow breather' and it was just south Jersey banging through. 'They all thought I was a hick.'

But a hick who had taken Blake and Whitman and Yeats to head and heart. She credits her hookup with the pianist Richard Sohl for putting the whole Patti together, not least because, like her, he was not a rock 'n' roll snob or for that matter any kind of snob. Classically trained, he 'loved show tunes. He'd play Bo Diddley and he'd play Mendelssohn.' She too has always lived in a broad universe of music. 'I loved R'n'B.' 'I work to Glenn Gould in the morning and go to sleep listening to *Parsifal*. But I've listened to "Rolling in the Deep" a million times.'

She was herself rolling along. In 1980, she married Fred 'Sonic' Smith of MC5, took a more political turn and wrote with him 'People Have the Power'. Politics didn't come naturally to her, she says, but she had worked for Robert Kennedy's senatorial campaign. When he was assassinated, she withdrew from the political world and it took the more activist Fred to quicken those combative political instincts. 'In my usual way I consulted Blake and the Bible. "The meek shall inherit the earth." I certainly got that.' Becoming interested in St Francis and making an informal pilgrimage to Assisi, she thought it something of a miracle when a pope came along who adopted the name and, apparently, the social evangelism that went with it. 'They said there would never be a Jesuit pope nor a Franciscan one. Now they have both.'

Every so often the old fury of 'Radio Baghdad' comes back. She remembers with quiet contempt a virtual conspiracy of media silence when a protest rally against the Iraq War, 100,000

strong, received barely any coverage. Though she rejoiced at
the election of an African American to the White House, like
millions of others on the left she has not forgiven him for keeping
Guantánamo open and prosecuting the war in Afghanistan.
'To me he's just like a good Republican.' The 'celebrity-driven,
materialist' culture saddens her, especially when she sees 'three-
year-olds being comforted by cellphones and video games instead
of being told stories'. The ongoing destruction of the environment
fills her with yet more bleak sorrow. With a little sigh she returns
to Blake. 'More than ever as I get older I can feel what it takes to
be him − a casualty of the industrial revolution while he sits at
home hand-colouring prints of shepherds.'

But then, she says, resolutely, pushing back the gloom, 'I am
still a very optimistic person. I continue to do work with joy.'
The Beethoven strain comes through. The first opera she saw
was *Fidelio*, a work so perfectly fitted to her temperament that
she wanted to make a film of it. 'I know the opening shots. I am
Leonore/Fidelio, with waist-length hair. I pick up the scissors
and cut it.'

It takes a bit of getting used to, the gentle humanism and eager
child's delight in life that is as much a part of Patti Smith's make-
up as the visceral fury. But then anyone surviving the succession
of hammer blows that hit her with merciless brutality from the
late 1980s onwards was bound to come out the other side either
lost to the darkness or bathed in new light. Mapplethorpe was
just the beginning of a series of losses. In 1990, at the age of
thirty-seven, Richard Sohl, apparently in perfect health, died
suddenly from the failure of an undetected faulty valve in his
heart. In 1994, her husband Fred succumbed to a long illness,
leaving her a widow with two young children. Hardly had her
brother Todd offered to take care of her and the children when
he was killed by a stroke.

How much disaster can any one person take? Only the imperative of looking after Jackson and Jesse gave her the strength to

endure. But that was all she could do. Creatively she dived into a void. The Mapplethorpe memoir was still unwritten, but that too was an invitation to pain. 'Anything I tried took me back to the centre of grief.' But a little light leaked back, through the lens of a Land camera. It was an instantaneous, almost effortless art and it began with a photograph of a pair of Nureyev's old ballet shoes. The music of things and then of places began to tune up gently for her. But she was stuck in Motown with the kids – possibly the only grown-up in Detroit who hadn't learned to drive. She had never been rich. Now, in every way imaginable, she was in bad shape, needing to find some way to make a living. Enter an angel: Zimmerman. In 1995, Dylan was touring and he asked her along. Was she nervous? 'Oh, sure. I didn't know if the audience would welcome me back; whether they would even remember me.' They did both.

At sixty-seven, Patti Smith's purchase on life and art has never been more secure. Her voice has developed an astonishing range that can suit whatever poetic tone her words call for. A bluesy, rhythmic elegy for Amy Winehouse ('This is the Girl') is the kind of thing the lost soul herself would have loved singing. 'Nine', written for her pal Johnny Depp, has an air of Irish pipe drone in the music. The women of the '70s and '80s – Chrissie Hynde and Debbie Harry too – have taken better care of their voices than the men. Dylan is scarcely more than a performing adenoid; the range available to Tom Waits's razor-shredded larynx is getting down to the last rasp. But Patti Smith – who once wanted to be an opera singer – has developed the depth and subtlety of her voice, and when she needs to, it can summon a velvety vibrato. She can roam the vocal range when she speaks that poetry as well. 'On the edge of the world in the desert heat/One shining star, sweet, indiscreet', she sings in another elegy, for the actress Maria Schneider. It's not that she's gone soft. She was never that hard. Tough, fierce, strong, sexy and forceful, but not hard.

When she was a little girl in south Jersey, dreaming wordy

dreams and telling stories to her brother and sister, her mother would sing to them in a smokey voice the Doris Day ballad, 'Que Será, Será'. And that, notwithstanding all that's wrong with the world now, and all those dear ones she has seen come and go, seems still to be the way she grips the world. Whatever will be, will be.

LEONARD COHEN

Tea and . . . what? Toast? Sympathy? No, oranges. From the start
Leonard Cohen was out to surprise by cunning. No wonder, then,
that he had to struggle for attention in the golden age of scream-
ers. Janis's ecstatic rasp, Hendrix's maddened guitar, Lennon's
glottal roar, even Dylan's adenoidal faux-country all made sounds
through which their lyrical inventions had to fight for air, and if
not quite up to snuff, those words could hide behind the wall of
noise. But Cohen's minimalist drone was the drowsy couch on
which his poetry lay, fully exposed, with nowhere else to go.

In the '60s, his lyrics grabbed attention through teasingly incon-
gruous unions: 'Like a worm on a hook / Like a knight from some
old-fashioned book'. For all I know, Suzanne did feed Leonard tea
and oranges, but it was the coupling of the prosaic and the exotic
(oranges, as Cohen well knew, did indeed come originally 'all the
way from China'), the yoking together of serenity and sharpness,
that makes the line jump from the chant. Suzanne is, after all,
'half crazy', so when she 'takes you down to her place near the
river' it may not be entirely for a picnic. On the other hand, 'that's
why you want to be there'. Okay, then, peel me an orange.

More than many great singer-songwriters of his generation
(Dylan excepted), Cohen made no bones about reaching for the
heavy literary hitters for inspiration. Lorca gave him the spooky,
beautifully sinister 'Take This Waltz' – although Cohen's free
translation of the Spanish arguably makes a more unsettlingly
powerful poem than the original – 'a forest of dried pigeons'

(Lorca) becomes 'there's a tree where the doves go to die'
(Cohen); 'take this waltz with its closed mouth' (Lorca) turns to
'take this waltz with the clamp on its jaw' (Cohen).

When Cohen did invoke the canon it's usually with a shrewd
knowledge of how it's been used and abused through the generations. Henry Wadsworth Longfellow's 'Sail On, O Ship of State',
the anthem on which Cohen's 'Democracy' builds to the marching
beat of a snare drum, was written in 1850 as fears for the endurance of the Union were grave. After the civil war, the poem, set
to music for choral performance, accompanied routine displays
of patriotic chest-beating. But the tone of Cohen's 'Democracy'
could scarcely be less rah-rah; it's more a scalding spit in the eye.
'It's comin' . . . from the fires of the homeless, from the ashes of
the gay . . . From the homicidal bitchin'/That goes down in every
kitchen . . . From the wells of disappointment/Where women
kneel to pray.' Compared to the freakshow ferocity that dominates 'The Future', in which Cohen turns porno-totalitarian:
'Give me absolute control/Over ev'ry living soul'; 'Give me crack
and anal sex/Take the only tree that's left/And stuff it up the hole
in your culture'. Democracy is, if not exactly warm and cuddly, at
least a qualified redemption: 'I love the country but I can't stand
the scene'. The starchy Longfellow anthem gets made over, in the
election year of 1992, into a disabused song of possibility.

For a while, projecting his own bouts of depressive melancholy
on to the state of things, Cohen specialised in acid-burn nihilistic
jeremiads, demonic impersonations of the forces of darkness,
growled at the mic. The Book of Revelation took over from New
Testament sweetness, which came as a relief to those of us who
had had enough of his gentle Jesus, the kind that shows up at
music festivals in knee-hole jeans smilingly beatifically, ready for
dope and three days of love. Cohen's gospel people stalk through
contemporary streets and bedrooms, so the card dealer of 'The
Stranger Song' turns out to be: 'Just some Joseph looking for a
manger'. But every so often the more adamant Yahweh of the

Old Testament shows up, bringing the year's transgressions to a mighty reckoning. A cohen is, after all, a high priest.

As seriously as he took this persona of Satan deploring sin, it's the more inward meditations on his favourite subject – 'L. Cohen' (as he styles himself at the end of 'Famous Blue Raincoat') – that have always drawn from him the most intensely felt and precisely visualised writing, and have challenged his melodic composition to go beyond minimalist dirge to match the force of the poetry.

Cohen's subjects in this vein of mutilated romanticism were the usual post-Renaissance suspects: valedictions, loss and remorse, emotional cruelty (inflicted and received), the insep-arability of tenderness and pain. Sometimes images, often of wistfully recollected visions – 'Your hair on the pillow like a sleepy golden storm', in 'Hey, That's No Way to Say Goodbye' – are allowed to hang in the song for the sheer metaphorical hell of it. They work so seductively they disarm the carping lit-crit who might pause to wonder if storms, unlike the lover, can actually ever be 'sleepy'?

If there's just a touch too much of happy self-regard about some of those early ballads, from the mid-'70s on, the onset of years Cohen saw in his musical mirror encouraged him to use imagery as building blocks in beautifully constructed, authenti-cally poetic narratives. In the sad love triangle of 'Famous Blue Raincoat', Cohen transfers a garment he wore to fraying point to 'my brother, my killer', who had run off with his wife, and had given her just 'a flake of your life/And when she came back she was nobody's wife'. In the strongest songs of this period, Cohen makes sure to skid away from self-pity – 'Well, my friends are gone/And my hair is gray/I ache in the places where I used to play' – into something more akin to rueful gratitude: 'I'm just paying my rent every day/In the Tower of Song.'

So perhaps it's not surprising that 'Hallelujah', the song in which music making and love making wrestle with each other, is the one most covered by other singers, and without draining the power of the piece into empty rhapsody. But to get the heart-ache you want from Cohen – and you know you do – you need to hear the old(ish) baffled, battle-scarred Cohen himself sing 'The minor fall, the major lift', his voice falling for the forbidden Bathsheba bathing naked on the roof, where 'Her beauty and the moonlight overthrew you'. But nothing works out as planned. The overthrow happens as the music soars, the omnipotent sovereign-psalmist is bound and shorn, and it's from that moment, when the composing-lover is pierced to the quick, that music gets born. Hallelujah.

TOM WAITS

I'm getting on. No time for messing around with the likes of Prokofiev or Trollope any more. The artists I have most time for now are those who have pushed the boundaries most bravely and inventively; who have made their chosen genre into something unanticipated, and who have done it so completely that, in your delighted amazement, you just scratch your head and say: 'Well, yeah, sure', as if it had been the most natural thing in the world. So I like what Thomas Carlyle did to historical writing, what Jackson Pollock did to painting, what Wallace Stevens did to poetry. It's not absurd to put Tom Waits, America's most eloquent poet-songwriter, in that company. Enough of Dylan already. Not that there's anything wrong with Dylan, but he's provoked volumes of heavyweight analytical bloviation second only to Freud, whereas people on both sides of the Atlantic have barely begun to give the singular Tom Waits his proper due.

Why should they? Because he has turned American music into the speech-song of ordinary men and women caught in that murky bad-smelling alleyway between the juvenile rhetoric of the 'American dream' and the unforgiving adult reality of contemporary life. You want the most heartbreakingly truthful, poignantly dismaying utterance on the predicament of the regular American Joe, caught in a war he can't fathom, but from which he can't honourably escape? Try Waits's 'The Day After Tomorrow' from *Real Gone*, where he drawls and growls his way through the unbearable lyrics with the raspy ruins of a

voice that is itself like a building shattered by shellfire and coated
with befouled sand. That voice, the organ of a much bigger man
than the slight, gaunt, delicately clownish figure (one of his
CDs features him in pierrot-face – this is someone who knows
exactly what he's doing), is one of the great sound instruments of
American art. Other very clever songwriters – Dylan, Leonard
Cohen – have also dramatised their laryngial damage in keeping
with the sharpness of their lyrics. In the opposite direction, Neil
Young's falsetto wail has become more painful as he has got more
desperately urgent. But none of them has, over the years, thought
about how they can make their voice into a sound portrait of a
country as intelligently as Waits – and then gone and done it. He
is imperial America's Kurt Weill (and, for a while, he studied
Weill a bit too strenuously), imitating the jangly percussive fury
of Weill's most abrasive songs.

But the comparison undersells Waits's originality, for there's
something almost Shakespearean about the breadth of Tom
Waits's take on modern American life, his astounding capacity
to get into the heads and lungs of, inter alia: barflies, hookers,
junkies, fairground barkers and burlesque crooners; veteran
soldiers with shrapnel-freckled limbs, reduced to selling their
tin stars on the sidewalk; Pentecostal thunderers roaring doom;
washed-up baseball stars wasted by booze; psychos on a short
fuse; woeful optimists losing it in the marinade of their martinis;
and, in one improbable case, a dead man singing sweetly from 6
feet under, asking his lover to come sit on his grassy grave. Only
Tom Waits could make an entire song out of a running string of
infomercials ('Step Right Up') and somehow turn the list into an
exhaustive, funny documentary on American credulousness and
American cunning: 'The large print giveth/And the small print
taketh away'.

And this is just a short list of his many incarnations. When
you dive into Waits's world, you're not, it's true, taking off for
la-la lullaby land; you're landed in a greasy-spoon diner as the

ashy dawn comes up over the trash-strewn car lot. In an intro to 'Eggs and Sausage' in a live performance in 1975, he warns of veal cutlets so 'dangerous they leave the counter to beat the shit out of the coffee that's too weak to defend itself'.

But though he's vinegar in the wounds of American pie-in-the-sky sentimentality, there's also plenty of tender passion bowling through the songs. 'Ol' 55', one of his earliest songs from his debut 1973 album *Closing Time*, is an ode to joy from emerging at 6 a.m. from a night of love ('My time went so quickly/I went lickety-splitly out to my ol' 55/and I pulled away slowly, feeling so holy/God knows I was feeling alive'). It is the single most beautiful love song since Gershwin and Cole Porter shut their piano lids.

Usually, though, Waits's love lyrics sting with salty disenchantment, and are all the more touching for it. 'Never Talk to Strangers' is a barstool duet with Bette Midler where the sad-sack's predictable routine ('I'm not a bad guy when you get to know me') gets pre-empted by her wise-ass knowledge of all his lines, even as they both fall for them all over again.

I came late to the troubadour of strip-mall ruin. A BBC director, adapting my book *Landscape and Memory* for television, set Waits's performance of Phil Phillips's 'Sea of Love' over archive images of floods in Venice. In place of the honey-drip croon was a feral roar turning the tone of the song inside out. (He does an even more astounding makeover on 'Somewhere' from *West Side Story*, so that you feel the utter hopelessness of adolescent grief in your bones.) I'd never heard anything like it. Who the hell was that, I asked the director. I've been hooked on Waits ever since. How could you not be hooked on a writer who comes up with a line like 'her hair spilled like root beer' and have you know just what he means?

Waitsomania is not a comfy addiction. His journey from the 1970s, when he was just another guitar-picking songwriter from the Midwest marrying up country and blues to his cornhusk voice, has seen him travel to ever deeper and darker places in the American psyche. While Dylan was lay lady laying, Waits was trying on tawdry, as he sang, ever so politely, 'I'm Your Late Night Evening Prostitute'. From there he descended all too predictably into the usual sump of booze and dope, eventually climbing out of it with the help of his partner-writer and co-producer Kathleen Brennan, who has been responsible for some of Waits's more brilliantly raw productions.

No one can touch him for evoking every kind of music, from carousel pump organ to lounge saxophone to Berlin cabaret, Italian Bel Canto, and lately African and Latin sounds. Sometimes he can push his furious refusal of songster-ingratiation to the edge of self-parody, so that the primal screams, grunts, howls backed by lid clanging and stock-banging percussion just collapse into a deep ditch of vocal rage. Listening to them is like chewing on barbed wire. And yet somewhere, in the middle of all the vocal carnage, is the heavily soiled innocence of someone who still reckons the good life can, after all, be just around the corner. The kid soldier, writing home to Illinois, weary with precocious, bloodily earned knowledge, sings:

> *I'm not fighting*
> *For freedom*
> *I'm fighting for my life*
> *And another day*
> *In the world here*
> *I just do what I'm told*
> *You're just the gravel on the road*
> *And the ones that are lucky*
> *Come home*
> *On the day after tomorrow . . .*

DEBBIE HARRY

'So did you perform at high school?' I asked the rock star.

'God, no,' she says, 'painfully shy.'

'That's hard to believe,' I say, thinking of the feline claws and purrs with which she launched Blondie, remembering the little rasp in the voice of the stalker: 'One way or another, I'm gonna getcha getcha getcha.' We took a look at her lines, sharp and curvy at the same time, and let the voice fall on us like a gladiator's net.

'Oh, yeah,' she comes back, 'sometimes I still get the shys.'

But not in live performance, not in Australia and New Zealand where Blondie – Debbie, plus two of the original band, Chris Stein and the great drummer Clem Burke – recently co-headlined with the Pretenders, the dream tour for anyone who likes their women rock singers fierce and full-throated, loaded with carnal knowledge. Chrissie Hynde one minute, Debbie Harry the next; it doesn't bear thinking about, does it?

But here's the dirty little secret about our favourite hard blonde: she is, in fact, a bit of a softie; easy-going, open, very smart, and no sweat to talk to. Debbie Harry is doing this interview in anticipation of the release of a brand new album, *Panic of Girls*. Sample some of the tracks from the web, especially 'What I Heard', and you know right away she and Chris Stein are back in brilliant form: edgy but full-on pop musicality. But she's also doing it because she has no problem talking about Blondie now and then. So she looks you straight in the eye; smiles, laughs that lightly smoked laugh; and gives off enough human warmth to light up a raw Manhattan morning when the fall has got its talons into the dying year.

We are sitting in the restaurant of a Midtown hotel. Around the corner are suits chowing down on their breakfast eggs. Amid this dull brassiness, Debbie Harry's genuine good nature burns bright. The cat-eyes still shine; the mouth that snarled 'Rip Her to Shreds', crooned 'Denis . . . un grand baiser d'éternité' and moaned 'Picture This' still does its lip magic. She's wearing a fine-spun loose thread white cotton sweater thrown over a dark T-shirt with just the carelessness that permanently beautiful women can effortlessly pull off.

Revisiting her classics, above all *Parallel Lines*, I'm struck by the range of her voice. So much has been noted and written about the Blondie-effect – its urban hipness; the sharp threads; the metallic sleekness of the sound – that you forget what an amazing voice it is that could open 'Heart of Glass' at the top of the register and dive into downtown chanteuse in 'Rip Her to Shreds'. 'I always approached singing as an actor,' she says, and while the persona she acted was all of a piece, she could make it sound brittle, volup-tuous and almost everything in between. Which is maybe why she occasionally flirts torchily with old-time standards. A version she did with Iggy Pop of Cole Porter's 'Well, Did You Evah!', written for Crosby and Sinatra, is – especially on video – an amazing per-formance. And I like a version of 'Stormy Weather', even though Debbie herself doesn't rate it.

'Funny,' she says, 'I was singing that song, driving in from New Jersey this morning.' I tell her it's what the business programme on National Public Radio plays when the market goes south. She laughs, because whatever storms there were – and there have been plenty – seem distant. She was an adopted child and I ask her whether she was in contact with her birth mother. 'Oh, I hired a private detective . . . but . . .' No dice. 'Did it bother you?' I ask, idiotically. 'Of course it bothered me,' she flares, 'but I didn't need a mother. I had a mother. One is enough.'

After the inevitable arts degree, and not yet bleached, she famously did a stint as a *Playboy* Bunny. 'Fun and horror . . . like most things.' Mistreatment? I ask, fishing. Only by women dates, she says; when they thought their men were hitting on the rabbits. She sang as a back-up in a folk band called Wind in the Willows, but she'd listened to rocking blues coming out of the radio in Newark: the Catman Hour and the great Cousin Brucie. Downtown beckoned in the early '70s; Velvet Underground and waiting tables at Max's Kansas City; the pre-CBGB cradle of punk. New York Dolls were primping and singing; a big Attitude Change was tuning up. One night, a friend asked her to front a band calling itself – what else? – Pure Garbage. 'Gee, that sounds good,' she said, 'better than Plain Garbage.' But by the time she showed up for the gig, the band had already broken up. It was when she hooked up, personally and musically, with Chris Stein that Blondie came to be born and triumphed. Though it's obvious they worked together, Harry always gives Stein the lion's share of credit for the lyrics of their strongest hits. But the perfect fit between how Harry looked, her body language, the attack voice dressed up in raw silk or brushed velvet, the super-smart – all that was, indivisibly, the work of a true partnership.

There was a third in the mix to make *Parallel Lines* the commercial as well as critical knockout it was: Mike Chapman, the Australian-born producer who, she says, had the pop-aesthetic they needed to go from downtown New Wavers into the mainstream. Plenty of DJs had checked out what Blondie had to offer and didn't like it. Chapman changed all that and, for a decent run, they never looked back. The genius designer Stephen Sprouse dressed her counter-intuitively; the more boyish she got with pencil lines, little suits and ties, scan-lines from a television printed on the fabric, the higher the sex-voltage.

This reinvention of the Blonde was waiting to happen. 'It was already in people's heads,' she says, from the movies: cocktail sipping, hard-talking, spirited give-no-quarter blondes in fitted pencil skits like Eva Marie Saint 'luring men to their doom', as an excited Cary Grant put it in *North by Northwest*. Warhol's Factory was stocked with bleach jobs but Nico sounds fey next to Blondie. 'I felt women in the '70s always sung songs about being victims.' Even the ones with the piled-up hair like Dusty Springfield, or the teary version of Marianna Faithfull. 'They just stood there.' Not Blondie. She made the moves. 'When you met me in the res-taurant/You knew I was no debutante.' The sappy pop opening line was the fake smoochy come-on, before the flick of the scarlet fingernail dug just where it counted. 'I will give you my finest hour/The one I spent watching you shower.'

It wasn't much of a stretch to wire up all kinds of pop currents to downtown punk and New Wave. Stein had been to London and come back full of reggae – cue 'The Tide Is High'. 'Heart of Glass' and 'Picture This' could not have been poppier. But then, a lot of what her friends the Ramones did might have come straight from the Beach Boys – 'Rock 'n' Roll Radio' or 'Rockaway Beach' – only much, much louder and much, much faster. All the same, Blondie's accessibility provoked inevitable accusations of selling out from old comrades of the CBGB era – Johnny Ramone ('always frowning') and Joan Jett ('one of the most vehement'). Harry bears no ill-will about this. 'She [Joan] was true to her colour . . . everybody was afraid of disco taking over.'

It was only four years from the release of *Parallel Lines* to the break-up of Blondie in 1982. Maybe they were running out of cre-ative steam; there were the usual management feuds, but it was a frightening, rare and initially undiagnosed auto-immune disease attacking Chris Stein's skin and eating into the rest of his body that ultimately made it impossible to go on. In their last concerts, she says, looking down, suddenly shadowed by the memory, 'he was 120lb' (less than 9 stone). Harry devoted a lot of her time to seeing him through a terrifying ordeal, which, though labelled pemphigus, still seems to defy most clinical analysis.

So it's good to report a happy ending. After recording some solo albums ('not spectacular' she insists, rebuffing a compliment), Blondie reformed with four originals including Stein, and Harry is unapologetically proud of the rarity of a band staying close, enduring through nearly four decades, and powering up their distinctive music again. Ultimately, this jubilant survival seems more important to her than any monster fame, the kind in which everything gets sunk into Brand. She knows well enough how a whole line of tough-cookie out-there rock chicks – Madonna, Lady Gaga – were all too Blondie-ishness where Debbie Harry wouldn't or couldn't go. She concedes this without any wistfulness or envy. 'I admire the completeness of their decision. It becomes a force, and we are all entertained by it. Even if we degrade it by gossip, we're still in awe of it.'

But if 'it' isn't for Blondie, what is, after all this time? If you weren't at the Isle of Wight Festival or Sydney last year, just check out YouTube and you'll see a fine, precious thing: a hard-driving band (Stein now silvery-haired but with all his rocking engine intact); and Debbie herself, prowling the stage, tough and tunicked-up, heavy metal (and sometimes a dagger) at her belt; gorgeously dangerous, but actually when she sings 'I'm not frightened by love' doing nothing more than celebrating, artfully, what men and women can get up to. If they damned well try, anyway.

HELEN MIRREN: *THE TEMPEST*

There's a moment in Julie Taymor's gender-bent film of *The Tempest* when Helen Mirren seems to come down hard on 'actors'. Briskly dismissing the masque summoned for the entertainment of the betrothed Ferdinand and her virginal daughter Miranda, 'Prospera', the enchantress, gently but firmly disenchants. 'Our revels now are ended. These our actors,/As I foretold you, were all spirits and/Are melted into air, into thin air . . .' It's a famous speech, often read as a valediction in Shakespeare's last play; the Bard, as it were, flicking the house lights on and off to boot out the late-night groundlings.

Mirren delivers the lines in a tone of benevolent clarity, as if breaking it to her innocent daughter that Santa isn't actually up there with the elves. In the London hotel drawing room where we're talking, her mother's mink collar wound round her neck, a slash of scarlet lipstick on her mouth, Mirren is warming up the bone-slicing cold with the sparks of her merry, articulate intelligence. I tell her, in case she hadn't done it consciously, that she lingeringly enunciates 'actors' with a curl of the lip. She breaks into one of her salty, estuary-girl laughs and says, 'Oh, really? I didn't mean to insult actors. I love actors and the whole process of acting.'

You believe her because she's a performer who reflects nonstop about what she's doing, on stage, film or television, yet without ever burdening her delivery with over-considered attitude. When I saw Gielgud do Prospero at the Old Vic in the 1970s, the

great man wandered about the stage in a state of vague irritabil-
ity, vocalising the 'cloud-capp'd towers, the gorgeous palaces'
as an inward, sombre meditation on the illusion-chamber of
the theatre itself. But Mirren's delivery is blade-sharp steel to
Gielgud's tarnished silver. The she-wizard is undeluded about her
conjuring because in the last resort she knows it is all nonsense,
even though, as Mirren concedes, 'nonsense is seductive'. The
nonsense-masters she had in mind, she says, are the wizards of
Wall Street and their like who kid themselves that they can make
castles in the air. 'The solemn temples,' she says, are 'Goldman
Sachs; the City . . . They seem so solid, don't they?' But, in fact,
they're just an 'insubstantial pageant' that can be 'melted into
air, into thin air'.

In the gender flip (which works so perfectly you don't give it
a moment's thought after Mirren's first appearance mantled in
raven-dark scales and plumes) this resolutely unbewitched tone
seems right for a motherly admonition to her dewy-eyed teenage
daughter. It's all very nice, the airy-fairy stuff, Prospera seems to
be saying, but look, kid, we'll be out of here before you know it
and if you know what's good for you you'll wise up in short order.
So when Miranda, confronted with a throng of tights and capes,
gasps 'O brave new world, / That has such people in't!' Prospera's
sidelong comment – ''Tis new to thee' – has the force of a different knowledge: the worldly kind.

Which isn't to say this is a prosaic film version of *The Tempest*,
and that Mirren's version of the spell-conjurer is flatly matter-
of-fact; womanly practicality, rather than magic monomania. It's
just that she inhabits a mindset in keeping with Jacobean culture,
finely balanced between visionary apparition and clear-eyed
pragmatism. It's easy, amid the spells and spirits, to forget that
this is a drama about power of various kinds – the kind of power
that needs the play of illusion as well as the impact of blunt force
to make itself felt. Mirren does both, but her blonde witch of
revenge certainly relishes the 'rough magic'.

I ask her, since she is seriously well-read, whether she was thinking of Renaissance women who gave no quarter – such as Catherine de' Medici? 'No, Simon,' she says, smiling, 'you would be thinking of that. I just thought of the human situation – who had betrayed you, had tried to murder you? Of someone who had lived with bitterness and anger and a desire for revenge.' She mentions as an inspiration Euripides' Medea, consumed with murderous rage channelled into bloody havoc. But her motherly Prospera is a mix of tough and tender, pretty much like the actress. 'Now [the end of the play with the plotters caught in the island trap], when you could exact the most horrible revenge . . .', she says, letting the sentence run out thoughtfully. It's not just the fact of the torturing cramps and stings the sorcerer visits on the captive Caliban, she says, it's the enjoyment of listing them – 'side-stitches that shall pen thy breath up' – that's so fierce.

It's this taste for physical and mental cruelty that the actress who played the Duchess of Malfi and guns down bad guys in Red recognises as an authentic side of the Bard as much as his complicated interior ruminations: 'Shakespeare opens fissures you don't want to look into.' Some of those openings, she says, are frankly sexual. Prospera inflicts torments on Caliban because of his attempt to rape the child/girl Miranda. 'All he wants to do is f*** her, really f*** her.' The mother pays him back the way a threatened mother would.

Prospera was Mirren's idea. Watching Derek Jacobi's Prospero in 2002, it struck her that 'a woman could do this and it wouldn't change a word' of meaning. She then went home and read through the text to make sure it wouldn't just be some sort of reflex feminist gesture. And she saw what might be gained: a different kind of protectiveness bestowed by a mother on her daughter; a different reason to make Ferdinand's road to nuptial bliss a thorny trial. 'She knows what sixteen-year-old girls are like, swoony and dreamy, because she's been one. She needs to make sure Miranda isn't cheaply won.' 'All thy vexations/Were but my trials of thy love', indeed.

Then there is the male terror, in the late Renaissance, of the book-learned woman; always close in contemporary minds (not least in that of King James himself) to the sorceress; privy to dark learning locked inside a hungry mind and a potent body. And there, too, is the unconscious ruthlessness with which the dethroned Duchess of Milan obsessively imprints on her adolescent child the sinister story of her displacement. 'Dost thou hear?' 'Oh, alright, Mum' – a daughterly eye-roll – 'go on, tell me again . . .' Mirren, who is happily childless, chuckles.

Meeting Taymor at a party, Mirren tried her idea out on her. 'I want to do Shakespeare and there aren't many parts. I'm not interested in Volumnia or Gertrude.' (Pity, since she would be a spellbinding Gertrude, trapped by erotic bonds to the murdering usurper.) Gert is a bit of a victim and Mirren doesn't really do victims. She does Lady Macbeth; the turn-on of blood. Taymor, who had already produced *The Tempest* twice, loved the idea but it took a year before there was the phone call telling Mirren it was going to happen. She assumed that the excited Taymor was talking about a staging, and the exhilaration of discovering it was going to be a film was tempered by a realisation of what she would now be taking on; a text of fiendish complexity and eccentric word order, even by the standards of very late Shakespeare. 'He's just riffing,' she says, of the whole coils of serpentine lines eating themselves: 'It's like late Miles Davis.'

Even though the chopped-up nature of filming didn't require it, Mirren decided to commit the whole play to heart before going near the shoot (on the lava-encrusted Hawaiian island of Lana'i). 'There was no way I could play the part and risk reaching for the lines.' Even then, she was worried enough about memorisation that she considered using an autocue. She didn't in the end but, she insists, 'I'm always terrified of forgetting lines.' Has she ever dried? 'Only once. In a modern play. David Hare's *Teeth 'n' Smiles*.'

It was Dave King, 'the classic washed-up, f*****-up comedian', playing the rock 'n' roll band's road manager, 'who saved my arse that night, so unlike the sweating panicky actor.'

But there is another kind of internalising that Mirren goes through, whatever role she plays. In this case she knew that Prospero's complicated relationship to Ariel and Caliban lies at the heart of the play, and Mirren's scenes with them (especially perhaps Ben Whishaw's nude teenage sprite) are poetically intense; charged with subtle erotic voltage. The two island creatures are, she says, the poles of human character: Ariel the embodiment of creativity, soul, spirit, imagination, 'things that take flight'. Caliban's world is sex and violence – 'equally part of our valid human experience'. But what Mirren needed to get the role right was 'a sense of what the other characters mean to you personally . . . what Ariel is to me, Helen, or what Caliban means to me, Helen. What the audience thinks, what Shakespeare thinks, doesn't really matter.'

In case we hadn't noticed: Helen Mirren is a robustly thinking actress, who, whether Queen Elizabeth II or Sofia, Countess Tolstoy (in the wonderful *The Last Station*), translates that care of thought into finely calibrated expression of voice and body language. So much steaming drool has been written about her undeniably permanent gorgeousness; the wide Russian eyes, the sonata of curves, the come-and-try-your-luck-sunshine Essex voice, honey on coal-tar, the voice I know from growing up almost down the road from her in Westcliff and Leigh-on-Sea (how the hell did I manage to miss her on the Southend mud or at the back of the Leigh cockle sheds?), that Mirren's exacting thoughtfulness gets short-changed.

She is, in the most unpretentious sense, creative. Very occasionally, she gets a script that 'reads like literature'. One of them was Barrie Keeffe's script for *The Long Good Friday*, a classical Greek drama of bloody disintegration set in late 1970s London gangsterland. Mirren was cast as Bob Hoskins' girl, and played it hard and tight, like a cosh wrapped in satin, until the inexorably baffling terror gets to her too. Mirren loved the script but saw 'there was one huge hole' – her own part, two-dimensional gangster's moll. When the revised version came back it was 'exactly the same'. So 'I became a real pain. I'd rewrite the scenes', turning the woman, crucially, into an upper-middle-class manager, the svelte polisher of Hoskins' rough diamond; in it for the arousing buzz of bad money and a real love of her pet thug. How did the rest of the crew feel about the rewrites? Oh, she says, Bob Hoskins is 'a great guy, supportive – other actors would have taken offence. Poor John [Mackenzie, the director]. I did feel sorry for him. But only I could do it.'

She comes by the tough-tender thing honestly. Her father, Vasily-turned-Basil, the son of a Russian army officer ('we had the Tsar and Tsarina on the wall in a wooden frame'), was, she says, like Tolstoy: 'thoughtful and gentle, a humanist'; while her mother, West Ham, butcher's daughter, was 'noisy and passionate'. You can feel that Essex home of the Mirinoffs: happy uproar and pensive wistfulness for the loss of homeland culture; carriers of old philosophy having to drive cabs for a living; mastering an unfamiliar kind of Knowledge. The distance from buttoned-up Englishness takes the form in Mirren of an expansive generosity about the human comedy, the observant openness to all sorts that gives her an unparalleled range. She argued with her father over his conviction that 'all cultures and races should become one'. 'Not a bad idea,' I say. 'No, not bad, but if all skins are the same colour it just becomes so much human porridge. Cultural difference is what's wonderful.'

Which makes her think again, of the episode in her acting life that bit very deep: the year with Peter Brook. She'd been clocked as a phenomenon early, lifted straight out of the National Youth Theatre to the RSC. I'd seen her sinuous Cressida; the only version of the part that made entirely credible her betrayal of moaning Troilus to the hard man Diomed. As an understudy she watched in spellbound amazement what Brook famously did with *A Midsummer Night's Dream*: sweeping the stage of all the distracting impedimenta – pasteboard glades and tussocks – liberating the bounding physicality of the action; letting the roaring poetry have its head in a wide open chamber of space and sound.

Mirren would later write a letter about the clutter of over-designed staging getting in the way of the drama that was very Brookian. In 1972, wanting a way to 'learn', to do something braver and broader than 'conveyor-belt kultcha', she went to Paris to join Brook's experimental group, which was already in the throes of his exacting improvisation routines that were meant to culminate in a dramatisation of the Persian garland of poems: *The Conference of the Birds*. The experience did not get off to a good start. 'I was a latecomer there. In my naiveté I thought, right, let's have a party, get drunk, do what we do in the pub, moan, gossip, complain. But the actors just stood around; no one spoke to anyone! It was a nightmare. Put me off giving parties forever!'

Chastened but inspired, Mirren went to north and west Africa with the Brook company, throwing down a carpet and improvising to unpredictable audiences. On one occasion, '2,000 Tuareg on camels showed up. We'd heard there was a festival. "Oh, let's all go and perform," we said! And there they were on their camels.' 'How did they react?' I asked. 'Oh, with gracious bemusement . . . Once in a blue moon we hit on a moment that did make for the common humanity Brook was after.' A Malian actor, Malik Bagayogo, had the inspired idea of taking off a shoe; stringing a line of shoes behind him and then we all just responded to that. The shoe show made a connection.' But it was hard. Unlike a script, 'there was nothing to hold on to except yourself and I didn't have that to hold on to either as Brook was constantly undermining, criticising . . . well, no' – she corrects – 'challenging'.

'I failed as an esoteric actress. I wasn't of that ilk; ultimately I'm not part of any group, not the Stanislavski group, the Grotowski group, the Brook group. I couldn't do the self-effacement. Brook thought stardom was wicked, self-deluding and tasteless. "Oh, f*** it," I said, "I want my name up there."' Shakespeare the actor doubtless felt the same way, I say. 'Yes, but, you know, I still do believe Brook is the great genius of the theatre of our time, so far ahead of everyone; doing what was unthinkable . . . He truly believes in common humanity.'

She pauses for a second, then adds, 'I believe in common humanity too: it's sex, violence and money.' Then, hastening to explain that by the 'money' bit she just means our material cares and pleasures, she gives up on the qualification, throws up her hands, and lets the Essex chuckle roll round the panelled room. 'Have another cup of tea,' she says. 'Have a bickie.' I do.

FALSTAFF

Of all Shakespeare's plays, *Macbeth* is the one whose performance history is notoriously strewn with disasters. But, as Dominic Dromgoole, whose new production of *Henry IV*, Parts I and II, has just come to the Globe, may have discovered, the Scottish Play is a cakewalk compared with the Henrys.

Unlike the other much-performed histories, they don't have one big theme and one big royal hero or villain to hold them together. But there is, of course, an outsize figure in the Henrys. Sir John Falstaff, the fat knight and leader-astray of the Prince of Wales, is the most immense of all Shakespeare's creations, his girth matched by his wit, his appetite by his cleverness. And there is a big theme, too: the journey of Prince Hal, from dissipated layabout to upright royal pragmatist.

Nothing in the Henrys is simple, though. We see Falstaff lie, rob, cheat, celebrate drunkenness, exploit pitiful soldiers, fleece an honest widow and, in his dotage, grope a whore. And yet we give him our heart. We see Hal throw off a life of idle lout-ishness and accept the mantle of sovereignty, and he turns our blood cold. The end of Part II, in which Hal becomes Henry V and repudiates his old companion in crime, is more shattering than any denouement of Shakespeare's tragedies. At the end of *Hamlet*, *King Lear* or *Antony and Cleopatra* the stage is littered with bodies. At the end of *Henry IV*, Part II, all we have is the broken heart of the fat old knight, and it is much worse. On coronation day, he gets his crushing put-down. 'I know thee not, old man,' lies the new king, and Falstaff, before our eyes, begins to deflate and die.

The Henrys are full of these sudden mood swerves between comic riot, bloody mayhem and unexpected falls into deep tenderness. They are also packed with some of Shakespeare's most pyrotechnically spectacular writing. The exchange of abuse between Falstaff and Hal, the sheer euphoria of slapdown insults, is alone worth the price of admission. But more minor characters all get startlingly powerful, funny and meaning-packed speeches, each in their own idiom.

The testosterone-driven young warrior rebel, Hotspur, brandishes hyperbole like a broadsword. The increasingly ill, guilt-racked Henry IV has the voice of desperate solitude: 'Uneasy lies the head that wears the crown.' Falstaff's sorely tried hostess at the Boar's Head tavern, Mistress Quickly, is given the 'so she said', 'so I said' broken diction of the gossip; Justice Shallow, who embarrasses Falstaff with memories of their scapegrace days as law students, has the wheezy cadences of ancient memory.

Shakespeare gives us his England in its completeness: the Eastcheap tavern world of Falstaff and his gang; the Gloucestershire village where he goes to press pathetic recruits; the lonely court of the insomniac King Henry IV; the feuding coteries of nobles who put him on the throne but now conspire against him.

So, much credit to Dromgoole for taking a crack at the cliff-face challenge that are the Henrys and to Roger Allam for taking a deep breath before padding his costume with Falstaff's mighty circumference. It's not a perfect production by any means, but, despite its flaws, it has – courtesy of Allam's fine, subtle Falstaff – the breath of life in it, hot and boozy and by turns exhilarating and devastating.

There's a special fitness about seeing the Henrys in the intimacy of the Globe, for the plays make shameless appeals to the audience's sympathy. Shakespeare always sets off the posturing of the nobles against the revelling of the simple and the earthy in the Boar's Head. The toffs think they are immortal. The boozers know they are mortal. Echoes resonate. The king hates the night. Falstaff and his company hate 'the sweetest morsel of the night' being stolen from them by a summons to arms.

Dromgoole's hardworking company do their utmost to get across this contrast between high emptiness and simple humanity. But the success or failure of any production of the two parts of Henry IV must turn unavoidably on the performance of Falstaff, the 'most completely good man in all of drama', as Orson Welles said of him.

Welles not so much acted as became Falstaff (as well as directing himself in the role) in *Chimes at Midnight* (1965). Falstaff has to be a magical compound of sweetness and cynicism, animal appetite and sharp-witted philosophy, appalling self-deception and fearless truth-telling. Anthony Quayle did it brilliantly, with ruthlessness and rapine uppermost, in various versions beginning in 1951 and continuing over two decades. Hugh Griffith turned in a roaring performance for Peter Hall and John Barton's Royal Shakespeare Company production in 1964, and Joss Ackland came close to definitive in ripe life-force eloquence in 1982.

So it is heartening to report that Allam's version stands comparison with the great Falstaffs, even the frighteningly titanic Welles. Allam's is a younger Jack, not so very plump, and grey-rather than white-haired; a Falstaff who could actually be the fifty-going-on-three-score he claims to be. This Falstaff is nimble-witted, graceful even, in the self-admiration of his cleverness, the voice rising and falling in collusion with the audience. The rumbustiousness is there but Allam soft-pedals the streak of real cruelty with which Shakespeare complicates Falstaff's make-up. On the other hand, his kinder, cuddlier Falstaff is fully convincing in the generosity of his love, not just for the likes of Doll Tearsheet (a scene played with exactly the right touch of mortal pathos) but, most fatally, for the prince. And no one, but no one, is ever going to do a better 'sherris-sack' monologue than Allam.

But at times Allam seems to be off by himself, acting in an altogether different company from a cast that all too often doesn't take the measure of Shakespeare's richly subtle text. Are there any other plays that depend so critically on getting ostensibly small roles right – the robotically cold-blooded John of Lancaster, for instance? Some of the cast, doubling up, do rise to the challenge. William Gaunt makes the Earl of Worcester, who has one crucial strategic moment in the events leading to the battle of Shrewsbury, plausible in his weary mistrust of the king; and then delivers a lovely uncaricatured version of Justice Shallow in Part II. Amazingly, Paul Rider is both a fabulously grunty Bardolph and a sinister Archbishop of York, and Barbara Marten in the perilous role of Mistress Quickly is pitch-perfect, in gossip and bony righteousness.

But there are some casting clunkers that turn the play's high poetry into pedestrian prose. Poins, Hal's laddish sidekick, the butt of the Prince's social hypocrisy and a creepy accomplice in his own repeated humiliations, can't possibly be played as Danny Lee Wynter does here, as an inane fop. You don't have to have a young Sean Connery to play Hotspur (as he did in the BBC's 1960 *An Age of Kings*), but, since the part is all about macho strut, you don't want to turn the character, as Sam Crane does, into a screechily petulant undergraduate.

The tonal music of the two parts could not be more different. Part I is all physical uproar and adrenaline rush. The deeper, more unsparingly anxious and painfully beautiful Part II is the mordant payback: pox, gout and an autumnal infirmity in which love struggles to resist being snuffed out by power. Written in 1596–97 after the death of Shakespeare's eleven-year-old son Hamnet, the two different plays are hinged together by the tortured dramas of paternity that will culminate a few years later in the ultimate father-son vindication ordeal: Hamlet.

The theme obsesses the playwright. Through the course of the Henrys, one father, the king, wishes out loud that there had been a changeling error that would allow him to claim Hotspur as his son rather than his own delinquent Hal. Hotspur's father Northumberland effectively condemns his own warrior boy to death by staging a no-show at the battle of Shrewsbury. Falstaff and Hal play at Dad–Bad Boy exchanges, Falstaff the deuterodad gushing the affection that will set him up for a lethal impaling by his 'sweet boy'.

The two parts of Henry IV are but half a masterpiece, however, unless we get a great Hal alongside a great Falstaff. At the Globe, Jamie Parker as Prince Hal gives decent merriment in the tavern scenes but never really rises above handsome affability into the realm of verbal violence and calculation with which Shakespeare has invested him.

The sudden sickening turn, during the play-acting scene in which Falstaff plays Hal and Hal the king, when the volley of invective loaded on to Falstaff is so violent that the laughs freeze mirthlessly, is performed at the Globe as just another round of chuckledom. Worst of all, the repudiation scene is flatly businesslike, as if the new king now had a Plantagenet PR adviser at his side telling him he has better things to think about than one surplus-to-requirement fat man. This is to cheat the audience of the tragedy of the moment, rather as if someone were to pop up with an umbrella for Lear on the blasted heath.

But what the production lacks in attentiveness to the text it makes up for in genuine ensemble fellowship, of the kind Shakespeare undoubtedly wanted for the Boar's Head scenes. You feel the warmth in the Globe production: there are precious moments when the hearty savour of Shakespeare's world takes possession of ours and bad, sad wisdoms of family, power, sex, larceny, drink and slaughter, country tables and urban pisspots, all become mysteriously real amid the heady delirium of words Shakespeare unleashes on us. And there in the middle is a truly great Falstaff: a performance of flesh and thought, inhabited equally by the ghosts of eros and thanatos. Now why in the world would anyone want to miss that?

SHAKESPEARE AND HISTORY

It may have been a frosty winter's Sunday but, on the RSC stage, thirteen-year-old Jack Gouldbourne was warming things up. 'O for a muse of fire,' he gamely chirped, 'that would ascend the brightest heaven of invention!' Jack was one of nine finalists in 'Off By Heart Shakespeare', a televised nationwide competition that had thousands of schoolchildren spouting off as Romeo, Macbeth or Portia. Anyone among the grumpy elders moaning about how the kids are slaves to the tweet would have been confounded by Jack and his peers, who had taken Shakespeare into their heads as well as their hearts. Even better, they weren't just declaiming; the teens had got to grips with the heady complications of Shakespeare's language games.

Given the daunting assignment of leading off the nine performances, our pint-sized Chorus Jack knew exactly what Shakespeare was up to: the seduction of that new thing, an audience, at the even newer place, the Globe. The very first word out of his mouth, the one-letter tease 'O', describes that venue, the 'wooden O' in which they are gathered. Jack rounded his mouth as if he was blowing smoke-rings. 'Pardon, gentles all,' he went on with just the right accent of mock apology; pretending that, for the duration of the performance at least, the groundlings were as good as the real gentles; that they were all in it together at Agincourt.

And when Jack asked permission for the actors, 'ciphers to this great accompt, on your imaginary forces work', I was transported back not to the vasty fields of France but the sooty streets of Waterloo in 1955. I was sitting, wide-eyed in the stalls of the Old Vic, next to my bardolater dad. Chorus, in the melodious notes of the late great John Neville, Mr Cheekbones, was swishing his scarlet cape in my direction, piecing out his imperfections (not that he seemed to have any) with my thoughts. It was the first Shakespeare I'd ever seen, though my father, the thespian manqué, was given to suddenly declaiming over breakfast while pointing to the silver tea strainer, 'The quality of mercy is not strained.'

That evening in Waterloo, the king was an up-and-coming Welshman called Richard Burton, whose versatile, slightly nasal baritone could do plummy and steely all within a single sentence. I inhaled deep what I thought was the dustymusty of the Elizabethan world, actually the mingy-dingy of the Old Vic wardrobe department. The price of this treat was my having to memorise one of the king's speeches, so for days on end my sister had to endure me squawking for England, Harry and St George.

Shakespeare awakened the historian in me. He seemed to deliver a certain idea of England at a time when all that was left otherwise was tea and cricket. In 1955, just ten years after the war, it was as though the Bard had scripted Churchill; that the original 'happy few' were prototypes for the boys who flew in Spitfires. What now looks like the shamelessly chauvinistic film version made by Olivier in 1944 as a morale booster for D-Day made perfect sense to us even after the war had ended. Hadn't we all been in it together, Exeter, Harry the King, George the King, Winston, Dunkirk, the Blitz, Normandy? 'We band of brothers, for he who today sheds his blood with me shall be my brother'! We needed the pennants of Agincourt and the Crispin-St Georgery of it all, for London was still a sooty pea-soup fog-shrouded place; bombed-out buildings in the city and East End sticking up like stumps of blackened teeth. Despite the brave face put on by the techno-driven, Comet-jet powered Festival of Britain in 1951, and the designation we all gave ourselves in honour of the graceful but unreachably impeccable young queen of 'new Elizabethans', we needed someone to tell us who we were as a country, even if that someone happened to have died three and a half centuries before. We were the winners, weren't we? So why was the Empire disappearing; why were we in hock to the Americans; why were the Hungarians beating us at football; what did the British do in the world now other than endlessly Troop the Colour?

A certain power endured but it was the power of English rather than England; and, when you went to hear and see Shakespeare, you drank deep on it and emerged heady with its elixir of confidence. If all the world really was a stage, no one could out-troupe us.

This peculiar sense of English belonging, kindled in the theatre and then projected onto the streets, fields and villages of the country, had begun in the time of the first Elizabeth, and Shakespeare was its great virtuoso. Just as Olivier had done his bit in a Plantagenet pudding-basin haircut at a time of military trial, so the Globe had staged *Henry V* in 1599, a time of unnerving crisis. There was a Papal fatwa out on Elizabeth I, commending for remission of sins anyone who would take the heretic queen out of this earthly world. The militant Catholic Counter-Reformation was closing in. The Earl of Essex had signally failed to defeat the Irish rebellion, and the rumours of a new Spanish Armada, launched by King Philip III, were serious enough for the militia to be mobilised. In the midst of this panicky atmosphere, the one figure needed to calm the national jitters – Gloriana herself – had gone missing, for whatever reason unable to do a repeat of the great Tilbury speech of 1588, when she had appeared in armour before the troops and promised to die, if need be, in the company of her dear countrymen. Almost certainly conscious of the charisma-vacuum, Shakespeare filled it with a pseudo-Elizabeth in the guise of Harry of Monmouth, who, like her, was presented as having the common touch – so when he promised to perish on the field of battle among his 'brothers' and 'dear friends', they really believed it.

Shakespeare would not be the great poet-philosopher he is were he not to have spoken to the universal condition of humanity, but at the beginning he didn't address himself to humanity at large but to the English. If his history plays fed off a need for national chronicle, ordained by the powerful and apparently craved by the powerless, they also brought that new sense of shared historical destiny to the public who thronged to the Rose and the Globe. Almost before there was a true political and institutional 'England', there was a theatre of England.

Sometimes we forget the startling fact that in the sixteenth century only the English had custom-built, site-specific commercial theatre. In Italy the peripatetic *commedia dell'arte* performed on the street; in Spain and the Netherlands plays were acted on decorated carts and wagons. The court and the church still summoned performances all over Europe. But the English had the Theatre, the Curtain, the Rose and the Globe, open to both the elite and ordinary for it cost just a penny to stand with the groundlings in the pit. In this way, the theatre filled the void left by the Reformation's destruction of the old Catholic spectacle, enacted in churches and on village greens, that had also been one of the few places where lords and lads mingled, though not physically cheek by jowl.

Socially, this creation of the theatre as a kind of profane national communion was a two-way process, both top-down and bottom-up, and that gave Elizabethan theatre its demotic, rough-and-tumble feel. Elizabeth, the ultimate drama-Queen, knew that her legitimacy depended on the magic of spectacle outside the court as well as in it, hence the royal progresses around the country. Impresarios of image such as the Earl of Leicester extended this sense of newly minted public spectacle by becoming patrons of travelling companies of players who performed in tavern yards in close proximity to popular entertainments like bear baiting. But in the 1560s and 1570s, in one of those mysterious transformational moments of cultural history that are ultimately impossible to pin down, what had been a royal and aristocratic entertainment took on a commercial life of its own. The first owner-manager to convert a tavern yard site into a true theatre was the grocer John Brayne, who established one at the Red Lion in the rustic suburb of Whitechapel. Ultimately, the Red Lion was just too far from the punters to make a go of it, but Brayne's brother-in-law, James Burbage, was a carpenter-joiner as well as an actor, and when they moved the enterprise to the more populous and buzzingly seedy area of Shoreditch, they took over the ruins of a Catholic convent for the new theatre. The symbolism of one kind of spectacle succeeding the other could not have been more eloquent. The Theatre in which Shakespeare found his place was a humming mix of hard business, rowdy spectacle, aristocratic slumming and – from the outset – English self-congratulation. For, although the early repertoire included comedy and blood-and-guts melodrama, what broke through to a mass public was history. Ten thousand people were said to have come to the Rose to see *Henry VI*, written (though not entirely) by the actor-cum-script-fixer-upper William Shakespeare. History became the country's new theology. There were, in fact, relics of the old Christian plays haunting the bloody chronicle of *Henry VI*: the mad and saintly king; the demonic Gloucester; the martyr-mystic Joan of Arc; and the knight-valiant Talbot. But the generation that flocked to the theatre was also the first to be able to read English histories in their own language. These, written in the 1540s, like that by Edward Hall, were aggressively Protestant, insular, chest-beatingly Tudor. Reliable literacy figures are impossible to come by, but the schoolmaster (of the kind that taught the young Shakespeare) was both the ally and the maker of this concerted attempt to forge a national, anti-Catholic common allegiance.

Under Elizabeth the mixed genre of 'England' books – part antiquarian tradition, part topographical gazette, part history chronicle of kings and queens – suddenly flowered. Hall was reprinted, joined by William Harrison's *Description of England*, and most famously Raphael Holinshed's *Chronicles* (especially in the cheaper 1587 quarto edition). Holinshed's work was not just one damned king after another; it pulsed with a meaty sense of England: our food, costume, sports and after-hours pleasures. And much of this rudimentary ethnography of what it meant to be English becomes earthy poetry in Shakespeare's history plays.

Though the scenes may have unfolded on the bare boards, they are very specific – from Eastcheap to the vale of Evesham – and countless groundlings who had immigrated from the hard-up countryside into the swarming shacks and tenements of London would have had no trouble in conjuring up the orchards and hedgerows. The plays smell of English cooking, too, especially in the verbal appetite of that incarnation of the national stomach, Falstaff, who describes a dullard as having a wit 'as thick as Tewkesbury mustard'. The sense of a language made from different voices and accents, some of them beyond England – the Welsh of Owen Glendower, the (cod) Irish of McMorris in *Henry V*, or the macho Geordie of Hotspur – all fed into the pot of national relish that Shakespeare cooks up with juicy gusto.

In Shakespeare's hands the cult of England is never a sentimental romance. It is easy to forget that John of Gaunt's famous ecstatic catalogue of 'this England's' imperishable virtues is, in fact, a bitter rant against the fact that it has perished. The enduring power of the histories, written by someone who had dwelled in various social worlds – small-town glover's boy, grammar-school swot, common thespian – lies in the comprehensiveness of their vision of how power is invented, manipulated, exploited; how it both panders to the cravings of those it rules and stamps ruthlessly on their frailties. No one was more daring in exposing the grinding machinery of politics (whoever plays Richard II has to work hard at making him so detestable as to merit his fate at the hands of the self-righteous puritan Bolingbroke). And in *Henry IV* Shakespeare makes sure that Bolingbroke's victory in *Richard II* has turned out to be pyrrhic. In the miserable hours of his guilty insomnia, any shred of vainglorious deception collapses.

Prince Hal/Henry V deludes himself that he can inhabit both the world of those who live by the courtly code (honour) and Falstaff's realm of disenchanted honesty (what is honour? A word. Air!): only to realise on assuming the crown that its first necessary victim is not just his old 'tutor of riot', but the human truth. The most important scene in *Henry V* is not the battle itself but the encounter between the king and Michael Williams, a common soldier who warns that 'if the cause be not good, the king himself hath a heavy reckoning to make, when all those legs and arms and heads chopped off in a battle shall join together at the latter day and cry all, "We died at such a place."' How that must have echoed with the groundlings recruited for the endless wars in Ireland across the Irish Sea.

The shock of the encounter moves Henry to soliloquise in the darkness, in the greatest speech of the play, on his moral burden: 'Upon the king! Let us our lives, our souls, our debts, our careful wives, our children and our sins lay on the king! We must bear all. O hard condition.' What have kings that 'privates hath not too,' he asks in this same sombre mood, 'save ceremony, save general ceremony?' It is an extraordinary achievement, this conjuring both of the craving for royal magic and the chilling knowledge of its shortcomings.

The first time that the name of Shakespeare appears in print is on the impure 1598 version of *Henry IV* published as a stand-alone drama. The histories were not just the making of the Bard, they were in some mythic but also deeply astute way the making of the English, too: our humour, our impatience with the pretentions of the mighty, our unforgiving insight into their deceptions, our perennially forgiving celebration of a sovereignty that shares the common sacrifice and mysteriously, irrationally, somehow incarnates that otherwise formless collective thing that is us, our mostly and, in spite of everything, happy breed.

BONDED TO BRITAIN

Fifty years of excitingly detonated hardware and women breathing 'Jaaames' in states of postcoital gratitude, thousands of air miles clocked en route to tropical lagoons where villainy lurks among the ravenous barracuda – and where has it gotten Bond? Trafalgar Square, that's where. There he sits in *Skyfall*, the latest, cleverest and most psychologically gripping of all the Bond epics – in London's National Gallery, in a mood of uncharacteristic pensiveness. A geeky tousle-haired twenty-something joins him on the bench, and to Bond's incredulity claims to be the new Q, the master of all those boxes of tricks that have gotten him out of impossibly tight spots over the past fifty years. He hands Bond the usual elegant leather case. But this time it appears, mystifyingly, to be . . . merely a leather case. Inside is a gun. And that's it. 'Not exactly Christmas, is it?' the agent says, looking like a small boy who has just been handed a present of socks. 'What were you expecting,' asks the baby Q with an expression of condescending pity, 'an exploding pen? Sorry, we don't do that any more.'

Conscious of having to mark the half-century of Bond without compromising the pure adrenaline rush of entertainment, *Skyfall*'s director (Sam Mendes, born anno *Thunderball*, 1965) has packed the movie so full of memories that watching it almost feels like experiencing the whole cycle of the films from the time when JFK (predictably an Ian Fleming fan) and Harold Macmillan were in power, through the death pangs of the Cold War, and into the age of cyberterrorism. At one point in the new movie Bond unearths his most cherished antique: the Aston Martin DB5 first unveiled in 1964's *Goldfinger*. 'Not very comfortable, is it?' complains Judi Dench's M, who herself has gotten to the point where creature comforts matter: 'Where are we going?' 'Back in time,' replies Daniel Craig's Bond, looking bony and haunted like the lone grey wolf he has become.

Time travel, as anyone who watched the opening ceremonies of the London Olympics (with its droll pageant of the Industrial Revolution) will know, is a British obsession. There was a point in the middle age of the Bond films (roughly coinciding with late-period Roger Moore) when mindlessly robotic futurism set in: all whooshing monorails and lame displays of whatever British techno-inventions – the (doomed) vertical takeoff Harrier Jump Jet in *The Living Daylights* (1987), for instance – could be wheeled out to advertise to the world that Bond's Britain was more than just an academy in advanced social deportment. But these sweaty efforts at rebranding missed the beating heart of Bond's enduring appeal, which was an updated personification of the British 'gentleman' in a world of murder, terror and imminent nuclear annihilation. Perfect tailoring and clipped wit, maintained even as Bond was either being tortured by, or dishing it out to, some sadistic monster. Brit brains could beat doltish megalomania any day.

In James Bond's universe, the delusions of common little people aspiring to be Masters of the Universe would always be their undoing. 'Little fish pretending to be bigger than they are,' Sean Connery sneered at the title character's heavily magnified aquarium glass walls in the series's first film (*Dr No*, 1962). In *Goldfinger*, Oddjob perishes from the steel-tipped bowler hat he so presumptuously wears along with his inexcusably ill-fitting suit. Commander Bond of Scotland's Fettes College (Tony Blair's alma) is not for a minute fooled by the old-school-tied psychopathic strangler Captain Nash, played by the great Robert Shaw in *From*

Russia With Love (1963). With every grating 'old man' Nash sends Bond's way, the less likely it is that he is really the British agent he claims to be. Ordering (O horror!) red wine with his fish in the dining car of the Orient Express just clinches the unmasking.

Bond, like his literary creator, Ian Fleming, is always a snob but never a bore. His obsession with correct style is a defence against the coarse vulgarities of a changing world in which a conspiracy of global power and money seem to have the upper hand. In the Bondian fairy tale, they come a cropper against Savile Row suits and mordant asides. To the lethal sirens – think of the flame-haired vixen Fiona Volpe in *Thunderball* or Xenia Onatopp in 1995's *GoldenEye* (like Dickens, Fleming loved making his names act out the part) – Bond delivers lashings of rough sex and death. But to the drippy D-cup Andromedas, chained to their rocks by some lunatic captor, he is always the liberating knight-gallant.

American movie mythology has occasionally gotten mileage from this romance of the anachronism, in the form of the cowboy who has outlived his time – Butch Cassidy or one of Clint Eastwood's stubbly *Unforgiven* antiheroes. But America has always been about the rush of the now, whereas almost everything creative in Britain, Bond included, has come from a dialogue between past and future, the antique and the cool (think *Sergeant Pepper*). James Bond was dreamed up as the British Empire was on its last legs, and like Churchill, it was painfully aware of its dependence on the American protector. Writing before the independence of the Caribbean colonies from his windowless Jamaican villa (named 'Goldeneye' after one of the wartime naval intelligence ops he was involved in, usually from behind a desk), Fleming was offering a placebo for the disappearing empire in the fantasy of a manly British style that would never be outmastered for seductive elegance. Nobody would do it better. Compared with Bond, Felix Leiter and the CIA looked like the duh-brigade, forever in need of catching on and catching up.

Bond was also the answer to another area where Britain felt challenged in the late 1950s: the shrinking manhood department. Films rehearsing the wartime heroics of escaping POWs or against-the-odds naval battles were an exhausted genre. The greatest generation wore trusses and had retired to the pub with a perpetual half pint of bitter. Churchill was doddering; his successors among the ruling class were ponderously tweedy. As Noel Coward once put it, 'Continentals have sex; the British have hot-water bottles.' Not Fleming, though. A sexual omnivore with a 'cruel mouth' and hawkish mien, he projected onto Bond and indulged a taste for the erotic whip that makes Christian Grey look like Mary Poppins. For years, Fleming carried on a long affair with the decidedly upper-crust Anne Charteris, then married to the media magnate Viscount Rothermere. When with regret she returned to London from 'Goldeneye', she wrote wistfully, 'I loved cooking for you, sleeping beside you, and being whipped by you.'

Fleming was not the only writer who used spy literature to explore the many shades of British impotence. In the early '60s, when the Bond movies were launched, John le Carré, who knew whereof he wrote, created the dark, treacherous, authentically chronicled world of the Cold War MI6. But there was also the under-appreciated and brilliant Len Deighton, whose 'insubordinate' agent (called 'Harry Palmer', and played by Michael Caine in the movie) perfected a street-smart insolence that couldn't have been more different from Bond. Palmer seduced as much with his Gauloise-smoking cockney attitude as he did with his cooking. (Deighton wrote excellent cookbooks meant to persuade men their virility was not under threat from knowing how to dice an onion or make a cheese soufflé puff and rise.)

Books by both authors generated movies, in particular two little 1965 masterpieces: *The Spy Who Came In From the Cold*, based on a le Carré novel, and the even more brilliant *The Ipcress File*, adapted from Deighton. The first, with Richard Burton as the self-destructive Alec Leamas, all grubby trench coat and hooded-eye hangover, operated from start to finish under a shroud of dingy, cynical gloom. *The Ipcress File*, even with its delicious poke in the eye at the camel-coated and bowler-hatted brigadiers of MI6, was too local and British for mass export, even with the irrepressibly chirpy Caine as its standard-bearer.

No one appreciated this more than the producer of *The Ipcress File*, Harry Saltzman. A Canadian Jew settled in Britain since the late 1950s, Saltzman was the power behind Woodfall Films, the fountainhead not of fantasy Britishness but of hard-edged social realism. Movie after movie set in industrial wastelands – including *Saturday Night and Sunday Morning* (1960), *A Taste of Honey* (1961) and *The Loneliness of the Long Distance Runner* (1962) – explored sex, class and all-around hopelessness. Each film spoke to the true condition of a Britain caught between post-imperial hangover and the aggravated yearnings of a generation crushed by exactly the old-school complacency Ian Fleming and James Bond personified.

But Saltzman had a hunch that the new Britain, breaking spec-tacularly free from its ancient crust of decorum – the England of the Rolling Stones and the Beatles, of Mary Quant miniskirts and Carnaby Street bell-bottoms – was up for something more roguish than dramas of back-street abortions and the Friday-night puke. Wherever you looked, tongue-in-cheek self-mockery was at the pulse of what the raffish jazz singer George Melly called 'revolt into style'. Satire invaded the stage with the hit review 'Beyond the Fringe' and flooded the television airwaves with *That Was the Week That Was*, a show so simultaneously cheeky and biting that it was suspended during the election campaign of 1964. *Private Eye*, the take-no-prisoners satirical magazine, is (along with the still hot but wrinkly Rolling Stones) the only venerable British treasure to last the full fifty years alongside 007.

What these hoary pensioners all have in common is the talent to send up Britishness even as they affectionately rejoice in it. On this side of the pond (with the honourable exceptions of Stephen Colbert, Jon Stewart and *The Onion*), you don't dare celebrate America by mocking it. In Britain, where during the Olympics the queen became the latest of the Bond girls to surrender to the gentle joke, it's virtually a patriotic obligation.

It's possible to overdo the caper side of Bond, and Roger Moore's broadly whimsical Bond did just that, with the lethal brutality of Connery's personable thug getting lost in all the bad puns and smirking. The stunningly shot and artfully written version of one of Fleming's best books, *On Her Majesty's Secret Service* (1969) – its lyric opening on a French beach as twilight hangs over the sea is evidence of the real gift Fleming could command when he chose – actually flirted with tragic tenderness. It was a quality Diana Rigg supplied but that was well beyond the talents of George Lazenby, who was cast as Bond after appearing in chocolate commercials. Timothy Dalton overdid the New Man's Bond, all feline edginess – though he was ill-served by formulaic writing, tinny scores, and low-budget action that exposed the strains in the franchise after Saltzman and his partner Albert 'Cubby' Broccoli had gone their separate ways. It was left to the looker Pierce Brosnan and the terrific writing team of Neil Purvis and Robert Wade to restore the ballsy merriment.

Daniel Craig and his directors have aimed for something leaner, meaner, darker and harder – though the blade edge of wit without which Bond wouldn't be Bond is still there. With *Skyfall*, Sam Mendes (and his writers Purvis and Wade, supplemented by John Logan) has done something genuinely remarkable. Summoning all those other spy ghosts from the time of Bond's creation – the Harry Palmer and le Carré moles – they have turned the epic inward, into Britain itself (where by far the greater part of the action takes place). The film isn't short on the standard supply of bang and splat, but the trajectory of the journey that Bond always takes is, this time, into the ruins of history, both public and personal. Freud rather than Blofeld lurks in the dystopian darkness, and the drive down memory lane is full of the pain of the orphaned.

Which might be said of Britain as well as 007. Bloodied and bashed about, where is its destiny supposed to lead these days? Not to collapsing Europe, but not across the Atlantic either, where the big boy is preoccupied with its own business. So Britain, like Bond, seems cut loose, a voyager on a sea of doubt. Which somehow does not make either Bond or Britain any the less riveting a story. It's just that these days, for them both, life is apt to seem shaken as well as stirred.

BONDED AGAIN

Scanning the dim interior of Le Caprice, the writer failed to see anyone answering the description of the man he was looking for. There were the prosperous bald lunching with the dangerously chic. A scented cloud of Guerlain hung over the room. 'You would be . . .?' asked the girl at the desk, looking steadily at the writer from beneath heavy mascara. 'The reservation should be under . . .' He tailed off, wondering if 007 had booked under his real name. Unlikely, he surmised. He was already feeling uncomfortable. It was unseasonably warm for April. Normally he would have lunched tieless but 007 was old school, so he had suited up and knotted a dark red silk tie at the strangling collar.

A light tap on the shoulder. The writer spun round to find himself faced by a feral smile set in a lightly bronzed face. The writer took mental notes: chin, cleft; eyes, chestnut with little specks of gold in the iris; black hair thickly swept back; sardonic eyebrows. 'Mr Horowitz, if I'm not mistaken?' The voice was low, studiously charming, a burr as soft as Scottish heather. Bond separated the syllables as if the writer's name was a private joke: Mister Horror-Wits. 'Shall we?'

Perspiring freely, Horowitz followed the dove-grey silk and wool suit to a corner table. 'Now tell me, Mr Horowitz, what makes you think you will succeed where others have stumbled? Not quite your usual line of work, is it?' The cat smile again. 'And the stakes are so high, aren't they? Mind you, I like a man with a taste for risk.' The writer felt a bead of sweat form on his brow and prayed it would not run down his nose. All appetite lost, he wondered for the first time if this had really been a good idea.

Oh, yes, it was! Anthony Horowitz has written a humdinger of a Bond story, so cunningly crafted and thrillingly paced that 007's creator would have been happy to have owned it. The screenwriter and novelist, a life-long fan, knows that, when he wanted to, Ian Fleming could turn on the literary juice with the best of them. The French beach scene that opens *On Her Majesty's Secret Service* is a brilliant piece of atmospheric writing, at once innocent and sinister like Fleming's whole project, and the ending of *You Only Live Twice*, with its debt to Nathaniel Hawthorne's fable 'Rappaccini's Daughter', is so unexpectedly off-kilter that, in the film, producers Saltzman and Broccoli had to replace it with the psycho-ferret Donald Pleasence version of Blofeld whizzing through his fake volcano on – the latest thing! – a monorail. But from his brilliant first chapter on, Horowitz is a pitch-perfect mimic of the Fleming one-line punch: 'Rain swept into London like an angry bride.' 'Silence sat in the room, an uninvited guest.' He even gets the clichés spot on. 'Just he and the Maserati, plunging into the green hell.'

Trigger Mortis (down to the tacky title, for Fleming revelled in tacky) is what you would call a Loving Tribute. Horowitz is a purist, so the mood is martini-nostalgic even if he gets the recipe a little off. The time is the 1950s, the Cold War; M is still pipe-smoking and dyspeptic; the Soviet secret service Smersh is up to no good and there are rockets to be interfered with. The book is the best Bond movie you'll ever see without actually having to see the movie. There is a nail-biter at the Nürburgring racetrack, the mother of all chases deep in the New York subway, and the obligatory procession of excitingly hard women, beginning with Pussy Galore and ending with Jeopardy Lane. (Pussy the bored tourist in London is an inspired touch.) The über-villain gets to deliver the usual lengthy autobiographical narrative explaining how he has come to be dead to all human feeling, and Bond, also as usual, responds in the most insulting way he can by brushing off the pathos as the self-indulgent ravings of a sociopath. As a result he is consigned to the kind of elaborately sadistic fate from which the wide-eyed reader cannot possibly believe 007 will escape, even as we all know he must.

Is this all too vague for you? Of course it is. But anything else would be a criminal spoiler and, take it from me, you really don't want *Trigger Mortis* spoiled.

'Well done, Anthony,' said Bond as he extended a hand. They were back at his watering hole. 'You certainly pulled it off. I must tell you there were doubters but of course I wasn't one of them. So now you won't take it amiss, will you, if I point out just one or two little errors . . .? Nothing serious, of course . . . Your Bond might indeed have been delighted to see a Château Pétrus 1950 on the menu of an English country establishment but, my dear Anthony, he would never have drunk it, not a mere seven years after the vintage. The 1945, on the other hand, was coming round nicely.

'And you know I wouldn't have perused the front page of *The Times* for news because, in 1957, you recall, there wasn't any on that front page . . .' The smile gleamed over the rim of his martini glass. 'Next time, why don't you send me the manuscript? Then I could save you your blushes.' He lifted the chilled glass on which vodka beads hung like crystals. 'Your very good health.'

PAUL BEATTY

Just how black can comedy get? Well, try this on for size. At the start of *The Sellout*, Paul Beatty's howl-a-page assault on the pieties of race debates in America, the black narrator is up before the Supreme Court for keeping a black slave. There was a time when African Americans did indeed own slaves, but not these days and not in a rustic corner of the ghettos of south-west Los Angeles.

The case file is 'Me vs The United States' — our narrator's father, the acting dean of a community college, having short-ened the family name of Mee to match his overdeveloped sense of historical calling. Just how the son got to be an involuntary slaveholder lies at the heart of Beatty's outrageous, hilarious and profound novel. We never do learn his real first name but his inamorata, the sumptuously foul-mouthed Marpessa Delissa Dawson, calls him 'Bonbon' and there never was a more soft-centred hero in all of African-American writing.

Bonbon's ghetto hamlet, Dickens, is known as 'The Farms': 'You know when you've entered the Farms because the city side-walks, along with your rims, car stereo, nerve and progressive voting record will have vanished into air thick with the smell of cow manure and, if the wind is blowing in the right direction — good weed.'

Bonbon's daddy's main project is his son, whose home schooling consists of lessons in the black experience, past and present, driven home by brutal exercises in conditioned response. Daddy mugs his own son to demonstrate that supportive bystanders fail to materialise when the victim is black; daddy has son self-electrocute when failing to answer history questions. An especially severe dose of voltage has a dramatic effect. 'What I discovered was that the phrase "evacuate one's bowels" is a misnomer, because . . . my bowels evacuated me. It was a faeces retreat comparable to the great evacuations of history. Dunkirk. Saigon. New Orleans.'

Daddy gets shot by the LA police in the usual random altercation, sociopolitical to the end, shouting, 'I'm warning you, you anal-retentive authoritarian archetypes.' Bonbon buries him in the farmyard, takes over the farm, and discovers a gift for raising luscious, if unorthodox fruit: the square watermelon for instance. But Dickens itself has been made to disappear from the official maps of LA. Bonbon mounts a rearguard action, posting exit signs from the freeway to a place that no longer officially exists, but the end of Dickens has a much more dramatic effect on long-time Dickensian, Hominy Jenkins.

The aged Hominy was once a child actor, featuring in *The Little Rascals*, an actual series of fifty one-reeler shorts in which a gang of kids – Spanky, Alfalfa and the black Buckwheat – get up to no good on a weekly basis.

Hominy never does get to stardom, outliving the age 'of the human golliwog' and the short. He survives on occasional fan mail and the odd pilgrim, undeterred by Dickens's fame as 'the murder capital of the world'. But these meagre consolations disappear along with Dickens's zip code, and one day Bonbon discovers him 'buck naked and hanging by his neck from a wooden beam'. Bonbon cuts the 'self-lynch[er]' down, in return for which Hominy implores, or, rather, demands, servitude, refusing to call Bonbon anything except 'massa'. Bonbon tries manumission but his slave uses it as toilet paper. However, it's a selective form of servitude. Hominy doesn't do a lick of work on Bonbon's urban farm, but shows up daily from 1 to 1.15 p.m. for a slavish genuflect and is so intent on punishment that he has to be taken off by 'massa' every Wednesday to receive a good whipping from certain parties specialising in that kind of thing, and who lay it on thick.

If you are already wondering 'what's funny about that?', caveat emptor, it gets worse (or better). Convinced that only resegregation will save the local middle school from educational disaster, Bonbon and assistant principal Charisma Molina ban whites. In a scene of reverse busing, five pearly white (or, rather, honey-tan) valley girls attempt to enter the school that has quickly become famous for academic excellence. The threshold is barred by a defiant Charisma, the barrio's answer to Governor Faubus. No writer since Tom Wolfe in his *Bonfire of the Vanities* years has such an eye for social farce.

Rival gangs, the 'Venice Seaside Boys' and the 'et tu, Brute Gangster Munificent Neighborhood Crips 'n' Shit' who used to rumble over turf possession in 'Hood Day' have been more effectively dispossessed by variable-rate mortgages and the attendant gentrification: 'wine bars, holistic medicine shops and [the houses of] edgy movie stars'. Now, in order to 'put in work' (i.e. shoot each other) they are forced to commute in to south-west LA 'from faraway places like Palmdale and Moreno Valley'. Exhausted by sitting in traffic for hours, the hoods are reduced to historical re-enactments, except instead of Vicksburg and Bull Run, the battles are the epic conflicts of gangland's yesteryear: 'the Lincoln Boulevard Skirmish' and the 'infamous Massacre at Los Amigos Park'. Voltaire and Laurence Sterne would have recognised a bro.

Sometimes (you know what I mean), the contemporary American scene is so operatically vicious, so murderously unhinged, so monstrously unjust, that only comedy can do it proper justice. It takes confidence to fight back with hot-wired polemics. But it takes a whole other level of sheer audacity to expose atrocious things through the play of wit. Beatty plays for very high stakes – but he wins. His brilliant, beautiful and weirdly poignant book knocks the stuffing out of right-thinking solemnities and he delivers droll wisdoms besides which the most elevated rants (if you'll forgive the expression) pale into ponderous sententiousness.

Comedy that delivers social truth through hee-haw is hard, maybe the hardest writing genre of all, and the condition for its success is steely literary grip. Beatty is knife-sharp. At the resegregation showdown everybody is 'as stubborn as grass stains'; after taking a slug himself, Bonbon says 'anyone who's ever described a bullet wound as superficial has never been shot'. Elsewhere he reflects that real slavery had to have been bad enough 'for someone to convince themselves that Canada wasn't that far away'.

As his career as avenging lord of misrule develops, Bonbon gets to enjoy himself and so do we. Marpessa throws Hominy a birthday party on the number 125 bus she drives, and takes it right onto the beach; Bonbon reinstates Dickens by surreptitiously painting its old boundary lines on the roads; to the sign for the trauma ward of a hospital famous for its indifference he adds dripping, horror-comic painted blood. Bonbon may slaughter everyone's sacred cows, but he is a farmer not a butcher, and he owes his innocent power to the incomparably luscious crops he raises.

If you needed one word to describe *The Sellout*, it would be: fruity. A judge sets his bail at 'a cantaloupe and two kumquats', while Marpessa gets all hot and bothered at night thinking of his plums and 'juicy-ass pomegranates'. Juiciness stains every lovely page of Beatty's mad, marvellous, toothsome book, which is just as well since we need all the sweetness we can get if we are going to survive this time of sour derangement.

WAR AND PEACE:
PRINT AND SCREEN

How should we live? That's the not unimportant question posed by Leo Tolstoy's masterpiece, and it makes *War and Peace*-niks terrible bores. But we can't help it: we need to evangelise, spread the word that there is no book quite like it; no book that encompasses almost the whole of humanity, and that collapses the space between ink and paper and flesh and blood so completely that you seem to be living it rather than reading it.

You emerge from this total immersion with your emotions deepened, vision clarified, exposure to the casual cruelty of the powerful sharpened. Which is not to say that the book is therapy for anything. In its pages the historical cavalcade looks like an unavoidable bad joke, while the search for a happy and meaningful life, embarked on by the clumsy hero Pierre Bezukhov, invites one torment after another. Only when he hits rock-bottom does a tantalising glimpse of light appear. And yet when Pierre backs into love, so do we, and the experience is overwhelming.

My first reading was a half-century ago. Weary of being told by a Cambridge friend that it was the best book ever written, that everything men and women do to each other was its subject, I gave in. I was stuck in a dull vacation job, the only straight in the village that was the soft furnishings department of a big West End department store. Every so often I would emerge from the back office cubbyhole to flog a thousand feet of plush curtaining to interior decorators for third-world dictators. But where I wanted to be was Bald Hills, Moscow, St Petersburg, the sanguinary, smoke-choked fields of battle.

Around the corner from the store was a salad-and-brown-rice lunch bar where you sat at tables of scrubbed pine and toyed with vinegary mounds of alfalfa sprouts. 'Excuse me, young man,' said someone parked opposite. The voice came from an elderly gent, salt-and-pepper whiskers, country-pub suit, regimental tie; not the brown rice type at all unless retired brigadiers were going vegetarian in 1965. I put the book down, trying not to seem put out by the interruption. 'I hope you don't mind,' said the brig-adier, adopting the courtly tone of Count Rostov transplanted to Tunbridge Wells, 'but I see you are setting off on the Long March.' (I was perhaps on page 100.) 'Would this, by any chance, be your First Time?' Indeed it would. 'Ah, so fortunate to have all that ahead of you.' His eyes shone with the benevolence of a gratified apostle. 'Do you know I myself will be setting off for the twelfth time this summer?' Sure, I thought, not believing him for a second. Now I do; the next time will be my ninth.

So if the BBC's new dramatisation sends millions to the book, we must rejoice and try not to wince when Andrew Davies's script improves on Tolstoy. Early in the second episode the newly mar-ried Pierre trawls his hand through the conjugal bedsheets. 'What are you looking at?' Hélène asks, as though baffled by a peculiar hobby. 'My lovely wife,' he whispers breathily, spectacles fogging with passion, 'you are an inexhaustible treasure full of wonderful, wonderful secrets and delights. The more I discover, the more it seems is left to discover, more secrets, more delights.' 'Actually,' says Hélène, glued-on smile going with the Notting Hill diction, 'one can get a bit tired of having one's secrets and delights discov-ered all the time over and over.'

This fifty-shots-of-vodka approach manages to miss the one passage of high erotic voltage that Tolstoy wrote describing the exact moment of Pierre's entrapment. At a dinner organised to get him to pop the question, an 'aunt handed him the snuffbox right over Hélène, behind her back. Hélène leaned forward so as to make room and smiling glanced round. As always at soirées she was wearing a gown in the fashion of the time, quite open in front and back. Her bust, which had always looked like marble to Pierre, was now such a short distance from him that he could involuntarily make out with his nearsighted eyes the living loveliness of her shoulders and neck, and so close to his lips that he had only to lean forward a little to touch her. He sensed the warmth of her body, the smell of her perfume, and the creaking of her corset as she breathed.' And that's how to script a sexual ambush.

But much of the essence of *War and Peace* is there in the new BBC adaptation, thanks to deeply thought-through performances by Brian Cox (Kutuzov), Jim Broadbent (Prince Bolkonsky), Stephen Rea (Kuragin), and brilliant Jessie Buckley in the thankless part of Marya Bolkonsky – all of whom give unmistakeable signs of having read the book, as does the perfectly pained Pierre (Paul Dano), whose every blink is a sonata of bewilderment. And if the casting director decided that the most frightening thing that could be done with Napoleon was to make him the spitting image of Malcolm Tucker, then that certainly works for me.

Never mind that adapting the 'monster', as Henry James lovingly called *War and Peace*, is an invitation to hubris; every generation must have a go and sometimes it costs them dearly. The Russian director Sergei Bondarchuk, who cast himself as Pierre in the seven-hour epic he made in the 1960s, survived two massive heart attacks towards the end of filming, during one of which he was pronounced clinically dead for four minutes. Touch *War and Peace* and you play with fire.

When he composed his *War and Peace* opera in the 1940s, Sergei Prokofiev knew he had to appease Stalin's taste for patriotic bombast but somehow managed to smuggle in the exquisitely poignant waltz so that the endurance of tenderness registers amid the dull boom of autocratic cannon. At the other end of the musical scale, the immersive 'electro-pop opera' *Natasha, Pierre and the Great Comet of 1812*, which I saw performed in a tent two years ago (with an on-cue snowstorm falling on Manhattan), hits everything important about the Andrei-Anatole-Natasha triangle with manic brilliance. Did we well up at the crucial moment of Pierre's speech to Natasha? You bet we did, and it was nothing to do with the thin vodka and cardboard *pirogis* that come with the show.

Film and television versions of *War and Peace* have to steer a tricky course between romance and reverence. The twenty-part BBC dramatisation in 1972 may have been a bit too much, beginning ominously with three minutes of a footman setting dinner plates on Count Rostov's table, though Anthony Hopkins inhabited Pierre's fumbling big-heartedness as though born for it, which is more than can be said for Henry Fonda in the 1956 King Vidor picture, basically *Gone with the Balalaika*. Bondarchuk's stupendous movie has been the most faithful to the book and, with 13,000 Soviet soldiers and a budget of at least $70 million in today's money, you certainly knew you were in a war zone. I first saw it in Paris in 1966 in two parts; the first ending with the battle of Borodino, after which the audience exited ashen-faced, not unlike the remnant of the Grande Armée departing Moscow. Later, it was hideously dubbed and butchered for anglophone audiences. But I screened a sumptuously restored, uncut print at my local indie movie house on a hot July day a few years back, with only a fifteen-minute intermission for a compassionate dose of Stoli. Not a soul departed before the end. Bondarchuk used breathtaking helicopter photography and dizzy crane shots. His cameramen roller-skated through the dancers in the ball scene, synchronising their movements with the lilt of the waltz. The battle sequences, in their chaotic din and hacking slaughter, are the most historically credible ever filmed and the Borodino sequence, nearly twenty minutes long, ends with one of the most astonishing aerial shots in all of cinema: cavalry charges performing an endlessly looping ballet of carnage, while fire blooms from the cannon and infantry stagger back and forth in blind futility. That Olympian top-shot, both omniscient and despairing, exactly translates into film Prince Andrei's brutal eve-of-battle exclamation to his ingenuous friend Pierre (come to see the battle dressed in a white topper). 'War', says Andrei, 'is the vilest thing in the world . . . [men] come together to kill each other, they slaughter and maim tens of thousands . . . and then they say prayers of thanksgiving for having slaughtered so many people . . . how does God look down and listen to them?'

Bondarchuk was also brilliant at the intimate moments and understood how important soundscape was to Tolstoy. We are first introduced to Andrei's father, the martinet Prince Nikolai Bolkonsky, as he walks through the autumnal woods of his estate. A Haydn minuet plays over the action; all very pretty. But then the camera tracks back to reveal an actual quartet playing for the prince beneath the trees, which is precisely what a serf orchestra used to do every time Tolstoy's maternal grandfather chose to go for a stroll. When the walk was over, as Rosamund Bartlett's fine biography of Tolstoy tells us, the serf violinists went back to feeding the pigs.

The uncanny physical immediacy of *War and Peace* is the result of Tolstoy bringing together personal memory, family history and dense archival research into the making of his narrative. His hero, he said, was truth. Before writing the Borodino chapters he walked the battlefield in the company of a twelve-year-old boy for several days. But other kinds of memory-archive came into play, too. His presence at the siege of Sevastopol in the Crimean War, both as soldier and war reporter, gave Tolstoy first-hand knowledge of what it felt and sounded like when shells landed and bullets came flying like 'flocks of birds'. The figure of his rustic 'Uncle''s Tatar mistress is drawn from Tolstoy's earlier service in the Caucasus, plus his own affair with the wife of one of his serfs, who bore him a child. Earthiness was everything. Where sensation was most intense in his memory, as in the book's wolf

hunt or the Christmas Eve sleigh ride, fake moustaches applied
with burnt cork, his prose takes wing.

With typical preference for honesty over kindness, Tolstoy
insisted that he and his wife Sophia, not long after their marriage,
read each other's diaries; his, of course, full of his sex escapades
recorded in hurtful detail. And yet the early years of that marriage – he began *War and Peace* in 1863, just a year after their
wedding – he believed to be his happiest. Tucked away in Yasnaya
Polyana, the estate he inherited from his mother's family, he was,
with Sophia's crucial help as amanuensis (for his handwriting was
so illegible he could hardly read it himself), at liberty to create
a masterwork. Six years on, the 5,000 pages of manuscript, 600
characters, three changes of title, and a complete alteration of
plot (1805 was originally the back-story to a tale of the doomed
Decembrist uprising of 1825) were delivered to the world. By this
time Tolstoy was already a successful writer and had committed
himself to changing Russia, freeing and educating the serfs, rather
than indulging himself in further fiction. So the moral zeal bled
into the pages of the book. In fact, he indignantly refused to call it
a novel at all, 'still less a poem and even less a historical chronicle',
but what the author wanted and was able to express in the form in
which it was expressed. Stylistically, it was also unlike anything
anyone else had written before: raw, richly inelegant, sometimes
directionless, bursting through the confines of good literary form
yet stained on every page with the juice of life.

Strenuous physical immediacy is but half of the book; its deep
core is concerned with the rest of us, the inner life, especially
of the passions and what happens to them when abraded by the
force of ambition, cupidity, vanity and violence. Accordingly, the
most radically exhilarating passages document the workings of
that inner life in broken diction, interior monologues (you even
get inside the wolf's head) and the repetitions and linguistic con-
tortions that form and unform in our minds. One such passage
has the young hussar Nikolai Rostov, on the eve of the impending

disaster of Austerlitz, fighting off sleep while still mounted on his horse, peering dimly at some sort of white spot in the darkness – a tache:

"Tache or no tache . . . Nat-asha, my sister, dark eyes. Na . . . tashka . . . (she'll be so surprised when I tell her how I saw the sovereign!) Natashka . . . take the tashka . . . Na-tashka, at-tack a . . . yes, yes, yes. That's good.' And again his head dropped to his horse's neck. Suddenly it seemed to him that he was being shot at. 'What? What? . . . Cut them down! What? . . .' said Rostov, coming to his senses. The moment he opened his eyes, Rostov heard ahead of him, where the enemy was, the drawn-out cries of thousands of voices . . .

All he can make out, however, is 'aaaa!' And 'rrrr!'

'What is it? What do you think?' Rostov turned to the hussar standing beside him. 'Is it from the enemy?'

Eventually, Nikolai realises he is listening to the full-throated acclaim of the enemy soldiers – '*Vive l'empereur*' – as Napoleon rides through the French camp. But Tolstoy has us hear the overture to calamity through Rostov's drowsy senses, as an obscure, distant hum and roar, the shapeless *aaaa* and *rrrr* of life into which we are inexorably pulled and through which we struggle, as best we can, to find a place of safety.

Politics, History and the Public World

'Why don't you just stick to history?' the trolls yell when they take exception to something I might have tweeted, or written in the pages of the Financial Times about Brexit or the giddy black comedy that is the Trump presidency. But, ever since Thucydides presumed to write about the war in which he had himself served, the division of labour between politics and history has never been clear-cut. It was precisely because he believed the political destiny of Athens was at stake that its greatest historian was moved to write his masterpiece; brimful as it is of the most fundamental arguments about right conduct in a democracy tempted to imperialism.

Generation after generation historians are warned by their peers to steer clear of political argument lest it contaminate the objectivity they are optimistically assumed to bring to their subject. And generation after generation they have been ignored by the strongest of their craft. For Machiavelli, political theory and history were inseparable; the same went for Macaulay, who saw no shame in tracing the lineage of the parliament of which he was a member back to the epic of the Glorious Revolution of 1688. At one and the same time the great nineteenth-century historian Jules Michelet presided over the newly founded Archives nationales, taught at the Collège de France, and made no secret of his ardent republicanism.

Sometimes this conviction that history actually is spoken citizenship comes at a price. The great historian of the Dutch revolt Pieter Geyl was *imprisoned at Buchenwald partly because the SS were worried about the possibility of his comparing Hitler to Napoleon in the historiographical study he was writing. Another of his countrymen, Johan Huizinga, was likewise held prisoner by the Nazis for refusing to recant his anti-fascist writings, and the Jewish historian whose work transformed feudal studies, Marc Bloch, joined the French Resistance, was captured and shot. Eventually canonised, all three were held at distance during the danger years by their temporising academic colleagues.*

Troubled times summon historians to join the fray. For Churchill, of course, history writing and history making were indivisible; the one informing the other. Far from his polemical journalism and brilliant television lectures compromising the scholarship of his work, A. J. P. Taylor saw them as the indispensable medium for making history count in contemporary political debate.

So historians have nothing to apologise for if they sound off in the maddened arena of contemporary politics or the whiplash tweet replaces argument with exclamation. If a president airily mouths a slogan like 'America First', or politicians and populist newspapers stigmatise opposition as enemies of 'The Will of the People', they need to be reminded that the first slogan was paraded by American admirers of the Third Reich and the second (coined by Jean-Jacques Rousseau) was used to legitimise the punitive tyranny of the Jacobins. It turns out, then, that our future has never more urgently needed the voice of those who, in less interesting times, might settle for communing with distant ghosts.

LIBERALISM, POPULISM AND
THE FATE OF THE WORLD

The Leslie Stephen Lecture, Cambridge, 2018

I first became an enthusiast for history more than half a century ago, when in our dim and dusty classroom at the wrong end of Hampstead – Cricklewood, in fact – we seemed to be getting instruction not just about the Enlightenment but directly from it. This was because our teacher bore an uncanny facial resemblance to Voltaire, or at least to the smiling face of the *philosophe* as modelled by the sculptor Houdon. That famous smile – repeated in almost every subsequent image of Voltaire – could be read in different, not necessarily irreconcilable ways: as the countenance of the black mirth of the author of *Candide*, chuckling at the cruelties and follies of mankind. But it could also be seen in a more benign light as the expression of someone convinced (as indeed, on his better days, Voltaire was) that stupidity might eventually yield to instruction. Humane reason, forcefully pressed, would get the better of animal brutality and theological fairy tales. This upbeat version of modern history was recited to us by our own Voltaire look-alike, who well knew that once we thirteen-year-olds had seen those pyramids of human bones bulldozed into limepits at Belsen, we would never get them out of our head. Nonetheless he turned to us one rainy afternoon in 1958 and declared, 'Well, boys, we don't really know what the future has in store but you can at least be sure of this: nationalism and organised religion are dead as dodos.'

So much for the prophetic powers of historians. But at the time there was good reason for this breezy confidence. Atavistic nationalism did indeed seem to have burnt itself out in the monstrous carnage of the Second World War. Works like the many books of Hans Kohn devoted to the sources and magnetic power of nationalism seemed virtually antiquarian. (How wrong we were about that and indeed about Kohn himself, a fascinatingly complex figure.) Henceforth conflict, even when frighteningly pushed to the edge of nuclear annihilation, would be driven by the collision of mass ideologies. Europe, for centuries the theatre of atrocious wars between nation states, lay shattered. Ancient enemies across the Rhine were, with the help of the Marshall Plan, piecing it back co-operatively. The expansion of Stalinist totalitarianism had been checked and, west of the Iron Curtain at any rate, liberal democracy and prosperity seemed to be mutually sustaining.

In short, history seemed to be going our way, and in 1963 when I arrived at Cambridge to study it, reasons to be cheerful or at least hopeful multiplied. In the brand-new Harvey Court one night in 1964, my friends and I watched as two political upheavals unfolded simultaneously, both we thought for the better: the sudden end of Nikita Khrushchev's rule in the Soviet Union (we were naive about what might follow) and the replacement of Conservative governments (which had been in power since my early childhood) with white-heat Wilson's Labour: a double dose of political euphoria.

It's become a commonplace lately to chuckle retrospectively at that complacency and to characterise the onward and upward trajectory of democratic liberalism as some sort of mirage. I don't happen to think that's true – three-quarters of a century without a major European war (the horror of Bosnia aside); the peaceful unification of Germany; and astonishing economic and social transformation are not to be written off as so much Panglossian wishful thinking. But that's not my immediate point – not yet anyway. Rather, it's about the appeal of historical study at that moment of 1960s optimism. Was its job to track the long, problematic, tortuous journey to the contemporary world with the historian as an unapologetically opinionated protagonist, or was that approach hobbled by what its opponents called 'presentism': a reading of the past reduced to the genealogy of now; the historian, a political scientist of the dead? Or, was its explanatory power based on something like the opposite assumption: the past as foreign country and the historian more like an ethnographer of parts and peoples unknown? The pure intellectual force and poetic power of the *Annales* school, driven by this more anthropologically determined methodology, settled the matter for many of us. Our history was to be social rather than political; it would be either micro (indeed nano) or macro, parasailing over epochs or parsing a single week in a single year in a single village; it would at any rate not deal in the medium term that was the standard measuring scale of political causes and effects. To the extent that history's field of play was the picayune comings and goings of parties and treaties, manifestos, wars and revolutions, it exposed itself as incurious. To be a partisan in the archive was shallow vulgarity.

This nose-holding continued despite the fact that J. H. Plumb would often remind us at Christ's that the discipline was inescapably civic; that it had all begun, as he put it, with 'Herodotus shouting in the marketplace'. The quality of Thucydides' history was hardly compromised, either by his having been a particpant in the epic he narrated and still less by his moral intensity. For that matter, Macaulay may well have been guilty of the otiose self-congratulation of his class and time but, considering the alternatives – let us call absolutism by its name – the epic he had traced of the rise of liberty and the defeat of despotism was something more than the self-serving fairy tale of the Whigs. Plumb also reminded us that some of the social and cultural historians we most passionately admired had made no distinction between intellectual craft and the duties of citizenship in free and even more in unfree societies. Some indeed had paid a terrible price for that conviction: Marc Bloch had been shot by the Gestapo; Emmanuel Ringelblum had perished in the 1943 uprising of the Warsaw ghetto; Johan Huzinga was ostracised by his own department at Leiden University and placed under house arrest during the German occupation; Benedetto Croce, who had turned from one of the bewitched to one of the adamant foes of fascism, perhaps had been right in his most famous nostrum: 'all history is contemporary history'.

Or so it seems to me now, more than ever, a profession of moral obligation as much as dispassionate investigation, hence the unpalatably sententious title of this lecture, unbecoming as many of you might think for a history professor who should better content himself with the causes and consequences of discrete phenomena, to which I can only say that there are times, and this is one of them, that try our vocation, the very norms of scholarly integrity – what is true and what false; what is fact and what myth; what is history and what propaganda – and ask something of us beyond the routine conventions of academic life. Pass the port and let the dogs of unreason bark their falsehoods; let Professor Trump lecture us on the career of Robert E. Lee; let Vladimir Putin criminalise any mention of Katyn Forest; let the le Pens demote the Holocaust to a footnote of history; let the Milorad Dodik, the current contender to be president of the Bosnian Serb republic of Srbska, claim that the Srebrenica massacre barely happened; let Nigel Farage claim in front of an Irish audience that Brexit is the equivalent of the Easter Rising. Yesterday the Brexiteer Daniel Hannan published an absurdly one-sided account of the result of the Battle of Hastings in which an innocently free and equal Saxon England was extinguished beneath the feudal jackboot of the Normans. Like it or not, from one end of the world to the other, history has become the fulcrum on which power turns. Perhaps it has always been that way; the question is, what do we do about it? In answer to which I call, as witness, one Leslie Stephen.

Stephen was thirty when he shook the hand of Abraham Lincoln. It was mid-September 1863. Trying to take Chattanooga from the Confederates, the Grand Army of the Union led by General William Rosecrans was about to mount an all-out offensive near the creek of Chickamauga in Georgia, a move that could culminate in catastrophic failure; actually a disaster for both armies, nearly 40,000 dead. Only Gettysburg was bloodier. Two days before the battle, Secretary of State William Seward brought Leslie Stephen to see the beleaguered president. Stephen described Lincoln in a letter to his mother as 'old Abe' (he was in fact fifty-four), 'tall and bony' and 'rather awkward', but 'more like a gentleman to look at than I should have given credit from pictures, with a particularly pleasant smile and a hearty laugh'. Lincoln could spare Stephen just half an hour prior to a Cabinet meeting, but the moment and everything Stephen had encountered in the American war radically changed his life. 'I took kindly to him,' he added, and well he might.

Before this momentous trip to America in 1863, the year of Gettysburg and Vicksburg, Leslie Stephen, the Trinity Hall don and ordained cleric, had come to the point of not really knowing what to do with his life. He was more sure of what he didn't want to do. He didn't want to follow in the footsteps of his father James Stephen, the under-secretary for the colonies, who worked so feverishly at his post that he became known as Over-Secretary Stephen and who briefly in the early 1850s had occupied the Regius chair of history, lecturing on French history. Leslie had taught maths at Trinity Hall for the best part of a decade, but was better known as a long-distance runner and marathon walker: the personification of 'muscular Christianity'. But in 1859 he read *The Origin of Species* and he began to harbour doubts about Noah's

Flood. His friend and fellow Trinity Hall mathematician Henry Fawcett, blinded in a shooting accident a year earlier, had become one of Darwin's most eloquent champions, a thorn in the side of soapy Sam Wilberforce, and in 1861 Stephen informed the master of the college that he could no longer in good conscience attend chapel, at which point he was asked to resign his tutorship, lest he corrupt the impressionable young with his scepticism.

What was he to do? Where was he to go? His father had wanted the unexceptional life of a clergyman for his son but this was now out of the question; and Leslie completed his divorce from Trinity Hall by resigning his fellowship in 1862. There was the law, but his younger brother Fitzjames was already the obligatory barrister in the family. However, all these personal issues were set aside to pay attention to the one moral cause, which had become paramount on both sides of the ocean and, as a Stephen, Leslie could hardly avoid: slavery. The Stephens like the Macaulays were Clapham Sect Evangelicals and waging war against the abomination of slavery had been their mission since the late eighteenth century, shoulder to shoulder with the other Wilberforce, Granville Sharp and the Clarkson brothers. At the Colonial Office it had fallen to James Stephen to draft the sixty-six sections of the draft bill abolishing slavery itself, which the over-secretary, with more than even his usual shot of zeal, duly completed between a Saturday and a Monday in 1834.

So when the expansion or containment of slavery became the critical issue threatening the destruction of the American Republic, Leslie Stephen was bound to become absorbed in the issue. Once hostilities began in 1861 with Britain declaring itself neutral, the matter became still more pressing for Stephen because much of Cambridge, like the majority of the governing and landed classes in mid-Victorian Britain, were unapologetic and very vocal supporters of the Confederacy. In his biography of Stephen, the great Cambridge medievalist F. W. Maitland reports his pupils at Trinity Hall goading him by boasting of their sympathies with the south. The exceptions were northern radicals, John Bright in particular, and the Lancashire cotton workers who were the most immediate economic victims of the supply 'famine'. But while ostensibly neutral, the government of Palmerston and Lord John Russell was south-sympathising and, most shockingly for Stephen, so was the selectively ethical William Ewart Gladstone, whose family fortune had been made in the slaving Caribbean.

What most offended Stephen was the insistence on the part of all those British friends of the Confederacy – then as now among the Stars and Bars wavers – that slavery and race were incidental as the principal *casus bello*. What it was really about, they claimed (and still do), was states' rights, which was a fight for Liberty comparable to the revolution that had created America in the first place. (This in spite of Article IV section 3 of the Confederate Constitution explicitly recognising the sacrosanct character of the institution of slavery.)

Stephen smelled rank hypocrisy in British protestations: a grossly material concern on the part of the rich and powerful, both the landed and manufacturing classes, fraudulently wrapping themselves in the rhetoric of liberalism. He almost certainly had noted that in 1860, both in the president's inaugural address that went out of its way to reassure slave owners that the federal government was not committed to abolition, only to precluding the expansion of slave states in new territories, and in his subsequent statements, Lincoln had shown himself to be an abolitionist zealot. Even when Stephen learned of the Emancipation Proclamation drafted in 1862 he thought it motivated more by a strategic desire to destroy the economy of the south than any tender-hearted moralism. The final proclamation had been issued in January 1863, and without at that stage knowing much of American history or literature (he would become a great champion of both, even writing the first study of 'American Humour'), Stephen set sail (as the battle of Vicksburg was raging in the summer of 1863) on what we would now call a fact-finding mission.

There was something almost comically earnest about this – like Tolstoy's Pierre Bezukhov showing up on the eve of the battle of Borodino in a white topper and getting a flea in his ear from his friend Prince Andrei to the effect that war was all about mutual murder and be off with you. Tolstoy would have understood Leslie Stephen's American odyssey perfectly. Predictably it began with the liberal great and good in Boston and Cambridge, Massachusetts, where he met James Russell Lowell the poet, Charles Eliot Norton, who would define the study of the humanities at Harvard, Henry Wadsworth Longfellow and the militant veteran warriors for abolition, Wendell Phillips and William Lloyd Garrison. Stephen wrote letters back to his mother, which, once she had digested the contents, were to be sent along to Henry Fawcett to be read out loud to the blind professor of political economy. One of those letters described a regiment of black Union soldiers, which could, I think, only have been the famous Massachusetts 54th Infantry commanded by Captain Robert Gould Shaw, being cheered through the streets of Boston on its departure. Stephen also told the story of the officer (again most likely Shaw) who in view of Jefferson Davis's vow to hang any white officer leading black troops, asked his mother whether she was content that he so serve. The reply, Stephen recorded, was that she would be even prouder of her son than if he was shot in battle, which I guess is one kind of motherly love.

The more he travelled, spending nights on trains and steamboats, and one night bivouacking with the troops of General Meade, the victor of Gettysburg, the more preposterous it seemed to Stephen that anyone could imagine that conflict was not, in fact, altogether about the great enormity of slavery.

So he was touched by the cordiality with which he was welcomed (especially as a friend and political ally of John Bright, whose letter of recommendation opened doors for him including that of the White House), since for the most part Britain was a dirty word. Before long it became apparent why: *The Times*, under its editor John Thaddeus Delane, was publishing a stream of reports by his star war correspondent, the internationally famous William Howard Russell, stories that were not only outrageously pro-Confederate but contemptuous of any real possibility that the Union would ever succeed in prevailing over the south. Even when General Sherman began his march on Georgia to the sea, Russell compared it to Napoleon's hubris in Russia. It was doctored news (if not actually fake) tailored to reinforce the anti-Yankee prejudices of the readers of *The Times* and coloured by undisguised gloating at the crash of the upstart American democratic experiment. A permanently divided America was a lot easier for the British Empire to swallow.

On returning to Britain, Stephen was determined to set this piece of history to rights and it was the making of his vocation as a radical liberal. In 1865, he published a thirty-page polemical pamphlet titled *The Times on the Civil War*, unsparingly recording its wilful, possibly knowing, perversions of the truth, its unprincipled evasion of the great issue of slavery and freedom – self-evidently, whatever Confederate apologists claimed, the reason for the death of more than half a million souls. The claim that secession should be understood as an act of liberal struggle was itself an act of moral infamy. Moreover, Stephen understood that in Britain, taking the part of the south was indivisibly linked to a gathering fear of democracy at home, in particular the resistance building to a second Parliamentary Reform Act.

If I've tested your patience with this long story I've done so not just because it was the turning of a don's life into a political life but also because it seems to me emblematic of many of the challenges to contemporary liberal democracy in which the integrity of history is necessarily implicated and calls for historians to defend it. Living in the United States and teaching at a university in which one of my most distinguished predecessors, Richard Hofstadter, specialised in what he called 'the paranoid strain' in American politics, I suppose I'm less embarrassed about this than I should be. But who else is to engage with the distortion of empirically documented truth; the exposure of race hatred beneath disingenuous rhetoric of libertarian self-government and states' rights; the equation of individual rights with self-armament; and more generally the demonisation of the project of knowledge itself as an 'elite' activity – if not us?

The late nineteenth-century American political movement that first called itself the People's Party, and in short order became known as Populist in some respects, was the diametric opposite of Donald Trump's assortment of ex-Goldman Sachs executives and Carl Icahn protégés, since it arose in the rural south and Midwest from a deep suspicion of eastern bankers' designs to de-monetise silver and replace it with the gold standard – hence the force of its most charismatic leader William Jennings Bryan's electrifying 1898 convention speech to the Democrats: 'They shall not crucify you on a cross of gold.' But, culturally, populism came to embrace characteristics you'll recognise as haunting us now: a mistrust of metropolitan life; a hatred of mass immigration (even though so many of its own adherents had come from immigrant stock themselves; which Americans had not?), itself an inheritance from the Know-Nothings of the 1850s; a devotion to scripture over science; revelation rather than reason. Bryan famously prosecuted the case against a Tennessee schoolteacher who had had the temerity to teach evolution to his pupils. (About half the present American population believe that evolution is no more than an unproven theory.) Tom Watson, the first and fieriest of populist leaders, opened his campaigns by forging an alliance between both black and white rural poor. But in the first decades of the twentieth century his political rhetoric turned venomously anti-Semitic and anti-black. The years 1915 and 1916 saw, inter alia: the refounding of the Ku Klux Klan; the screening of D. W. Griffiths' paean to the Klan, *The Birth of a Nation*, with its grotesque caricature of goggle-eyed, jumped-up negro Reconstructionists; the lynching in Georgia of Leo Frank, the Jewish factory manager convicted, but innocent, of murdering a Catholic girl worker by a crowd responding to Watson's incitement; the publication of Madison Grant's *The Passing of the Great Race* – the most vitriolic anti-immigrant treatise arguing that mass immigration (especially by Jews) was bringing crime, disease, political violence and religious contamination to America and beginning the irreversible decline of its 'civilisation'. The corollary was that the 'true, civilised America' was in danger of eclipse at the hands of invasive aliens, an unholy combination of big-city money men; lice-ridden non-English-speaking migrants and – as always – those eternal cosmopolitans, the Jews. (Nigel Farage has just warned America it should be more worried about what he calls the 'Jewish lobby' than any Russian interference in its elections.)

When I first learned about those populists – in Cambridge in the 1960s, taught by my Jewish American history supervisor Jonathan Steinberg – they seemed an anachronistic relic, along with the authoritarian xenophobes who had strutted through Europe in the 1930s. Not just the Nazi Brownshirts but Italian fascist Blackshirts and other European legions that swiftly pushed democratic liberalism aside to embrace the doctrines of national purity, violent militias and charismatic dictators claiming to represent the will of the people – Mussolini's fascists of course but also Ionescu's Romanian Iron Guards, or Engelbert Dollfuss's Fatherland Front in Austria, which outlawed all political parties other than itself. But whereas the defeat of the Third Reich had apparently flushed those toxins from the European bloodstream, in America they continued to mutate generation after generation. In a weirdly paradoxical way, the very innovativeness of American life, far from seeing off the feverish mythologies and demonologies, actually refreshed them as responses to every wave of new technology. If you were Henry Ford you could be at one and the same time a great innovator and an even greater anti-Semite, the acknowledged inspiration of Adolf Hitler. This may not be as paradoxiçal as it seems. Ford's obsession after all was with uniformity, both of automobiles and those who made them on his production line, the ethnic pot fully melted into his version of all-American ethnic wholesomeness. The very latest media could at one and the same time be trigger and weapon for your successful ethno-xenophobe. Hitler had Leni Riefenstahl's cinematically choreographed battalions of muscle; the anti-Semitic Father Coughlin was the first of the manic wireless shock jocks; Huey Long dressed his personal militia in the standard boot and brownshirt populo-fascist kit. They were in the end all thwarted in their presidential ambitions, but it was a closer thing than you could imagine. And in some sense, long-term, they succeded, for their violent anti-immigrant paranoia (inherited from the first generation of populists) shut the doors against Jews in desperate need of asylum from those who threatened and then executed their annihilation. *Kindertransport* aside (and remember that was conditional on children being taken from their parents), the same was true in Britain. 'Hurrah for the Blackshirts' shouted the front page of the *Daily Mail* in 1938, the year of Kristallnacht and the Anschluss. None of this ended with the war. Much of the rhetoric of McCarthyism presupposed a covert invasion of America by communists who by definition were not American and a disproportionate number of Jews. In the 1960s, George Wallace noted that in the forefront of those who were betraying the white race by attacking segregation and Jim Crow were Jews. And Wallace – who made his own run for the presidency of course – articulated more clearly than anyone the populist creed that nation and a rough and ready sense of popular sovereignty trumped any sort of constitutional restraint. 'There is one thing more powerful than the constitution,' he declared, 'and that is the will of the people.' ('If people choose to abolish the constitution it is their right . . .'). Today, opinion polls show an astonishingly high percentage of Republican voters prepared to suspend constitutional protections if the president (that is to say *their* president) deemed it necessary.

So, fellow historians, it's one of those Leslie Stephen in the White House moments; time to strap on the buckler and shield. The notion that the fundamentals of liberal democracy are not under assault in the name of Will of the People, that all this is just so much snowflake panic, whiffs a bit of Weimar, does it not? Especially when we are unequivocally told by Viktor Orban that liberal democracy has had its day and is about to be (or already has been) replaced by an illiberal democracy prepared to sacrifice the traditional constraints of liberal institutions to the higher needs of the national popular will. Those who take another view are to be regarded not just as opponents but traitors. Orban is right in one respect: illiberalism is in the driver's seat from the Philippines to Brazil. List the places that were once functioning free democracies and have turned authoritarian and you quickly run out of fingers: Turkey, Venezuela, Nicaragua, Poland (there is a sinister book by a Polish historian equating liberalism, or rather what he calls 'liberal imperialism', with communism).

Liberal democracy isn't just some sort of vague feel-good state of mind that comes with a subscription to *The Guardian* or the *Washington Post*. It rests on specific bedrock principles and practices, all of which have been fought for at great cost and sacrifice over the centuries: the independence of the judiciary and the truism that no political power is above the rule of law; the prohibition of detention without showing due cause; the obligation to treat all citizens equally under the law; freedom of conscience, speech, publication and assembly; the presupposition that laws are made by freely elected legislatures; the integrity of electoral votes; the peaceful alternation of opposed governments. Virtually all of those irreducible characteristics of a liberal democratic

state are now under siege; have been threatened however blus-
teringly and incoherently by President Trump and actually done
away with from China to Saudi Arabia. And it seems to me that
Trump's indifference to those violations, in fact his admiration
for authoritarian regimes, has made leaders more shameless in
their contempt for democratic restraints on dictatorship. So that
the most likely winner of the presidency of Brazil in two weeks,
Jair Bolsonaro, is quite open in expressing his preference for dictatorship over democracy.

A quick run through the fracking of those democratic bed-
rocks makes the success of creeping Putinism depressingly clear.
Despite widespread popular protests, the independence of the
judiciary has been fatally compromised in Poland by the Law
and Justice Government (a wonderful Orwellian inversion of
descriptive language) and in Hungary, whereas in Russia the
essential requirement is political loyalty rather than misguided
independence and where, featured on campaign posters at bus
stops and railway stations, is the face of the cosmopolitan enemy,
the eternal Jew, George Soros, who will stop at nothing – witness
his founding and endowment of a *university* – that purveyor of
treason in the guise of knowledge. Donald Trump has made
no secret of the fact that absolute and unconditional loyalty is
what he expects of his own Department of Justice, and its capacity to conduct an impartial investigation into Russian collusion
during the 2016 presidential election will undoubtedly be tested
should the Democrats fail to win back their majority in the House
of Representatives. A critical factor in the nomination of Brett
Kavanaugh for the Supreme Court was the expansive view he
takes of presidential power and its immunity from prosecution
or even investigation.

Then there is the integrity of elections. Possible collusion aside,
there is no longer any question that Russian hacking and voter
targeting in both the election campaign of 2016 and almost certainly the Brexit referendum of the same year likely affected the

outcome of both processes. The gerrymandering of redistricting in the United States (a long-established practice by both parties, it is true) has reached outrageous proportions with the control of a majority of State houses by the Republicans. State power – in the hands of lieutenant-governors – has been deployed in all sorts of inventive ways to depress turn-out, especially in districts with a high percentage of minorities – from naked purges of the electoral rolls (especially brazen in states like Indiana, Georgia and North Carolina); restricting voting hours and polling stations; depriving voters of early voting; insisting on photo IDs in districts where Hispanics in particular don't invariably possess driving licences and go to work in car or truck pools. This is to say nothing, of course, of the Niagara of money pouring into PACs since the Supreme Court ruled that restricting the flow was an unconstitutional abridgement of the First Amendment.

Even after the votes are in, the sanctity of elections can be compromised by completely groundless accusations of voter fraud. One of the most startling moments in Trump's 2016 campaign (which is saying something) was his refusal of an unconditional acceptance of the result should his opponent win. If the Democrats succeed in flipping the House (by no means a certainty or perhaps at this stage even a probability), it's a sure bet that Trump will demand an investigation into fraud and 'irregularities'.

Then there is the demonisation of opposition as by definition quasi or wholly treasonous, a conspiracy funded by malevolent foreigners (naturally George Soros, who has had American citizenship for over half a century, has been accused of engineering the protests against the confirmation of Brett Kavanaugh to the Supreme Court) and much else besides. You could hear such accusations daily on hard-right talk radio in America decades ago; and of course it's the standard modus operandi of authoritarians like Vladimir Putin and Recip Erdoğan. A genuine sign that quasi-fascist politics are replacing democratic contestation is a preference for rallies over debates where rapture can be orchestrated, the press threatened (often physically), and where the Dear Leader leads the chants of 'Lock Her Up' – the Trumpian remix of '*Sieg Heil*'. The fuel of these staged exercises in mass hysteria and verbal violence is the energy fascism exploited to great effect in the 1930s – the glee, the pure adrenaline rush of punitive hatred. The more horrified liberals become at these kind of antics the greater the surge of that hatred, juiced as it is by personal verbal abuse of the kind Trump has imported from reality TV and shock-jock radio. Plaintively during the primaries the relatively sedate Jeb Bush said to Trump, 'Oh, so you're going to insult your way to the presidency, is that it?' Trump merely emerged from behind his lectern, and smirked.

Leading the perp walk in any authoritarian system of course is the free press itself. Trump has made no secret of wanting to reform the libel laws to make it harder for that press to say disagreeable things about him, but in the age of short attention span he has already succeeded in stigmatising factual reporting as fake news. The only media exempt from the charge are those that hang on his every word in slavish adulation; not just Fox News but also the enormous Sinclair Broadcasting Corp with 173 stations in eighty-one markets, which instructs its news anchors to parrot the White House Line. Together, Fox and Sinclair have pretty much created state broadcasting in the United States.

The great casualty of the attrition of an independent critical press is of course the status of truth; the factual knowledge project that, in the end, was the alpha and omega of the Enlightenment. Every appeal to free expression as a mighty defence against tyranny – from Milton's *Areopagitica* ('Though all the winds of doctrine were let loose to play upon the earth, so Truth be in the field, we do injuriously by licensing and prohibiting to midoubt her strength. Let her and Falsehood grapple; who ever knew Truth put to the Worse in a free and open encounter?') or Jefferson's draft statute on 'Religious Toleration for Virginia' ('Truth is great and will prevail if left to herself'). But then Milton and Jefferson could not have foreseen Twitter. Hannah Arendt on the other hand, in her 1951 *Origins of Totalitarianism*, did:

> In an ever changing incomprehensible world the masses had reached the point where they would at the same time believe everything and nothing, think that everything was possible and nothing was true. Totalitarian leaders based their propaganda on the correct assumption that one could make believe the most fantastic statements one day and trust that if the next day they were given irrefutable proof of their falsehood they would take refuge in cynicism; instead of deserting the leaders who lied to them they would protest they had known all along that the statement was a lie and admire the leaders for their superior tactical cleverness.

The greatest damage to a governance resting on truth is perhaps not even the willingness of the cult worshippers to believe anything they're told but the refusal of the members of Trump's own party to contradict him. Thus not only could he claim that he and Republicans were the protectors of Medicare from Democrat assaults on the system, when the opposite is true, but he bet correctly that his own party would embrace the lie; the categorical reverse of the truth as a campaign tactic. The consequences of this debasement are profoundly Faustian. Despotism does indeed depend on political actors willing to overlook falsehood, and the demonisation or criminalisation of truth tellers, for the sake of gaining or retaining power.

The biggest lie of all, of course, the one with the most potential to corrupt, erode or destroy the norms of liberal democracy, is the one about race and immigration; the relationship you might say between nature and nation. Trump launched his campaign with two immense lies: that the rate of crime among Hispanic immigrants was monstrously higher than the white population – the cry against Mexican rapists and murderers – when in fact it is demonstrably statistically lower, as it has been with almost all immigrant populations striving for some sort of social stability and upward mobility. Most homicides, he insisted, were committed by blacks on whites, when this too was demonstrably false. But it served to stoke the fear and paranoia that are the battery charge of this kind of politics, and since then race paranoia has been the great engine of his success, just as appeals to the ethnic homogeneity of nations – from Indian Assam and Buddhist Myanmar to Benjamin Netanyahu's Nation state statute (infamous to this passionate Zionist) – have been dependable rabble-rousers. Donald Trump's entree into politics was as the champion of 'birtherism' – the belief that Barack Obama could not possibly have been born in the United States; that he was most likely a Kenyan Muslim disguised as an American. Even when confronted with an unimpeachable birth certificate, Trump's default position was that it must have been a fake. It was simply not natural for an African American to occupy the White House. Similarly, the DNA evidence produced to exonerate the five African Americans originally convicted for the horrific rape and murder of a jogger in Central Park did nothing to shake his belief in their guilt.

The radical narrowing of who is *naturally* a citizen (it's always struck me as telling that the process by which immigrants become citizens in the United States is called *naturalisation*) has of course been taking place all over the world: Muslims in Assam deprived of Indian citizenship; the Rohingya in Myanmar ethnically cleansed; Jews in France unable to wear a skull cap in public; Israeli Arabs told, in contradiction to Israel's original Declaration of Independence, that their state is essentially meant for Jews only; declarations that it is impossible to be a Bavarian Muslim; crosses nailed to the wall in every government office of that state; minarets banned in Switzerland; Hungarian and Austrian prime ministers claiming they are in the front lines of protecting Christian Europe from an Islamic invasion.

Arguably, though, the effect of this urge to ethnic homogeneity (quixotic though it will ultimately be) is most profoundly damaging in the United States because from Crèvecœur at the end of the eighteenth century to Horace Kallen in the early twentieth, and on to JFK's (ghostwritten) *A Nation of Immigrants*, the historical grandeur of the United States lays precisely in its indifference to geographical origin, language, religion, ethnicity: all that was required for that naturalisation was acceptance of a set of political principles – those, indeed, of liberal democracy enshrined in the Constitution.

But heterogeneity, cosmopolitanism, it turns out, is most easily embraced by intercontinental historical winners: the great metropolises – Sydney, New York, Manchester, Chicago, London. Its obverse, a state of grievance, is fed by a sense of loss, and dispossession; and the aching romance of defeat – those wounds that kept open and bleeding: the 'Lost Cause' of the south; Kosovo, Dunkirk. Also, of course, the greater loss of empire: British India; French north Africa, the Soviet empire; the post-dynastic miniaturisation of Hungary and Austria. Much of the friction in racially and religiously mixed societies comes from imperial blowback: the migration of ex-colonial subject populations to the metropolitan centre. Migrants desperate to reach Italy come from territories – Libya, Somalia, Eritrea – which we sometimes forget were part of the Italian empire. It was from an exaggerated, in fact wholly unrealistic, belief that imperial cultures – Marshal Lyautey's *mission civilisatrice* in the Mahgreb for instance – had struck deep roots in colonised societies that for a while it was assumed immigrants from those former colonies could be unproblematically assimilated into the metropolitan homeland.

Look at our world now – with the eyes of a long-lens historian – and it's a truism that we are beset with three immense problems: the slow degradation if not slow death of our planetary habitat; the drastic inequalities of subsistence between the developed and undeveloped world; and not least the great gulf between those who wish only to live with people who look, sound, dress,

speak and pray (if they do at all) like themselves, and those who
are happy to live alongside people who aren't. In fact, all these
conditions are functionally linked. Climate change has destroyed
entire ecosystems, radicalising its casualties – long years of
drought did that in the upper Jordan basin sending migrants
into Syrian cities that couldn't find work for them and ending as
recruits for both sides in the most terrible of contemporary civil
wars; famines in sub-tropical Africa have created the multitudes
of desperate people setting off for Libya and calamity; the same
is true of Central America and the tragic odyssey north. And
eventually – this I suppose is the good or at least not apocalyptic
news – all the walls, fences and moats in the world will not be
capable of dealing with the deep roots of the disaster and the vast
waves of transhumance it has generated.

But in the meantime, what do we do about embattled liberal
democracy? The challenge is all the more difficult because the
world wide web turns out not to further world wide truth and
transparency but instead has been a perfect nesting place for
communities of self-reinforcing myths, lies and conspiratorial
fantasies. And that in turn points to two different directions
on which democracy might stand its ground. The first, already
mobilised in the United States, is identity politics, known in an
even unlovelier phrase as 'intersectionality' – a constellation of
linked constituencies each concerned in the first place with the
defence of their own group, and making strategic alliance with
equally threatened or disadvantaged groups. But then there is –
and no prizes awarded here for guessing where I want to plant
my flag – the unapologetic reawakening of universal ideals of
democratic freedom, and justice – those after all were the same
values blazoned on the battle flags of Mandela, Gandhi, Martin
Luther King – and for that matter and for all their manifold shortcomings, Milton, Locke, Voltaire and John Stuart Mill. Their
history has, it sems to me, its own epic; why should the legions of
the aggrieved, the defeat cultists, the martinets of ethnic purity,

have all the best stories when in fact they don't? But that history, our history, needs to be rhetorically re-armed — and not just in the halls of academe, not just in books, but the places where most people get their stories. Out of the ivory tower then, my friends, and into battle, for this fight is not for the faint-hearted; but it is — as I venture to presume — one that Leslie Stephen, whose life was changed by a handshake with old Abe, would sign up for. What, after all, is the alternative — the resignation of the quietly right-minded? No, up and at it. *Écrasez l'infâme.* And soon, while we're at it, lest it be too late.

MID-TERM TRUMP

Ten days before the mid-term elections in America, murder came to the Tree of Life. Shouting, 'All Jews need to die,' a neo-Nazi gunman with an animus against the Hebrew Immigrant Aid Society slaughtered eleven Jews gathered at their synagogue in Squirrel Hill, Pittsburgh. Two days earlier, pipe bombs had been sent to fourteen critics of Donald Trump by a man who had turned his van into a rust-bucket shrine to MAGA and its great apostle. One day previously, Gregory Bush, thwarted in his attempt to enter a black church in Louisville, Kentucky, had shot and killed two African Americans at a local supermarket. Before he was arrested, he shouted, 'Whites don't kill whites.' All three perpetrators believed they were engaged in saving white America.

This onslaught of actual and attempted killing, along with Trump's unanticipated revelation that he would like to abolish birthright citizenship for the children of undocumented immigrants, has decisively changed the character of what was in any case a mid-term election like few others. At the last post it has come down to a conflict between two mutually hostile visions of national identity. Battles like this are presently raging worldwide, from the removal of Indian citizenship from Muslims in Assam to the Brexit debate over just what it means to be British. But because the US has historically been seen, generation after generation, by those who have dreamt of getting there as the immigrant haven par excellence, this battle between a heterogeneous and a homogeneous patriotism has been engaged with unforgiving intensity.

It can all be summed up in two contrasting scenes from contemporary American life. On the one hand there is Squirrel Hill, where the Tree of Life synagogue sits between two Protestant churches; where a Palestinian street food truck sells falafel outside the orthodox Jewish Shaare Torah synagogue; where Irish and Italian Catholic families share the neighbourhood with Asians and African Americans; and where Taylor Allderdice High School has been one of the most integrated institutions in the city.

Like many other Jewish organisations in the US and around the world, HIAS – which began its career helping to resettle destitute Jewish immigrants fleeing pogroms in the 1880s, and went on to assist Soviet Jews making the same odyssey – has helped resettle asylum seekers, overwhelmingly Muslim, from war zones in the Middle East and elsewhere. This has been deemed a *mitzvah*, a duty.

But for Robert Bowers, as he prepared to point his AR-15 at elderly worshippers, this was, as he put it, 'sugar-coated evil'; 'genocide'; participation in an 'invasion' bent on slaughtering 'my people'. As far as he was concerned, Trump, with a Jewish son-in-law and converted daughter, was in thrall to the 'kikes'. But Bowers's poisoned beliefs were nonetheless the fruit of accusations about Jewish complicity in immigration. From the phobic obsession with George Soros, who has replaced Hillary Clinton as the object of punishment chants at Trump rallies, it has been a natural progression to blame Jews generally for the racial adulteration of America.

Soros is regularly described, not just in alt-right ravings but on Fox News media, in terms out of the classic literature of nineteenth- and twentieth-century anti-Semitism: the secret manipulator of money and men, plotting the destruction of Christian civilisation. In Connecticut, a Republican candidate

for congress, Ed Charamut, sent out a mailer with the face of his
Jewish opponent on it, a crazed look in his eyes, hands stuffed
full of dollar bills.

In particular, Soros has been described as the financier and
mobiliser of the immigrant caravan moving north through
Central America. When asked whether he believed Soros was
behind it all, Trump replied, 'I wouldn't be surprised.' So the
scene that might be pictured as the symbolic opposite of Squirrel
Hill would be trucks full of troops being sent to the Mexican
border to repel the 'invaders'.

Setting aside, for a moment, the comically gratuitous mobilisa-
tion of up to 15,000 soldiers to face a sad procession of families,
many of them mothers and children, fleeing terror and violence
in Honduras, almost 1,000 miles away from the border and rap-
idly dwindling in number, the gesture is controversial since the
Posse Comitatus Act of 1878 disbars regular troops from any
kind of domestic police action. Even Fox News anchor (albeit a
rogue for the facts) Shep Smith felt it necessary to say straight out
that the 'invasion is coming' panic along with the troop movement was a crude pre-election stunt. 'There is no invasion,' he
calmly declared; 'there is nothing at all to worry about . . . we're
America, we can handle it.'

The contest between two definitions of American nationhood – one embracing immigration, and one insisting on white,
principally Protestant homogeneity – has been a constant in
the history of the US. The Know-Nothings of the 1850s based
their party on animosity towards Irish and Italian Catholics.
The charismatic leader of the Populists of the late nineteenth
and early twentieth centuries, Tom Watson, began his career by
attacking eastern bankers and the gold standard in the name of
the rural poor, both black and white. But by the second decade
of the twentieth century, Watson had turned anti-negro and
bitterly anti-Semitic. It was his animus against the Jews that, in
1915, encouraged a mob to lynch Leo Frank, wrongly convicted

of murdering an Irish girl, Mary Phagan, at the Atlanta factory where he was foreman.

That same year, 1915, was another climactic moment in the battle for American identity. D. W. Griffith's cinematically inventive but historically grotesque *The Birth of a Nation*, with its caricatures of goggle-eyed blacks polluting white America in the Reconstruction years, was the overture for the refounding of the Ku Klux Klan on Stone Mountain near Atlanta.

Meanwhile two publications encapsulated anti- and pro-immigrant visions of American nationhood. Madison Grant's *The Passing of the Great Race* was an elegy for racially pure America steadily contaminated by diseased, criminal hordes swarming off the boats. The other was an article published in *The Nation* by the philosopher Horace Kallen: 'Democracy versus the Melting Pot'. His essay coined the term 'cultural pluralism' and argued against a cookie-cutter version of American identity. Instead of uniformity, Kallen argued that American exceptionalism lay in its capacity to reconcile patriotism with the preservation, not the erasure, of cultural identity.

Trump is betting that a majority of voters disagree with Kallen. Startling even to his own party, he has, at the last minute, sought to capitalise on white grievance by raising the possibility of depriving the children of undocumented immigrants of their 'citizens' birthright' under the provisions of the Fourteenth Amendment to the Constitution. Those, including George Conway, the husband of Trump's adviser Kellyanne Conway, who have taken strenuous issue with this proposal, have reminded the public that the Fourteenth Amendment was passed after the Civil War expressly to erase the legacy of the Dred Scott decision of the antebellum Supreme Court denying the possibility of citizenship to slaves or the descendants of slaves. But it is also Trump's gleeful discovery (as he imagines) that he can bring about this radical alteration by executive order that has turned the immigration debate into one concerned with the abuse of executive power.

The possibility of a Yankee Duce has been a perennial anxiety in history. In the first number of *The Federalist Papers* in 1787, Alexander Hamilton cautioned that 'those men who have overturned the liberties of republics . . . have begun their careers by paying obsequious court to the public, commencing as demagogues and ending as tyrants'. Nine years later, in his farewell address, George Washington warned not only against the blandishments of an authoritarianism stoked by 'ill-founded jealousies and false alarms [which kindle] the animosity of one part against another', but also, with shocking clairvoyance, the 'foreign influence and corruption, which finds a facilitated access to the government itself through the channels of party passions . . .'

Whether Trump has had any part in 'facilitating access' is for Robert Mueller's investigation to determine, but (admittedly a small consolation) the president is too lazy to be a successful tyrant, his authoritarian instincts tempered by the alternation of indolence and impulsiveness. All he truly craves, aside from endless rounds of golf, is the gush of flattery delivered by his Cabinet, the obliging parrots of Fox News, and the rallies to which he is addicted: those overloaded cheeseburgers of his psychic engorgement.

Put those anxieties together – self-promotion posturing as protection from immigrant invasion, and the demonisation of opposition, especially the media, as 'enemies of the people' – and you have Trump's unrepentant script in this most fateful election. But will it catch fire with the voters as it did two years ago? Will history look back on the cult of Trump as no more than a hot flash in the pan? Or does the Republic risk mutating into the illiberal state that Viktor Orban and his admirer Steve Bannon have proclaimed to be The Future?

If the Democrats hope to put a brake on this lurch towards illiberalism, they will have to flip twenty-three seats in the House of Representatives. Until very recently, the dream of a 'blue wave' has been looking just that. A switch of majority in the senate seems out of reach, but it's a different story in the House of Representatives. Republican seats that once looked safe, such as Utah 4th and New York 19th, appear to be turning bluer as election day draws near. Across the country, and away from their bi-coastal citadels, the Democrats have been able to mobilise a range of fresh, articulate talent that has bitten into red strongholds. The 'elite' in many of these contests are Republicans on the defensive. In the deep red state, Utah, Republican Mia Love is struggling against the popular mayor of Salt Lake County, Ben McAdams. In West Virginia 3rd, which went for Trump by fifty points, Richard Ojeda, a veteran from a mining family who voted for Trump but has turned fierce Democrat, is now in a close race with the Republican candidate Carol Miller.

The re-localisation of politics back to material concerns such as healthcare is good news for the Democrats, a way for them to reboot their connections with middle- and working-class voters and move away from the white noise of the culture wars. It's even more marked in the all-important gubernatorial races, where the Democrats may pick up as many as seven state houses: among them Florida, Wisconsin and Michigan, all of which went to Trump two years ago. But for any or all of this to happen will depend on the turnout of Hispanic and millennial voters, habitually missing in action from mid-term polls, matching or exceeding Trump's core voters, who are likely to show in 2016-scale numbers.

There are other obstacles in the way of blue-tinting the electoral map, not least strenuous efforts by the Republicans to minimise or suppress the vote. Georgia's secretary of state, Brian Kemp, the party's candidate for governor, who has refused to step down from overseeing the arrangements for voting, was caught on audio worrying about losing the race should all those entitled to vote actually do so. He has the substantial African-American population of the state especially in mind, since his opponent Stacey Abrams would, if elected, be the US's first African-American woman governor in history. Kemp is doing his best to see this doesn't happen. It is thought that as many as a million and half voters may have been purged from the electoral rolls on the grounds of not having recently exercised their vote. Needless to say, most affected potential voters are black.

There are other ways, too, in which a democracy can be hobbled, not least through an assault on truth, leaving voters at sea about whom to believe or else cynical that the facts of the matter can ever be securely established – the 'he said; she said' courtroom conundrum applied to an election. The arbitration of discoverable truth has been a bedrock of the liberal tradition from its founding. But Bannon's answer to John Milton's optimism in *Areopagitica* – 'whoever knew truth put to the worse in free and open encounter?' – or Jefferson's version in his draft Virginia 'Statute for Religious Freedom' that 'truth is great and will prevail if left to herself, she is the proper and sufficient antagonist to error', has been, in his own confident instruction: 'flood the zone with shit'.

In the hands of the president, it has worked a treat. Trump inaugurated his political career with the claim that Barack Obama was no American at all, having been born in Kenya, a falsehood that for a long time no birth certificate could gainsay. When DNA evidence exonerated the African Americans wrongly convicted of raping and assaulting a Central Park jogger, Trump continued to insist on their guilt. For him, whether a matter of law or the fate of the Earth's climate, science is just another opinion. It is, to be sure, a truism that most politicians treat the truth as a matter of convenience.

But there has never been a president for whom the falsification of fact has been to such an extent the driving engine of allegiance. In the past two weeks alone, by way of bolstering the notion that the caravan of migrants is a national security threat, Trump insisted there were 'Middle Easterners' among their numbers, before conceding that there was no evidence to support any such thing. On the stump, fantasies have cascaded down: non-existent riots in California against sanctuary cities; a tax cut for the middle class to be acted on 'before November' — which is news to congress since it is out of session.

So will the sensationalist strategy used to stunning effect in 2016 work again, or could it have worn out its electoral welcome? Instead of taking fright at the phantom army of invaders, the Democrats are hoping Americans are more worried about decent healthcare. If that turns out to be the case and large numbers of voters act on the hunch that perhaps it was not such a good idea entrusting all the branches of government to one party, then the Founding Fathers can rest easy in their tombs, and democracy in America, as they wisely devised it, will yet have a robust future.

ROYAL WEDDINGS

When a low-rent paparazzi scam briefly threatened to derail the Windsor wedding this week, the irony would not have been lost on Britain's royals. They, after all, are heirs to an institution whose modern image has developed in step with photojournalism. The momentous rebranding, which, in the reign of Victoria, transformed a ruling dynasty into a royal family and turned its household calendar — the cycles of marriages, births and deaths — into national events, depended crucially on a nice balance between publicity and privacy. On the one hand, remoteness, if not actual invisibility, helped preserve the royal mystique; but on the other, selective exposure, fed to the public as a steady diet of family occasions, gave the monarchy the impression of accessibility, necessary to tie the emotional bond between crown and people.

This balancing act was always going to be a challenge but, historically, it was just the latest edition of a problem intrinsic to the crown's 'two bodies' — the 'body natural' and the 'body politic' that historian Ernst Kantorowicz identified as both the strength and vulnerability of the medieval monarchy, which persisted well into the age of image-management inaugurated by the Tudors. With her 'body natural' failing to produce an heir, the fantasy creation of an ageless Queen Elizabeth, celebrated rather than despised for her virginity, was but the first exercise in producing portraiture designed to mobilise affectionate allegiance in a divided realm.

More invested in divinely anointed authority than human accessibility, the Stuarts hired image-makers such as van Dyck who would reliably turn out masterpieces of courtly grandeur, editing where necessary a queen's stained teeth or a king's limited stature to fit the image of gods on earth, visions in watered silk. But though those who would have seen the great paintings were limited to a narrow circle of princes and aristo-crats, Charles I's own family feeling produced the first beautiful images of royal children, every lovingly rendered kiss-curl a chuckle in paint.

The real push to overcome the indifference generated by royal invisibility or, worse, the demystification of printed satire came from the monarchs for whom family feeling was not at all an opportune affectation but something of a mission: George III and Queen Charlotte. As Janice Hadlow makes clear in her won-derful *The Strangest Family*, no one toiled harder, or against such steep odds, to replace the image of the Hanoverians as mistress-swamped creatures of voluptuary indulgence with one of the ideal sentimentalised family. Charlotte was not just queen but *uber-mutti*, producing fifteen children, with whom the monarchs conscientiously played (sometimes down on the carpet with the toddlers) as per contemporary instructions on how to best secure domestic happiness.

It didn't work. In revolt, the Prince of Wales grew into a pet-ulant, bloated, waddling creature devoted to gratifying needy appetites, publicly estranged from his rejected wife and stalking his inamorata, the widowed Mrs Fitzherbert, until she surren-dered to the marriage ceremony in Mayfair that both parties knew would not stand as legal. Though public affection for his father ran broad and deep, the years of Farmer George's demented seclusion took him out of public view, and the more the country saw of the Prince Regent, the less it liked him. When, as George IV, he looked likely to expire childless, his middle-aged brothers ditched their mistresses in an unseemly bolt to the matrimonial altar with

suitable aristocratic brides in hopes of producing legitimate heirs.
This was especially hard on the actress Dorothea Jordan, who had
borne the Duke of Clarence, later King William IV, no fewer than
ten illegitimate FitzClarences.

Two marriages made in heaven came to the rescue of the
British monarchy. The first, of course, was the passionate love
match between Victoria and Albert; the second was between
the crown and the popular press, reinvented in the 1830s with
steel engraving and lithographic illustrations. Circulations
were transformed by images and, now, by pictures of the royal
round, a crown still selectively removed from the everyday, yet
somehow connected to the basic instincts of bourgeois family
life. The rejoicings and griefs of Victoria's family thus became a
national cult, published and promoted at exactly the time – the
'Hungry Forties' – when Britain was most socially divided by
brutal economic distress.

Moved by both emotional instinct and shrewd calculation,
Victoria and Albert made sure to take their brand of family
connection out of London: to the Midlands in 1843, Lancashire
in 1851 (mindful that not everyone could get to the Great
Exhibition in the Crystal Palace, notwithstanding special reduc-
tions in train fares), and to Leeds in 1858. It was unthinkable
that the Hanoverians would have opened the new docks at
Grimsby, but Albert made a beeline for the occasion in 1849,
just as he revelled in opening the great Manchester art exhibition of 1857.

It was a renovation of the Elizabethan progresses for the industrial age but, unlike the strict control imposed by that queen's
council on the production and circulation of royal portraits,
Victoria, Albert and their children embraced photography as a
way of making their presence familiar. This didn't mean that
the private life of the royals was now an unregulated public
spectacle. Images of queen and consort, dressed like a respect-
able middle-class couple, were carefully selected and edited for

cartes de visite: little photographs printed on stiffened paper that could be kept in a purse or wallet, which sold, initially, in tens of thousands, then in millions. Some of the most appealing of those images were startlingly informal. The most touching of all was of Princess (later Queen) Alexandra, the wife of Bertie, the Prince of Wales, piggybacking her second son. The child who, as King George V, would be notorious for his brusque formality (and severity with his own children), looks out from the photo with a toddler's imperious unease, but the face of 'Alix' — herself a keen photographer — is maternal, larky joy, Diana before Diana. More than any other photograph I know, this is the icon that turned the British monarchy into a royal family, and it was so popular that the little boy's eventual princess bride, Mary of Teck, repeated (or should we say 'staged'?) the pose, carrying the future Duke of York and father of the present queen, Albert, who looks no happier on the ride.

The wedding of Bertie and Alix in 1863 was the first in the modern era to be held in St George's Chapel, Windsor. The enormous late Gothic space is, as television viewers will see, hardly chapel-sized and was more associated with funerals and burials. The two mortal adversaries of the Wars of the Roses, Henry VI and Edward IV, were both entombed there, as were Henry VIII and the remains of the beheaded Charles I. Most recent royal nuptials had been held in the Chapel Royal of St James's Palace, including the first great wedding of Victoria's reign, that of her eldest daughter Vicky to Friedrich, the Crown Prince of Prussia, in 1858. And there was, as the queen herself gloomily noted, an atmosphere of desolation hanging over the moment. Prince Albert had died in 1861, and Victoria was convinced that the cold he had caught while marching his wayward son around in the Cambridge rain ordering him to abandon his mistress, Nellie Clifden, had been responsible for the tragedy.

Before the ceremony, the queen had taken the couple to the recently completed Frogmore mausoleum, and had joined their hands over the tomb of the Prince Consort to signify, by close proxy, his blessing on their union. In the chapel, Victoria, attired in black with a miniature of Albert pinned to her dress, looked down on the proceedings from the balcony-box 'Royal Closet' built in 1510 for the doomed Catherine of Aragón. Guests were told to wear nothing brighter than grey and mauve. The only note of insubordination was supplied by the four-year-old Prince Wilhelm of Prussia, later the Kaiser, biting the legs of two of his British uncles.

But Britain had had enough of weeping. There was such public demand for a procession through London to the train bearing Alexandra to Windsor that hasty rearrangements had to be made to accommodate it. A route was designed to take the carriages and lengthy military escort from the City through Trafalgar Square, Piccadilly and Hyde Park to Paddington. But even those orchestrating the event were astonished at the size of the crowd; so dense that there were serious injuries in the jostle and crush including six fatalities. As had been the case with Vicky and Friedrich, the readers of the *Illustrated London News*, the *Telegraph* and *The Times* couldn't get enough of the illustrations detailing the bride's dress (Honiton lace was a must), her jewels, bouquet (orange blossom obligatory) and – especially – the elaborately tiered wedding cake (more or less invented by the Victorian royals) with its columns of icing sugar, towers and spires.

Thereafter, royal weddings were often designed to shake off national melancholy. In 1923, the marriage of the Duke of York to Elizabeth Bowes-Lyon was a conscious coming-out from the obsequies of the Great War, and was held in Westminster Abbey to maximise the jubilation. The same held for the marriage of Princess Elizabeth (the present queen) to Prince Philip in 1947, with the country deep in post-war austerity. It may be too much and too unfair to expect the rejoicing around this latest royal wedding to lighten the weight of two burdens: that of the memory of the Diana-tragedy, and that of the anxieties of a nation headed for an exit without any clear sense of destination. Of all the family, Prince Harry has recoiled most sharply against the inevitable intrusions of the hungry lens. But spirits-lifting, as he knows, goes with the job. And if, for a fleeting moment, images of the Harry and Meghan show can turn the union of past and future from political cliché into human love story, then what could possibly be the harm in that?

BILL CLINTON

How do you begin a conversation with the man who knows everything? Steering clear of female literacy rates in Bhutan, the daily amount of clean drinking water available to slum dwellers in Caracas, or the rate of coral bleaching on the Great Barrier Reef, the sort of thing Bill Clinton recites in his sleep or sings in his shower, I try something less expected. 'Do you ever think much about John Quincy Adams?'

'Oh, sure,' he says, with his most disarming smile. 'The first ex-president to do something active afterwards; eight terms in congress, led the anti-slavery movement.' And then he's off, as unstoppable in his historical enthusiasms as he is in almost every other subject you can imagine. Sitting next to me at a Dimbleby Lecture dinner some years ago, Clinton used dessert time to offer an exhaustive analysis of the Kashmir conflict, sketched with a marker pen on a paper napkin.

The motormind is still racing. It's quickly apparent that not only has Clinton given thought to his activist ex-presidential predecessors but that he has established a kind of personal comradeship with them across the generations. Jimmy Carter? 'Magnificent . . . Thirty years since he left the White House; must be eighty-seven now . . . he just goes chugging along . . . Saw him just before he went down to Haiti to build houses.' Some presidents walk alone; Clinton was made to bond, even with the dead. William Howard Taft? 'Went to the Supreme Court . . . suited him better than the presidency I think . . .' Herbert Hoover? 'Left office around the same age as me . . .' It's as though he had got them all together for chinwags over coffee and doughnuts.

Amid the club of ex-presidents, Clinton likes to confound stereotypes by hunting for good amid Republicans reviled by his own Democratic side. So he singles out Hoover not as the president who claimed that 'prosperity is just around the corner' while America was on its knees, but as the young idealist-engineer trying to lift a world from its bloody prostration after the First World War: the reformer later drafted by Harry Truman to reorganise the federal civil service. Even more improbably, Clinton invokes George W. Bush as an environmentalist techno-geek. As governor of Texas ('and not a lot of people know this') he signed legislation to make it more attractive to put up windmills, 'so that Texas is now the number one producer of wind energy in America. On a good day, when the wind is blowing, Texas gets 25 per cent of its baseload of electricity from wind.' This is the sort of thing that makes Clinton's wonky heart jump with joy.

Seven years ago, that heart gave out on him, requiring emergency quadruple bypass surgery. As he got back on his feet, the fleshy Clinton face became sharply chiselled and the rest of him followed suit. At sixty-five, standing tall in the office of the Clinton Global Initiative in a Harlem skyscraper, he is now trim rather than gaunt, the hot dog ravening replaced by vegetarianism. 'He's a near-vegan,' his aide Craig Minassian tells me, a concept about as persuasive as near-virgin. Trying to interrupt Clinton in the full spate of Exemplary Data is like trying to lasso a tornado. But amid the onrushing info storm – the amount of energy generated by the waste that would otherwise have been dumped in landfills in São Paulo; the amount of pollution Walmart has eliminated by reducing its packaging by 5 per cent, 'the equivalent of taking 211,000 dirty, diesel-burning trucks off the road and saving its supply chain $3 billion' – I put it to him that, however right all these causes championed by the Clinton Global Initiative are, the problem right now in America is that cool factuality has been swept aside by the hot vehemence of Belief. Right-wing radio and television shows with audiences of millions chortle daily at 'environmentalist wackos', while for the Tea Party, climate change is just another stratagem by which liberals mean to turn the US into Sweden West. Confronted with militant antediluvianism, why would Clinton assume that evidence-based arguments would have any impact on those whose avowed goal is the neutering of the entire American governing system put in place since Theodore Roosevelt? Isn't the real challenge, I suggest, one of counter-persuasion; the battle for reason itself? Perhaps, then, Clinton might yet follow John Quincy Adams' example and run, as he is constitutionally entitled to, for a seat in the House? There, amid the flat-earthers and holy rollers, he might yet make the case for American governance. President Clinton could morph into Speaker Clinton. Think of the apoplexy of the foe!

Amused, he doesn't take the bait. 'I don't think so, no. There are plenty of well-qualified people in congress who can do a good job, but not a lot of people who could do what I do [with the Global Initiative] – just because of the life I've had.' Still, he concedes that classic American governance, so institutionally brittle on paper, so forgivingly elastic in practice, is now not just sclerotic but paralytic, at exactly the time when the economy has gone into a vegetative state and the social fabric is fraying. 'We're living in a time when there is a disconnect between the way both politics and many of the communications channels work, and what works for the economy and society. Basically we know what works to create jobs and grow prosperity is networking and co-operation, but it's not a very exciting segment on the evening news and it doesn't get blood boiling in elections.'

Clinton characterises the core problem as the dominance of 'ideology' over 'philosophy'. In his book there is nothing wrong with genuinely philosophical debates in American politics. 'Everyone should have a political philosophy . . . it's good to be a little bit liberal or a little bit conservative, or a lot liberal and a lot conservative. The problem with ideologies is that you've got all the answers in advance, so evidence is irrelevant, experience is irrelevant, how the competition is doing is irrelevant.'

For that matter, 'criticising the government is the birthright of every American,' Clinton says, since the nation was born, after all, 'in response to what we believed was an irresponsible abuse of power . . . that was the number-one obsession of the Founding Fathers'. But as much as the framers of the Constitution wanted a system that would protect Americans from those abuses, they also wanted 'a government that could be strong and flexible enough to do what needed to be done through all times and ages. They understood that if you want entity, someone has to provide the glue.' Virginia, he says, was the founding generations' version of Angela Merkel's Germany, called on to assume the debts of much poorer ex-colonies with which it had nothing in common. But it cut a deal to do just that by having a capital city on the Potomac. So attacking governments is hardly new. By now 'we've got enough barnacles on our institutions that everyone can find a tax that was too high, a programme they think is a waste of money, a politician they believe abused power'. But as much as Americans have always been leery of too much government, they 'have always wanted enough government, so the real debate is about "what is enough and what is too much?"'

So why, I ask, isn't that debate actually happening and why isn't President Obama leading it? Partly because there's money in hot air, Clinton thinks. The polemicists of the airwaves may well believe what they believe, but they push to the extreme because raw conflict entertains. 'There's a disconnect between politics and the media and economic success.' The latter comes from building networks and doing deals, but what angry politics builds is 'attention deficit disorder'. And the fast-food psychology of governance doesn't help either.

If you ask Americans, Clinton says, they claim to like the idea of divided government; the White House and the congress held by different parties, preventing each other from lurching too far to the left or right. In more or less normal times that system is made for deals across the aisles. Apparently brittle, the governing culture is usually elastic; friendly to compromise. 'There are only two things Americans should never see being made,' Clinton quotes Mark Twain as saying, 'sausages and laws'. But both deliver the goods. Now all that is imperilled, not least because what Teddy Roosevelt called the bully pulpit has got a lot smaller. 'When I was first old enough to vote, the president got between thirty and forty-five seconds every night on the news. Now it's less than eight seconds.'

Some of the hysteria against government Clinton discounts as commercially astute entertainment. Rush Limbaugh, the most successful of the ultra-conservative radio jocks, is, he says, 'a very smart man. I don't mean he doesn't believe any of this, but he gets market share by ideology and the extreme.' But even if the orches-trators of the anti-government chorus do it mostly to annoy, the arrival of Tea Party ideologues sworn never to raise revenues has pushed Republican leadership in the House of Representatives so far to the truculent right that their spanner-throwing can seize up the works of government altogether. In some deep, theologi-cal sense, the Tea Party faithful want to hasten the Last Days of federal government.

'The Tea Party', Clinton says, 'is the most extreme incarnation of the thirty-year cycle that began when Ronald Reagan said in his first inaugural that government isn't the answer, government is the problem. But the real issue is not that the Tea Party is in control of the country, has captured the airwaves or represents a majority of public sentiment; the problem is that something [the deal-making system] that has worked for the American people in the past isn't working now.'

And the ideologues haven't had their 'Waterloo moment to break the fever', such as the two shut-downs of the federal gov-ernment engineered by Speaker Newt Gingrich and the incoming House Republicans in 1995. That triumphant phalanx assembled beneath the banner of the Contract with America to which they vowed to remain uncompromisingly faithful. But the public hated the shut-downs and blamed Republicans to the point when it became apparent they had actually taken out a contract on themselves. It was Gingrich, not Clinton, who was ousted, the president winning re-election a year later. The manufactured spat earlier this year over raising the debt ceiling had Waterloo-moment promise, but the prospect of the US defaulting for the only time in its history and the risk of sending the already stressed bond market over the cliff meant that Obama, unlike Clinton, couldn't call the naysayers' bluff.

So what can be done about this latest edition of Know-Nothings? 'You can't convert the ideologues because they don't care what the facts are. With the world as it is, you have to fight the fight you can win, and the fight you can win is economics.' Clinton gets intense at this point. 'There isn't a single example of a successful country on the planet today – if you define success as lower rates of unemployment, higher rates of job growth, less income inequality and a health system that produces the same or better care at lower cost – that doesn't have both a strong economy and effective government that find some way to work in harness with each other . . . If you don't do that, if you don't have a system by which the poor can work their way into it, then you lose the social cohesion necessary to hold the country together, and that is a big problem.'

'The answer for America has got to be to do the things that we know are good economics.' The Clintonian trump card is just the arithmetic of jobs generated by intelligent investment. 'For $1 billion invested in a new coal plant, you get fewer than 900 jobs, for solar you get 1,900 jobs, for wind turbines 3,300 jobs and [for] retrofitting buildings, 7,000–8,000 jobs. These kind of projects represent a process of natural co-operation between the private and public sectors. I just say, "Here are the jobs, here is the investment. Are you really against it?"'

It's not something, Clinton realises, that can be legislated (though legislation can surely enable it); but it works when it comes about 'organically'. Which takes him to Orlando, Florida, a subject on which the ex-president waxes lyrical. 'Go down there tomorrow and, with the exception of a slight drop in visitors, you'd have a hard time knowing there was a recession.' The reason is not just Disney, but the Department of Defense, which makes an annual investment there of $5 billion in research and training. What is it that Disney, Electronic Arts, the video-game kings, and the military all need? 'Computer simulation!' he exclaims. 'If you and I joined the air force tomorrow we'd have to go down there and train on simulators.' Add to the mix a technology-savvy institution of learning and research – the University of Central Florida, 56,000 students strong, devising programmes so that its graduates can fit right into the nexus – and you've got the perfect positive feedback loop between the public and private sectors and NGOs that make for an incontestable economic powerhouse. 'Now why would you look at that model of success and reject it?'

When we turn to education, Clinton lauds a national inner-city programme called Kipp (Knowledge is Power Program). For the bright kid from Hope, Arkansas, it's always been about knowledge; the Jefferson in William Jefferson Clinton the personification of that eighteenth-century belief, shared by both the Scottish and French Enlightenments, that informed understanding will conquer all; poverty; a wreck of family life; the disadvantages of the held-back. The particular magic of American optimism has been the seeding of that conviction amid the millions of immigrants, enslaved and destitute, generation after generation, sustained by the gospel that learning is the condition of upward mobility. Like the current incumbent of the White House, he is both the advocate and the personification of that principle, though somehow Clinton has always worn his learning more lightly than Obama. No one has ever accused him of sounding professorial.

But he also recognises that we are in a populist moment when a display of intelligence can be a political liability. His response to the television debates of the Republican aspirants is 'you know . . . wow'; each of them (to borrow Joe Klein's verb he loves) 'empretzelling themselves' to be further to the right than each other: 'We heard that Social Security is a Ponzi scheme.' Ron Paul, the libertarian, was asked – since nothing run by the government can be good – whether he would close the Grand Canyon? 'That's a trick question,' he exclaimed with the pain of a cornered sophomore. As for 'poor Jon Huntsman' – the former governor of Utah who was also Obama's ambassador to Beijing – Clinton says sympathetically, 'Disqualified by being Obama's ambassador and speaking Mandarin?! I believe in God and know what they mean about intelligent design, but looking at those debates I had to wonder.'

He had his own way of defusing the madness. In 1999, on the thirtieth anniversary of the moon landings, 'when there were still raw feelings . . . the impeachment . . . I got NASA to loan me a moon rock, carbon-dated 3.6 billion years old. I put it on the table in the Oval Office and when people started the crazy stuff, I'd say, "Wait a minute, guys. See that rock, it's 3.6 billion years old. We're all just passing through, take a deep breath, calm down, let's see what makes sense." It had an incredible calming effect!' Should Obama try the moon rock strategy? 'Well, when he thinks they're off the reservation he should stand up to them, break through the ideological fog and get back to deciding things.'

I ask him whether school budgets aren't taking the biggest hit from the savage cuts in every state across the union. Aren't we wasting our seed corn?

'Yes, we are,' he concedes. But he also says that it isn't just a matter of throwing money at the problem – there are structural, systemic problems of accountability that need to be addressed. 'We are still living with a farm calendar. Only Belgium has a shorter school year.' But 'we still have a pay structure based on getting all the smartest women in America for free. Women

were the last low-cost, high-quality labour pool feeding into the
supply. Now they are on company boards, in medicine and law.'
More seriously, the baby-boomer women teachers are all about to
retire. 'Money matters to recruit young people to teach, even if
for just five years,' but it isn't the whole answer. An overwhelmingly African-American high school in one of the poorest counties
in the country, in the Mississippi Delta, but a Kipp school that
emphasises innovative methods of instruction and social behav-
iour got to rank second in Arkansas; a testimony to inspired
teaching, not a bank of dollars.

Which leads Clinton to pull another melancholy reflection
from his own bottomless barrel of knowledge. When Franklin
Roosevelt became president in 1933, he reminds me, it was the
old who were the poorest Americans. But their plight was transformed by the great accomplishment of the New Deal, Social
Security, and Lyndon Johnson's creation of Medicare in the 1960s,
the two institutions that stick most in the craw of conservative
believers in the absolute supremacy of the market. For the past
two decades, Clinton points out, it's the young who constitute the
poorest social cohort in America: whether as children deprived
of adequate health insurance or the basic high-school education
that would give them some chance in the employment market.
'It's a metaphor,' he says, for prosperous countries, valuing the
present over the future.

'So, Mr President,' I say, 'do you really think America has what
it takes to get out of this deep hole?' He shifts his chair closer to
me. 'I'll give you an honest answer. I'm absolutely confident we
have what it takes. But I'm more worried now than I have been
for many, many years . . . because we have both a short-term crisis
of horrible unemployment and long-term issues about education,
healthcare and tilting the economy a little more to production.
But here's what I know . . . People have been betting against
America for 200 years – it's a maddening country – and they all
wound up losing money. They said Washington was a mediocre

surveyor with a set of false teeth; on the way to his inauguration an Illinois newspaper said that Abraham Lincoln was a baboon, he'll ruin the country ... Khrushchev said he'd bury us, the Japanese in the 1980s were going to bury us too.'

But, and something like a sigh escapes the optimist – 'this is a different sort of challenge. It's short-term and long-term, it's complicated and we need a narrative that allows people to buy into America. The best I can do is tell you that what works in the modern world is different from what works in politics. When I'm asked what's the one thing I'm proudest of, it was moving a hundred times as many people from poverty into the middle class as in the previous twelve years, because that was clearly the product of economic policy. That's what this country is all about; the idea that if you work hard and you're an honorable person you get a chance to live your dream and give your children a chance to chase it.'

The aides close in, calling time. Clinton wants, of course, to carry on talking, especially about the fate of the young in America, not just as some sort of abstract policy issue but as if he were one of them himself, which, of course, the Comeback Kid in many ways still is. He walks over to the windows of his office and looks down to a scrap of green amid the urban grit. 'See over there? That park? That's Marcus Garvey Park. Tough spot. But that's where the Harlem Little League team plays. And some years back, they made it all the way to the World Series. Just imagine!' Which is what, for all his worldly political wisdom, Bill Clinton still irrepressibly does. Imagine.

ARIANNA HUFFINGTON

It's the eve of the 2010 mid-term elections. In the sunlight of an autumn Monday afternoon, downtown New York City, the last bastion of beleaguered liberalism, seems to be shrugging its shoulders, resigned to the worst; relieved that the Hudson River separates it from the madness it thinks is about to descend on the rest of the country. SoHo goes about its usual business. Sidewalk vendors are selling ersatz Vuitton bags; there's a traffic jam inside Dean & Deluca for the Catalonian olive oil; tourists lug bags full of designer jeans out into the blaring traffic. But for some of us unrepentant liberals it seems time to circle the wagons and hunker down. Already we can hear the cackles of the right-wing radio ranters as a rain of Tea Bags buries us alive.

Arianna Huffington doesn't do hunkering. In her sunny office, she stands tall – literally – in high-heeled black suede boots. The rest of Huffington is also dressed in Manhattan black, close to her trim figure, but with an edging of purplish-indigo-chiffon between bust and throat that says something more than corporate know-how. Mostly, as she turns from a window looking down on the SoHo street, she gives off waves of improbably invincible happiness. But this is the way she looked forty-plus years ago when we first met in Cambridge.

Arianna Stassinopoulos struck me then as the kind of Greek who wanted to tell Aeschylus to cheer up: a warm-hearted girl, impervious to toffish sarcasm and quaintly convinced that *Homo sapiens* is by and large a good thing. Not much of that essential

Arianna has changed. The dark hair is now a shade of California poolside honey and falls straighter to her shoulders. The mascara is generous but then it always was. Her laugh still proves you don't have to smoke to sound smokey. And her demeanour is, as it was then, open and generous, baffled, if not wounded, by cynicism.

If she wants to rally the American centre-left she has her work cut out for her right now. But having been on both sides of the political spectrum in her career, Huffington is likely to take the populism of the Tea Party as evidence of an energy still running through the circuits of American social life. She simply wants to harness it for the Good Guys and the Good Cause. On this particular day she thinks she has. She is just back from the 'Rally to Restore Sanity and/or Fear' proclaimed by the political satirists Jon Stewart and Steve Colbert, which drew a quarter of a million to the Washington Mall.

For Huffington the latest rally was 'not just an exercise in point and counterpoint' but 'something much bigger': a call to restore the civil society she wants to see replanted in an America polarised between destructively competing demonologies. And she was not going to be a mere bystander either. The *Huffington Post* – the über-blog she created in 2005, two years after an unsuccessful campaign for governor in California, which has become an indispensable way to ride the news cycle – mobilised its own community of enthusiasts to travel to Washington in a fleet of specially hired buses. 'How many buses?' I ask, having heard there were twenty or thirty. 'Two hundred,' she says, the lilt rising triumphantly, '20,000 people!'

The *Huffington Post* fleet was a vindication of everything its founder is trying to do to detoxify American politics. When I needle her a bit about whether there wasn't too much oil poured on troubled waters at the rally, too much feelgood reassurance when there isn't a whole lot to feel good about, Huffington disarms me with another statement of impassioned practicality. 'It's not that we were all nice people,' she says, but 'it brought out the best' in the midst of the scapegoating that is the stock-in-trade of hard times' demagogues. The aim of the *Post* and of the rally, she says with almost evangelical resolution, is to ask 'how can we activate a countervailing force' to all that corrosive, aimless, 'mad as hell' negativity?

She cites admiringly the case of Seth Reams, unemployed in Portland, Oregon, who, turning to the only commodity he had left, founded wevegottimetohelp.org, an online community that gets the jobless working – providing childcare, creating community gardens, mobilising lawyers to prevent foreclosures. The *Huffington Post* has given Reams a 'Game-Changer Award', but, more than just pinning a gold star on him, it's enabled seventy-five cities to multiply his mutual-help organisation in their own backyard. The *Post* is now raising money so that Reams can 'scale up' his whole operation.

Huffington is sometimes mocked for her interest in anti-materialist spirituality, but she knows that this kind of social religion has deep taproots in American culture, especially in the nineteenth century when local voluntarism and mutualist communities got fired up for causes such as temperance, abolitionism and women's rights. Huffington says she wants people to re-examine the callowness of 'consumption'. 'When people have their back against the wall they re-evaluate their lives and what matters to them. That's the positive to the dark side.' But she doesn't want to come across as some sort of online Pollyanna in designer boots. She is, she says, the last person to make light of a genuinely tragic moment.

There is 'a deep crisis in the lives of millions of people'; a middle class that has been 'shorted' by the delirium of sub-prime derivatives; a whole generation now forced to deal with downward social mobility, the blighted hopes of their unemployed children; the assumption that cuts the heart out of the American dream – that the lives of the next generation look certain to be less fortunate than those of the last. Reflectively, she looks out of the window but her mind is further off surveying the wrecked landscape of the middle and working classes: 27 million unemployed or under-employed, 5 million foreclosures by the end of this year.

Her answer to the crisis: a combination of rekindling the spirit of community in America (she is much intrigued by David Cameron's 'Big Society', though puzzled about how it might take effect) plus bold action by the federal government, the latter not exactly the flavour of the month this side of the Atlantic. Usually – as in Britain – these options are alternatives not complements, but Huffington is determined to make them fit. The trouble with Obama is that he 'has two Achilles heels – if you can have two,' she says, laughing at the image. 'Bernard [Levin, her famous, exactingly brilliant journalist partner of ten years] used to say, when I mixed my metaphors, "Draw me a picture."'

We never get beyond the one Obamian heel: his reticence to use the power of the federal government forthrightly enough to promise success. Instead, guided by people like Timothy Geithner and Larry Summers, who as Wall Street loyalists had been gung-ho for deregulation, Obama doomed the stimulus package to half-hearted inadequacy. She quotes Lloyd George to the effect that 'you cannot jump across a chasm in two leaps' and I am so surprised by her choice of aphoristic model I forget to ask her, apropos of what?

Of the $800 billion committed, $300 billion, she points out, came in the form of tax cuts designed to win the support of the business community, who promptly stashed it in their vaults or delivered it to lobbying campaigns against financial regulation. She says that Obama is hobbled by his 'very deep reverence for establishments', whether Wall Street or the military. She professes astonishment that he insists on sticking with 'an unwinnable war' in Afghanistan to the tune of $2.8 billion a week.

That Arianna Huffington has gone from being a campaigner in her then husband Michael Huffington's conservative campaign for the senate to an anti-war, pro-government activist seems, to her, not especially fantastic. Ralph Waldo Emerson's 'a foolish consistency is the hobgoblin of little minds' might be the motto of her life to date. But then she comes honestly by her impulsiveness. Her journalist father was punished with incarceration in a concentration camp for running a Resistance paper during the Second World War, after which she says he decided 'he could do anything', including much philandering and a separation, though the kind in which Elli, Huffington's mother, would be as likely to cook him dinner as show him the door.

Living in a tiny apartment in Greece, a picture of Cambridge in a magazine, with the usual punts and boaters and floppy-haired Jamies, gave Huffington the idea, with no English to speak of, that this might be a fine place to go to university. Much laughter greeted this notion except from Elli, who thought it would be just the thing. An application was sent off, much intense language tuition followed, and then a recce by mother and daughter into the fens. A telegram duly arrived telling Huffington she had been awarded an 'Exhibition', which seemed to be a good thing, despite an uncertainty about what exactly she was supposed to exhibit.

She soon found out: determination, eloquence wrapped in a thick Greek accent, a thick-skinned confidence in the rightness of what she was saying at the Union (a manner that hid hours of anxious swotting), a refusal to be abashed, a willingness to laugh at herself and to make the most of a persona that was something other than crumpets and bicycles. This all translated first into becoming the third female president of the Union and then to the world of radio and TV, where she met the Schubert-and Wagner-crazed Levin. Invited to dinner, she plunged into non-stop homework 'on Northern Ireland' and *Die Meistersinger*. The improbability of the statuesque Greek and the gnomic Jew delighted friend and foe, but Huffington speaks with wistful sweetness of ten years with her soulmate and of the strength it took to leave him when he refused to have children. Why is it that very clever people can also be myopic idiots, you think?

Translated to New York, along with her mother, Huffington dated property and publishing tycoon Mort Zuckerman (no pussycat) and wrote controversial biographies of Maria Callas and Picasso, with commercial success but not unanimous acclaim. Nothing about Huffington has ever got bogged down in cautious deliberation. In Los Angeles in 1984 she was introduced to oilman Michael Huffington, with whom she says she fell immediately in love and went off to lead the billionaire life in neoReaganite southern California. Two daughters arrived, but so did Michael's political ambitions.

In 1994, a 'wave' of Republican mid-term victories broke over the foundering Clinton presidency, exceeded in force and scale only by this year's election. But despite megabuck funding, and after a bitterly contested count, Huffington failed to surf to victory in southern California. The discovery of an illegal Latino nanny – now a regular source of political undoing – did not help. Huffington never got over the dismay and neither did the marriage. You get the distinct impression he blamed his wife for the nanny embarrassment, but his bisexuality, only discovered during the divorce, she says, must also have been part of the problem. But Arianna Huffington is not one to let these sorts of thing cast long and lingering shadows over family life. She and Michael remain close and will spend Christmas together with their girls, as they always do.

Unlike the current president, she never does things by halves. Asked when she moved left, she says 1996, but adds that she had long been interested in steering her conservative friends towards social activism and the problems of worsening inequities in American life. Increasingly treated as a traitor to conservatism, she found herself cold-shouldered at a Washington dinner party. 'Why is she here?' one conservative matron complained.

Soon she would give them something to complain about. First

an ill-starred campaign in 2003 against Arnold Schwarzenegger for governor of California. Huffington's showtime instinct billing it as 'the Hybrid against the Hummer' was cute, but not cute enough to offset the obstinate thickness of her accent – absolutely unchanged after thirty years in America – and the electorally lethal combo of lightly worn wit and left-liberal polemics. In retrospect, though, this all seems a prelude to her 2005 founding of the website that would change the whole institution of news journalism in the US. Asked why and what she had in mind, she answers the question in three parts, suggesting a well-practised response, but one that makes a lot of sense in the way of all great ideas that seem, in retrospect, obvious but were in fact unthinkable until someone came along to act on them.

She could see 'how conversation' about politics 'was moving online' and wanted to 'create a platform' that would organise its speakers and its audience. But she was also motivated by a strong sense that the old media had betrayed their calling by complaisance in the face of the two great crises of the Bush years: the run-up to the Iraq War and the financial crash. In the first case, those who prided themselves on investigative journalism had traded in their mission to cheerlead for the president's policy, turning a blind eye especially to the lack of hard evidence of WMDs. The blind eye was followed by a deaf ear to the many predictions of financial disaster.

But beyond responding to this abdication of responsibility, the *Huffington Post* was created as a way to allow writers blocked from print culture by the formality and laboriousness of essay-writing to 'deposit something in the cultural bloodstream' with minimum fuss and time. 'I called Arthur Schlesinger [the revered octogenarian historian of the New Deal and liberalism who had been close to JFK] and he said "What's a blog?"' He confessed he still wrote by typewriter. 'That's alright, Arthur,' Huffington said. 'Fax me.' Up came an unfortunate allusion to Yalta in presidential remarks and Schlesinger (who could have been there) hit the keyboard and got his retort to the *Post* in twenty minutes flat. 'Exactly what I had in mind,' she says, smiling fondly at the memory of the world's oldest intellectual blogger – who died in 2007.

Other issues matter a lot to her and give the *Huffington Post* its strong presence: a refusal to adopt 'a contrived neutrality' even while adhering to all the traditional ethics of traditional journalism; and an eagerness to respond to a new way to engage with the news. 'People don't just want to consume the news: they want to share it and evolve it, be part of the story, and the mainstream media don't understand this.' This organic self-seeding, an unruly liberation of the news beyond the tight control of papers and networks, is indeed something that rattles the old guard because it presupposes an alteration much bigger than simply transferring traditional content online.

But the democratic openness of the blogosphere comes with its own problems: the unreliability of stories that can come hurtling in; the meteor shower of junk data and anecdote. Huffington employs thirty people, in addition to 190 regular staff, precisely to monitor this dodgy abundance. They weed out all the e-dreck she so hates – conspiracy theorists, malicious slander, ad hominem attacks. Editors, she concedes, are needed more than ever as gatekeepers of the truth in a digital world where every prejudice comes armed with imagined rights to be heard. Does the future belong exclusively to the *Huffington Post* and Tina Brown's *Daily Beast*? She doesn't think so. The future, she says, 'will be hybrid'. There will be fewer printed papers and those that survive will be the ones that can properly integrate their reports and essays into the online world.

I take a stroll with Huffington through her football-field-sized open office and the scene – kids out of college, beavering away in their e-baronies, food, entertainment, business, the arts as well as economics and politics – sure looks like the future to me. One of the many things that may change for good in the present crisis is reporting itself. 'If you just look at the papers you would have no idea what is really going on out there in America,' she says with some justification. The *Post*, though, has reporters assigned to cover stories of heartbreak and courage around the country in its hardest of hard times. This may be nothing new, but the possibility of thousands of 'citizen journalists' giving those who log in to the *Huffington Post* a whole panorama of social pain most certainly is. From outposts of hardship from coast to coast, bloggers write in to give their best to her reporters whom they feel have looked closely and sympathetically at their troubles. Whatever this is, she is right to be proud of it as something other than the mindless self-reinforcing herd mentality in which 'enormous amounts of oxygen get consumed' on something as inanely picayune as the Florida pastor's threat to burn the Koran.

Arianna Huffington may not single-handedly be changing the nature of journalism in American life, but against the shit-storm of hatred and rage that is currently engulfing the country, the 'countervailing force' of the *Post* does good strong work. So it's not just the flashing wide smile, the merry look in her eye and the proffered cheek that, as we say our goodbyes, makes me feel warm in the happy hour; it's that brand Arianna, with its unrepentant embrace of social indignation and its laying about the fatuous and unjust, has exactly what these miserable times call for: intelligent high spirit delivered with no mumbling or shuffling or equivocation. And then there's that other thing she gets out online 24/7 and is not to be slighted: the truth.

HENRY KISSINGER

To whom should we look for guidance, in the toils of our Afghan perplexities? Well, obviously, the Duke of Wellington. So, at any rate, Henry Kissinger thinks. Don't go imagining this has anything to do with the Indian empire, either. Ten minutes into our conversation he remarked that policymakers should be thinking . . . Belgium. Yes, Belgium. Pausing for a moment between observations delivered with a rumble so basso that it automatically sounds profundo, the Doctor waited to see if the history professor would get it.

And suddenly I sort of did. Never mind the weird vision of the Hindu Kush relocated to the Flemish mud, both have been states that have never quite been made; theatres of contending languages and faiths, doormats for unscrupulous neighbours – the Scheldt! the Meuse! Waziristan! 'Throughout the eighteenth century and earlier,' Kissinger resumes, like a patient tutor, 'armies had marched up and down through Flanders.' As indeed they had, triggering appalling, endless wars. What was Wellington's answer, at the dawn of Belgian independence in the early nineteenth century? Internationally agreed neutrality. 'It lasted for eighty years.' We should be so lucky, the Doctor implies, with Afghanistan.

At eighty-seven, Henry Kissinger, who has an epic and, in some places, surprisingly moving book out on China, is history, but certainly not in the sense of past and gone. Quite the opposite. In his office at Kissinger Associates in midtown Manhattan, he invites me to sit on his left, advising that one eye no longer works as well as it should. But there is precious little evidence of much other infirmity. The wavy hair is snowy, the broad face is more lined, but the analytical mind is still razor-keen, delivering serial judgements at a steadily thoughtful pace; the reflections of an old magus, Yoda rescripted by Machiavelli. Kissinger lives, technically, in Manhattan and Connecticut, but his real abode seems to be in a Parnassus of classical statecraft, where, on a daily basis, Bismarck tips his hat to Metternich while a somnolent Talleyrand, from beneath powdered wig, winks knowingly at Zhou Enlai.

There are good and not so good aspects of this lofty perch from which he surveys the panorama of national foibles. On the one hand, the Olympian prospect enables Kissinger to see the bigger picture. On the other hand, a lifetime's immersion in the studious formalities of official business, the diplomatic obligation of wariness, has planed his conversation smooth of the knots and scuffs of the human condition. In the China book, though, human reality is very much present in his warts-and-all portraits of Mao and Zhou, Deng and Ziang Zemin. Kissinger chuckles deeply, as if gargling with pebbles, when he remembers the aged Mao, not going gentle, declaring theatrically that 'God will not want me', or insisting that he wanted to be 'cursed', to prove that even at the end he was imperially potent enough to provoke fear and rage.

I have tried my best not to like Henry Kissinger for the usual Nixon/Cambodia/Chile reasons, but more than once I've been comprehensively disarmed. Seventeen years ago I was assigned the review of his book *Diplomacy*, which I anticipated would be an eye-opener about the culture of the craft; the ways in which momentous decisions can turn on picayune matters of ostensibly trivial protocol. I had in mind the lengthy debate, at once absurd and weighty, over the shape of the table in the Vietnam peace talks in Paris. Were there not telegrams whose poor wording triggered disaster? Cocktail party fiascos that had turned into international incidents? Instead, *Diplomacy* turned out to be a fairly conventional but elegant narrative of nineteenth-century foreign policy; the statecraft of the grandees of European power. In its way it was just fine: often illuminating, especially about Bismarck, on whom Kissinger had done much research at Harvard, and the 1815 Congress of Vienna, which had been the centrepiece of his *A World Restored*, still the best thing on its subject. I said as much in the review, while regretting the missing sociology of diplomatic practice.

A week or so after the review appeared, the phone rang. The courteous voice was deep, dark and German. *Oh, sure*, I thought. Two days earlier a mischievous friend had impersonated Kissinger on the phone convincingly enough to dupe me into believing I was being berated for the review, before I got wise to the trick. When a second call came, I was on the verge of answering with my own, pretty good, Nixon impression before realising, in the nick of time, that this was, in fact, the actual Doctor, expressing a polite mystification about the sort of book I had wanted him to write and asking me if I would consider explaining more fully in person? After the deep breath I thought, *Hell, why not?* At the front door of his apartment, I told myself: this might be a bad idea, but it was too late. With one hand Kissinger (rather than the expected Manhattan flunky) hospitably opened the door and – this was the moment of disarmament – with the other dropped a dog biscuit into the open and appreciative mouth of a floppy hound. Wars have been averted with less.

Disconcertingly, nearly twenty years later, Kissinger remembered the incident (his memory remains prodigious), continuing the Schama-Disarmament programme by telling me that he'd tried to incorporate some of the insights I had wanted in his new China book. Caught off balance by the light touch of the flattery, I recalled that I had indeed noticed passages that dealt with the display of Chinese power as a kind of cultural performance: the banquets, the toasts, the exquisite calibration, inherited from imperial precedents, as to how and when foreign envoys might be admitted to an audience with The Chairman. Without this shrewd attentiveness to what he nails as 'hospitality as an aspect of strategy', Kissinger believes the opening to China might never have happened; and the world would be a very different place.

The China book, then, is different from anything Kissinger has hitherto essayed in print: a journey towards cultural empathy by two powers that seemed, at the outset, prohibitively ill-equipped to acquire that knowledge. Looking at Nixon and Mao, listening to their utterances, they should have been the oddest of odd couples. But paving the way for the 'quasi-alliance' were Kissinger and Zhou Enlai, and the heart of the book is the story of their personal rapprochement, born of a mutual effort to understand an alien and incomprehensible culture.

But then, of course, the first alien and incomprehensible culture that Henry Kissinger had to negotiate was that of the United States of America. He was already fifteen when his family arrived in New York in 1938, fleeing the Nazi Reich. There were ways and communities to ease the shock: a lively crowd of German-Jewish expatriates on the Upper West Side, the *stammtisch* by the Hudson, the cosmopolitan City University of New York, and then the band of military intelligence interpreters, full of people like him. At Harvard, it was another story: the parched cerebrations of the college Brahmins. It was an unlikely mentor, William Yandell Elliott, of Murfreesboro, Tennessee, who was Kissinger's first and lasting guide to the American mind at its most exacting. 'He was a big personality,' Kissinger recalls, a member of the 'Fugitive Poets' of Vanderbilt University, a gang that included Allen Tate and John Crowe Ransom. Elliott had brought his outsize personality and tough mind to Washington for Franklin Roosevelt and stayed connected with that world. Harvard undergraduates, perhaps especially ones with thick German accents and earnest intellectual urgency, may not, initially, have been his shot of bourbon. 'He made it quite clear when I was assigned to him that that was one burden too many,' says Kissinger, smiling wistfully. 'He said, "Why don't you go write an essay on Kant?" The Categorical Imperative and the Practice of Politics?' Right up young Henry's street even when the ex-Rhodes Scholar Elliott required him, Balliol-style, to read it out at their next meeting. When he had finished, the Fugitive Poet conceded, 'You really have an interesting mind.' 'In effect he said he would now look after my intellectual development. As a first step he made me read *The Brothers Karamazov*.'

What Kissinger took from Elliott was that without grasping the long arc of time, any account of politics and government would be shallow and self-defeating. That long view is on full display in the China book, which insists – entertainingly – on going back to the origins of Chinese classical culture and on through the many dynasties of the Middle Kingdom before even touching the epoch of decline, dismemberment and revolution. Kissinger smiles at the scene with which he opens his book, in which Mao gathered together the leaders of the party to listen to his account of a war that occurred during the Tang dynasty. 'It would be like one of our leaders going back to the wars of Charlemagne.' And you get the feeling that Kissinger believes that it would do them no harm if they did. Instead he laments that 'contemporary politicians have very little sense of history. For them the Vietnam War is unimaginably far behind us, the Korean War has no relevance any more,' even though that conflict is very far from over and at any minute has the capability of going from cold to hot. 'This [the United States of Amnesia as Gore Vidal likes to call it]', he sighs, 'is a tremendous handicap . . . when I talk to policymakers and I cite some historical analogy they think, "There he goes again with his history."'

Kissinger's *beau idéal* of analytical thinking informed by deep historical knowledge remains the formidable circle of advisers around Harry Truman. Their commanding figure, George Kennan, says Kissinger, had 'a beautiful mind; magnificent scope. Kennan's article on containment [the famous Long Telegram of 1946 on the ambitions of the Soviet Union] was', he says, 'seminal; you wouldn't change a comma.' But as a diplomat, Kissinger recollects Kennan was a hot temper in the Cold War; never quite able to control the rush of blood, shouting tactlessly at Tempelhof airport that conditions in Moscow were still 'just like Nazi Germany'. 'He thought in more or less absolute terms,' Kissinger says, smiling. 'The contingencies that might arise were unbearable to him.'

Mastering contingency is what Kissinger's style of foreign policy has been all about, never more so than in the Chinese scenario. The objective historical situation in which the mutual suspicions of the Russians and the Chinese were bound to lead to explosive conflict was always there. But it took Kissinger and Zhou, counter-intuitively in tandem, to follow the logic of the situation to achieve a breathtaking realignment. Knowing what we do now about the self-destructive overreach of Soviet power, were Chinese fears of Russian aggression, Mao's 'ill waters', overdone? Not at all, Kissinger responds. Both sides were nervous, which is what made the situation in 1969 genuinely dangerous. Brezhnev, he says, exuded 'a sense of ominous danger emerging out of China'. Stalin's last years were haunted by the same conundrum, never 'solving the problem of how their influence in China would continue'. Mao was sufficiently alarmed at the imminence of a pre-emptive Soviet strike that 'he dispersed all his government ministers over China and only Zhou remained in Beijing'.

How much did Kissinger know about Chinese history and culture when he set off for his first rendezvous with Zhou? 'Oh, at the beginning . . . nothing.' Since at that point secrecy was paramount, Kissinger was denied any briefing from the usual agencies. Back to Harvard he went, hoping for a crash course from the great scholars of modern Chinese history, J. K. Fairbank and Owen Lattimore. 'They wanted to talk to me about why China should be admitted to the UN and gave me all sorts of methodologies by which we could ease the admission, which I am sure was very wise but nobody sat down and said, "Now you really ought to understand how they think."' What followed, then, was intensive self-education, but also Kissinger's certainty that if anything was to be accomplished he had to shrug off the bureaucratic and State Department default obsessions of raising legalistic issues of claims and indemnities and the like with the Chinese, instead moving directly to first principles, beginning with the mutual agreement that there was, in fact, one China not two, a position then upheld by the Nationalist government in Taiwan as much as by the communist government in Beijing.

Kissinger talks about this momentous shift in global alignments as though it could only be accomplished through the kind of personal interaction customary to classic nineteenth-century statecraft. But at the centre of it all (not to forget the strange, turbulent, contorted personality of Nixon) was, after all, Mao, whose magnitude, for good or ill, Kissinger never wants to sell short. What about the deranged contradictions in Mao's imperial fiats: decreeing a Great Leap Forward that condemned millions to die in an engineered famine, or unleashing the trauma of the Cultural Revolution only to slam on the brakes once it threatened to bring down the state itself? 'They were a rebellion against mortality,' Kissinger says, a little gnomically, but offering an interesting addendum. It is Deng's generation – and Deng himself, twice purged and who lost a son to the fury of the Red Guards – that has been permanently scarred by the 'unimaginable abomination'. But their children are beginning to think that perhaps Mao 'was on to something . . . but as always pushed it too far'. With the misery and terror of the Cultural Revolution just a parental memory, the next generation, Kissinger says, feels 'nostalgic for . . . an alternative sense of community'. 'There is in Chongqing right now', he tells me, 'a party secretary, Bo Xilai, who has been leading a kind of Maoist philosophical revival. One of my associates who has been in China tells me that university graduates who ten years ago all wanted to be Goldman Sachs executives now want to be government officials.' And what would Mao himself have made of contemporary China? 'I think he'd be troubled. He really did believe in an ethical mission for the Chinese. I think the selfishness of the Chinese yuppies would bother him.'

Shouldn't the obstinately brutal record of the Chinese government on human rights give us pause when we cosy up to them? As if sensitive to all those accusations that he has been, at times in his career, insufficiently moved by these issues, Kissinger says, 'I periodically raise human rights issues, usually on behalf of individuals, always without publicity. But for the advocates of human rights, publicity is a moral imperative because it puts us on the right side of history. I respect them for that.'

Not so much, though, as to get in the way of treating China as an indispensable element in any stabilisation of perilous situations in Korea and Afghanistan. Without China's active participation, any attempts to immunise Afghanistan against terrorism would be futile. This may be a tall order, since the Russians and the Chinese are getting a 'free ride' on US engagement, which contains the jihadism that in central Asia and Xinjiang threatens their own security. So was it, in retrospect, a good idea for Barack Obama to have announced that this coming July will see the beginning of a military drawdown? The question triggers a Vietnam flashback. 'I know from personal experience that once you start a drawdown, the road from there is inexorable. I never found an answer when Le Duc Tho was taunting me in the negotiations that if you could not handle Vietnam with half a million people, what makes you think you can end it with progressively fewer? We found ourselves in a position where to maintain . . . a free choice for the population in South Vietnam . . . we had to keep withdrawing troops, thereby reducing the incentive for the very negotiations in which I was engaged. We will find the same challenge in Afghanistan. I wrote a memorandum to Nixon that said that in the beginning of the withdrawal it will be like salted peanuts; the more you eat, the more you want.'

Kissinger laughs even as he sketches a scenario for an Afghanistan even grimmer than anything anyone has yet imagined, where the presence or absence of al-Qaeda will be the least of its problems. What might happen, he says, is a de facto partition, with India and Russia reconstituting the Northern Alliance, and Pakistan hooked to the Taliban as a backstop against their own encirclement.

Suddenly, spring goes chilly. The prospect looms of a centennial commemoration of the First World War through a half-awake re-enactment. Not Belgium but Sarajevo. Think proxy half-states; the paranoia of encirclement; the bristling arsenals, in this case nuclear; the nervous, beleaguered Pakistanis lashing out in passive-aggressive insecurity. 'An India–Pakistan war becomes more probable. Eventually,' says the Doctor, his voice a deep pond of calm. 'Therefore some kind of international process in which these issues are discussed might generate enough restraints so that Pakistan does not feel itself encircled by India and doesn't see a strategic reserve in the Taliban.' He looks directly at me. 'Is it possible to do this? I don't know. But I know if we let matters drift this could become the Balkans of the next world war.'

Suddenly the irrefutable clarity of his pessimism makes Dr Strangelove look like Dr Pangloss. Around America this week, biblical placards are appearing proclaiming that the world will definitely end on 21 May. If they're right, you won't be reading this. But if Kissinger is right, they may yet have a chance to move the date back a bit. Don't say history and Henry Kissinger didn't warn you.

THE BALFOUR DECLARATION:
100 YEARS ON

My father was sixteen years old, just two shy of being conscripted for the trenches, when he – and the rest of Whitechapel – heard about the Balfour Declaration. The letter, sent by Foreign Secretary Arthur Balfour to Walter, Lord Rothschild, expressed the British government's support for 'the establishment in Palestine of a national home for the Jewish people', but added the proviso, 'it being clearly understood that nothing shall be done that may prejudice the civil and religious rights of existing non-Jewish communities in Palestine'.

The initial response of Chaim Weizmann, the Zionist leader, when Sir Mark Sykes came bounding out of the Cabinet Office on 2 November 1917, holding the document and announcing, 'It's a boy', was disappointment. 'Well, I did not like that boy at first,' he wrote in his memoir *Trial and Error*, 'he was not the one I had expected.' Weizmann had wanted 'establishment' to be altered to 're-establishment', by which 'the historical connection with the ancient tradition would be indicated and the whole matter put in its true light'. That true light was meant to shine on something nobler than an opportunistic transaction of imperial strategy.

Weizmann's own misgivings quickly gave way to euphoria when what had been done sunk in. That evening he and his colleagues sang what were described as 'Hasidic songs' and danced in celebration. A week later, when the document was made public by the Zionist Federation, my father saw the same singing and dancing erupt in the streets of the East End, from Mile End to Whitechapel. Something propitious, something providential, had happened, but also something against the odds.

At the time of the declaration there were probably only about 5,000 members of the Zionist Federation across the country and the organisation's offices were a few small rooms on Piccadilly. But equally there is no doubt that emotional support was much broader. If British Zionism did not make the declaration, not unaided anyway, there is no doubt at all that the declaration made British Zionism. A place the Jews could call their own swam into excited vision, and not a colony in east Africa but the birthplace they had never relinquished in memory, ritual, language.

That East End street party – 'a kosher knees-up', Dad called it, lots of fried fish, cake and shouting – was all instinct and no thought, but then sometimes instincts are the real story. Arthur remembered the 'Hatikvah' being sung outside a synagogue close to the family house. A month later the same song brought the crowd to their feet in the Royal Opera House. My father stood outside amid a huge throng beside sacks of the next day's cabbages.

He knew all about the Jewish opposition: anti-Zionists, the grandees of the Anglo-Jewish Association and the Conjoint Committee – Claude Montefiore and those Rothschilds, Leopold in particular – who were on the wrong side of the argument. He was especially horrified by the public accusation of Edwin Montagu, one of the two Jewish members of the Cabinet (the other was the pro-Zionist Herbert Samuel), that the Balfour Declaration was tantamount to being anti-Semitic, since in Montagu's eyes it presupposed divided loyalties, especially heinous during the war. Others among the anti-Zionist lobby felt the same way, in particular the historian Lucien Wolf, who had actually been questioned about his true nationality by a policeman in 1915 and never quite got over it.

For my father, the defensiveness of the anti-Zionists was a

symptom of the gulf dividing West End Jews from East End Jews. The declaration's sixty-seven words, he thought, could be boiled down to one – the word 'home', *bayit*. It was all very well for the likes of Edwin Montagu to complain that their indivisible sense of a British home was now vulnerable to charges of divided allegiance, but Montagu's home was manorial: avenues of oak and elm, game birds flushed from the bracken, dropping to Home Counties guns.

For my father, who had *shul* on *Shabbes* and Shakespeare on Sundays, it was perfectly possible to be indivisibly British and Jewish; British and Zionist. In fact his whole life and those of all his friends were built around that unproblematic possibility. The meeting of minds, as he supposed there had been, between Arthur Balfour and Chaim Weizmann, between the philosophical patrician politician and the 'little yid' from Motol, as Weizmann described himself, was not only possible, but somehow a histor-ically predestined fit. Britain was, after all, a country in which a Jew, thinly disguised as a church-goer, had been twice prime minister, the towering figure of Victorian conservatism.

Everything turned then, as it still does, on that one emotively loaded word, 'home' – both for celebrants and mourners. For Jews it was as if the doors of the ancestral home where Hebrew and Judaism had been created had finally been opened after being barred and locked – most recently in the 1880s, when the Ottoman Empire put severe restrictions on immigration to Palestine. But for the Palestinian Arabs, the establishment of a Jewish national home already seemed an early notice of evic-tion. Whether or not that pessimism was justified at the time or whether it became a tragically self-fulfilling prophecy is still being argued. But in the midst of our unapologetic celebrations, we owe it to the moral case for the declaration to put ourselves in Palestinian shoes as well as our own.

For the poorer Jewish communities of London and the prov-inces, the terror of homelessness was not just a debating point.

Many had come recently from the terror of pogroms in Russia and Romania, or had witnessed the rise of political anti-Semitism in cities like Vienna. They were altogether less sanguine about domicile being granted in any but a provisional and conditional way. Even in Britain there were reasons for apprehensiveness. There were anti-Semitic riots in Bethnal Green and Leeds in 1917. In the *National Review* there was always space for literary anti-Semites like Hilaire Belloc and G. K. Chesterton to vent their witty malice. The anti-immigrant demagoguery of organisations like the British Brothers' League had pressured the Conservative government led by Balfour himself to enact an Aliens Act in 1905, imposing strict curbs exactly at the time when they would be most damaging. In 1914, the Aliens Restriction Act had made those controls even tighter.

The East End, too, had a good idea of what was unfolding on the Eastern Front of the war, where millions of Jews found themselves caught between the rolling military machines of the Austro-Hungarian army on the one side, the Russians on the other. No fewer than 600,000 were deported from territory in the war zones, especially in the Ukraine. These upheavals were accompanied by other merciless pogroms, especially murderous when the Russian army was in retreat. Estimates of the civilian Jewish dead range from 50,000 (the most conservative figure) to as high as 200,000. The Russian Revolution brought no respite; the opposite in fact. The civil war saw 1,300 separate pogroms perpetrated by the Whites, the anti-Bolshevik Volunteers and the Poles; 106 by units of the Red Army, in particular Budenny's 1st Cavalry. When Red Army officers tried to stop the attacks they were either stabbed or shot. When Jewish fatalities from the two back-to-back wars are put together they could come to half a million.

So Jews could be forgiven for thinking there was no safe position for them to take and in extremis nowhere for them to go. Jews have not been the only people to have suffered uprooting.

But they have been the only people in the world eternally unable to find a place where shelter would not be given on sufferance, conditionally, provisionally, liable always to be withdrawn, terminated along with many lives, at short notice. No one in countries inheriting the legacy of the expulsions and the doors shut against the desperate – as they were in Britain after the Aliens Act or as they were in the US after 1921 – is in a strong position to question Zionism's legitimacy.

In 1915, the Yiddish writer S. Ansky, who had been one of the founders of the Social Revolutionary Party, went to see for himself the scale of the catastrophe, while trying to publicise the miseries and help organise relief for the multitudes of starving and homeless. He discovered whole towns in blackened, scorched devastation, often nothing left of the Jewish districts. In Brzostek he heard of a father and son taken out to be summarily hanged. The son was told his life would be spared if he personally hanged his father. He refused but the father begged him and, unhinged with distress, went through with it, while the soldiers sat around and laughed before stringing up the son anyway.

Ansky saw that these enormities were not just the result of disintegrating order in the country. Though other populations – ethnic Germans in particular – suffered deportation, the worst horrors were selectively perpetrated on Jews because of the grip of the most paranoid strains of anti-Semitism, intensified during wartime. The usual suspicions attached to 'rootless' Jews morphed into full-on accusations of treason. Yiddish was held to be synonymous with German, which then turned every Yiddish speaker into a potential or actual spy. A whole mythology of treason circulated throughout the war zone, shared not just among the ranks and the local country people but, as Ansky discovered, by the officer corps, even right up to some of the command itself.

So for Ansky and many others, being Jewish meant, sooner or later, being a homeless refugee or worse. This fate could befall even professionals and commercial Jews who had been permitted to reside in Moscow, beyond the Pale of Settlement. In 1891, much of that population was summarily expelled. Did this belated insight make Ansky a Zionist? Not exactly, or not immediately. For a while, he imagined the demonisation of the Jews would disappear with the dawning revolution of workers and peasants – until, that is, the Bolsheviks outlawed Hebrew and stigmatised Zionism as a reactionary crime.

And although the atrocities in the east seemed yet more evidence of the selective cruelty perennially meted out to Jews, their entrapment in permanent homelessness, that alone would never have ensured that the Zionist case would prevail with the British War Cabinet. As all historians have noted, imperial strategy had a great deal to do with the decision. The year 1916 had been a bad one for the Allies at Gallipoli and the Somme. The next year looked to be no better. Weizmann, who, as a chemist, had been engaged in producing acetone for munitions by Churchill, had shamelessly played up the role the Jews might have in persuading the US to enter the war.

But if there were compelling humanitarian and strategic reasons for the British government to support a Jewish national home, it was also true that the case for this to be planted in Palestine, notwithstanding simultaneous British encouragement of Arab nationalism, owed something to history and emotion. Weizmann won Balfour over in person because he persuaded him that such a national home would only take root if it grew from the millennia-long, unbroken connection of the Jews with the place where their identity had been created and their language formed. Alternatives that had been offered in east Africa and El Arish on the Sinai coast would indeed have been exercises in colonialism. But British enthusiasts of a Jewish return knew well that Jews were not only not absent from Palestine, but actually had constituted the majority of Jerusalem's population for some time and were living in communities of thousands in

the Galilean towns they had built in the sixteenth century like
Tiberias and Safed.

But they were still vastly outnumbered by the Palestinian Arab
population, who saw a Jewish national home in Palestine as an
outrage. How, then, could the British persuade themselves that
somehow the ambitions of both Jewish and Arab re-awakenings
could be reconciled? The answer of course lay in that crucial proviso
added to the declaration: 'it being clearly understood that nothing
shall be done that may prejudice the civil and religious rights of
existing non-Jewish communities in Palestine'. In all likelihood
this was written not by Balfour but by the political secretary to the
War Office, Leo Amery, himself a secret Jew who had belatedly
discovered his mother's true identity, and who wanted somehow to
square the circle in such a way that it was conceivable to reconcile
the aspirations of both national communities in Palestine. The other
element of the declaration to which an optimistic reading could be
attached was that crucial little word 'in', meaning a Jewish national
presence in part but not the whole of the country: a shared place,
then, not the monopoly of one or the other.

Most of the answers given by historians, shadowed by
knowledge of how all this would play out during the Mandate, are
bleakly pessimistic, if not downright cynical. But at the time, the
possibility of two national awakenings coexisting side by side, and
at the very least refraining from mutual destruction, was not out
of the question. This is because, contrary to most polemical histories, at least some figures in either camp were paying attention
to the other and not invariably from a stance of intransigent hostility. Weizmann's friend Ahad Ha'am, the great seer of 'cultural
Zionism', had warned in the 1890s after visiting Palestine that the
future of the entire project would turn on Zionists understanding the sensibilities and rights of those who were already there.
In 1905, at the seventh Zionist Congress, Yitzhak Epstein – who
lived in one of the earliest Jewish villages in Galilee – called it
the 'one issue [that] outweighs them all'. He had seen first hand

that the purchase of land from Arab landowners resulted in the dispossession of their tenant *fellahin*, so Epstein optimistically proposed that Jews bought only uncultivated land for their settlement and development. He also argued that Zionists should appreciate the Palestinian Arabs' own sense of home and negotiate with them on that basis of mutual respect.

Weizmann tried to do just that when he went to see Emir Faisal, the son of Sharif Husain of Mecca, to whom the British had promised sovereignty over a great pan-Arabian state following the war. Travelling by boat, camel and foot in the broiling heat of June 1918, Weizmann spent two hours in discussion with Faisal at his encampment on the Jordanian plateau. With the help of T. E. Lawrence, who believed it could all somehow be managed, a document was produced in which Zionism and Arab nationalism were represented as complementary and mutually beneficial.

A similar understanding was reached at the Paris Peace Conference when the two men met again, although an essential rider was added that, should British promises of Faisal's Arab kingdom in Syria not be realised, any such understanding would be null and void. Notoriously, of course, earlier secret negotiations dividing the region between French and British interests set those promises cynically aside, putting Syria and Lebanon under a French zone of influence and ultimately delivering the Palestinian Mandate to Britain, both with fateful consequences.

It was, then, the briefest honeymoon and 100 years on there seems always to have been a shadow cast over the declaration. The issue of whether or not the country from the Jordan to the sea is to be the home of one or two peoples, in one or two states, raised in vague outline in 1917, is still the essence of the matter in 2017. For Jews, what grew from the seed of the Balfour Declaration has been in so many ways an astounding miracle: for all its flaws and failings a vibrant, contentious, if embattled democracy and the retort in living humanity to the Nazi ambition to wipe out not just the bodies of all Jews but their culture and memory, too.

But as many Zionists have known and argued, the fulfilment of a national home will turn not just on power but on ethics, in which case the humanity of the other people of the land needs to be respected, too. This week brings another anniversary with it, one of equal solemnity: that of the murder of Yitzhak Rabin, who was among the greatest of Israelis to come to that conclusion and who paid with his life for daring to put it into practice. A possible peace or even the retreat of hatred and violence may seem right now so remote as to be in the realm of miracles. But then that first dawning of a Jewish home a century ago was proof enough that sometimes, even in the field of fire that is the Middle East, such things may happen.

TZIPI LIVNI

It's a long, lonely walk to the entrance of the Israeli parliament, the Knesset. You cross a bald plateau of paving alongside an avenue of Star of David flags, and on the way try to fight off an attack of seasonal metaphors. But you fail, for it's spring in Jerusalem. Sprays of almond blossom riot against the blonde limestone walls. '*Hatikvah*', the Israeli national anthem, means hope, and, however many times it's been dashed, this is the season when it's no shame to fall for it all over again, what with multiple sproutings going on from the Maghreb to the Gulf. Could Passover, the freedom festival, herald liberation from the bondage of defensive assumptions, starting with the received wisdom that any serious move towards peace with the Palestinians is bound to deliver more jeopardy than security?

The party Tzipi Livni leads calls itself Kadima – Forward – a name that turns a military order into an exhortation to break with dead-end truisms; a march to the future. No one could accuse its first leader, Ariel Sharon, the epitome of military ferocity, or its third, Livni, the ex-Mossad agent, of being soft touches. But she wants to redefine bravery as more than reflex military impulse; rather as the co-existence of Palestine and Israel: 'two states for two peoples'.

'Time is not on our side' is one of the refrains of her conversation. The possibility that the United Nations General Assembly will independently recognise a Palestinian state in September has given the need for movement on the negotiation front a burst of urgency. It is beginning to sink in that Prime Minister Benjamin Netanyahu's default mode of standing pat could confront Israel with unpalatable alternatives: either the acceptance of imposed borders, or the drastic consequences of refusing to recognise the frontiers of a sovereign fellow member of the UN.

Even without this incentive to action, Livni does not believe that a perennial defence of the status quo best serves the survival, let alone the prospering, of the Jewish state. She makes no secret of her frustration with Netanyahu, whose opposition to the talks that she and the former Kadima prime minister Ehud Olmert had with the Palestinian leadership in 2007 and 2008 was, she believes, expedient rather than principled. 'I have no idea (other than rejectionism) what he wanted,' she says, a bemused smile settling on her face. 'Actually, I still don't know.'

Their difference has the unforgiving sharpness of a family feud, but the family in question is ideological. Both 'Bibi' Netanyahu and Livni come from the same political cradle: the Revisionist Party founded by the charismatic orator and writer Ze'ev Jabotinsky in the 1920s out of disgust with what he thought was mainstream Zionism's cowardly pragmatism; its refusal to embrace a sovereign Jewish state – on both sides of the Jordan – as the unequivocal goal of the movement. Bibi's father, Benzion Netanyahu, a distinguished historian of the fate of Jews under the Spanish Inquisition, who celebrated his 101st birthday last month, was Jabotinsky's secretary, a pedigree that gives the Netanyahus an almost dynastic claim to the succession of hardline Zionism.

But Livni's father, Eitan, the operations chief for the Revisionists' paramilitary wing, the Irgun, was hardly a compromiser. It was the Irgun that blew up Jerusalem's King David Hotel in July 1946, and today it would unquestionably be classified as a terrorist organisation. But when Livni argues to the Israeli people that their true security is best served by evolving away from a dug-in obduracy, she can invoke her father's Irgun commander, Menachem Begin, whose history of militancy did not prevent him from evacuating the Sinai Peninsula, shaking the hand of Anwar Sadat, and signing a treaty of peace with Egypt in 1979. It was that larger vision, she thinks, that was the stamp of true leadership. By contrast, Netanyahu's outlook seems morally puny and historically self-defeating.

Livni points to another hard man of the right – Sharon, who was prepared to uproot settlers from Gaza – as an additional precedent for the courage of changed minds; Revisionism revised. If the ultimate goal is the simultaneous preservation of Israel as a Jewish state and a democracy, then the Land will have to be divided. Otherwise demography will destroy democracy.

She knows this is a hard sell, especially in light of a recent upsurge in atrocious violence. This month an anti-tank missile launched from Gaza fell on an Israeli school bus. The subsequent counter-strike killed several Palestinian civilians. In March, Livni went to the *shiva* mourning at the West Bank settlement of Itamar for the Fogel family, whose slaughtered included small children, the youngest three months old, throats cut as they slept in their beds. 'Though the settlers have very different views, I had to go, to express my grief and that of the nation,' she says.

The bereaved told her that at such a time she and her party should unite with the government. She tried to explain that murder only deepened her conviction that there could be no papering over the profound differences between which policies would deliver true security.

Almost the first thing the smiling Livni asks me as she comes into her modest office is whether I'd seen the framed document on the wall. I had been too busy looking at the photographs of her handsome, hawk-faced father and her mother, Sarah, to pay the letter much attention. But now I saw it was dated 1929 and was from Jabotinsky himself. My ragged Hebrew made out the word 'nashim' – women – but not a lot more. Livni smiles again. 'He's writing to the town council to say he wouldn't be paying any more taxes until women were hired.' 'Was he true to his word?' I ask. 'I bet!' she laughs.

Tough women are Israel's history. Golda Meir, whose successor as prime minister Livni hopes to be, existed on a diet of cigarettes and six-inch nails for breakfast and made veteran generals look limp-wristed in comparison. Sarah Livni (née Rosenberg), with her thick knot of swept-up hair, wide, dark eyes and a delicate button nose, is drop-dead beautiful. I say so, and the daughter enjoys telling me about the firebrand's vanity. 'She lied about her age.' 'How much?' I wonder. 'A lot!' At Sarah's *shiva* a few years ago, veteran comrades from the Irgun made sure to tell Livni that some people called the dead Sarah 'the mother of the traitor'. 'Did you find out what she said in reply?' I ask. 'Yes, they told me that my mother said "She's my daughter and my daughter is always right."'

Tzipporah means bird in Hebrew, and the daughter has her father's prominent, slightly beaky nose and the keen, intensely blue eyes that give her a look of avian alertness. The plumage is elegant: a sweater-dress in the black the photographers had expressly banned. She laughs at her disobedience, knowing that the stretch fabric shows off her trim, curvy figure. She wears indigo-blue tights and strappy grey suede shoes brightened with a little inset band of gold. The mother of two boys, she looks a lot younger than her fifty-two years and acts young too; merrily tough, easy body language. In conversation she's animated and relaxed, the unhesitant English running along like water over stones. I had been warned by friends in the Israeli media that our conversation would be stolidly unmemorable. 'That Livni,' said one of them, 'she's less than meets the eye.' Boy, was he wrong.

In Israel, politics invariably comes back to families, solid and fractured, devastated and enduring. Tzipi Livni is no exception. 'You know how my mother and father met? In a train robbery!' Women were recruited by the Irgun to join the heists so that they could stuff the loot inside their clothes and pass – so the folklore has it – for pregnant. Both Eitan and Sarah were subsequently arrested and imprisoned, but it took more than barbed wire to keep Livni's mother cooped. Incarcerated, Sarah found someone to spike her milk with whatever it took to mimic the symptoms of appendicitis. Transferred to hospital, she jumped from the second-storey window of her ward to liberty. Livni would later meet someone who took her mother in while on the run, still in her hospital pyjamas. Songs were written about the exploits of the legendary 'Sarah *katon*' – little Sarah. 'Want to hear one?' asks Tzipi, switching on her iPod. On comes the marching song and massed chorus, over which the daughter translates the lyrics of sentimental martyrdom . . . 'If they are going to hang me, don't cry. This is my fate; instead of tears, take your gun close to your heart.'

Eitan, who made his own escape in the Acre prison break in 1947, was the hardest of the hard. Serving for many years in the Knesset as a Herut (the forebear of Likud) party member, he was displeased by Begin's peace deal but abstained rather than vote against, 'out of respect' for his old commander. His will specified that his gravestone should bear the emblem of the Irgun, a raised rifle over the 'greater' Eretz Israel along with the slogan '*Rak kach*' – 'Only thus'. Perhaps it's exactly this family history of fanatical militancy that makes it possible for Livni to understand the Palestinian version, and to be so committed to getting beyond the romance of blood.

In any case, she says, the likes of her parents were less hypocritical in their daily dealings with Palestinian Arabs than the self-righteous Mapai party-affiliated left that dominated Israeli politics and governing institutions in the first three decades of Israel's existence. Tzipi grew up in a Tel Aviv district where politically correct neighbours were disconcerted to see Arabs coming to tea with Eitan, who spoke their language. 'As a kid, I led a double life,' she says. It didn't do to own up to a Herut family when all of her friends were Mapai. Betar, the youth movement inaugurated in Israel by Menachem Begin, had been notorious for kitting out its cadets in brown shirts, chosen to symbolise the soil of the Land of Israel, but, as the Mapai-niks were quick to remind anyone, bearing a telling resemblance to the uniform of the Nazi SA stormtroopers. Baffled by being called a 'brownshirt' at school, when she was wearing the revised uniform of blue (for the skies of Zion, naturally), Tzipi came home to ask her parents what this was all about, and got from them, she says, a strong sense of a marginalised minority. Occasionally, the young Tzipi made a stand. In observance of May Day – a socialist occasion that, to her parents' indignation, had been turned into a national holiday, Israeli schools were shut. 'I demonstrated against this.' 'How?' I ask, hoping for some act of hellfire revolt. 'By going to school!'

Tzipi would not stay so well-behaved, joining Mossad at twenty-two, just out of the army. Around the time she was with the Israeli intelligence agency, in the early 1980s, an atomic scientist working in Iraq showed up dead in Paris. Although she may have been nothing more than a safe-house manager, it's not hard to imagine Tzipi glamorously dangerous. Since there's no point trying to get anything out of her about the Mossad years, we talk of more important things, none more so than the clandestine discussions with the Palestinian Authority leadership undertaken in 2007 and 2008 by Olmert and herself, details of which were leaked earlier this year by al-Jazeera.

For a long time it was an article of faith for almost all Israeli governments that the hardest issues – the fate of the settlements, the military status of Palestine and, above all, the possibility of Jerusalem being something other than the exclusive and uni-fied capital of Israel – should be set aside pending some sort of preliminary agreement. But, Livni says, 'I don't do interim.' Postponing the hard stuff was not only cowardly; it would guaran-tee the unravelling of any more generalised agreement. In Sharm El Sheikh, Olmert and Livni said farewell to procrastination. Nothing, not even Jerusalem, was off the table. She stresses that an agreement over the city was not reached between her and the Palestinians; and that if she is to respect the promises of confidentiality made to their leadership, she can't discuss any details of the al-Jazeera leaks, which they themselves have not put on the record. But her revolutionary willingness to countenance the possibility of a shared Jerusalem is one reason why Livni is not prime minister today. The price of forming a coalition with the ultra-orthodox Shas Party was to take the indivisibility of Jerusalem off the table – and this she steadfastly refuses to do.

The breakthrough at Sharm El Sheikh with Mahmoud Abbas and Salam Fayyad was one of psychological temper. Livni insists, refreshingly, that peace, or even the cessation of mutual mutilations, cannot turn on a choice of competing narratives; that the endless competition of unspeakable calamities, such as the Holocaust and Nakba, was a ball and chain that would hobble the lives of children yet to be born. Enough already!

'We began by talking about rights,' she says, 'our rights, their rights', and then decided to stop doing that and talk instead about possibilities. 'It's said that the devil is in the details, but in our case it was God instead . . . We made lists – the kind of lists, for example, of the kind of weapons they would need to defend themselves and the weapons we couldn't let them have, and we found we could do those lists!' 'Did their flexibility on these kind of matters surprise you?' I ask. She gives me one of her high-wattage smiles: 'This wasn't the first time I met with them.'

She gives me an example of the difference this made on one notoriously thorny issue: the demilitarisation of Palestine. To ask as much was, initially, an outrage to the Palestinian leaders, who retorted they would never accept being a 'minus state'. 'At that point we could just have given up, and left the room, but we didn't. We talked history. "Look," I said, "has Germany been an impotent 'minus state' for limiting its army and armaments? Has Egypt been disadvantaged by a demilitarised Sinai?"' And so they hashed out those lists. The same concrete approach went for territorial exchanges. What seemed irreconcilable changed when representatives from both sides went to walk the line, to physically look at villages, olive groves, roads.

You get the feeling Livni thinks this kind of bargaining can make headway on all the issues that conventional wisdom has for so long decreed to be unresolvable. And that while men like to thump the table and shout grievances, women get on with the mundane practical matters in hand that constitute the realities of daily life. So she thinks about what those realities might be like for Palestinians as well as Israelis. 'It's not in our interest that Palestine should be a failed state.' Or, she adds, 'an extremist state'. That, she explains, is the true conflict at the heart of the Middle East, one even bigger than the enmity of Jew and Arab: the genuinely irreconcilable clash between theocratic and autocratic regimes, and liberal democracies. Right now, and for a little time perhaps, an Israeli party of reason might be able to make the peace with its Palestinian counterpart. Evidently there has been something like a meeting of minds across the 'security fence'. But not forever. No one knows which side – Islamic militancy or democratic secularism – will emerge from the Arab Spring. But that uncertainty only makes the need for an early settlement more, not less, pressing.

Not least because Israel, too, has a domestic cultural conflict on its hands that is undoing assumptions about what kind of Jewishness the Jewish state is supposed to embody. Between the Jerusalem ultra-orthodox Haredim, for whom the only true Jewish state is one based on rigid obedience to *halacha*, the precepts of the religion, and those whose Israel is pluralist and secular, there is as wide a gulf as between the Muslim Brotherhood and the Tweeters of Tahrir Square. The two crises – of the outer borders of the Jewish state and its inner identity – Livni sees as organically connected. It says something about her forthrightness as well as her optimism that Livni wants a written Israeli constitution that would make a clear demarcation between synagogue and state.

But then she is a great believer in the strength of principle, championing an international code of practice to govern elections in newly born democracies. Recalling that in Israel the expulsionist Kach Party was disbarred from participating in elections, she wants the same principle to apply to parties in Muslim countries that use democratic means to overthrow democracy. Hitler, she remembers, came to power through the ballot box. 'This would not be patronising or imperialist,' she says. 'They can all do what they like. But if they want to participate in an international community they should abide by those conventions.'

It's this kind of reflectiveness that makes one feel Livni is a mould-breaker, even though when you say this around Jerusalem and Tel Aviv, you are met with sceptical chuckles. But perhaps it's the worldly straightforwardness of Tzipi Livni's emotions that might make it possible for her to translate political heresies into a working version of what the majority of Israelis crave, the *shalom*, the *salaam* that is the first thing out of the mouths of Jews and Arabs alike. Don't tell me gender has nothing to do with this; the difference between Netanyahu's reverence for his father and his famous hero-brother Yonatan, killed in the 1976 Entebbe raid, and Livni's life as a Mossad agent become mother. A few weeks ago she went to see her younger son, Yuval, graduate as an officer in an elite combat unit of the army. To make the moment more intense, he had signed on for a four-and-a-half-year service rather than the mandatory three. Talking about this, her face softens and she reaches into her wallet to show me a photo of handsome Yuval and his curly-haired elder sibling Omri. The ceremony was in the Negev desert but it was a chilly winter day. 'Of course I was conflicted. I was so proud of him but my heart was in terrible pain so I added my tears to the rain.'

There's nothing trite about this. What Livni wants for herself, for Yuval, for Israel, she wants so that the tears, as well as the blood, might finally have some chance of stopping.

FOOD

I suppose there are good cooks who don't like to talk about their cook-
ing, but I can't say I've ever met one. Though my favourite food writer,
M. F. K. Fisher, begins one of her essays by confessing 'the first thing I
cooked was pure poison' (a ghastly milky blob-pudding made as an act
of protest against her mother's pregnancy), for the most part cooking is
itself a form of communication, usually delivered as an act of generosity,
an invitation to company, whether prepared for one or many. It's not
surprising, then, that as British cookery flowered in the 1960s, the
kitchen, at least in the glossy imagery of weekend magazines, became
the social centre of the home. But when I started to cook in earnest in
my last year as an undergraduate at Cambridge in the early 1960s, all
I had to work with was a single gas ring in a cupboard-sized space at
the end of a corridor.

    But I also had a shelf of words: Elizabeth David's French
Provincial Cooking *and the first volume of Julia Child's* Mastering
the Art of French Cookery, *out of which on that gas ring I could*
whistle up soups, stews, fricassees and ragouts, all served in Portmeirion
pottery bowls that came in shades of burned orange or bilious green.
Pretty soon it became clear that a novice cook could either follow the
way of Child or the path of David, which is to say, studious discipline
or forgiving improvisation. No prizes for guessing which way I went, but
it was at least as much about the words and the places they conjured as
the food. Before I knew anything about their lives I admired Julia (whom
I later got to know when I was living in Boston in the 1980s) and her

cordon bleu rigour, but I lusted after Elizabeth, who reassured me that 'delicious meals can be cooked with the sole aid of a blackened frying pan over a primus stove' even as she was leading me to something more ambitious. Her attitude to quantities was unreliable, her directions casual, her gossip meandering, her memories savory. But when I knocked up a garbure *or a* coq au vin, *the damp college corridor turned into a tiled kitchen in Provence and I'd been to market that morning with Elizabeth, who'd leaned over a stall and popped a perfect olive into her greedy mouth.*

The cookery shelf quickly expanded into a whole library, with particular favourites: Alan Davidson, Jane Grigson, but especially the originator of the grand style of cookbooks, Bartolomeo Scappi, chef to Renaissance cardinals and popes, and whose enormous Opera *published in 1570 will handily tell you how to spit-roast the head of a suckling calf, not forgetting to replace the tongue with a slab of prosciutto or a saveloy sausage; cook up a pottage from bugloss and mugwort (who wouldn't?) and give you 'various ways to cook bear meat', something that would have come in handy for my mother-in-law, who actually regularly fried, stewed and roasted bear shot by my father-in-law in the mountains of Nevada. A descendant of that helpful tradition is Magnus Nilsson, whose* Nordic Cook Book *will be a godsend for anyone eager to make 'a stew of shaved reindeer meat', 'braised guillemot' or — and this has to be a must, I think — 'Icelandic Rotten Shark', the rather special aroma of which has Nilsson weighing his words with the care of a poet: 'just a little fishy, a little rancid, a bit like old cheese and fish oil and dark harbour water, but not really in a very bad way'.*

Most of the recipes and essays that follow were published in GQ *magazine as a result of its hospitable editor, Dylan Jones, offering me a regular berth as cookery writer. By way of testing his faith, I suppose, the first offering I delivered was all about British bison, as it happens one of the most nutritious and flavour-heavy meats you can cook, just so long as you don't let it dry out. Dylan wanted little essays as well as recipes, which took me to a farm, not far from Salisbury Plain, where I saw, unforgettably, a small herd of West Country bison plodding* through a weedy duckpond: the Archers meeting Zane Grey. The pieces that followed were a labour of love but one of the most exacting genres to which I've ever turned my hand, not least because I became obsessively perfectionist about the illustrations, insisting on photographing the food as it was actually being cook-tested. This we did in a basement kitchen studio in Battersea with only the occasional mishap, as when for instance I dry-roasted four different kinds of Mexican chili pepper, the smoke from which went straight through the ceiling and into the yoga class of the photographer's wife. An evacuation of coughing and wheezing yoga punters ensued, not many of whom were giving me sun salutations as they fled into the street coughing and rubbing their eyes.

I can't imagine a life without cooking any more than a life without writing — the two kinds of nourishment mutually sustaining. Carême knew what he was talking about when he wrote, 'From behind my oven I regard the cooking of India, China, Germany and Switzerland and I feel the ugly edifice of routine crumbling beneath my hands.'

LUNCH WITH MICHAEL POLLAN

'So, did you eat the in-flight meal, then?' I cheekily ask Michael Pollan, mainly because he looks fresher and rosier and happier than any 55-year-old has a right to after thirteen hours on a non-stop flight from San Francisco. The writer is in England to talk about his new book, *Food Rules: An Eater's Manual*.

Nearly all of Pollan's rules ('eat slowly, eat well-grown food from healthy soils') are routinely broken by the junk served to paying hostages trapped behind tray tables and wired like battery chickens to the dictates of the flight schedule. Feed NOW. Watch movie NOW. Get drunk on 15 per cent Tempranillo NOW (but only so much that it will help you to snooze so the crew can have a giggle in the galley while chowing down). Pollan owns up to ordering the Vegetarian Special, which, he says, was in a beet-rooty way 'not too bad'.

We agree that at least this got him out of being stuck with the supremely depressing Seasonal Salad, which is not much of either: usually ancient leavings from the school of suicidal cucumber keeping company with leaves wilted in grief at having been torn from the life support plastic bags in which, as Pollan explains in his 2006 book *The Omnivore's Dilemma*, inert gases have unnaturally prolonged their existence. At least the Salad of Despond obeys Pollan's cardinal rule that we should eat 'not too much and mostly plants' – since you'll never want to eat much of this stuff, which technically is 'mostly plant'.

Pollan and I are sitting in Acorn House Restaurant, on the

ground floor of a nondescript corner office block in an unglamorous patch of King's Cross. The establishment describes itself as London's first 'truly eco-friendly training restaurant' and is owned by the Shoreditch Trust, which does genuinely decent things in urban communities. So it seems just the kind of place that Pollan, who spends most of his life trying to alert the American public to the inexorable food-death brought about by the empire of agribusiness, might like: civic but tasty.

The kitchen, manned by two breezy cooks having a suspiciously good time, is open to view. The wood is blonde, the seat backs are done in the zesty green of primary-school romper rooms. Wall shelves are weirdly stacked with items not usually associated with the organic food movement: bottles of Worcestershire sauce, tomato ketchup and boxes of bog-standard dried pasta. Either there's some irony going on here or the ambience trainees need a bit more work.

Pollan and I had already met fleetingly, though neither of us can remember exactly where, some time shortly after he had published his first book, *Second Nature*, in 1991. This features at its heart an epic battle with a woodchuck that was treating Pollan's garden as his personal canteen. The struggle for supremacy between resolute gardener and resourceful rodent builds to a titanic climax with the Man of the Soil emptying cans of gasoline down the varmint's burrow and setting light to it like some deranged garden Nazi bent on a backyard *Götterdämmerung*. Pollan's essay was wonderfully out of keeping with the solemnities of American nature writing, and so deeply Jewish in its mischievous self-regard that it was as if Henry David Thoreau had had an encounter with Woody Allen and never been quite the same since.

Pollan's day job is Knight professor of journalism at UC Berkeley, where he's been since 2003. After Bennington College in Vermont, and a year in Oxford, Pollan did a Master's degree in English literature, specialising in American nature writing

and Thoreau, at Columbia University. For a while he was a TV
critic but then 'I realised people who read didn't watch TV and
people who watched TV didn't read.' So in 1983 he went to work
with Lewis Lapham's relaunched *Harper's Magazine*, a publication
famous for commentaries of high moral purpose expressed in
tough, elegant writing.

But Pollan's winning way with food polemics is all his own,
coloured by an easy-going humane generosity. The reader never
feels hectored into gastric virtue. Guilt is not Pollan's trip. This
is a writer who wants to restore the culture of true eating but
who can own up to a shot of pure pleasure at a home-cooked
plate of fries.

He's taller and rangier than I remember, bald in the way that
makes bald handsome. He has the open manner that makes you
feel, somehow, family, so I ask him about his, in particular about
his son Isaac, who coined the term 'cornography' as the genre his
father has made his own. I wonder whether Isaac had been into
food in the same way my own kids were, both of whom, in their
twenties, have become impressive cooks. Pollan smiles one of his
tenderest smiles and says, 'Not always.' For much of his childhood, while Pollan was going green, Isaac (who is now seventeen)
ate strictly white: rice, noodles, breakfast cereals submerged in
milk. At the same time, he would wear exclusively black clothes
(dark-blue socks excepted) and favoured in particular a kit of black
leggings from which he could not bear to be parted. Pollan, who
in *Food Rules* insists on the importance of the family all eating
the same food (rather than junior with a defrosted pizza and sis
upstairs nibbling on a choc bar in front of the computer while
mum and dad moodily shovel their penne in the eat-in kitchen),
shrugs his broad shoulders and concedes that he, 'er, customised
Isaac's food during that time'.

Isaac's black-and-white obsession got so serious that Pollan's
friend Alice Waters, the owner-cook of Chez Panisse (the
Berkeley restaurant that was revolutionary in its commitment to

seasonal organic produce), offered to lend a hand introducing the boy to what non-white food could actually be. Dutifully, the great cook grilled up some choice steak (undoubtedly grass-fed), and served it, carefully cubed. Isaac toyed with it more in a spirit of filial duty than pleasure. Waters was unconcerned and reassured Pollan that in a few years he would be 'an eater'. At fourteen Isaac did a stint as an intern in the kitchen at Chez Panisse, prepping veggies and trimming quail wings. His father knew that Alice Waters's prediction had come true when Isaac came home one evening announcing, 'I much prefer squab.'

For all the charm of his writing, Pollan is in deadly earnest about what he sees as the imprisonment of American foodways in the corporate imperatives of agribusiness, above all in the industrial mega-production of corn that has all but obliterated the possibility of a truly omnivorous diet. If we are what we eat, then most Americans are corny even when they think they are eating meat. What they are actually eating – in their beef, their poultry, even their fish (in addition to scrapings of other animals) – are livestock as processing tubes for a corn surplus. The result has been a victory of profit over nature. In *The Omnivore's Dilemma*, Pollan describes how, in the 1970s, the livestock industry was altered to use up huge corn surpluses that were depressing the price of grain. Cattle were no longer to be raised on pasture but shackled immobile to feedlot railings, standing in lagoons of their own faeces, pumped with grain, not grass, and brought to kill, fatter and faster than ever before.

The price paid for this industrial supply of cheap meat has been a population of the obese and the chronically diabetic, waddling along, stuffed with the chicken nuggets and burgers that are the ultimate product of this relentless corn-chain. There was a time when the cornfield was the emblem of American wholesomeness. Now, as Pollan describes, it seems more like the mortuary of American nature.

It is just because Pollan is so deeply and lovingly invested in the culture of his country that he mourns the loss not just of its alimentary health but the sense of domestic community destroyed by the supremacy of fast food, of cooking that has been surrendered to the dictates of convenience industries. Nineteen per cent of all American meals are now eaten in a car, which is why the nugget that can be consumed with one hand was the dream product for the corporate food marketeers. Of the thirty-eight separate ingredients that constitute the McNugget, thirteen, Pollan found, are corn-based.

There is, of course, the corn-fed chicken, grown to reach its prime slaughter-age as fast as possible, when, as giant breasts on exiguous legs pumped full of antibiotics, they are 'processed' to their date with supermarket trays. But then in the chicken nugget world there is also the corn starch used to hold the things together; not to mention the Brobdingnagian servings of sweet fizzy drinks that are nothing other than carbonated high-fructose corn syrup.

One part of Michael Pollan is in awe at what agribusiness has achieved: the delivery of low-cost food on an unprecedented scale. But the better part of him is appalled. 'What's happened is Walmartism: the reverse of Fordism,' he says. 'Ford raised the pay of his assembly line workers so they would buy his cars. Walmart pays low wages, knowing workers can always get bad, cheap food.' The result is a burger- and jumbo-sized cola-addicted population. No one is better than Pollan at giving the devil its due, conjuring the unmistakeable, almost narcotically addictive 'fry-fragrance' to which junk food junkies helplessly gravitate. It is, he thinks, a kind of ersatz 'home': some imagined smell of childish security in that oily-crunchy, burgery squishy provision – as if fast-food momma was one gigantic American tit on which the infantilised masses of America placidly suck.

Anyone who has read Pollan's coda to *The Omnivore's Dilemma*, called 'A Perfect Meal', knows he is not just a historian and prophet of food but a hell of a cook too. So I ask him about the paradox of our time in which the obsessions of food – celebrity chefs, food columns in every newspaper and magazine, the marketing of gourmet kitchens – has somehow coincided with people cooking less not more. Television cooking we both think has become a kind of manic gameshow, in which star turns of charismatic rage and an emphasis on feverish speed has made it harder, not easier, for family cooks to transfer what they see to their own kitchens.

The one exception to the bleak outlook is the rise and rise of local farmers' markets, and what Pollan calls 'Big Organic' stores such as Whole Foods Market, where accurate source labelling is crucial to shopping decisions. From his perch in Berkeley he is under no illusion that somehow this salutary revolution is going to reach the mass of American people in recessionary times, but Pollan is tired of hearing from the better off that the reason the hired help defrosts yet another pizza, or lugs the kids off to a Happy Meal – while the gourmet trophy Viking stove goes begging – is shortage of time. The average amount of time spent on cooking, eating and cleaning up a meal, he says, is thirty-one minutes; the average daily non-professional time at a computer is two hours, and in front of a television three hours.

Pollan sighs. 'You know, we have been drilled to believe that only in the workplace do Americans produce something. But when we cook we are producers too. It's sad that we are supposed to be just consumers.'

While sharing the dirge, splashed by London sunlight, Pollan and I have been sampling the Acorn House's 'Antipasti Platter'. There's a tangy salami, but a 'Speck d'Aosta' that's no better than ho-hum. The rest are seasonal offerings that promise more than they deliver: new potatoes with spring onions in an anodyne mayonnaise; spinach and wild-garlic yoghurt with not much evidence of the wild. The one item that sings out loud is – this must be Pollan's luck – beetroot, some dark and bloody, some pink and fetching. We have also ordered Dorset mackerel 'pan-fried' (where else are they going to fry it?), but the manager makes a sudden appearance. An ingredient has failed to show up. They thought maybe mint would do and then thought, no, it wouldn't. Would we mind if the fish was chargrilled with some green tomatoes and cannellini beans? The happy boys in the open kitchen do their thing and amid the half-empty restaurant a little miracle of simplicity happens: the fish is mouth-wateringly meaty, the skin crispy, the white beans as they should be, a touch soupy.

Pleasure arrives. But then so does the minder from Pollan's publisher, and she's looking uninterested in pleasure. He is ushered away.

But Pollanation has happened. Over a moody rhubarb sorbet I brood on our conversation. 'There's a big tragic social theory lurking in your work, isn't there?' I'd said to him. 'We're stuck with a culture that militates against your dream of restoring a sense of community through cooking and eating together at home. TV dinners and movie popcorn are the opposite of real eating; our restaurant fetish lets someone else do the cooking; and the gym hours spent to make us feel good give excuses not to make dinner. So what the hell can we do?'

'Oh,' he said, summoning one of his most expansive smiles, 'we can tell stories.'

LAMB WITH POMEGRANATES

Is it just me or does anyone else wonder what famished desperation led to the unlikely discovery that globe artichokes were edible? Is this what happened? Starving omnivore stumbles over giant thistle, stoops to grasp its leaves, which repay his curiosity by puncturing his hand. Does he kick and curse and go on his way? No! He thinks, wow, boil up that sucker for an hour or five, scrape the ends off, and it's going to be really yummy.

Weird things hanging from trees must have sorted the wary from the greedy. How hungry or perverse would you have to have been to bite into a rambutan, so very like a hairy testicle? And if you've seen an unripe pomegranate, green and leathery, surmounted by its tough crown, it's hard to imagine how anyone thought to bother. But then a transformation happens and the ripening fruit develops, first its coy, rosy blush and then that deep ruby glow – an irresistible invitation to interior inspection. But what was discovered within was – and is – a challenge.

Where, exactly, is the flesh? Nowhere. Instead, it is packed with hundreds of brilliant gem-like red seeds, encased in a pithy membrane so bitter that if you get a bite of it, the sumptuous sweetness of the juice will lie like tannic poison on your tongue.

Look harder at the seed and beneath the translucent jelly of the red you'll see the unforgiving toughness of its core. Could it be this split personality of the pomegranate – nice and nasty, sweet and sour, sacred and profane, seductive and deadly – that accounts for its universal cultural allure? It seems much likelier that the forbidden fruit in the Garden of Eden was a pomegranate rather than an apple.

You're the Satanic serpent; which would you proffer to Eve: a blood-red squirter or a Granny Smith? The abundance of the tightly packed seeds has made the fruit a universal emblem of fertility.

Talmudic sages declared that dreams of pomegranate seeds were a prophecy of prosperity. But they have also been the grains of sorrow and death. In a replay of the Genesis story, Demeter has her daughter, Persephone, restored to her from the underworld only to have her future blighted when she accepts six measly pomegranate seeds from the wily Hades to doom her to return to his realm of the dead for three months of every year. Persephone's tragedy is our good fortune, though, as pomegranates are an autumn and early winter fruit. Many overlook the vast potential of cooking with the juice, seeds or the dense pomegranate molasses you can now find in speciality (especially Middle Eastern) food shops. The most efficient way of extracting the juice is to roll the pomegranate on a hard surface, your palm on top. You'll hear and feel the seeds squishing. Then, with the fruit over a bowl, make a small puncture or slit and the good stuff will come gushing out. You'll probably need eight pomegranates for 500ml. It's easier than it sounds so don't be deterred from the pleasure of cooking up some beauties from Iranian cuisine – the place where the pomegranate is said to have originated. Try the spectacular tenderising and flavouring got from marinading and slow roasting a leg of lamb in molasses, or the Persian dish *fesenjan* – a bird, usually chicken or duck, simmered in a blend of fresh pomegranate juice and ground walnuts.

And now you can do yourself, and the world, a favour by buying juice and molasses from Pomegreat, which imports it from Afghanistan.

Pomegranate is one of the oldest fruits in existence. The first records date back to 100 BC. A pomegranate tree can grow to 15ft in height and may live for more than 100 years. The antioxidant potential of the pomegranate is thought to be up to three times higher than that of green tea and red wine.

In 2009 a state-of-the-art juice-processing plant, Omaid Bahar, was opened in Kabul, supplied by 50,000 farmers from the embattled country. American aid agency US AID has helped plant nearly 1.5 million saplings and, in a triumph of good over evil, farmers growing pomegranates make many times the income they would from cultivating opium poppies. Afghan pomegranates are said to be the richest, juiciest, most delectable in the world, so wouldn't it be 'Wonderful' (the name of the most popular cultivar) if the blood-red fruit contained within it the seeds of a new life for a tormented people?

Pomegranate marinade for roast lamb
(Prepare 1–3 hours before grilling)

- A bone-in leg of lamb (around 2kg)
- 300ml pomegranate molasses diluted with 100ml water
- 3 cloves of crushed garlic
- 2 tbsp light olive oil
- 1 crumbled dried red chilli
- 1 tbsp sumac

Method
After breakfast: strip away all fat and silky membrane from the lamb; score the meat with incisions over the joint; mix ingredients of the marinade, season, and set the roast in a glass bowl to steep for 3–4 hours. At eleven o'clock, turn it over. Around three o'clock: heat the oven to 210°C (410°F; gas mark 6); set the roast in a deep roasting tin, keeping the marinated bits clinging to it; turn the oven down to 110°C (230°F; gas mark 1/2) and roast

very gently for three and a half hours, turning once. The flesh should be spoon-soft without falling off the bone. While the lamb is resting (20 minutes or so before serving), deglaze the remaining marinade and a few tablespoons of water, scooping up the bits in the roasting tin; adjust the seasoning; strain and you'll have a fine rich dark sauce. There are few things I like less than cold roast lamb – but this is an exception. The pomegranate stays perfuming the meat. It works brilliantly with a winter salad of chicory and shredded, spiced cabbage.

BISON IN WILTSHIRE

Big carnivore, are you? Partial to a nice plateful of blood with a choice chunk of wagyu reposing in the middle? Reckon you need that lavish marbling of fat to deliver a hit of flavour? Think again. There's one meat that will knock you sideways with a richness of flavour your palate never dreamed of, and its meat almost entirely without fat. It's that heavy-haunched, brown-eyed, grazing protein pack, draped in what looks like the remains of your Aunt Edna's carpet: *bison bison*.

Until you've got stuck into a rib-eye or a filet mignon so tender you could use a spoon on it, or wrapped your face around an oozy bisonburger, leaking good stuff into the bun, you have absolutely no idea how satisfying deep meat can be. Is it like venison? No. Is it gamey? No again. What *is* it like? Take the subtlest, most luscious beef you can imagine, a symphony of flavour that has your taste buds weeping for more, and then add a delicate tang, a grace note of savoury muskiness underneath. The B-spot it hits is about two-thirds to the back of the tongue, and after the meat has paid it a friendly visit, it will never be the same again.

That's the tang of happiness, because raised right, bison are exclusively pasture munchers, but that doesn't mean pure grass. Bison are nature's weed whackers. They thrive on scrubby growth – sagebrush and thistle – that no beast but Eeyore would give the time of day to. Which means not only can you feast off the best meat you've ever eaten, but you get to be sanctimonious back to the vegetarians because you've done your bit for an ecologically benign food chain (although these days only if you're eating British bison, which can be seen roaming the range in cowboy country such as Wiltshire or the badlands of Melton Mowbray). Don't expect bison to show up in Waitrose or Sainsbury's any time soon, though. The herds are still modest, and raised by what the head of the British Bison Association's Colin Seaford calls 'enthusiasts', albeit farmers like him who make a decent living from selling frozen meat online and to visitors.

In America, the return of the bison began as a romantic-penitential restoration programme of prairie grassland and the beasts that once numbered tens of millions. It started as a vanity project by the likes of CNN founder Ted Turner, but promoted as a healthy and humane alternative to beef, bison meat is now routinely found in supermarkets across America where most buyers are under the impression that they are eating a piece of the nation's heritage miraculously restored to life. Yes and no. The bison business has been compromised by its own success. With demand outstripping supply, the pressure to bring the animals to slaughter weight faster than traditional leisurely grazing allowed has meant, inevitably, fattening them in confined feedlots, where they have undergone the same fate as beef cattle: unnaturally grain-fed, accumulating layers of fat and depleting their flavour. Over 90 per cent of bison meat retailed in the markets is industrially fattened. It's still possible to get the real McCoy, but you have to go online to get it from South Dakota's Wild Idea Buffalo Company.

But on this side of the pond, the only bison you'll order from the Seafords' Bush Farm or from their British colleagues will be field-raised animals.

Seaford got his first bison from America via Belgium more than twenty-five years ago, but he is quick to point out that they were European beasts before they were American, and that recent excavations in the West Country have yielded troves of prehistoric bison teeth. So there were shaggies roaming what is now Salisbury Plain.

Seaford, who fantasised as a boy about bringing a piece of the

Old West to the West Country, took me to meet their modern counterparts – Big Georges the bull (who really is titanic where it counts) and the cows (Amy, Ruth, Clementine), who are either in calf or have their tawny offspring in tow. A happier, healthier bunch of animals you could hardly imagine.

After giving us the once-over they trotted off down a hill in single file like schoolchildren on a field trip. Outlined against the Wiltshire sky they looked a picture of contentment. 'I never get tired of looking at them,' said Seaford. And once you've tried the steaks, the mince or the sausages (the Seafords also raise American elk, which make a fabulous sausage), you'll never tire of eating them, either.

Because bison meat is substantially lower in fat than beef, it will dry out more easily, so barbecueing is a very bad idea (as it is for decent hamburgers, for that matter). Instead, use a cast-iron ridged grill pan, lightly oiled and brought to just below smoking heat. The subtly musky flavour will not survive the addition of aggressive ingredients, so lay off the tabasco, Worcestershire sauce and garlic. Don't add salt to the mix as this will pull out the juices to waste in the pan rather than in your mouth.

Ingredients
(For 4 patties of a centimetre or so each)

- 500g bison mince
- 1 tbsp grated red onion juice
- I tbsp finely chopped parsley
- A few grinds of pepper to taste

Method
1. Mix ingredients lightly without kneading. Shape into course, flat patties and make a shallow depression in the top (this prevents them from swelling bulbously, but don't ask me why).

2. Set onto a very hot grill pan. However much you fancy yourself as Grill Man, resist the temptation to pat, poke, or in any way molest them.

3. After a mere three minutes (for rare) flip them carefully with a spatula. Your burgers will have caramelised stripes on the outside and will be running with ruby goodness on the inside. Mercy!

4. Underplay the bun: just a slice of late-season tomato (that you've not made the mistake of keeping in the fridge), another of red onion. Home-made salsa, with rehydrated New Mexico chillis, a few green tomatillos, a splash of oil and freshly squeezed lime juice blitzed together won't kill you or the big boy in your bun.

5. Serve with posole hominy (white corn kernels) if you can find it (those in Goya tins are terrific, especially gussied up with a pinch of sweet smoked paprika); a mess of black beans you've lovingly cooked in the morning; and guacamole mashed in a bowl, not processed to a paste.

RHUBARB

Come springtime in Intercourse, Pennsylvania, the folks have just one thing on their mind: rhubarb. So in May they organise a festival: the oldest of its kind in America, brushing aside amateur competition from rival rhubarb fests in Aledo, Illinois, Conrad, Montana and Silverton, Colorado. Locals and rhubarb pilgrims do the Rhubarb Stroll; a rhubarb Derby (alas, just sticks on wheels) gets raced; bulky men wear pink with no fear of being misunderstood. Along with the usual pies and jams, there are weirder concoctions.

Fancy a spicy rhubarb barbecue cocktail hot dog or a rhubarb turkey Monte Cristo panini? Off to Intercourse with you, posthaste!

We have our own celebration, but wouldn't you know; it's a gritty, wintry affair, staged in February in the capital of English forced rhubarb: Wakefield. No chance of the Rhubarb Stroll in Wakefield. Instead, you can enter darkened forcing sheds, inspect their pallid, light-deprived shoots and take in a vegetable silence so absolute that, according to the local rhubarb eulogists, 'you can hear it growing'.

Native to the high mountain country bordering China and Siberia (where Marco Polo found it), it came west in the sixteenth century, mostly as the dried root, prized in China as – and this I really don't get – both a cure for dysentery and a laxative. Either way, the rhubarb vendors are in with one sort of killing, and given the fierce nature of late Chinese imperial politics they may well have prescribed the lethally toxic leaves to anyone organising the other kind.

The vegetable (as all rhubarbores will remind you, it is no fruit) was a latecomer to the British table. A variety planted in Edinburgh's Royal Botanic Garden in the mid-eighteenth century was still thought of as medicinal. It was only when the botanist John Lindley grew the plant in his garden at Banbury in the 1770s, then published his recommendation, that rhubarb became a popular pudding.

It still took another two generations for it to become a working-class staple, thriving, apparently, on the soot and ash of the industrial north that is still used as a fertiliser. But it was wide-spread enough in the national diet to make Commissioner Lin Zexu in China, making a brave stand against the opium-dumping British Empire, imagine he could make the drug merchants desist by threatening to cut off exports of the two products indispensable to the English: tea and rhubarb. 'What noxious substances have we sent you,' he wrote with pained indignation to Queen Victoria, 'that you should make drug slaves of the Chinese?' Should the long-suffering Middle Kingdom deprive the British of their tea and rhubarb, desolation and constipation would be their punishing lot!

Junks were blown out of the water. Hong Kong happened, and rhubarb – with its sidekick, custard – became the staple many of us love. The gleaming, slip-sloppy, pink-stringy chunks sitting in their bath of Brown & Polson was the dish I couldn't get enough of.

Rhubarb was not just a blushful cheery thing in the brown dimness of the '50s, it went all the way to comical. The Goons pounced on this, so that mirthful rhubarb took to the skies in 'Wings over Dagenham' while riotous choruses of 'rhubarb' were punctuated by occasional eruptions of 'custard' by Peter Sellers and Spike Milligan. But the rosy-red stalks are no joke. They are, in fact, packed with sumptuous flavour; both astringent and toasty; as deep, dark and peculiar as the maddened crimson of the most gorgeous stalks. The most forgiving of foods, a sugared pan of chunks will collapse into melted tenderness in five minutes. You just have to guard against their going green. In a friend's kitchen, I once attempted a rhubarb soufflé with youngish stalks that emerged from the oven a ghastly jade and immediately regretted not adding some pureed raspberry.

There are all kinds of things you can do with it – sweet and savoury – without resorting to Intercourse's unfortunate rhubarb quesadillas.

There's a lamb khoresh stew that uses its flesh and juice; and you can make a killer granita or sorbet to freshen up rhubarb tart. The recipe below – which, in honour of the Goons, adds a custard to the pink stuff – offers a startling way to make the pastry shell that, to those who think chilling everything is the condition of decent shortcrust, will seem the craziest of heresies. I did, too, when I caught it online on the breezy website of Chez Panisse's former pastry chef David Lebovitz, who in turn got it from Paule Caillat in Paris. But it works and makes a dessert worthy of John Cleese's hymn of praise: 'The principles of modern philosophy/ Were postulated by Descartes/Discarding everything he wasn't certain of/I think, therefore, I'm rhubarb tart.'

Ingredients
For pastry shell:

- 90g unsalted butter, cut into dice
- 1 tbsp vegetable oil such as safflower or canola
- 3 tbsp water
- Good pinch of salt
- 170g plain flour

For the filling:
- 500g rhubarb cut into 3cm chunks
- 30g unsalted butter
- 50g caster sugar
- 1 tbsp lemon juice

For the custard:
- 3 large eggs
- 200ml double cream or whole-milk yoghurt
- 1 tbsp vanilla extract
- 50g caster sugar

Method

1. Pre-heat oven to 210°C (410°F, gas mark 6) and grease 22cm tart pan with removable bottom. Mix rhubarb, sugar and lemon juice in a glass bowl – leave for 15 minutes.

2. Melt the butter in a medium-large saucepan. Add the rhubarb mixture and cook on a medium heat for about 5 minutes or until the chunks are tender but still intact. Don't leave the kitchen! You don't want the rhubarb to disintegrate, which it does very quickly. When tender, remove from the heat and allow to cool.

3. In a processor, whizz eggs, cream or yoghurt, vanilla extract and sugar to thicken, and smooth the custard.

4. Set the diced butter, water, oil, salt and sugar in an oven-proof bowl. Heat for around 20 minutes until the mixture is bubbling and just beginning to brown.

5. Remove – remember those oven gloves – and quickly stir in the flour with a wooden spoon or spatula. It will – amazingly – cohere; work it into a ball that comes away from the sides of the bowl with the spatula. Set the pastry blob in the middle of the tart pan and flatten a little.

6. When cool enough to handle – this will happen quicker than you think – press the pastry ball over the base of the tart pan, working with the heel of your hand from the centre towards the

sides. More miracles – the pastry will stay fairly intact as you do this. Go for it, using fingers to press the pastry up the grooved sides of the tart pan. Prick a few fork holes in the bottom of the shell; set in the oven and bake for about 15 minutes until golden. Turn the oven down to 185°C (365°F; gas mark 4).

7. Using a rubber spatula, fill the tart shell with your rhubarb mix; then pour the custard over, leaving chunks of rhubarb poking above the surface of the tart. Bake for around 40 minutes until the tart is golden – take care it doesn't brown. Cool on a rack, or leave in the refrigerator until you can safely and carefully remove the pan bottom.

ULTIMATE CHILI

Does the thought of chocolate in your chili con carne appal you? It shouldn't, because, although you can now buy tough-guy bars of dark, 80 per cent cacao chocolate studded with pimento, the idea isn't newfangled at all. It stretches back to the earliest use of both the hot and the dark in Central and South America, where both were native.

When you combine them with that other American indigen, tomatl, you are paying tribute to the New World foods that conquered the earth. The Spanish may have taken Mexico, but Native American plants colonised every other cuisine. Without them, there would be no heat in Thai, Indian or Chinese food; no red in Italian cooking; no Sachertorte; no Mars bars.

The combination of chili and chocolate is very ancient. In the eighth century, Mayans were already splitting the big oval cacao pods, roasting the seeds, crushing them and whisking them in water to make the froth that was, for them, the whole point of the drink they called chacacahoua. The tree itself was sacred to their gods, but mortals were allowed a precious sip, flavoured and intensified with chili, when the calls of either fighting or loving (or both) commanded. It seems never to have occurred to the Maya to have sweetened chocolate, but centuries later the Aztecs gave it the Nahuatl name of tchocoatl, and had enough of a sweet tooth to add honey to it, as well as ground maize, which they drank cold. No one in their right mind would have thought the addition of milk anything but an act of sacrilege. That had to wait for the British and the Swiss.

Christopher Columbus stumbled on both chili and chocolate, but failed to give either their due; like many of the conquistadors who followed, he was more interested in the yellow than the black gold of the New World. From the time of Hernan Cortes' conquest of Mexico, though, the cult of the 'black almonds' caught on among the Spanish, and it was through them and the Portuguese that both chocolate and chili began their journeys through the foodways of Asia and Europe. While Europeans disdained the notion of cacao as treasure, the harvest feast of the Aztecs – in which chocolate was drunk from 2,000 golden cups presented by as many naked virgins – did succeed in capturing their attention. By the third quarter of the sixteenth century, the king of Spain was drinking it. A Frenchman in London first sold it as a 'West Indian drink' in 1657. And Samuel Pepys drank it every so often in the early morning, in little china demi-tasses.

Today, 80 per cent of cacao comes from west Africa, where the hardier *forastero* is dominant. But there are a few precious, isolated pockets of the much older, purer growths descended from trees originally found in Central America that have somehow miraculously survived. One such plantation is on the island nation of São Tomé and Príncipe, where the Italian grower Claudio Corallo makes a truly sublime product. From Corallo you can carry off the 100 per cent beans that are seriously grown-up flavour hits and, needless to say, 80 per cent cacao shavings studded with chili, the old style. If you must have something sweeter, the 75 per cent shavings have within them minute crystals of unrefined sugar, which you crunch on as though you're munching chocolate-covered powdered glass. It's better than it sounds.

Cooking meats in a chili-chocolate sauce would have been tantamount to blasphemy for the Maya and Aztecs, but that needn't stop us, since it hasn't prevented their descendants in Mexico from creating fabulous combinations. The most famous of these is mole, which, if done right (and in many Mexican restaurants it isn't), is good with chicken. But since I had the best chili of my life

from a shack near San Antonio in Texas that used a decent amount
of unsweetened chocolate, I've always done the same.

And although chili con carne is a Texas 'thang' – invented
sometime in the middle of the nineteenth century – the addition of chocolate preserves a folk memory of how it got going.
After the annexation of Texas in 1848, the border town of San
Antonio still had its population of *norte* Mexicans who would sell
chili-meat stews off pushcarts in the streets. Aside from the beer
and the chocolate, the heart of the matter was a sampling of the
hundreds of varieties of dried and fresh chili: the smoky *chipotle*;
the subtly fiery dark-green *poblano*; the fever-inducing *árbol* and
the pungently rich *guajillo*. At all costs avoid the useless, generic
'chili powder', which will do nothing for the stew except deliver
heat. The idea is a slow burn in which flavour is enriched, not
masked, by fire. In fact, the whole mess (a complimentary term
in chili-land) is like most good things – best cooked low and slow
and savoured lengthily over many days as the winter cold starts
to eat at our happiness.

~

Ingredients
To serve 4–6

- 2 dried *chile anchos* (mild, earthy)
- 2 *chile guajillos* (mild, tangy)
- 1 large dried *chile mulato* (mild, spicy)
- 2–4 *chile chipotle moritas* (depending on desired heat)
- 1–2 *chile árbols* (hot; use if you are feeling brave)
- Handful of cumin seeds
- 6 ripe tomatoes
- 1 tbsp olive oil
- 2 fresh green *poblano* peppers (optional)
- 2 sweet red peppers, chopped

- 2 sweet yellow onions, finely chopped
- 4 cloves of garlic, finely minced
- 1 tbsp grapeseed oil
- 750g beef mince
- 1 tbsp salt
- 1 bottle of Mexican beer
- 250g unsweetened chocolate, 80 per cent cacao
- 50g masa harina flour
- 2 tbsp smoked paprika
- Handful of fresh coriander leaves, coarsely chopped
- 1 can of pinto or red kidney beans (optional)

Method

1. Dry roast all the chiles in a hot frying pan just long enough for them to exude their aroma: 30–45 seconds. If they smoke, avoid inhaling the fumes – they will hurt.
2. In separate glass or earthenware bowls, cover each of the types of chile except *árbol* with warm water. Soak for 20 minutes.
3. Remove the chiles, saving the soaking water (crucial for flavour), and coarsely shred, removing seeds (use rubber gloves).
4. Dry roast the cumin seeds until they start to colour and give off their aroma, then grind coarsely in a spice grinder.
5. Blacken the tomatoes under the grill or in a frying pan with the barest smear of oil.
6. On a medium heat, fry the *poblanos*, if using, the sweet peppers, onion and minced garlic till they soften, around 15 minutes. Set the mixture aside in a bowl.
7. In a cast-iron casserole or Dutch oven, heat the grapeseed oil to almost smoking and add the beef, browning. Drain off excess fat.
8. Add to the casserole the softened vegetables, the roasted cumin, blackened and smashed tomatoes, salt and chiles (except the *árbol*), along with their soaking water. Stir well, bring to the boil, lower heat to medium and cook for 5 minutes.

9. Stir again, add the bottle of Mexican beer and simmer for another 30 minutes.

10. Coarsely grate the unsweetened chocolate and add to the chili, mixing in well.

11. Add 1 tsp warm water to the masa harina to make a thick paste and stir into the chili.

12. Taste for flavour and heat (the *chipotle moritas* will have given quite a kick) and add, depending on your inclination, 1–2 *árbol* chiles and, if using, the pinto or kidney beans. Simmer for another hour, stirring every 15 minutes or so.

13. At the end of cooking, scatter the coriander over the top of the chili.

14. Serve with rice or corn tortillas heated in napkins in the oven and – does this need saying? – tequila.

TWO BIG EATERS

Lunch with Adam Gopnik

1. France

SIMON SCHAMA: Your writing is dominated very powerfully by France. Is this particularly because you're from Canada?

ADAM GOPNIK: Well, I grew up in Montreal and there I had a period of being colonised by French cuisine. There was one great guy at Chez Bardet, which was a place my parents took me on my birthday when I was a kid but that was not at all the native cuisine of Quebec, which is nothing like French cooking. It's truly a sort of northern peasant cuisine.

SS: More like Breton?

AG: Yes, exactly. Shepherd's pie and that sort of simple thing. But, yes, I grew up with French around me all the time, so in that sense it was second nature.

SS: Did you cook as I did? You know, as a student?

AG: Cook to impress girls?

SS: Yes, absolutely, I mean shockingly. When I realised, to my astonishment, that I was very impractical – I wouldn't know what a carburettor was if it fell on

me; lousy at sport – I got more interested in cooking
for girls.

AG: I cooked excessively when I was a kid and it was an
unusual skill when I was growing up but it took me a
while to learn that, if the girl is paying any attention
to you at all, then she's as impressed as she's ever
going to be, and there is nothing more you can do after
that to impress her.

SS: In the 1950s my parents would take us out and it would
be to high-end places like the Savoy Grill where we'd
have Dover sole, lots of silver tureens. It was essentially
high French cooking.

But a decade later, in the 1960s, we're talking about
1965 really, there was a sense of there being – thanks
to Elizabeth David, and also thanks to Robert Carrier,
who had a restaurant in Islington and whose laminated
cookery cards I religiously collected – another kind of
French food altogether: provincial, native, much more
forgiving and generous.

So when you say [in *The Table Comes First*] about it being
later when British cooking improved, in the 1970s, you're
mostly right, but in London and out in the countryside
there was a lot of good cooking even in the late 1960s.

AG: My memory is I had two siblings in Oxford in the 1970s
and I would often see them and didn't enjoy the food
there; whereas now, when you go to Oxford, it's hard
not to eat well. In fact, and it's a painful truth for a
Francophile like myself, on the whole you can eat better
in London now than you can in Paris.

SS: Yes, that's true. I do go to Paris but not a lot.
[Anselm] Kiefer has this little Italian place he goes
to. It's sweet but basically what they do is cover
everything with white truffles and it's just absolutely an
avalanche of them.

AG: Who can complain, and yet?

SS: Exactly, you just can't say anything else.

AG: One of the strange things I recognise about the decline
of French food is that the civilisation of the table in
France is to my mind incomparable, and one of the
things I love about it is the French habit, which is so
unfamiliar to Americans particularly, of shaping a
restaurant around yourself – in other words, to find
a place to go that is yours, and then the restaurant
grows around you rather than you being a supplicant
to the restaurant. The first thing that any American
who comes to Paris says to you is, 'Where shall we go,
what's fashionable?' No French friend I have would ever
speak that language. They might sidle from one place to
another . . .

SS: They'd go to Chez Georges . . .

AG: They'd go to their place, wherever it might be. They
usually have two places – they have a fancy place and
a canteen, and they go to those two places. And the
beauty of it is that there's this wonderful warmth – but
the terrible part of it is [the food] is always the same.

But, as I say, I still would rather eat in Paris than
eat anywhere because you feel the beautiful force of a
wonderful modern adventure in a restaurant and the
culture of cooking. You can still feel it. It's not that it's
an ancient rural continuity you're in touch with, but it's
the beginnings of urbanity.

And I still feel, if I'm having a brasserie meal at the
Balzar or having a great meal at Le Grand Véfour, I feel
not that I'm stepping back but that I'm sort of stepping
in to what modernity was meant to be and then took
another turn.

2. Menus, Fasting

AG: Let's choose what we're going to have. I could do the salmon but it's a bit boring, isn't it?

SS: No, not at all. Salmon swims through the pages of your book really.

AG: Yes, it does, I'm a Canadian boy.

SS: So, salmon and broccoli purée. I don't get broccoli at all. It's the only thing I have in common with George Bush. I can't bear it in any form. I've tried to stir-fry the s**t out of it, done everything I can but . . .

AG: My mother, bless her, hates broccoli, but one way to do broccoli that I thought I could get my mum to eat is to do it as a purée, lots of crème fraîche and sea salt.

SS: Oh, yes, well, I'll try it. Verbs [on the menu] are sometimes [off-putting]: I have a rule, which is never order anything that has more than one verb in it. Do we want our water chestnuts shaved? I don't know. And draped? The sea trout sashimi is actually draped!

AG: You see, this has become the new manner of every classy menu, that is not descriptive but – what's the word? You know – comma-bound, like a Hebrew text, so you're not putting it into verbs.

SS: Yes . . . I want to have the celeriac Meyer lemon tea but do I really know what it's going to be?

AG: Is it Meyer lemon tea, that is to say a tea made from Meyer lemon? Is it Meyer tea? Or is it a tea-based flavour ornamented with Meyer lemon? Because I love tea flavours added to rice.

SS: Right, exactly. That's why I thought I'd have it, but I mean you can't make tea out of Meyer lemon. I mean what are you supposed to do, stand around for months while the zest dries? And then, let's see . . . this is my

pre-fast meal [ahead of Yom Kippur] . . . beef would
really stand me in good stead . . .

AG: I would go for that, with the fasting ahead of you.

SS: It's easy, except you can't drink water for twenty-
four hours. And, actually, at the end of it, you feel so
undeservedly smug. I always break my fast on a glass
of milk, an apple and a slice of any kind of soft white
bread, challah if possible, with no butter, nothing
on it. All one's tongue receptors are just sitting up
and begging for gratification, and you'll never taste
an apple as good as that one. There is a kind of four
o'clock trough. Partly it's bad because if you're still at
synagogue, you're listening to the Book of Jonah while
you're at the low point in the welter of food deprivation.
You feel something has eaten you . . . okay, I am going
to go for the beef.

AG: It's funny; on my way here I was thinking about your
fast, and about how much you're doing that as a symbol
sums up what I was trying to say [in the book] about
the role of food in our lives. You don't literally believe,
I think, that God is taking out his book and writing
the names of those who are going to live or die in the
coming year.

SS: No. That would be horrible predestination.

AG: Right. But you do think, I would imagine, that
attaching yourself to that kind of ritual is an incredibly
powerful, necessary thing as a symbolic act. It connects
you to the continuities of our common past?

SS: Yes.

AG: And then [there is] also the suggestion that, in this
world of secular choices in which I live a largely
secularised life, by seizing on this symbolic ritual of
food, I sharpen, narrow and define who I am . . .

SS: I suppose that's right. It is quite an eternal theme: there

is this line at the opening of Kol Nidrei [the evening
service that opens Yom Kippur], which is all about
summoning all Israel to stand before you, and I do think
about that as this huge indefinite roll call of the living
and the dead and my parents. It's just actually stepping
outside the routine . . .

AG: What I mean is that it seems to me that we're often
given the false choice between what food choices we
should make – we're told that a diet has to be rational
and justifiable. It's got to save the planet. And it seems
to me that most of the choices we make about food are
at some level symbolic. They're not going to save the
planet or our lives. And that was the point I was trying
to make in the chapter about localism: that it may well
be that all those carbon miles are not saved. That the
planet would be better off if we all ate lamb from New
Zealand. But we would not be better off if we didn't
have the experience of going to the farmer's market and
talking to the guy.

3. The Cult of Origins

SS: Not long ago there was a very strange restaurant in
London called Konstam [closed in 2010], of a sort it's
impossible to imagine in New York. Almost everything
it served came from within or near greater London,
beyond which it would not serve or cook anything at all.
It was preposterous, really.

AG: My favourite instance of that, and I've eaten his food but
never been to the restaurant, is Noma in Copenhagen.
[Chef René Redzepi] did a lunch in New York, so I got
to taste the cooking. It was a totally ersatz environment,
and, if you think it's difficult to source just around
London, imagine sourcing just around Copenhagen

in February. And the question then becomes, 'What
in February?' And the question then becomes,
'What does that all mean?' Because we tell ourselves
that we're making a commitment to the planet, to
sustainability, but there are, as you know, very potent
arguments to suggest that that's an illusion at best, or an
exaggeration at best.

SS: That you're robbing farmers in Kenya of the possibility
of selling haricots verts.

AG: Yes, exactly. And Adam Smith solved this problem
several centuries ago about specialisation and
comparative advantage. But the part that's frustrating
for me about this question is the misunderstanding:
people tend to think that either you're saying, 'Oh, I
believe that there's one way to eat and there's a system
of importance that we need to demand where the beef
came from, because it may have come from a dog'; and
then there's the alternative, that it's all fashion. It's all
just absurdity and manners, and we and our obsessions
about asking where the beef came from is just as
ridiculous as our great-grandfathers at Delmonico's who
wanted to eat strawberries in December. And the point
I wanted to make is that's not a real choice. That's not
how human life is organised. The most important things
we do are symbolic gestures. That's what gives meaning
to the race.

SS: Well, you make one caveat, which is that there are taste
issues. Is asparagus, eaten one week late, say mid-June,
rather than late May – and grown just within London's
perimeter – is it actually going to be that much better
than getting it from, I don't know, California? Actually,
it probably is – there's nothing worse than long-distance
Californian asparagus!

AG: But every cohort in every faith from Judaism to

localism demands extremely minute and, in some
way, arbitrary rules, which just show that it is a faith.
To show that what you're doing is subscribing to a set
of beliefs.

ss: And they are arbitrary? There are things to do with
memory that I am obsessed with, and it's entirely to
do with the emblematic: strawberries and asparagus,
for instance, because I remember the intensity of
strawberries in a very, very narrow band of time –
June, July, Wimbledon on TV, things like that.

AG: The point about the emblematic is the emblematic
is essential. For me one of the great intellectual
revelations from you [in *Citizens: A Chronicle of the French
Revolution*] was when you started talking about all of the
emblematic aspects of the French Revolution, dress,
hairstyles, ways of speaking, and all those things, and
the point was that they weren't secondary effects. They
were essential to what the revolution was about. It
was through the manipulation of that surface that the
revolution for good and ill had its life.

Similarly, the trivial question, 'What are we going
to have for dinner tonight?', which may simply be part
of the comedy of manners of over-privileged people,
is quite profound in the sense of the way it indicates
what we believe and how we choose to behave within
our lives.

I do this terrible thing. I end up at the supermarket,
and I'm facing the farmed salmon, and the bagged
greens, and I say to myself, 'Is my faith' – I'm like a
Jewish kid, looking at a hot dog in Philip Roth – 'Is
my faith, my secular faith, deep enough to lead me
three blocks away on this weary night so I can get the
wild salmon?!'

4. *The Table Comes First*

AG: One of the ironies of the food revolution in America is that it's powered out of all that kind of old-fashioned, puritanical, moralistic energy that makes America America. It's not sybaritic and luxurious as the similar movements have been in England. It's very much about improving your life. It's in the best sense puritanical in its impulses; I mean puritanical in its pleasure, believing that life should be a series of missions, and improvements.

SS: The emblem of that in terms of language, and something that has always bothered me, is waiters who come over to you and say, 'Are you still working on that?'

AG: Yes.

SS: And I also really want to correct parents who tell children who clean their plate, 'Good job.' They're four! They don't have a job. It's much too soon. I want to say, 'No, I'm not working on this, I'm f***ing eating it!' It's just so bizarre.

AG: It's bizarre but reflective: it's an Americanism you would never find anywhere else in the world. I can't imagine a French waiter saying that. Although a French waiter will say, 'Monsieur, is it satisfying?' Which is a polite way of saying, 'Is it not satisfying? Is there something wrong?'

SS: Yes. My favourite joke; you must have heard it. And this is so short it's barely a joke at all. The waiter comes to two old Jewish ladies who have been eating in the same place for years and he comes over and says, 'Is anything alright?'

AG: [Laughs] Yes.

SS: So let's talk about [the food writer] M. F. K. Fisher —
you feel as strongly as I do about her, don't you?

AG: Yes, absolutely.

SS: Fisher is a great writer. And she keeps on being
rediscovered but never properly rediscovered, and the
writing, the quality is just astounding.

AG: It's extraordinary. I think the single best thing ever
said about writing about food is 'When I write about
food, I write about hunger.' There's something deeply
melancholy about it.

It's like a story I tell about A. J. Liebling, who was my
beau ideal, everything a food writer can be. I said to Phil
Hamburger [a former *New Yorker* writer], 'Oh, my God,
I just love reading his food stuff so much.' And he said,
with a wince, 'I can never read Joe's stuff on food because
I've watched him eat himself to death.' And that was the
other side of the experience, which — in the alchemy of
writing, becomes jovial and joy-giving on the page — but
was reflections from his overeating himself to death.

And I gather with Fisher, too, that she was a deeply,
deeply melancholy woman, who found release in food.
It's the same as we can all read Larkin because we find
release in his melancholy, but he had to live with the
melancholy every minute of his life. We can find joy in
her ability to treat food elegiacally but she had to live
with the elegiacal mood all the time.

But I love her work . . . love the way it exposes
something that's part of this experience, right? It's the
illusion of continuity, which is essentially a truth of
commodification, right? We're sitting here, in a false
warmth, [having] purchased time, space and food. And
that's how we spend our lives in restaurants. And we
delude ourselves that the warmth of the greeting as we
come in reflects our irresistible nature.

SS: Yes, well, that's why I could stand it if all the restaurants in the world closed down but I could not stand it if I were paralysed, somehow disabled from cooking. I mean if that were the ridiculous choice . . .

AG: No, no. One nice thing is that, over the years of marriage, you unconsciously tailor your cooking to your spouse. So, though my children give me a polite approval, my wife loves what I cook.

SS: Yes, that's probably true.

AG: It's not that you've set out to please but you learn, and it's like you know that, in the next thirty years, we'll have that as a common thing.

In 2017, Damien Hirst asked me to contribute an essay for the catalogue of his *Treasures from the Wreck of the Unbelievable*. In the spirit of the project, I wrote the following . . .

INVENTORY

I blush to think that Amotan of Antioch (or Amotanius as Pausanias calls him), the greediest of antiquity's collectors, only came to my attention a quarter of a century ago, and then by the most roundabout route.

A steady rain was falling on The Hague as it often does in July. Clouds of gnats were spinning above the murky waters of the Hofvijver, the urban lake that washes against the brick walls of the Dutch parliament. Trams were making squealing turns around the Tournooiveld, the leafy square where, after a hard day's slog in the National Archives or the Royal Library, I'd ponder the day's work over a tall glass of pilsner and a plate of the *bitterballen* you pop into the mouth on the end of a toothpick.

On this visit, I had been trawling through the Royal Library for a rare Dutch book – never, to my knowledge, translated – on bezoars, those coagulate or stony masses that lie in the stomachs of large animals, and were thought precious by Renaissance natural philosophers as an antidote to poison.

This quality, often tested, seldom successfully, recommended the collection of bezoars to princes fearful (with good reason) of their vulnerability to being poisoned. Anatomists and alchemists were also drawn to bezoars for their curious forms and occasional beauty.

The book I was after was the work of a peripatetic physician, Martinus van Busselen, who had ministered to Tsar Peter the Great during his time in Holland. Van Busselen had been a friend of Dr Frederik Ruysch, whose cabinet of curiosities, including stillborn foetuses draped in silk and preserved in formaldehyde, became the gem of the Tsar's own chamber of curiosities. I had seen a reference to van Busselen's book *Over het bezoar of de knobbelen in de darmen* in a nineteenth-century scholarly work on the collection of other curios: outsize, creamily marbleised gallstones and the agates whose random veining suggested mysterious heavenly landscapes.

The great historian of such fancies, and one of my heroes, Jurgen Baltrusaitis, evidently knew van Busselen's work on the bezoar, but advised in one of his eccentric bibliographies that it was to be found only in the Royal Library in The Hague. There too, however, I was disappointed. It was indeed listed in the old handwritten card catalogue, but after lengthy waits, occupied by perusing seventeenth-century reports of double-headed sheep and women giving birth to rabbits, the librarians, embarrassed, as well they might be, confessed that, alas, van Busselen's book was not where it was supposed to be shelved, nor anywhere else they could find in the collection. They would, they said, make further searches and promised to let me know should the book be found.

Later, I sat at the Posthoorn café, glumly dabbing the crispy *bitterballen* with smears of hot mustard. I was halfway through the pile when a sudden memory gave me new hope. My fascination with the collecting of bezoars had been long-standing. I had meant to include the subject in my book about seventeenth-century Dutch culture, *The Embarrassment of Riches*, probably in the section about popular omens, alongside stranded whales washing up on the North Sea coastline. But I was at a loss to find van Busselen's all-important reference book. I had mentioned it to the one person whose incomparably encyclopaedic knowledge of the darker, stranger side of Renaissance and Baroque culture made her a likely source of help: Professor Frances Yates of the Warburg Institute, author of many works on the hermetic tradition, alchemy and the occult.

I had not been disappointed. Professor Yates and I were in the Old Combination Room of my college at Cambridge, following a lecture she had given on Giordano Bruno. Putting down her glass of claret a little too hard on the table, so that drops of it flew onto the polished mahogany, she gave out a little shouted laugh and remarked how extraordinary it was that I should ask. She explained that just the day before she had seen van Busselen's book listed in the catalogue of her favourite Dutch antiquarian bookseller and meant to snap it up – but now that I had expressed interest, that I should do so.

This of course I should have done, but I didn't.

Things intervened as they do: other papers, other passions. But sitting in the café in The Hague I recalled not only Professor Yates's tip-off but also that the bookshop was itself a short walk away from where I was sitting, in one of the side streets around the corner from the Mauritshuis art gallery. I summoned the waiter, paid in a hurry and marched to the premises of Felix de Vos, *Antiquariaat*. I had passed the shop many times during research stays in The Hague but the seventeenth-century maps and fine-bound editions of Renaissance texts had been priced so far above my means that I had never crossed its threshhold. The *Antiquariaat* seemed as it had been in the 1970s, the last of the old-fashioned shops in the narrow street, sandwiched uncomfortably between frying-oil cafés and woofing music stores like a dowager on a bus sitting between pierced teenagers. There was wood trim around the display window that exhibited, on faded green-velvet cushions, a pair of spectacular Romeyn de Hooghe caricatures of Louis XIV. Like music from the past, the door gave a tiny bell-tinkle as I went in.

De Vos – as he introduced himself, extending a softly cushioned hand – emerged from a back room, puffing on a small cigar, clearly undeterred by the possibility of sending his inventory up in smoke. His hair was white and thick; his cheeks rosy; rimless glasses hung halfway down his fleshy nose. I told him of my failure with van Busselen and that some years before her death in 1981, Dame Frances had been kind enough to mention that she had seen the item in one of his shop's catalogues. Of course this was a long time ago, I said, but given that it was an item unlikely to have much interest for any but the most specialised collectors, perhaps he might still have it somewhere in his stock?

'*Ach ja,*' he said, puffing and shrugging. '*Jammer!* What a pity, the van Busselen was still here up until just a few weeks ago when I had an order from a gentleman in Abu Dhabi, and I am afraid I sent it off to him just a little while back.' A long silence of disappointment hung in the air.

'But would you like a *kopje koffie*, and a look round to see if anything else might interest you?' I accepted the offer, and he came back with two little white cups emitting a good strong aroma, with the inevitable (but delicious) Speculaas biscuits sitting on their saucers. De Vos sighed a little sigh and said, 'It's such a shame that Dame Frances is no longer with us. Do you know I thought of her just the other day because I made a little discovery concerning a particular interest of hers: the collector Amotanius. She spoke to me often of how appealing the story had been to Renaissance patrons like Alfonso d'Este and Cosimo de' Medici, the Duke, who recognised in the educated greed of that erstwhile slave something of their own cultural encyclopedism, the craving to bring together the myths and magic of the entire world under one roof, so that when they interlocked, the deep secret of the organisation of the universe might be revealed. It was that impossible ambition, such hubris for a slave, which had foundered in a shipwreck at the very point of realisation.

'Of course the story was so morally charged that notwithstanding Pausanias treating it (on the basis of a conversation with an elderly scribe in Jerusalem) as true, everyone since had assumed both the Collector and his ship to be just a colourful fable. I remember Dame Frances chuckling when she spoke about the spell it had exercised on her popes and princes as they sent men out to scour the ruins of antiquity for their own collections, or instructed Dominican missionaries and Jewish spice traders on the Coromandel Coast or in distant Ethiopia to hunt for the esoteric remains of Indian and Egyptian antiquities, without which they could scarcely hold up their heads as masters of universal knowledge. Every so often, fragments of alabaster figurines would be sent to their courts, their suppliers pretending them to be of great antiquity – stolen, they said, from Amotan's cargo before his ship had sailed to its destruction. But, of course, when the pieces were washed of their crust of dirt, it took little cunning to see them for the outrageous fakes they were.

'It was,' De Vos went on, 'just a morality tale, no? We all thought so, Dame Frances especially. But then a week ago I got a letter from my old friend Mrs Hewlett – Horatia; let me see if I can find it for you.' He disappeared into his back office and returned with the letter. It was written in a tiny, neat hand on pale-blue notepaper with only a slight trace of the spideriness that comes over the best writers as they become old and arthritic. Before I could read much of it, De Vos took it from me.

'She was, you see, clearing out her cottage in Gloucestershire – ah, so many times I have sat in that garden . . . such an English garden . . . the big hollyhocks, the delphiniums – because she said she could no longer manage on her own and had sold the house, where so many memories lived. The gardener helped her with boxes brought down from the attic, to decide what would go on the bonfire and what she would like to keep. One of those boxes contained letters and diaries from her mother Cynthia, Lady Cynthia Tremain.

'Before that lady had married James Tremain, the poet, Cynthia Fitzgerald, as she then was, had been a friend of Gertrude Bell – yes, the "Queen of the Desert" – and Rebecca West, and like them had been fearless in her travels. You may have seen photographs of her, in high boots standing in the Hindu Kush, one hand on a rifle. Horatia thought she had read all of her mother's writings on her journeys, the books and her personal letters. But somehow she had missed the journal for 1910: "My Travels in Cappadocia". So, she says here', he poked his cigar-stained finger at the sheet of blue notepaper, 'that when she opened the diary, a little parcel of folded papers, bound with a purple ribbon, fell out. There were four pages, covered top to bottom with a long list of strange objects:

Medusas, crystal, gold, malachite and more Andromeda, monster
Sphinx (various, two) Hermaphrodite
Foot of Apollo Scorpion, jewelled
Hydra and woman warrior

. . . and finally at the foot of the fourth page, you see, the explanation:

"The cargo of the freedman Amotanias, as loaded onto his vessel Apistos."'

De Vos noticed my startled expression. 'Yes, I was very surprised; very surprised. It could be a joke, you know, but if it is not, then this is the inventory – of course a copy of the original document – of the great lost treasure, drawn up before its owner set sail. You know, Mr Schama, I am a Dutchman. We are the most sceptical people in the world. To know a fake at first sight, this is in our blood. And at night sometimes I wake up and laugh at my silliness. But there are other nights, many other nights, when I wake up as though someone had shaken me and then I think, *Why not?* Look, you can read these entries from Cynthia's diary, copied by Horatia, for yourself.'

And so I did.

15 October 1910 – Cappadocia
A brief stop to dismount from the mules, ease our rattled bones and drink a little water from the leather bags, which over the past few days have made its taste foul. We drink it all the

same. I am writing this sitting on the boulder most hospitable for my aching posterior. We trot through a universe of ashen lava; wind-driven dust. The terrain is so hard, the weather so harsh and the mules so temperamental (as I suppose all mules must be) that for the first time since we began this journey I wondered whether, after all, it would be worth it; whether the mosaics of St Basil would be as extraordinary as Richard Burton tells us. Exaggeration was second nature to him. My throat aches, my eyes are sore from blowing grit, the grey waste seems to go on forever.

Victoria, slight though she is, endures these trials with more fortitude than I. There she is on her mule swatting away the flies, eager to start again up this endless rubble-filled mountain track. Monty does his best to keep our spirits up but it is of course Victoria for whom he has undertaken this ridiculous pilgrimage, and with every kindness he extends to me I feel the weight of his resentment at having to bring his fiancée's friend along, especially since her reputation for bearing hardships with equanimity seems unfounded. Still, I am grateful for the schnapps he has brought with him in that silver flask. It burns my throat but, oddly, the smart of the scouring makes me feel better. By Monty's reckoning we should arrive at the cave monastery, or at least see it, within the hour. But I feel so obliged to his solicitousness (not a feeling to which this woman is accustomed) that I dare not ask him if we can indeed expect to reach shelter before dark. I refuse to give him any reason to condescend to our sex.

16 October 1910 – The Monastery of Saint Macrina
Cynthia (unlike the fresco of the Christ Pantokrator) much restored! Even after a sleepless night – for who needs sleep when one has found a treasure?! The monks are long-bearded and kindly. Their coffee is turbid and their goat cheese stinging. None of this, however, matters beside an astonishing

revelation. One of their number – very old, Minas by name – spoke a broken but understandable English in a piping little voice. After our supper of chickpea soup and some bitter greens, this Minas – who had smiled at me through the meal – beckoned me aside and asked me if I would like to share a tea of mountain herbs with him and talk a little 'of times past'. Really I had no idea what he meant or what he wanted but Monty thought I should listen to what he had to say.

The floor of the monk's cell was covered with rugs, and he had placed icons on small shelves cut into the soft cave rock, which glowed in the candlelight. Pleasantries were passed between us, together with the sweet tea, drunk from tulip-shaped silver cups. The old man went to a chest on the floor, arranging his robe so he could kneel on the rug, open the lid and pull from it a folded length of crimson velvet. He had some difficulty standing again but brushed off my help. He set the velvet cloth on his lap, opened it and beckoned me to come closer. Inside was a tawny-brown sheet that I recognised right away to be ancient papyrus. It was divided down its length into three columns, each written in a different language. The left column was the fine, clear lettering of Syriac; the middle I could not recognise.

'Azania, from people of south, Africa,' Minas said, and the third, startling me, I made out to be Greek.

On the first line I could read 'Medusa' and with it was a drawn likeness of the Gorgon's head: open-mouthed, snake-haired.

'Treasures,' Minas said. 'All the treasures of the slave and his ship; the famous story.' And immediately in the cave-cell, the story – nonsensical fable I had always thought – of Amotanias and his vast cargo of the world's myths, magic and monsters, came to me in all its fantastic detail. But none of those who had related the disaster – not the author of the Periplus of the Erythrean Sea, not Pausanias, not Claudius Ptolemy – had ever

listed the contents of the cargo. How indeed could they have
done, since they all supposed it to be a fable?

Of course this long list before me might have been the retrospective fancy of someone adding detail to the tale. Or a
laborious hoax? But why then would it be in three languages
and why the painstaking list of every item? No, it must have
been – and the thought struck me like a thunderbolt – an
inventory drawn up before the monstrous cargo was loaded
aboard Amotanias's stupendous vessel. The story of the treasures might then be true! Why should it not be? Was it, after
all, any more improbable than the immense collection of the
occult-hungry Emperor Rudolf II: animalia and naturalia;
mandrakes in miraculous form; vast statues of Pagan deities?
That immense collection of marvels was also meant to coalesce
into some cosmic illumination, and it too had fallen to disaster,
plundered by the Swedes when they took Prague in 1648. Why
should an erstwhile Roman slave not have anticipated a Holy
Roman Emperor? Why should he not have been driven by the
same unconquerable appetite to possess the marvels of the universe, the terrors of men's minds, the omens of nightmares?

Thunderstruck as I was, I could not ask the old monk to
allow me to take his papyrus to scholars who might confirm my
excited suspicions or confound them. So since I could make out
the ancient Greek, I asked him if I might remain there through
the night, transcribing the papyrus lists into English.

'But you must sleep,' he said chuckling.

'No, I must write,' I said, laughing in my turn. And so I did,
the treasures coming into the vision of my dumbfounded mind
as I set them down, one by one, a hoard of more than a hundred
pieces, yet with only the Medusa drawn to illustrate them.

Why then have I said nothing to Monty and Victoria of my
revelation? Why have I tucked the inventory into these pages
secretively – and in case something should befall this book,
memorised the treasure as well? Because I am afraid of being

laughed at for a gullible fool, a woman lost to idle dreams, another victim of a tall tale? Because I want this to be my secret alone until I am ready to bring it into the light of the world?

That was all that Horatia Hewlett had transcribed for De Vos. She had ended her letter by saying that her mother must have decided to postpone the revelation of her discovery forever, and had the diary not lain there in her attic box, it might never have seen the light of day at all. Cynthia had taken no photograph of the papyrus at the Cappadocian monastery. All that she had was her English transcript and that she must have felt was not strong enough to withstand the scepticism or even ridicule of the scholars. But what did he, Felix De Vos, make of it? Might there be something to it? Might Amotan have lived? Might his treasure lie somewhere beneath the waves?

'I have written to Mrs Hewlett that I didn't know what to think, but I did know that her mother, Lady Cynthia, had written a beautiful story, true or false.

And then I heard nothing at all back from her. Letters to Gloucestershire came back unopened. She had gone.' He sighed and lit another cigar. 'They all go: wonderful Dame Frances – never another like her; Mrs Hewlett; me too, not long I think, and this *Antiquariaat*.' He waved a fleshy hand through the smoke. 'No one comes, no one wants all this; if they do I can send them volumes wrapped up in brown paper, from my home. This, this is too much.'

When I got back to Boston a few weeks later, a letter was waiting for me at my Harvard office from Felix De Vos. I opened it excitedly, thinking perhaps that he had more information about old Mrs Hewlett and her mother's journal. But no, it was merely the name of the Abu Dhabi buyer of van Busselen's book on bezoars, should I wish to ask him if he would consider selling it. But my bezoar quest had faded; and like Lady Cynthia Fitzgerald, I also felt the improbability of the story too strongly to ventilate it,

even as a fantastic entertainment. I set it aside in a back drawer of
my own memory cabinet.

Until, that is, a year ago, when I learned of the gold monkey
caught in a fisherman's trawl off the east African coast some
years earlier. This could easily have been a luxury curio, a table
charm belonging to one of the merchants who thrived in the
busy trading port of Rhapta, the submerged ruins of which lay
not far off from the fisherman's catch. But something about the
object pricked at my memory and I remembered, with a sudden
leap of the pulse, that just such a golden monkey had been in the
cargo inventory translated by Lady Cynthia, after, I believe, *foot
of Apollo*, and *hermaphrodite*. So when I heard that an expedition
had been launched to explore the seabed around the find, and
then, almost unimaginably, of the staggering trove hauled from
the waters – colossal sculptures, monsters from the deep, rearing
serpents, jewelled scorpions, objects drawn from the entirety
of the ancient world – I had no doubt that this was indeed the
encyclopaedic collection of the ex-slave Amotan, and that what
had been for centuries dismissed as mere fantasy had actually been
the realised passion of an art-crazed madman.

I doubt Amotan was the first, and he was certainly not the
last, to hunger for such a memory theatre, a great arena to house
the phantasmagoria that sprang from the myth-bearing mind of
men. Lords of many realms from Africa to central Asia: phar-
aohs and the kings of Persia must have embarked on comparable
conquests of the empires of wonder; dragged back to their palaces trophies in onyx, jasper, marble, malachite and gold; arrays
of gems; mountainous confections of bronze. Some must have
been sealed up inside their tombs. The anomaly of Amotan was
merely his original servitude and the lust of the freedman parvenu
to acquire the magic of the universe. Brought to light now, his
bloated excesses, his feverish passion to acquire, his pornographic
ecstasy in the writhing of serpents and the torment of mortals –
all seem pretty much in tune with the tastes of our time, do they

not? And, for that matter, of all times, so long as men are unafraid to make themselves ridiculous as they abandon themselves to the delirium of obsession.

I wonder now, if I could have been on the dock while crate after crate of the slave's treasure was being loaded to its doom, and had been bold enough to help myself to one of his objects, what might it have been? Something, I think, on the small side. For the gigantism of heroes and monsters wears me out. I would take something that miniaturises rather than magnifies: perhaps the little golden elephant that may have come from ancient China, carrying as it does, its burden of memory, and to judge from the sudden upthrust of its trunk, and its expression of gloomy resignation, an understanding that art, like life, lies somewhere between an accident waiting to happen and a joke yet to be cracked.

ACKNOWLEDGEMENTS

First and foremost, to my hospitable editors and colleagues at the *Financial Times*, home for my journalism this past decade, especially my comrades in the *Weekend* edition (Jan Dalley, Caroline Daniel, Alice Fishburn, Lorien Kite, Rebecca Rose, Alec Russell and Fred Studemann) and the paper's great editor, Lionel Barber, for giving me a berth in the pink in the first place. Other editors who have been kind enough to give me work are: at the *New Yorker*, David Remnick and Emily Stokes; at *GQ*, Dylan Jones; and at *Harper's Bazaar*, Lucy Yeomans. Putting together a collection like this is a whole lot more exciting than you (or I) could imagine, and it could not have happened without the devotion of Marta Enrile-Hamilton, Laurie Robertson and my brilliant, timeless agent, Caroline Michel. And my thanks to Iain MacGregor and Melissa Bond at Simon & Schuster for publishing *Wordy* may be taken as read, but never for granted.

CREDITS

Essays

Matzo Ball Memories: *Financial Times*,
17 February 2012

Otto Dov Kulka in Auschwitz: *Financial Times*, 25 January 2013

The Emperor of Lies: *Financial Times*,
15 July 2011

The Remains of That Day: *Financial Times*,
2 September 2011

Neil MacGregor: German Memories:
Financial Times, 19 September 2014

Orhan Pamuk: The Museum of
Innocence: *Financial Times*,
16 August 2013

The Palace of Colour: This essay first
appeared in the *New Yorker*,
3 September 2018

Gold: *Financial Times*, 2018

Blue: *Financial Times*, 2017

Hercules Segers: *Financial Times*,
17 February 2017

Hokusai: *Financial Times*, 26 May 2017

Mondrian and De Stijl: *Financial Times*,
17 December 2010

Robert Hughes: Originally published on
the *Daily Beast*, 8 October 2012

Sally Mann: Photo Traces of Cy
Twombly: *Sally Mann Remembered
Light*, Cy Twombly in Lexington
(New York, Abrams and Gagosian,
2016)

The New Whitney: *Financial Times*, 8 May
2015

Prints USA: *Financial Times*, 3 March
2017

Cindy Sherman: *Financial Times*,
3 February 2012

Tacita Dean: *Financial Times*,
30 September 2011

Rachel Whiteread: *Financial Times*,
1 September 2017

Beasts: *Financial Times*, 15 October 2010

Quentin Blake: *Financial Times*, 13 June
2014

Whitney McVeigh: Courtesy Eykyn
Maclean; exhibition info: New York,
Eykyn Maclean, *Whitney McVeigh: Elegy
to Nature*, March–April 2018; Simon's
essay within the catalogue: S. Schama,
'The Happenstance of Illumination' in
Whitney McVeigh: Elegy to Nature (exhib.
cat.), Eykyn Maclean:
New York, 2018, pp. 5–9

Cai Guo-Qiang: First published in 'Flora
Commedia: Cai Guo-Qiang at the
Uffizi', Florence, Giunti, 2018

Rijksmuseum Reborn: *Financial Times*,
29 March 2013

Civilisations: What Were We Thinking?:
Financial Times, 26 January 2018

Patti Smith: *Financial Times*,
24 January 2014

Leonard Cohen: *The Guardian*, 28 June 2008

Tom Waits: *The Guardian*,
9 December 2006

Debbie Harry: *Harper's Bazaar* (UK), 1
  March 2011
Helen Mirren: *The Tempest*: *Financial
  Times*, 25 February 2011
Falstaff: *Financial Times*, 16 July 2010
Shakespeare and History: *Financial Times*,
  9 June 2012
Bonded to Britain: *News Week*,
  29 October 2012
Bonded Again: *Financial Times*,
  28 August 2015
Paul Beatty: *Financial Times*, 17 June
  2016
War and Peace: Print and Screen: *Financial
  Times*, 8 January 2016
Liberalism, Populism and the Fate
  of the World: The 2018 Leslie
  Stephen Lecture at the University of
  Cambridge, delivered in the Senate-
  House, 15 October 2018
Mid-Term Trump: *Financial Times*,
  2 November 2018
Royal Weddings: *Financial Times*, 18 May
  2018

Bill Clinton: *Financial Times*,
  14 October 2011
Arianna Huffington: *Financial Times*,
  10 December 2010
Henry Kissinger: *Financial Times*, 20 May
  2011
The Balfour Declaration: 100 Years On:
  Financial Times, 2 November 2017
Tzipi Livni: *Financial Times*, 15 April 2011
Lunch with Michael Pollan: *Financial
  Times*, 11 June 2010
Lamb with Pomegranates: *GQ*,
  29 March 2012
Bison in Wiltshire: *GQ*, October 2010
Rhubarb: *GQ*, May 2011
Ultimate Chili: *GQ*, December 2011
Two Big Eaters: *Financial Times*,
  28 October 2011
Inventory: *Treasures from the Wreck of the
  Unbelievable* at Punta della Dogana and
  Palazzo Grassi, Venice (Italy, Other
  Criteria Books/Marsilio, 9 April–3
  December 2017)

Plates

The Remains of That Day: Visualization by
  Squared
The Palace of Colour: Copyright Jason
  Fulford/*New Yorker*
Gold: National Archaeological Museum,
  Athens (Greece) / Photo © Luisa
  Ricciarini / Bridgeman Images
Blue: Rijksmuseum, Amsterdam
  (Netherlands) / Bridgeman Images
Hercules Segers: Courtesy of
  Rijksmuseum, Amsterdam
Hokusai: © The Trustees of the British
  Museum
Sally Mann: Photo Traces of Cy Twombly:
  © Sally Mann / Courtesy of Gagosian
Cindy Sherman: Courtesy of the artist and
  Metro Pictures, New York
Tacita Dean: Courtesy of the artist, Frith
  Street Gallery, London, and Marian
  Goodman Gallery, New York and Paris

Rachel Whiteread: © Rachel Whiteread
Beasts: National Gallery, London (UK) /
  Bridgeman Images
Quentin Blake: © Quentin Blake, 2011,
  www.foliosociety.com
Whitney McVeigh: Photos by Oman
  Rotem / © Whitney McVeigh
Cai Guo-Qiang: Photo by Yvonne Zhao /
  Courtesy of Cai Studio
Civilisations: What Were We Thinking?:
  Courtesy of Jewish Museum, Prague
Patti Smith: © Brigitte Lacombe
Tom Waits: Aaron Rapoport / Getty
  Images
Helen Mirren: © Jake Walters
Bill Clinton: © Stefan Ruiz
Two Big Eaters: © Erica McDonald